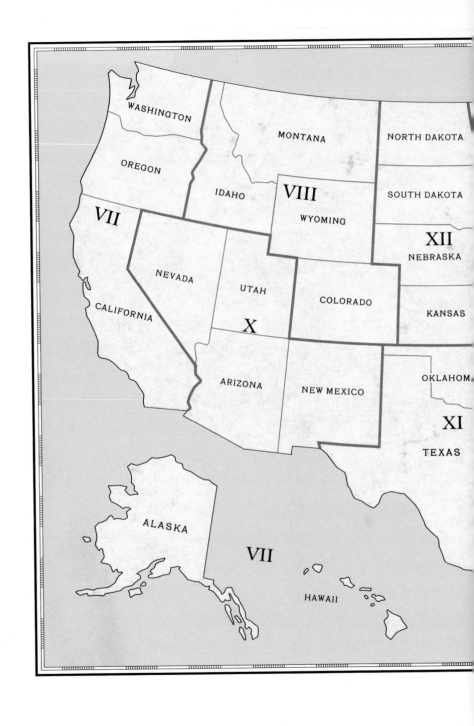

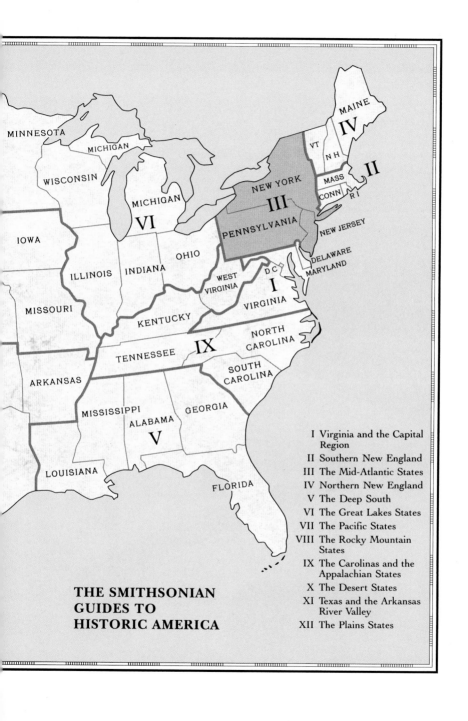

I Virginia and the Capital Region
II Southern New England
III The Mid-Atlantic States
IV Northern New England
V The Deep South
VI The Great Lakes States
VII The Pacific States
VIII The Rocky Mountain States
IX The Carolinas and the Appalachian States
X The Desert States
XI Texas and the Arkansas River Valley
XII The Plains States

**THE SMITHSONIAN
GUIDES TO
HISTORIC AMERICA**

# THE
# SMITHSONIAN
## GUIDES TO
# HISTORIC AMERICA
## THE MID-ATLANTIC STATES

TEXT BY
MICHAEL S. DURHAM

SPECIAL PHOTOGRAPHY BY
MICHAEL MELFORD

EDITORIAL DIRECTOR
ROGER G. KENNEDY
Director Emeritus, the National Museum of
American History of the Smithsonian Institution,
former Director of the National Park Service

Stewart, Tabori & Chang
NEW YORK

Published in 1998 by Stewart, Tabori & Chang, a division of U.S. Media Holdings, Inc., 115 West 18th Street, New York, NY 10011.

Due to limitations of space, additional photo credits appear on page 494 and constitute an extension of this page.

Front cover: main photo—Uris Library, Cornell University, Ithaca, NY.
inset 1—Fallingwater, Mill Run, PA..
inset 2—Thomas Edison's laboratory, West Orange, NJ
inset 3—Smithfield Street Bridge, Pittsburgh, PA.
inset 4—Unisphere, Flushing, Queens, NY.
Half-title page: Inkwell, Independence Hall, Philadephia, PA.
Frontispiece: Hopewell Village National Historic Site, Berks County, PA.
Back cover: Hasbrouck House, New Paltz, NY.

**Series Editors:** Henry Wiencek (first edition), Donald Young (revised edition)
**Editor:** Mary Luders
**Photo Editor:** Mary Z. Jenkins
**Art Director:** Diana M. Jones          **Cover Design** (revised edition): Nai Chang
**Designers:** Joseph Rutt and Paul P. Zakris (first edition), Lisa Vaughn (revised edition)
**Associate Editor:** Brigid A. Mast          **Editorial Assistant:** Barbara J. Seyda
**Cartographic Design & Production:** Guenter Vollath
**Cartographic Compilation:** George Colbert          **Data Entry:** Susan Kirby
Text revisions throughout this edition by the series editor.

Library of Congress Cataloging-in-Publication Data

Durham, Michael S. (Michael Schelling), 1935–
    The Mid-Atlantic states / text by Michael S. Durham ; special photography by
Michael Melford. — Rev. ed.
        p. cm. — (The Smithsonian guides to historic America ; 3)
    "Text revisions throughout this edition by Donald Young"—T.p. verso
    Includes index.
    ISBN 1-55670-634-0
    1. Middle Atlantic States—Guidebooks. 2. Historic sites—Middle Atlantic States—Guidebooks.
I. Melford, Michael. II. Young, Donald. III. Title. IV. Series.
F106.D95          1998
917.404'43—dc21                                                                96-40540

Distributed in the U.S. by Stewart, Tabori & Chang, 115 West 18th Street, New York, NY 10011. Distributed in Canada by General Publishing Co. Ltd., 30 Lesmill Road, Don Mills, Ontario, Canada, M3B 2T6. Distributed in all other territories by Grantham Book Services Ltd., Isaac Newton Way, Alma Park Industrial Estate, Grantham, Lincolnshire NG31 9SD, England. Sold in Australia by Peribo Pty Ltd., 58 Beaumont Road, Mount Kuring-gai, NSW 2080, Australia.

Printed in Japan

10 9 8 7 6 5 4 3 2 1

Revised edition

# C O N T E N T S

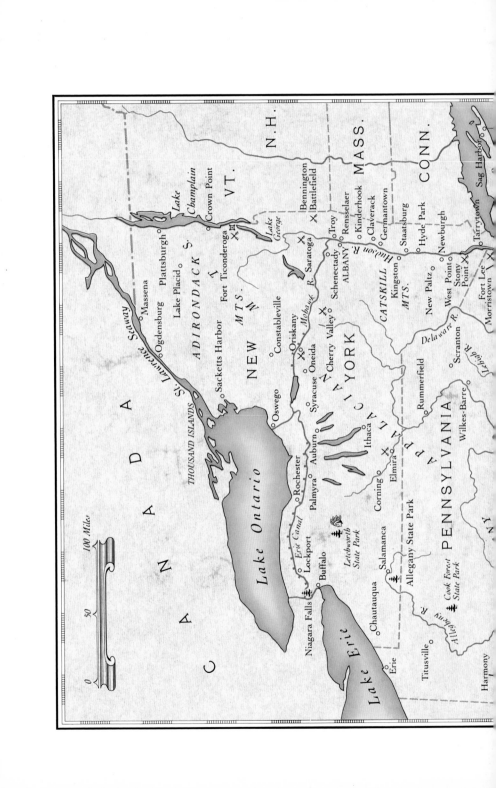

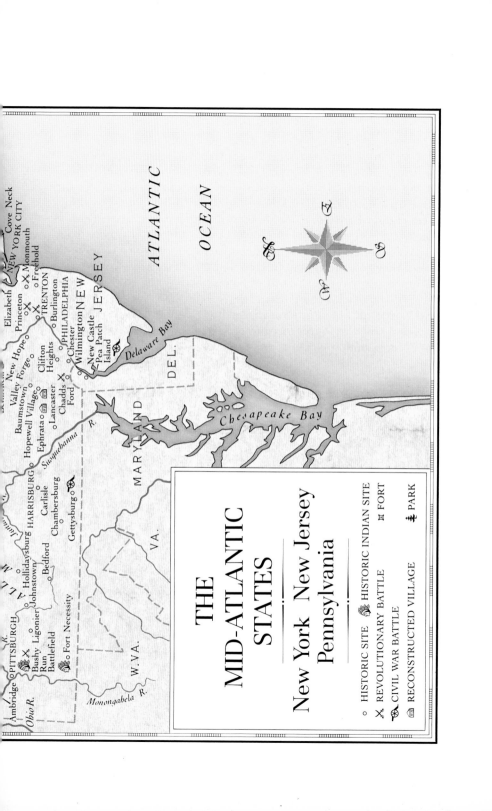

THE
MID-ATLANTIC
STATES

New York  New Jersey
Pennsylvania

○ HISTORIC SITE   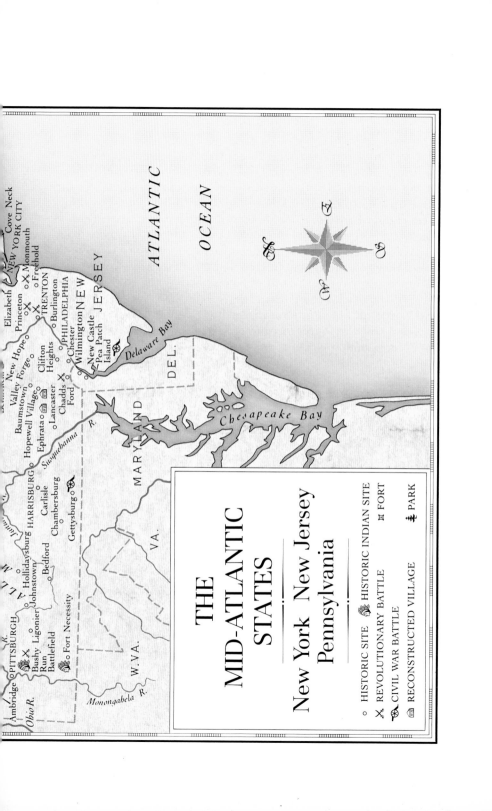 HISTORIC INDIAN SITE

✗ REVOLUTIONARY BATTLE     ⌤ FORT

⚙ CIVIL WAR BATTLE

🏛 RECONSTRUCTED VILLAGE     ⚲ PARK

ATLANTIC

OCEAN

Cove Neck
NEW YORK CITY
Monmouth
Freehold
Elizabeth
Princeton
TRENTON
Burlington
PHILADELPHIA
Chester
Wilmington NEW
New Castle
Pea Patch
Island

Delaware Bay

JERSEY

DEL.

Chesapeake Bay

New Hope
Valley Forge
Baumstown
Hopewell Village
Clifton
Heights
Lancaster
Ephrata
Chadds
Ford

Susquehanna R.

MARYLAND

HARRISBURG
Carlisle
Chambersburg
Gettysburg
Holidaysburg
Johnstown
Bedford

Harrisburg

VA.

W.VA.

Ambridge PITTSBURGH
Bushy
Run
Battlefield
Ligonier
Fort Necessity

Ohio R.

Monongahela R.

# I N T R O D U C T I O N

ROGER G. KENNEDY

If we could resurrect the villages that once lined the shores of upper Manhattan Island, Queens, Brooklyn and the Bronx— before urban growth erased them—we would find, to our surprise, an atmosphere redolent of the West Indies. The typical East River cottage had a long, Caribbean verandah; some larger country houses, like Alexander Hamilton's The Grange, had fragile tropical plants under glass, and hardier species out of doors. (Hamilton, one of the most prominent of New Yorkers in the early years of the Republic, was from the island of Nevis.)

It is startling to come upon survivals of this period, such as the Van Cortlandt house at Croton, or the Dyckman House on upper Broadway, or the southern wing of Hyde Hall near Cooperstown; such creole buildings seem out of place, until we recall that New York once paved its streets with a tax laid upon the importation of slaves.

Much of the prosperity of the English mainland colonies had been based upon such trade. Sugar and slaves made the Hudson Valley Livingstons rich; one branch of the family devoted themselves entirely to their plantations on Jamaica. The lordly Clarkes, rivals to the Livingstons, presided over more than 100,000 acres scattered about their mansion, Hyde Hall. The Clarkes and their relatives, the Hydes, derived most of their income from the 1760s until the 1820s from Jamaica, and spent it in London and New York.

The slave-and-sugar economy was followed by the trade in furs. That lively, though subsidiary, interest on the part of the European trading companies created some apparent geographic anomalies. Fort Orange (Albany) was established before New Amsterdam (New York) for the same reason that a Dutch stockade known as "The House of Hope," near Hartford, preceded settlements at the mouth of the Connecticut River, and the French built a post at Natchez before they founded New Orleans. Upriver trading stations could turn a profit in trade-goods with the Indians, while all that was needed at the points the rivers issued into the sea was a safe harbor for refitting vessels bound for the lucrative West Indies.

A set of odd facts recalls to us the cat's-cradle of trade that held the Middle Atlantic States together with the West Indies. New

Netherland was not a colony of Holland, but of the Dutch West Indies Company. New Sweden was to be a base for Swedish assaults upon the Spanish West Indies. Even Canada was, for a time, ruled by the French West Indies Company. In 1699, William Byrd of Virginia, himself a shipper of foodstuffs to the islands, noted that "Pennsylvania has little trade with England but pretty much with the West Indies, and are not precise in consulting what trade is lawful and what is not." William Bingham, one of the three most eminent men in Philadelphia, made his fortune privateering on Guadalupe. (The other two were Stephen Girard and Robert Morris, both of whom were traders with the West Indies.)

New Netherland kept looking southward after it became New York. As late as 1780, there were more slaves per capita in Dutchess County than there were in North Carolina, and many of the sweet "Dutch Colonial" houses along the Hudson were built by them. It is noteworthy that in the nineteenth century there were slave cabins upon the Roosevelt estate at Hyde Park.

Today, the counties of the central Hudson valley show the consequences of the history of their original ownership. The area remained sparsely inhabited throughout the colonial period largely because a manorial system of land tenure discouraged settlers. Elsewhere land lay all about to purchase, but along the Hudson a poor man, even after he got a little money together, could only be a tenant. That was not why land-hungry Europeans had come all that distance.

Though the Dutch West Indies Company had not been much interested in colonizing, it did reward some of its investors with ample landholdings, carrying titles more capacious than their responsibilities. These "patroonships," despite their name and despite much sentimental nonsense written about them, were not feudal. The merchants who received them took title not from the Crown but from a slave-trading commercial company and the States General. At the core of feudalism was the lord's obligation to defend his people, who, in turn, were expected to show deference to the lord in all matters legal, social, and economic. The early patroons had no rights to administer justice, nor were they expected to raise, sustain, or rally armies of tenants. How could they? The first generations of Van Rensselaers, Van Cortlandts, and Philipses were not expected to live upon their American grants, and did not do so. Kiliaen Van Rensselaer, safe in Amsterdam, had no intention of leading anybody into battle on the frontier; and he could expect no more deference from his tenant farmers than that imparted by ready cash. The patroonships lapsed into mutual rancor, enriching their owners but discouraging settlement.

When the British took over New Amsterdam, some of the patroons were still holding on, in a kind of rural capitalism that was more "modern" than the system that next was battened upon the land. Governor Thomas Dongen reversed the capitalist Dutch pattern, attempting to settle experienced captains in little domains along the borders. They were expected to keep order from their own garrisoned houses, where grain might be stored and to which villagers could go for shelter in time of trouble. The local seigneur, knight, or squire sat as justice of the peace and judge of courts for civil, criminal, and administrative cases. And, by George, he would brook no seditious curates; all clergymen must have his approval.

Near Kingston, Captain Thomas Chambers was given a "manor" upon which he was expected to maintain a mansion-house defensible against the French and Indians. The French authorities in Quebec also made grants, parcelling out most of what is now western Vermont and that portion of New York lying along Lakes Champlain and George. Some New Yorkers still hold chains of title reaching back to Dongen and the Marquis de Beauharnois, governor of New France.

Much of Putnam County was held by Tory manor-lords, whose property was confiscated after the Revolutionary War and divided into a multitude of small holdings. Farther north, the great sweep of countryside on the east side of the river and north of the Highlands all the way to Troy remained closely held by a few landlords who chose the winning side—largely the Van Rensselaers and Livingstons. To this day it is a land of great estates.

In New York, New Jersey and Pennsylvania the absentee landlords were never farmers on a large scale until Stephen Van Rensselaer and George Clarke became so after reading the novels of Sir Walter Scott in the nineteenth century. They were speculators, holding land with little intention of cultivation, squeezing tenants for high rents and hoping for windfalls as the tenants' improvements reverted to the owner after a lease expired. This system led to revolts in Ireland in the seventeenth and eighteenth centuries, and in New York in the 1840s.

The Hudson Valley "Antirent Wars" began in 1839 when the Van Rensselaer family demanded $400,000 in back rent from their farm tenants. The farmers rioted, leading Governor Seward to call up the militia. The violence continued intermittently until 1846. In a throwback to pre-Revolutionary methods of giving vent to grievances, the farmers disguised themselves in Indian clothing and tarred and feathered the deputy sheriffs who delivered eviction papers. In 1845 a deputy was murdered in Delaware County, prompting the governor to declare that district to be in a state of rebellion. The farmers won a victory in 1846, when the new state constitution forbade the issuing of leaseholds.

New York and Pennsylvania both benefited from three quite distinct Irish immigrations, well before the potato famine led to the great removal of the Irish peasantry to America and even before New York benefited from cheap Irish labor upon the Erie Canal. The first of these earlier settlements began in the seventeenth century, and was led by tough Scotch-Irish frontiersmen. The second brought to the fore equally hard but considerably more affluent and courtly Irish squires. The third produced, in Pennsylvania, a number of Irish artisans.

The Scotch-Irish, Presbyterian, plantation-trained military clans began to arrive in force in the 1730s. Some indication of their presence can be found in place names like Londonderry, New Hampshire, and New York's Orange and Ulster counties; but it was in western Pennsylvania that they began their occupation of the Appalachian valleys. From there they spread south and west into western Virginia (where one of their number, George Croghan, grew to be a squire after he and his partners acquired 2,500,000 acres), and on into the Carolinas, Tennessee and Kentucky. Though they carried with them the bitter memory of being ground between Anglican landlords and Roman Catholic peasants, and though their early photographs make them all seem as grim as Stonewall Jackson and John C. Calhoun, they knew how to laugh as well as how to scalp.

Some of them, and some Catholic squires as well, rose to become the dominant landowners in the inland empire of New York and Pennsylvania, managing huge estates on the edge of Iroquois holdings, from the Adirondacks to the Genesee and the Ohio. The Johnstons, Warrens, Constables, Lynches, Croghans, Duanes and De Lanceys vied with the Van Rensselaers and Livingstons until 1783, but many of them took the losing side in the

Revolutionary War. They left behind only their names upon streets and villages. Nonetheless, it is arresting to recall how different was the social status implied by a brogue in 1800 in the streets of Lynchville (Rome), Constableville, Warrensburg, Johnstown, Duanesville, or along Delancey Street, from what it implied after the Famine and the Erie Canal.

We know very little about the Irish glass-making elite who dominated the cultural life of Pittsburgh in its early days, but we do know of the generosity of George Croghan's heiress, Mary Elizabeth Schenley. She clung to two hundred acres in the heart of that city, but did not cling to all the revenues she derived therefrom. She was a great philanthropist, almost matching the benefactions of Stephen Girard at the other end of the state. Two rooms from her Picnic House, Pittsburgh's finest Greek Revival interiors, were rescued recently and flown up, in a kind of seraphic adaptive re-use, to repose on the upper floors of the University of Pittsburgh's "Cathedral of Learning." Her gift of land for a great cemetery still provides green relief for the citizens of the city, and offered employment to John Chislett, a practitioner of the English Regency style who was the city's most distinguished architect until the advent of Henry Hobson Richardson, fifty years later, in the 1880s.

There are places where this region can be seen much as it was before anybody arrived. An Adirondack crag or scree is unlikely to be much altered over centuries, unless bearing metal and, thus, drawing lightning. Pine barrens are very little affected by the centuries of human intervention, and there is wildness in thousands of acres of bogs contained in the granite uplands of central Pennsylvania.

But there is something especially consoling in large trees. So we will look for them. In New York, old growth timber is not so common as, nor is it to be found where, one might think. The largest tracts are near Claryville, on the west side of the Catskills. In the Adirondacks, depleted by a century of providing both fuel and lumber for cities downstream, there is much that has been abandoned to the wild, but not much virgin timber. One patch lies at the end of a good half-day hike near Wanakena.

Stretches of moorland, like Tug Hill, southwest of Watertown, and the duneland along Lake Ontario have miles of open land, remarkably unspoiled, and one can find a quarter-mile or so of primitive Long Island, though no one would mistake Montauk for a wilderness. For that, one has to go to northern New Jersey, which has some fifty-acre stands of climax hardwoods, one tended by Rutgers University near New Brunswick, and the pine barrens.

Pennsylvania has lost most of its accessible forest cover several times, but remnants of the old world can still be found. Around State College there are many patches of old growth trees. At the Alan Seger Natural Area, in Huntingdon County, there is a half-mile trail through old hemlocks along Stone Creek. Ricketts Glen Natural Area, in Luzerne County, is larger, more remote, and with huge white pines as well as hemlocks.

Any American who wishes to show a European friend why the rural areas of this country are different from the Old World's, and in a positive way, should get away from the homogenized international cities and into the countryside, anywhere from Lakes Erie and Ontario to Altoona, Schenectady and Cooperstown. This interior empire centers upon the incomparable beauties of the Finger Lakes, America's supreme pastoral landscape, and the Hellenic subtleties of its villages. Niagara Falls will do; so will the World Trade Center. But Geneva or Cooperstown, Skaneateles, Baldwinsville, Aurora, Ovid, or Poolville do not need to raise their voices to make their point. We can leave to others description of the urban accomplishments of the twentieth century. They are easy to find, from Buffalo, with its anthology of works of genius by Richardson, Louis Sullivan and Frank Lloyd Wright, to the parade of vanities along lower Park Avenue and "Arragansett." Let us focus, finally, on the wonders of the interior and limit ourselves to the Greek Revival.

There was a time when Elias Baker in Altoona, William Gurley Strong in Geneva, and ten thousand less affluent people could build clean, clear, classical houses, full of justifiable pride in a common achievement. Isaac Meeson had shown them the way as the century opened, in a somewhat earlier style—his house, Mt. Braddock, languishes, south of Pittsburgh, though it is the finest Georgian house west of the Appalachians. But the inland empire did not organize its aesthetics fully until the resumption of American self-confidence in the 1820s, a psychological and economic event expressed in a hundred thousand sudden columns. Go and see! This classicizing coincided with the settling of the uplands, and with the creation of the vineyards and orchards that continue to provide us with wine and fruit, and a well-tended, deliberate landscape today.

# NEW YORK CITY: BATTERY PARK
## TO
# MURRAY HILL

OPPOSITE: *Near Madison Square Park, the Appellate Division of the New York State Supreme Court is housed in a small but lavishly decorated marble building.*

"Ｎew York, thy name's Delirium," a poet once wrote, and never have truer words been written about any city. But it wasn't always so. When the first minister arrived from Holland in 1627, he found a half-starved Dutch settlement living in bark huts on the southern end of Manhattan. The 270 inhabitants struck their pastor as being a sorry lot, shiftless and without ambition. In 1627, New Amsterdam was two years old. The year before, Governor Peter Minuit secured his place in history by "purchasing" the real estate on the island from the Indians for $24. Since the Indians did not regard land as real estate, but as a place to live, fish, and grow crops, the "purchase" price was meaningless to them. Both Manhattan and Staten islands were home to prosperous Indian communities, but they were decimated by European diseases.

The original colony settled on the flat plain on Manhattan's southern tip, a particularly windy and exposed spot overlooking New York Bay, which would become one of the great harbors of the world. Starting about where 57th Street is today, two long ridges run north to the end of the twelve-and-a-half-mile-long island. They form a diagonal valley through which runs Broadway, the one thoroughfare that goes the entire length of the city. Manhattan reaches its highest elevation of 267 feet in Washington Heights. This strategic point—once important to the Indians—had reverted to the wilds and was still so a century and a half later, when the Americans lost it to the British during the Revolution.

In a series of relatively bloodless swaps of territory, the English took Manhattan away from the Dutch in 1664, ceded it back to them in 1673, and regained it the following year under the Treaty of Westminster. Under the British, New York became less a trading post and more a permanent settlement. All the time, the city was growing, pushing northward from the foothold on the tip of the island. The city took on a cosmopolitan air early: In 1644 a resident priest recorded eighteen languages spoken in the city.

The British found New Yorkers unruly and hard to govern. In 1689, Jacob Leisler, who was eventually hanged for treason, actually overthrew the Crown representatives, and, during his two-year rule, launched an attack upon the French in Canada. In 1734, the printer John Peter Zenger was jailed for "seditious libel," having criticized his British rulers, but he won the case, establishing the principle of a free press in the process.

In the colonial years, New York City ranked behind Boston and Philadelphia in both population and trade; besides, a sense of

*This painting of lower Manhattan as seen from Brooklyn was done about 1757 when the city had "2 or 3,000 houses and 16 or 17,000 inhabitants."*

their city's cultural shortcomings rankled New York's prominent citizens. In 1754, for example, Columbia University was started to give New York some of the qualities William and Mary gave Virginia, Yale gave Connecticut, and Harvard conferred upon Boston. Cultural striving grew with the city and led to the founding in the next century of such institutions as the Metropolitan Opera, the Museum of Natural History, and the Metropolitan Museum of Art.

Though New York was a center of Tory sentiment, American grievances against the mother country—particularly the desire for representation in matters of taxation—were as strong among some merchants in New York as among their counterparts in Philadelphia or Boston. In order to raise revenue for the defense of the colonies, Parliament passed the Stamp Act in 1765 requiring stamps on legal, commercial, and other papers. In response, the rowdy Sons of Liberty, a secret society of workingmen, rioted and burned the royal governor in effigy. The Stamp Act Congress, consisting of delegates from nine colonies, met in New York in October to protest taxation by a Parliament in London and assert their rights, as "Englishmen," to be taxed by their own representa-

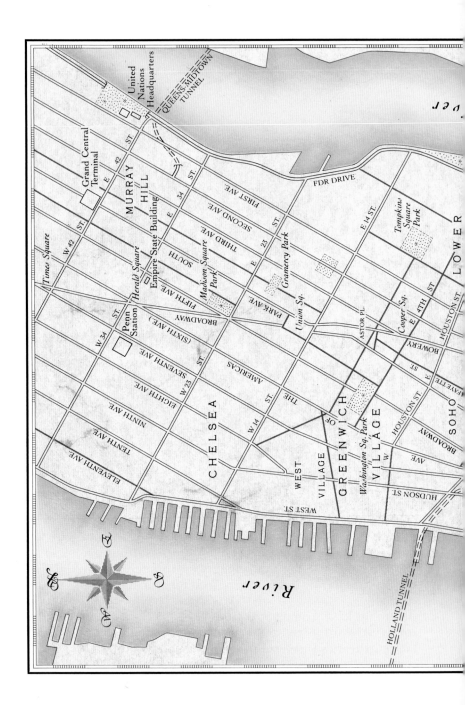

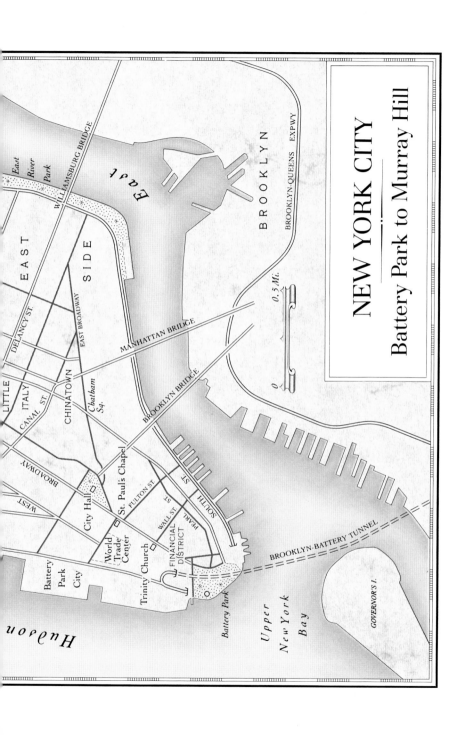

NEW YORK CITY
—
Battery Park to Murray Hill

tives. New York staged its own Tea Party in 1774, and on July 9, 1776, rioters toppled the statue of George III in Bowling Green and melted it down into bullets that, legend says, killed four hundred Redcoats during the Revolution.

Because it was strategically placed at the mouth of the Hudson River, New York City was a valuable prize in the early days of the Revolution. In April 1776, Washington moved from Boston to New York with a force of 19,000. In June and July, General Howe landed 31,600 men on Staten Island, supported by a fleet commanded by his brother, Admiral Lord Richard Howe, which controlled the waters around Manhattan. With this ominous presence literally within view, all Washington could do was dig in and wait for Howe to show his hand.

In late August, Howe began landing men in Gravesend Bay on the part of Long Island that is now Brooklyn. On August 27, Howe opened the Battle of Long Island at Brooklyn Heights by advancing on the American positions, which had been reinforced with additional troops from Manhattan. The Americans held off the first British attack on their right, but soon found themselves attacked from the rear by a column of ten thousand men that had marched unopposed through an undefended pass further to the east. In the fierce battle that followed, some 1,300 Americans were either killed, wounded, or captured. Some historians assert that Howe could have ended the Revolution by pressing his advantage; instead he hesitated—for him, a typical reaction to victory—and settled in for a siege. The respite allowed Washington to ferry his men back to Manhattan during the night of August 29–30, before the British realized the evacuation was underway.

On September 15, the British landed at Kips Bay on Manhattan's East Side (about 34th Street). They met almost no resistance from the retreating Americans, his men's poor showing inspiring one of Washington's displays of rage. However, Howe's caution—or the fact that he stopped for tea at the farm of Mrs. John Murray—allowed the five thousand Americans stationed in Lower Manhattan enough time to escape up the West Side.

The Americans put on a better show during the Battle of Harlem Heights the next day. There two thousand Americans beat back five thousand Hessians and British in a confrontation in a

OPPOSITE: *Federal Hall, Wall Street . Washington took the presidential oath on the balcony of the original building in 1789. The statue is by J. Q. A. Ward.*

*A Currier & Ives view of New York City, 1879 (detail).*

buckwheat field (present location: about 119th Street between Broadway and Riverside Drive), but accomplished little except to delay Howe's advance and raise American morale. A month later, after the first British attempt to envelop his position, Washington concluded he could not hold the line, and on October 18 began to evacuate his army to White Plains. Of the three thousand men left at Fort Washington, fifty-three were killed and the rest captured when the fort fell to the British on November 16.

The fall of Fort Washington two months after the British landing at Kips Bay ended the American presence on Manhattan. The city itself was all but destroyed by two serious fires—the first on a September night of 1776, the other two years later. The British occupied New York for the rest of the war—until November 25, 1785, when Washington and his army triumphantly paraded down Bowery Lane (shortly thereafter Washington said farewell to his officers at Fraunces Tavern). For years, Evacuation Day was a major holiday in New York City.

New York City was the state capital until 1797, the capital of the Confederation from the year 1785, and, for a year after Washington was sworn in as president in 1789, the capital of the new republic. In the first federal census of 1790, New York's population was some 33,000, smaller than either Boston or Philadelphia. Two years later twenty-four brokers operating under a tree on Wall Street formed a stock trading organization that became the New York Stock Exchange in 1817. But in 1792, Philadelphia was still the nation's financial center.

In 1807, the Legislature appointed a planning commission in an attempt to regulate the city's unruly growth. The Commissioners' Report of 1811, which covered the city from about East Houston Street north to present-day 155th Street, imposed the grid system of the newer portions of the city to cover most of the rest of the area with uniform blocks two hundred feet deep. Critics at the time attacked the plan for making no allowances for the city's irregular terrain and jested that the commissioners had come up with the grid by laying a mason's sieve over a map of the city. Frederick Law Olmsted, architect of Central Park, later attacked the senseless "tyranny" of the plan. He also claimed it was responsible for the development of the tenement, a narrow, deep building that gave residents awkwardly shaped rooms with little light or air.

By the census of 1820 New York was the largest city in the nation, with 123,706 people, but the city's preeminence became clearer after the Erie Canal opened in 1825. The canal, which connected the Hudson River (and thus New York City) to the Great Lakes at Buffalo, brought goods flowing through its port, attracted capital to its financial markets, and transformed New York City into the transportation center of the country. All this, in turn, attracted people. In twenty years, New York's population more than doubled—to 312,710 in 1840—and doubled again—to 696,115 in 1850. In 1898, the Bronx, Queens, Brooklyn, and Staten Island voted to merge with New York City, an addition that made Manhattan, with 22.5 square miles, the smallest borough. Interestingly, only the Bronx is attached to the mainland; otherwise New York is a city of islands—some fifty in all.

At midcentury, the city's population was swelled beyond imagining by the greatest wave of immigration that history has ever seen—a new wave of Irish fleeing the potato famine in 1846, followed by Germans, Jews from Eastern Europe, and Italians in the 1880s, to name but a few. In 1886 the Statue of Liberty was presented "to the American people," the writer O. Henry wryly observed, "on behalf of the French government for the purpose of welcoming Irish immigrants into the Dutch city of New York."

Officially the statue was given by the French to commemorate the
French-American alliance during the Revolutionary War, but it
soon became a symbol of freedom for new Americans.

The immigrants, crowded into slums and tenements, were
grist for the political mill. The notorious political machine known
as "Tammany Hall" originally got its start as a charitable organization to help the newcomers. After William Marcy Tweed took it
over in 1860, it controlled the police, politicians of both parties,
newspapers, the courts, and state and local government. The
Tweed Ring may have stolen as much as $200 million from the city
treasury. In the end, Tweed lost control of the Democratic Party to
Samuel J. Tilden and died in jail in 1878.

In 1871, the first office building elevator was installed in the
Equitable Building on Broadway (this building burned and was
replaced in 1915); some twenty years later, the first building in
New York using steel construction went up. These two developments made it possible for the city to grow skyward. Although
Chicagoans maintain the skyscraper was actually born in their city,
it matured in New York with such colossal monuments as the
Woolworth Building (1915) and Chrysler Building (1930). Skyscrapers of this era were either symbols of corporate power or
expressions of individual ego, with the builders placing a premium
on height. For example, when Frank W. Woolworth put up his own
building in 1914, he ordered his architect to make sure it was taller
than the Metropolitan Life Tower, then the tallest building in the
world. His reason: The Metropolitan Life Insurance Company had
once denied him a loan.

From 1879 to 1917, the art of architecture flourished in New
York in what was immodestly called the American Renaissance. No
firm was more successful in these heady years than McKim, Mead
& White, founded in 1879. They built mansions, libraries, universities, clubs, and civic buildings, and the celebrity of their leading
partner, the urbane Stanford White, was only increased when he
was shot to death in the roof garden of a building he had designed,
the original Madison Square Garden. Richard Morris Hunt, designer of the monumental central portion of the Fifth Avenue
facade of the Metropolitan Museum of Art, Cass Gilbert (U.S.
Custom House), Bertram Grosvenor Goodhue (St. Bartholomew's
Church), and his partner Ralph Adams Cram (Cathedral of St.
John the Divine) were other prominent architects of the period.

New York City's crowding, its frenetic pace, its unrelenting
quest for what poet Delmore Schwartz has called "more: more and

more: always more" are not to everyone's taste; architect Frank Lloyd Wright and the novelist Sinclair Lewis were two well-known figures who simply didn't like New York. Wright ill-naturedly suggested that demolishing New York City might solve its problems, while Lewis, irked as are so many by the city's high prices, complained in 1937 that "eighty cents still seems like too much to pay for orange juice."

More often writers and artists have turned to the city's streets for inspiration, sometimes declaring allegiance, as F. Scott Fitzgerald did when he wrote after sailing into the harbor in 1932, "that New York, however often I might leave it, was home." Frequently writers drew on their knowledge of other cities in an attempt to capture an elusive New York City in words. "New York is nothing like Paris; it is nothing like London; and it is not Spokane multiplied by sixty, or Detroit multiplied by four," E. B. White wrote in 1949. His words echo the sentiments Theodore Dreiser expressed in 1929: "Not London. Not Paris. Not Moscow. Not any city I have ever seen. So strong. So immense. So elate."

In 1909 essayist Edward S. Martin unwittingly bestowed a nickname on the city when he compared it to a big apple that gets "a disproportionate share of the national sap." These days New York City also gets a disproportionate share of the national problems, but New Yorkers generally don't complain about the distribution. Most agree that life in The Big Apple is impossible, but, they stoutly maintain—despite the noise, the dirt, the crowding, the crime, the traffic—they wouldn't live anyplace else.

The New York City chapters are organized, like the city itself, by its many neighborhoods and districts, each with its own character, history, and architecture. The entries start at the southernmost tip of Manhattan and proceed north, followed by the outer boroughs—the Bronx, Brooklyn, Queens, and Staten Island. However, nothing in the city is permanent: SoHo, for example, was until recently a factory and warehouse district; today it is the center of the city's artistic life. Similarly, many of Park Avenue's apartments and hotels have been replaced by office buildings, some, like the Seagram Building, modern masterpieces. Other architectural monuments, such as Pennsylvania Station, are simply gone, replaced by buildings no one would care to look at twice. And even as this chapter is written, Chinatown is spilling over into Little Italy, and the slums of the Lower East Side are being gentrified by young urban professionals, the city's newest sociological phenomenon.

# L O W E R     M A N H A T T A N

## BATTERY PARK

Situated on landfill at the foot of Manhattan, Battery Park commands a splendid view of New York Harbor with the skyscrapers of Lower Manhattan and Wall Street rising to the north. The Park, which extends west of State Street across from the Custom House, takes its name from the battery of artillery pieces that once protected the original port. The **Netherlands Memorial Monument,** a gift to the city from Holland in 1924, is a flagpole immortalizing the tale of Governor Peter Minuit "buying" Manhattan Island for $24 from the Indians. The Park is also the site of Castle Clinton, right next to the departure point for the ferries to the Statue of Liberty and Ellis Island and a short walk from the World Trade Center, where visitors can orient themselves from the observation decks.

At the foot of Whitehall Street a few blocks east, the three-slip ferry terminal with its three monumental arched openings and sweeping loggia was built in 1909 to provide ferry service to Brooklyn. Now called the **Battery Maritime Terminal,** the landmark building is also the landing for Coast Guard ferries to **Governor's Island,** today a Coast Guard installation not open to the public. In colonial times, the island was home to both English and Dutch governors. **Fort Jay,** at one time the city's main point of defense, was completed about 1798 with volunteer labor from Columbia College and trade organizations. Like Castle Clinton, its matching fortification on Manhattan, Governor's Island's **Castle William** was part of the fortification fever preceding the War of 1812.

### Castle Clinton National Monument

The land on which Castle Clinton now stands was originally an island two hundred feet off the tip of Manhattan. The United States built the fortress in 1808–1811 to prepare for war with England, but its guns have never been fired in anger. The fortress was named Castle Clinton (in honor of DeWitt Clinton, city mayor and state governor) after the War of 1812. In 1824, it was renamed Castle Garden and opened for public ceremonies, demonstrations, and entertainment. Samuel F. B. Morse demonstrated his "wireless telegraph" here, and P. T. Barnum's "Swedish Nightingale," the soprano Jenny Lind, made her American debut here in 1850.

*The Statue of Liberty's distinct features were inspired by the sculptor's mother, supposedly a formidable personality.* OVERLEAF: *The Battery Maritime Terminal, built in 1909, where ferries to Governor's Island depart.*

In 1855, the island was connected with Manhattan, and the castle became an immigration center. (At that point, processing immigrants was still the city's responsibility.) Eight million immigrants passed through here until the federal government took over the job and moved the facility to Ellis Island in 1890. In 1906, the architects McKim, Mead & White remodeled it for an aquarium, which lasted until 1940. In 1946, the federal government opened it to the public as a national landmark. Inside is a circular courtyard and a small museum dedicated to the history and many lives of the massive structure.

LOCATION: Battery Park. HOURS: 8–5:30 Daily. FEE: None. TELE-PHONE: 212–344–7220.

## STATUE OF LIBERTY

No symbol of America is more beloved than the Statue of Liberty, and none defines so well why the United States is unique among nations. Ironically, it is the creation of another country, France, which presented it to the United States in commemoration of the friendship between the two nations. But the statue quickly came to represent much more. Standing as it does, in New York Harbor,

*Detail of ceremonial "Ghost Dance" dress, made of painted buckskin, from the collection of the Museum of the American Indian.*

at the portal of the New World through which millions of immigrants passed, it bore silent witness to the arrival of people in flight from many countries who dreamed of a new life in the land of the free.

In her poem "The New Colossus," Emma Lazarus acclaimed the "mighty woman with a torch . . . her name / Mother of Exiles. From her beacon-hand / Glows world-wide welcome." From silent lips, the poet heard the statue say, "'Give me your tired, your poor, / Your huddled masses yearning to breathe free, / The wretched refuse of your teeming shore. / Send these, the homeless, tempest-tost to me, / I lift my lamp beside the golden door!'"

The historian Edouard Laboulaye and the sculptor Frédéric Auguste Bartholdi conceived the idea of a statue as a gift from France. The French people, impassioned advocates of political liberty, contributed all the money. Bartholdi may have used his mother as a model for the face, his wife for the figure. Gustave Eiffel, builder of the Eiffel Tower, designed the interior iron support structure of the statue, which was built by the Paris firm of Gaget, Gautier & Company and covered with hammered copper sheets 2.5mm thick. Americans chipped in to pay for the 89-foot-high base, designed by Richard Morris Hunt.

The display of the hand and torch at the Centennial Exposition in Philadelphia in 1876 and of the head and shoulders in Paris in 1878 generated great anticipation. The base and statue were assembled on what was then called Bedloe's Island, and dedicated on October 28, 1886. Light first radiated from the torch that evening. The statue is 151 feet in height; it weighs 450,000 pounds. A restoration, completed in time for the 1986 centennial, was celebrated with an international flotilla of ships and a blizzard of fireworks.

> LOCATION: Liberty Island, New York Harbor. HOURS: Ferries from Battery Park: 9:15–5 Daily. Extended hours and New Jersey ferries June through August. FEE: For ferry. TELEPHONE: 212–363–3200.

## ELLIS ISLAND

After the federal government took over the job of processing immigrants in 1890, it established a center on Ellis Island in 1892. The present brick-and-limestone buildings, opened in 1900 after a fire destroyed the earlier facility, were overwhelmed by the flood of new arrivals from Europe. In 1907 alone, more than one million immigrants passed through Ellis Island. World War I and laws restricting immigration drastically reduced the flow in the 1920s. The facility, thereafter underutilized, closed in 1954.

In 1965, Ellis Island (212–269–5755) was made part of the Statue of Liberty National Monument. The main building was refurbished for the 1992 centennial. Thirty galleries feature photos, oral histories, ethnic music, and other exhibits relating to twelve million immigrants who account for one-third of the U.S. population. The American Immigrant Wall of Honor has 420,000 names, the world's largest wall of names.

## U.S. CUSTOM HOUSE

The Custom House is on the site of Fort Amsterdam, built by the Dutch in 1625. Government House was built here in 1789 for President George Washington, but he and the government moved to Philadelphia before it was completed. After the state government moved to Albany, the building was torn down. The Beaux-Arts Custom House (1907) was designed by Cass Gilbert. Sculptor

Daniel Chester French created *The Four Continents* on pedestals on the ground-floor level. The cartouche with the U.S. arms over the main entrance is by Karl Bitter.

## National Museum of the American Indian

The George Gustav Heye Center of the museum, established in 1989 under the auspices of the Smithsonian Institution, is in the U.S. Custom House. The center was conceived as a place where indigenous peoples of the Americas can celebrate their heritage and share with others something of what it means to be an Indian.

The collections, assembled largely by Heye, cover ten thousand years of Native heritage. Among thousands of masterworks are intricate wood, horn, and stone carvings from the Pacific Northwest; hides and garments from the Plains; pottery and basketry from the Southwest; ceramic figures from the Caribbean; carved jade from the Olmec and Maya peoples; textiles and gold carvings from the Andes; and featherwork from the Amazon.

Visitors may meet artists, elders, and storytellers from the Americas and Hawaii, and see films and videos from native producers. School groups may attend educational programs.

LOCATION: U.S. Custom House, One Bowling Green. HOURS: 10–5 Daily. FEE: None. TELEPHONE: 212–668–6624.

**Bowling Green Park,** just north of the Custom House, became the city's first park in 1733 when it was leased to private citizens for an annual rent of one peppercorn for a favorite pastime of the era, outdoor bowling. Before that it was a cattle market and parade ground. The gilded lead fence erected to protect the statue of George III still stands, although the statue itself was pulled down by patriots on July 9, 1776 and turned into bullets.

South of the Custom House, at 7 State Street, the **James Watson House** is the last of a row of elegant homes in the Battery District; its two wings were designed in 1793 and 1806. It is now the Rectory of the **Shrine of Saint Elizabeth Ann Seton** (212–269–6865), the first American-born saint.

Lower Manhattan is often described as a sunless canyon of towering buildings bordering on narrow streets. Many older commercial buildings are architecturally and historically important, such as the

1921 **Cunard Building** (25 Broadway), with Renaissance facade and ornate interior, and, across the street, Carrère & Hastings's 1922 **Standard Oil Building** topped by a structure shaped like an oil lamp. The Zoning Resolution of 1916, a watershed law requiring setbacks in tall buildings, was passed in reaction to the 1915 **Equitable Building** (120 Broadway), which rises straight up for forty stories, blocking out light and air. The required setbacks gave New York's early skyscrapers their distinctive look.

South of Wall Street is **Hanover Square,** once an exclusive residential enclave where one of Trinity Church's parishioners, William Kidd, lived before he was hanged for piracy in England in 1701. The square is graced by the noteworthy Italianate **India House,** now a private club, built in 1854 for the Hanover Bank. As a plaque in the Square notes, a fire that destroyed 650 buildings began in the vicinity in 1835.

# WALL STREET

This internationally famed thoroughfare marked the Dutch colony's northernmost limit when Peter Stuyvesant had a protective wall built there in 1653. By the mid-nineteenth century it was the country's banking and financial center and went on to finance this nation's industrial expansion. From this period of unprecedented financial activity emerged the great financial barons—such men as Jay Gould, Jim Fisk, Daniel Drew, Jim Hill, E. H. Harriman, and the elder J. P. Morgan. These years were also marked by periodic scandal and financial collapse, as with the attempt by Gould and Fisk to corner the gold market, causing the Panic of 1869.

Imposing buildings designed to reflect financial stability, integrity, and prosperity line the street's few blocks. In addition to the Federal Hall National Memorial and, just off Wall Street, the New York Stock Exchange, are the 1913 **Morgan Guaranty Trust Company Building** (23 Wall Street), its facade still scarred from an unexplained bomb explosion that killed thirty-three people in 1920; the 1929 former **Bank of Manhattan Building** (40 Wall Street), intended to be the world's tallest building; and the 1842 former **First National City Bank Building** (55 Wall Street), with its massive granite columns and domed central hall. First the Merchant's Exchange, and then a custom house until the new one opened in 1907, the building was extensively remodeled by architects McKim, Mead & White.

*A World War II–era parade up Broadway. New York traditionally welcomes heroes, celebrities, and sports champions with a march up this historic street amidst a shower of tickertape.*

## Federal Hall National Memorial

The British City Hall, begun in 1699, originally stood at this site. In 1735, the printer John Peter Zenger was tried and acquitted there, in the first trial for freedom of the press, and, in 1765, delegates from nine colonies gathered in the hall to protest the Stamp Act. The building, renamed Federal Hall, hosted Congress under both the Articles of Confederation and the new constitution, from 1785 until the government moved to Philadelphia in 1790. Washington was sworn in as the first President on the second-floor balcony on April 30, 1789. The building was demolished in 1812.

Built as a U.S custom house in 1842, this fine Greek Revival building designed by Town and Davis later served as a subtreasury (1862) and is now a museum displaying Washington-era artifacts and administered by the National Park Service. The statue of Washington was sculpted in 1883 by a leading American artist of the late nineteenth century, John Quincy Adams Ward, and is placed approximately where he was sworn in.

LOCATION: 26 Wall Street. HOURS: 9–5 Monday–Friday. FEE: None. TELEPHONE: 212–825–6888.

# New York Stock Exchange

A sculpted tree commemorates the exchange's founding under a buttonwood tree on May 17, 1792. The present building was designed in the style of a Greek temple in 1903 by architect George B. Post. The sculpture by J. Q. A. Ward on the pediment is a placid scene depicting *Integrity Protecting the World*. Exhibits on the history and operation of the exchange are on the third floor; the trading floor—one of New York's great interiors—can be seen from the visitors' gallery.

The New York Stock Exchange grew to prominence after the construction of the Erie Canal, which was completed in 1825, and when Philadelphia lost the Bank of the United States in the 1830s. The Civil War and the financial battles over control of the expanding railroads further stimulated its growth while fortunes were made by men like Morgan, Vanderbilt, Harriman, and Gould. A period of unprecedented growth and optimism after World War I came to a sudden end in October 1929, with the stock market crash.

LOCATION: 20 Broad Street. HOURS: 9:15–4 Monday–Friday. FEE: None. TELEPHONE: 212–656–5167.

# Fraunces Tavern Museum

At the end of the American revolution, George Washington led his triumphant troops back into New York City and said farewell to his officers at this location on December 4, 1783. Built in 1719 as a residence for the merchant Stephen De Lancey, member of the powerful New York family that would lose its extensive holdings because of its Loyalist sympathies, the Georgian building was turned into a tavern in 1763 by Samuel Fraunces, a West Indian who became Washington's steward after the war.

Only the brick in the west wall is original. In 1904, the Sons of the Revolution purchased and reconstructed the building, based on what little evidence remained. Today the building houses a museum on the upper floors that includes period rooms, mementoes of Washington and his farewell dinner, and information on the building's history. A restaurant occupies the ground floor.

LOCATION: Corner of Pearl and Broad streets. HOURS: 10–4:45 Monday–Friday, 12–5 Saturday. FEE: Yes. TELEPHONE: 212–425–1778.

*The interior of Trinity Church, designed by Richard Upjohn.* OPPOSITE: *The graveyard at Trinity Church, where Alexander Hamilton and Robert Fulton are buried.*

## Trinity Church

Completed in 1846, Richard Upjohn's Trinity Church and James Renwick, Jr.'s Grace Church gave America a new set of Gothic Revival monuments. The former's 280-foot spire was for years New York City's leading landmark until surrounded and dwarfed by skyscrapers. Richard Morris Hunt based the design of the doors on those of the Baptistery in Florence. Since the roof vaults are made of plaster and need no extra support, the flying buttresses are merely decorative—as they are at St. Patrick's, uptown.

This is the third Gothic church on the site. The first, built in 1697, was destroyed in the great New York fire of 1776. Many prominent New Yorkers are buried in the graveyard: Robert Fulton, Alexander Hamilton, and James Lawrence, whose dying words, "Don't give up the ship," became a slogan for the War of 1812. A small museum in the church contains communion silver and items related to the history of the church. As the result of a land grant from Queen Anne in 1705 that included a good portion of Lower Manhattan, Trinity is still one of the area's most benevolent landlords.

LOCATION: Broadway and Wall Street.

## SOUTH STREET SEAPORT MUSEUM

By preserving some of the early-nineteenth-century buildings in this waterfront district and establishing a museum, the South Street Seaport hoped to salvage something of the era when it was known as the "Street of Ships" and the bowsprits of clipper ships docked in the East River nearly touched the buildings on shore. (In the days of sail the East River, which is better protected from the elements than the Hudson, received most of the city's shipping; steamships shifted to the deeper Hudson.) Three historic vessels—two large sailing cargo ships, *Peking* and *Wavertree,* and the lightship *Ambrose*—are open for tours. The 1885 schooner *Pioneer* sweeps visitors across New York harbor several times a day in season. The 1893 fishing schooner *Lettie G. Howard* offers training programs for teenagers and adults.

The area includes **Schermerhorn Row** on the block bounded by John, Front, Fulton, and South streets. These fine buildings were built in 1811–1812 by the merchant Peter Schermerhorn on tidal land that he filled. The **Museum** (207 Front Street) is included in an eleven-block historic district filled with Greek Revival, Georgian, Federal, and Victorian warehouses and buildings.

LOCATION: Fulton Street at the East River. HOURS: April through September: 10–6 Friday–Wednesday, 10–8 Thursday; October through March: 10–5 Wednesday–Monday. FEE: Yes (for ships and museum). TELEPHONE: 212-748-8600.

# C I T Y      H A L L      A R E A

In colonial times, **City Hall Park** was New York City's village green. Much of the protest against British rule was focused here. On the west lawn is a **Liberty Flag-Pole Marker,** a tablet and flagpole commemorating the poles the Sons of Liberty defiantly erected in the years between the passage of the Stamp Act in 1765 and the Revolution. The park also contains an 1890 **statue of Nathan Hale** by Frederick MacMonnies. Before the British hanged him as a spy, Hale proclaimed the now-historic lines: "I regret that I have but one life to lose for my country." (Scholars still argue over the location of the gallows, although a plaque at 44th Street and Vanderbilt Avenue claims to be near the spot.) A **statue of Horace Greeley** (1890) by J. Q. A. Ward in the park shows the newspaper publisher in a typically disheveled state. Greeley's *New York Tribune* and the other major dailies of the city were published on **Park Row**—in buildings facing City Hall Park—during the heyday of New York City newspapers in the late nineteenth and early twentieth centuries. The building that still stands at 41 Park Row was occupied by the *New York Times* from 1858 to 1904.

# CITY HALL

City Hall has been New York's seat of government ever since the building opened on July 4, 1811, a remarkable example of continuity in a city marked by constant change. Designed by Joseph Mangin and John McComb, Jr., who won $350 for submitting the winning plans, it is also one of the city's most architecturally distinguished buildings. Inside, the beautiful **Rotunda** has a circular staircase and dome supported by ten marble Corinthian columns. On the second floor, the **Governor's Room,** originally used for visits by the state governor, can be visited by the public. Among the American paintings here are a portrait of George Washington on Evacuation Day, November 24, 1783, and eleven other paintings by John Trumbull, as well as works by John Wesley Jarvis, Thomas Sully, John Vanderlyn, Samuel F. B. Morse, and George Catlin.

*City Hall: fine art and architecture amid the bustle of New York politics.*

On the second floor, the **City Council Chamber** was opened
when the five boroughs joined to form Greater New York in 1898.
The elegant **Board of Estimate Chamber** on the building's west
side is arranged like an eighteenth-century courtroom. Both chambers are open to the public on the days of hearings.

City Hall faces south, toward the small but appealing City Hall
Park and the skyscrapers beyond. On the front steps the mayors
perform one of their more pleasant duties: Here they greet the
guests of honor after they are escorted through Lower Broadway's
"canyon of heroes" in traditional ticker-tape parades. Those wel-
comed to City Hall include Charles Lindbergh after his 1927
transatlantic flight, General Douglas MacArthur, royalty, and
championship athletic teams. Abraham Lincoln, Horace Greeley,
and Ulysses S. Grant all lay in state in the rotunda.

LOCATION: City Hall Park. HOURS: 10–3:30 Monday–Friday. FEE:
None. TELEPHONE: 212–788–6865.

The City Hall area is rich in other historic architectural sights. **St.
Paul's Chapel** (Broadway at Fulton Street) was designed in 1766 by
Thomas McBean, a former employee of the English architect
James Gibbs. Clearly based on Gibbs's London masterpiece, St.
Martin's-in-the-Fields, its subdued exterior, large windows, and
cheerfully lit interior provide an outstanding example of Georgian
architecture and the only surviving colonial church in New York
City. George Washington attended services here after his inaugu-
ration as president in 1789; his pew in the north aisle is preserved.
The interior has an altarpiece by Pierre Charles L'Enfant, who
designed Washington, DC.

The **Woolworth Building** (233 Broadway at Barclay Street)
was designed by Cass Gilbert, who derived the building's Neo-
Gothic architectural detail from the nineteenth-century Houses of
Parliament in London. With a soaring 400-foot tower (beginning at
the twenty-ninth floor) topped by a delicate crown rising from its
base, the building is a masterpiece of proportion and grace. At 792
feet, it was the tallest building in the world from the time it was
opened in 1913 to the completion of the Chrysler Building in 1930.
The marbled lobby, which rises three stories, is almost as spectacular as the exterior. The vaulted ceilings are covered with mosaics
like those of Byzantine churches in Ravenna, Italy, and the Gothic

OPPOSITE: *The Woolworth Building, from 1913 to 1930 the tallest in the world. F. W.
Woolworth himself oversaw the details of its construction.*

decorative details include whimsical bas-relief figures of Woolworth counting his nickels and Gilbert peering through a pince-nez
at a model of the building.

Woolworth, who paid for his "Cathedral of Commerce" with
$13.5 million (in 1913 dollars) in cash and supervised such details
as bathroom fixtures and mail chutes, also saw to it that his building
was taller than the tower built earlier by the Metropolitan Life
Insurance Company.

Just north of City Hall is the former **New York City Courthouse,**
better known as the infamous "Tweed Courthouse" (in the park
facing Chambers Street) for William Marcy "Boss" Tweed who,
with his cronies, milked the city for millions during its construction.
Finished in 1872, the building cost twenty times the budget, and
the resulting scandal precipitated Tweed's downfall. The three-
story Anglo-Italianate building was long neglected by the city.
Now, the fine rotunda is open, and restoration is continuing.

**Surrogates' Court,** or Hall of Records (31 Chambers Street), is
an elegant Beaux-Arts building with an interior faced in Siena
marble and mosaics by William de Leftwich Dodge. The elegant
fifth-floor North and South courtrooms are lined with exotic
woods and have marble fireplaces.

At Center and Chambers streets, the 1914 **Municipal Building** was designed by McKim, Mead & White to be a focal point of
the Civic Center north of City Hall. Like the nearby Woolworth
Building and other skyscrapers of the era, it consists of a base, a
tower, and an elaborate crown—for maximum impact on the skyline. The Municipal Building is topped by a twenty-five-foot-high
gilt statue, entitled *Civic Fame,* by Adolph A. Weinman. Inside,
there is a monumental subway entrance with a vaulted ceiling.

## CHINATOWN

Chinatown, originally an eight-block area bounded by the Bowery
and Mulberry, Worth, and Canal streets, continues to grow today.
Although the low, four- or five-story buildings—some housing
sweatshops out of a previous era—are architecturally undistinguished, the narrow streets are atmospheric and lined with restaurants and shops selling aromatic herbs and Oriental culinary
specialties.

The first Chinese began to settle here in the 1850s; before
that, the area was known as the Plough and Harrow District, after a

tavern of that name. Settlement increased, as racial problems on the West Coast of the United States drove more Chinese east. The first Chinese were attracted to the laundry and restaurant businesses. Self-help associations, the Tongs, developed into underworld gangs, whose conflicts, the so-called "Tong Wars," damaged their reputation. The Tongs are now merchants' associations, and Chinatown is one of the city's more stable areas.

Chinatown's few historic sites include the **Edward Mooney House** of 1785–1789 (18 Bowery), the city's oldest rowhouse. The mid-winter celebration of the lunar New Year is the community's happiest time; a wild parade, punctuated with fireworks, features dancing men in lion masks and the crashing of cymbals.

## LITTLE ITALY

The area around Mulberry Street was settled by immigrants from Sicily and Naples in the peak Italian immigration between 1880 and 1915, and many of the tenement buildings date from those years. Although it has lost territory to Chinatown, and many residents have moved on, Little Italy steadfastly refuses to disappear.

The area is not noted for its architecture, although a visit should include **Old St. Patrick's Cathedral** (260 Mulberry Street), the city's first Roman Catholic cathedral, and the ornate, trapezoid-shaped former **Police Headquarters** (1909) at 240 Centre Street, a delightful and surprising anachronism amid the narrow streets and low buildings of the quarter. The 1816 **Stephen van Rensselaer House** (149 Mulberry Street), a Federal house with original dormers, was the governor's city dwelling. The interior lobby of the first-floor restaurant retains the original Federal archway. **Engine Company 55** (1898), at 363 Broome Street, provides an excellent example of a Renaissance Revival public building.

## L O W E R     E A S T     S I D E

In colonial times, most of the Lower East Side belonged to two landowning families, the Rutgerses and the De Lanceys, but by 1800 wealthy merchants and ship captains had begun to build homes in the area.

Next came the immigrants—first the Irish in the 1840s, then the Germans at midcentury. To house them, landlords developed the tenement form of rental buildings that produced maximum return for the space provided. Then, starting in the 1880s and

peaking in the early years of the twentieth century, Jews from
Russia and Eastern Europe poured into the area. The influx produced conditions common to all slums—overcrowding, poverty,
lack of privacy, crime, sweatshops, and suffering. The miseries
endured by the immigrant population were chronicled by Stephen
Crane, in *Maggie, A Girl of the Street* (1893), and other writers and
attracted the attention of reformers like Jacob Riis.

Amid appalling conditions, the Lower East Side supported a
rich intellectual life: The Yiddish theater thrived on the Bowery,
and publications included anarchist Emma Goldman's *Mother Earth*
and the still-thriving Yiddish-language *Jewish Daily Forward.* Many
successful Americans came from these surroundings. The labor
leader Samuel Gompers was born here. Mark Rothko and Jackson
Pollock were among the famous artists who kept studios or studied in the area. Tammany Hall political boss William Marcy Tweed
was born here, and died in the Ludlow Street Jail, now torn down.
The **Lower East Side Tenement Museum** (90 Orchard Street,
212–431–0233), in an 1863 tenement once occupied by twenty-
two families, interprets the immigrant experience and offers walking tours of the area.

The Lower East Side's historic main thoroughfare, **the Bowery,** was once a rural road leading to Peter Stuyvesant's farm, or
"bouwerie." During the Revolution it was also an evacuation route
for American troops stationed in the city—then entirely on the
lower part of the island. When it quickly became clear that Washington's troops were not going to stop the British landing at Kips
Bay on September 15, 1776, General Israel Putnam rode south to
evacuate the five thousand men under his command. Hessian
soldiers did capture three hundred Americans, who were heading
north, at the present intersection of 23rd Street and Park Avenue,
but Putnam's aide-de-camp, Aaron Burr, warned the general of
the threat and the rest of the detachment was diverted from the
Bowery west to Broadway, then called Bloomingdale Road. Had
General Howe moved quickly across Manhattan, he certainly could
have cut off the Americans on the lower part of the island. Instead,
he stopped to take tea at the Murray farm, thereby giving the
Americans time to escape up Broadway and join Washington in
northern Manhattan.

In the early nineteenth century, the Bowery became an affluent residential area, then a lively theater district. After the 1870s,
decline set in until the Bowery became the archetypical skid row.
During the Great Depression of the 1930s, in particular, it attract-

ed numbers of the unemployed and dispossessed. The classic **Bowery Savings Bank** (130 Bowery), with its grand Corinthian exterior and banking floor illuminated by a skylight, is one of the few landmark buildings in the area. It was as much an anomaly in the neighborhood when it was built in 1894 by McKim, Mead & White as it is today.

At 14 Eldrige Street, the **Congregation Khal Adath Jeshurun with Anshe Lubz** (Community of the People of Israel with the People of Lubz), a Moorish Revival synagogue built in 1886 by a prosperous congregation of Polish Jews, has undergone restoration. The **Henry Street Settlement Houses** (263, 265, and 267 Henry Street) are typical Greek Revival residences, with much detail remaining on the middle house. The Settlement, founded in 1893 by Lillian Wald, was one of the country's first social service agencies. The philanthropist Jacob Schiff aided the Settlement and donated two of the buildings. The institution adapted well to the changing ethnic makeup of the Lower East Side and is still extremely active in the neighborhood today.

The prestigious architects Carrère & Hastings designed the **Manhattan Bridge Approach** in 1912, three years after the 1,470-foot span was opened. The arch is a copy of the Porte St.-Denis in Paris, and Bernini's colonnade at St. Peter's Square in Rome was the inspiration for the colonnade of the bridge approach.

# SOHO

Like most neighborhoods in lower New York City, SoHo has had many lives, but nowhere have the recent changes—from 1960s abandoned factory and warehouse district to today's chic artists' colony—been swifter or more dramatic. SoHo—an acronym for "south of Houston Street"—was briefly a smart residential district in the 1840s. In the 1850s fashionable hotels and stores began to appear along Broadway, until they, too, moved uptown. The district is famed for its cast-iron buildings, built as factory lofts between 1860 and 1890.

James Bogardus, who also invented a mechanical pencil, was the first American to receive a patent for a complete cast-iron building; **85 Leonard Street,** several blocks south of SoHo, is attributed to him. Parts of cast-iron buildings were prefabricated and painted to imitate marble or limestone. Manufacturers offered many architectural details such as pilasters, balustrades, and fluted columns that provided builders with great flexibility and variety.

*The exterior of the Little Singer Building is distinguished by terra cotta panels and delicate wrought iron.*

Finally, in a process that was both cheap and quick, the prefabricated pieces could be bolted together around a steel framework.

The so-called **"King of Greene Street"** (number 72–76) and **"Queen of Greene Street"** (number 28–30) are two notable cast-iron buildings—both designed by J. F. Duckworth—on a street noted for its cast-iron architecture. The Queen's large mansard roof dominates the longest unbroken row of cast-iron buildings in the city, 8–34 Greene Street.

A masterpiece of cast-iron elegance, the **Haughwout Building** at 488 Broadway was designed by John P. Gaynor for the china and glassware merchant, Eder V. Haughwout and featured an Otis steam-driven elevator. It is possibly derived from Sansovino's Library in Venice.

At 561–563 Broadway, the **Little Singer Building** (1903) is a twelve-story landmark by architect Ernest Flagg with a facade of cast iron, terra-cotta panels, and plate glass. It is called "little," because Flagg, who designed the Corcoran Gallery of Art in Washington, DC, also designed what was once the tallest building in the world: the earlier Singer Building (1899) and Tower (1908), now demolished, at Broadway and Liberty Street.

In 1970, the city permitted artists to move into the empty cast-iron buildings in SoHo, thereby legalizing a movement that had been going on since the early 1960s. In 1973, twenty-six blocks, the largest concentration of cast-iron buildings in the country, were designated the SoHo Historic District.

## ASTOR PLACE DISTRICT

Although not historically part of Greenwich Village, this vaguely defined, architecturally diverse area is on the East Side, between 14th and Houston streets and east of Greenwich Village, and thus is sometimes called the East Village. In colonial times, the entire area was the farm of Peter Stuyvesant: Its most famous landmark, **St. Mark's-in-the-Bowery** (Second Avenue and 10th Street), is believed to be on the site of Stuyvesant's own chapel. The church, built from 1795 to 1799 with a steeple added by architect Ithiel Town in 1828, is the city's second-oldest church, after St. Paul's Chapel. It was recently reopened after fire gutted it in 1978.

In the late 1780s, Stuyvesant's great-grandson, Petrus Stuyvesant, developed part of the estate, including what is now Stuyvesant Street. Here, at number 21, he built the splendid Federal **Stuyvesant-Fish House** for his daughter before her 1804 marriage into the Fish family. In the 1830s, the area was home to some of the city's finest families—the Astors, Delanos, and Vanderbilts among them. The socialite-architect, James Renwick, Jr., built the group of sixteen privately owned, red-brick rowhouses now called the **Renwick Triangle** (112–128 East 10th Street and 23–25 Stuyvesant Street) in 1861.

A short distance to the southwest near Astor Place, the **Cooper Union Foundation Building** (East 7th Street between Cooper Square and Third Avenue) was built in 1859 by the self-made philanthropist Peter Cooper to provide a free education for deserving youths of both sexes. The institution is still operating and still offering full scholarships. Among his many accomplishments as industrialist and inventor, Cooper built the first American locomotive, Tom Thumb. Cooper Union is also the oldest remaining building in the country built from wrought-iron beams, made by a process Cooper developed to manufacture train rails. Near the main entrance is a **statue of Peter Cooper** (1897) by a former student, sculptor Augustus Saint-Gaudens. Abraham Lincoln delivered his famous Cooper Union "Right Makes Might" speech in

the building's **Great Hall** in 1860. The building was completely gutted in 1974 and, although the renovation was successful, the interior bears no relation to the original.

**Colonnade Row,** the sole surviving example of an architectural type of residential construction that was repeated elsewhere in the city, is a block to the west at 428–434 Lafayette Street. Four of the original nine townhouses with Corinthian columns aligned along the exterior remain. Built in 1833, they were once owned by such prominent New Yorkers as Warren Delano, grandfather of Franklin Delano Roosevelt.

Across the street, the **Public Theater** (425 Lafayette Street) was built between 1853 and 1881 in three stages as the Astor Library, the only gift to the city from the parsimonious John Jacob Astor. When the collection became part of the New York library system in 1912, the building housed the Immigrant Aid Society until converted to theatrical uses in l965 by Giorgio Cavaglieri, an early advocate and practitioner of adaptive reuse for old buildings.

## *Merchant's House Museum*

Built in 1832, this three-story brick townhouse was purchased in 1835 by the prosperous seaport merchant Seabury Tredwell. Owned by the Tredwells until the last family member died in 1933, it remains the city's finest house of the Greek Revival period to survive with its interior ornament and furnishings intact. The home has been meticulously restored.

> LOCATION: 29 East 4th Street. HOURS: 1–4 Sunday–Thursday; group tours available by appointment. FEE: Yes. TELEPHONE: 212–777–1089.

The 1899 **Bayard-Condict Building** (65 Bleecker Street) is the only building in the city by Chicago architect Louis Sullivan, and reportedly one of his favorites. His ideas influenced the design of skyscrapers for years to come.

Finally, on the district's southernmost border is the 1885 **Puck Building** (295–309 Lafayette Street). A fanciful, well-restored Romanesque Revival building of rich, red brick, it was once headquarters of the humor magazine *Puck,* and features the mischievous sprite over the main entrance.

OPPOSITE: *St. Mark's-in-the-Bowery, the city's second oldest church. Peter Stuyvesant, who once owned the land, is buried in the graveyard.*

# GREENWICH VILLAGE

Greenwich Village was once a distinct neighborhood cut off from the rest of the city by its location and the choice of its residents. Today, its main thoroughfares, such as Sixth and Seventh avenues, look the same as others in Manhattan. However, a block or so in either direction are areas that have retained the famous Village charm—often quiet, tree-lined, winding streets that provide pleasant relief from the monotonous grid imposed on the city to the north. Here is an ever-interesting mixture of "low-rise" architecture, including late-nineteenth-century residences, restaurants, cafes, and coffeehouses. The Village retains an atmosphere of unconventionality and a lively street life, partly due to its large gay population, but the area's heyday as a center of American intellectual artistic life is long since past.

*Doorways of Washington Mews, on a quiet street in Greenwich Village.*

When the Dutch colonists arrived in New York, Greenwich Village was the site of an Indian village called Sapokanican. The Dutch established farms here and, after the English took over in 1664, the area became the domain of large landholders like Admiral Peter Warren and his kinsmen, the De Lancey family. The area was named Greenwich, or "green village," about 1713. In 1825, a smallpox epidemic sent well-to-do, native-born New Yorkers fleeing north to settle here and the area became known as the American Ward. After 1850, several waves of immigrants made the character and population largely foreign.

Shortly after the turn of the century, the Village's old-world charm, its isolation from the rest of the city, and its low rents began attracting bohemians, artists, writers, performers, and thinkers who professed to be disaffected by American materialism. Here they lived—or tried to live—a life free of restraints, experimented with new artistic forms, and, in the Village's many cafes and restaurants, discussed radical ideas of the day, such as socialism, free love, and feminism. Of those who lived there before 1914, a remarkable number left their mark on American intellectual and artistic life.

World War I ended the Village's physical and intellectual isolation and drew many artists, whether they liked it or not, into the mainstream of American life. After the war, the Village became more accessible to the rest of the city when Sixth and Seventh avenues were extended into its precincts. Many rowhouses were torn down and replaced with apartment buildings, rents went up, and the artists and writers moved out to be replaced by middle-class citizens—many looking for freer lifestyles and less conventional surroundings. At the same time came the tourists, in search of a Greenwich Village that didn't really exist anymore.

The narrow and twisting streets of the Village are rich in historical associations; every one seems to have had famous residents. Theodore Dreiser, for example, had four Village addresses. Sherwood Anderson was his neighbor on St. Luke's Place, e. e. cummings a fellow resident on the tiny mews called Patchin Place. In 1845, long before artists moved here, Edgar Allan Poe lived in a house that still stands at 45 West 3rd Street. In 1837 he was treated for a cold at the 1831 **Northern Dispensary** (Waverly Place and Christopher Street), one of the city's few architectural survivors from the Federal period. In more recent times, Dylan Thomas frequented the **White Horse Tavern** (567 Hudson Street) and died in a Village hospital after one of his famous binges.

# WASHINGTON SQUARE

Some black slaves, freed by the Dutch in 1644, were among the first non-Indians to reside in Washington Square. Later it was used as a potter's field, and a hanging and parade ground. **Washington Square Park** was laid out in 1827, and soon elegant homes were being built on its borders. The handsome Greek Revival houses along Washington Square North between Fifth Avenue and University Place were built between 1831 and 1833. Known as **The Row,** the red-brick houses with marble trim are set back twelve feet from the lot line and protected by ornate iron fences. Edith Wharton, William Dean Howells, and John Dos Passos all lived on The Row.

In 1889, a wooden arch was erected in the Park at the foot of Fifth Avenue to commemorate the centennial of George Washington's inauguration. The residents of the area liked it so well that they commissioned Stanford White to design the present **Washington Arch,** built of marble and dedicated in 1895.

A half-block north on Fifth Avenue, **Washington Mews,** a private alley, the buildings on the north side being converted

*Detail of Washington Arch; the frieze includes a succession of stars and the initial W.*

stables, extends to University Place. The **Church of the Ascension** (36–38 Fifth Avenue at 10th Street) was built from brownstone in 1840 by Richard Upjohn, and remodeled in 1888 by Stanford White. A splendid **mural of the Ascension** by John LaFarge is over the altar, and two Tiffany windows of his design are preserved. At the corner of Fifth and 12th Street, the **Forbes Magazine Galleries** (212–206–5548) in the Forbes Building feature the Fabergé gallery as well as toy boats and toy soldiers in imaginative displays.

## NEW YORK UNIVERSITY

Albert Gallatin, Thomas Jefferson's secretary of the Treasury, and other prominent New Yorkers founded New York University in 1831 as a nonsectarian alternative to Episcopalian Columbia University. NYU is now the largest private university in the country. NYU's **Brown Building** on Washington Place is a former factory, where fire killed 146 workers, many of them young immigrant girls, of the Triangle Shirtwaist Company in 1911. The **Main Building** is an undistinguished replacement for a beautiful Gothic Revival structure, torn down in 1894, where Walt Whitman and Winslow Homer lived as students.

The **Judson Memorial Baptist Church** (1892), designed in Romanesque Revival style by Stanford White with stained-glass windows by John LaFarge, stands out in contrast to the modern buildings of Washington Square South. At 133 MacDougal Street, the **Provincetown Playhouse** is a former stable. From 1917, actors and writers produced plays, including those of Eugene O'Neill, a member. Restored by NYU in 1997, the Playhouse is a performance space for young people and a venue for young playwrights.

## WEST VILLAGE

The **Jefferson Market Courthouse,** with its pinnacles, gables, and arches, is an outstanding example of the Gothic Revival style. Built in 1877 by the firm of Vaux & Withers, it stands on the site of a nineteenth-century market. Preservationists fought long and hard to save the courthouse, which was restored to modern use by Giorgio Cavaglieri, architect of the Public Theater renovation. It is now a branch of the New York Public Library.

After she won the Pulitzer prize in 1923, Edna St. Vincent Millay and her husband lived at the nine-and-a-half-foot-wide **75½ Bedford Street,** the narrowest house in the city. The bizarre **Twin**

**Peaks** (102 Bedford Street) opened in 1926 as a haven for artists, actors, and writers. At the ceremonies, the house was christened with a bottle of champagne by an actress sitting on one of the peaks. Between 10 and 12 Grove Street is the entrance to **Grove Court,** an engaging enclave of brick-fronted houses built in the 1850s for workingmen. On Hudson Street, **St. Luke's in the Fields** (1822) is the third oldest church in the city, after St. Paul's Chapel and St. Mark's-in-the-Bowery.

The house at **6 St. Luke's Place** is still marked by two "mayor's lanterns," traditionally the sign of the mayor's residence. This was the home of the debonair James J. "Jimmy" Walker, New York City's popular, songwriting, fiscally dishonest mayor from 1926 until his forced resignation in 1932. The beautiful row of Italianate houses on St. Luke's Place was built for wealthy merchants in the 1850s. In 1916, Theodore Dreiser moved into a sparsely furnished apartment at number 16 and worked on *An American Tragedy* at a desk made from a piano.

# CHELSEA

Clement Clarke Moore, distinguished Hebrew scholar and developer of Chelsea, is best remembered for his beloved poem, *A Visit from St. Nicholas.* After inheriting the land from his grandfather, he laid out residential streets with houses set back ten feet, banned manufacturing from the area, and donated an entire block, between Ninth and Tenth avenues and 20th and 21st streets, to the **General Theological Seminary,** where he was on the faculty. The first building was erected in 1826; between 1883 and 1900, Charles Haight designed the Gothic Revival quadrangle, which provides an oasis from the busy streets. The Chelsea Historic District also includes the fine stretch of Greek Revival houses, completed in 1840, known as **Cushman Row** (406–418 West 20th Street).

Chelsea's vague boundaries run from West 19th to about 29th street and from Eighth Avenue to the Hudson River. In the 1870s theaters began to appear on West 23rd Street, and before World War I Chelsea was a center for moviemaking. Studios included the Famous Players Studio, which moved to Queens after a fire destroyed its West 26th Street home in 1915.

The **Chelsea Hotel** (222 West 23rd Street) is a reminder of the quarter's heyday and an artistic landmark that is still going strong. Built in 1884 as a cooperative apartment house for artists, the eleven-story building was, at the time, the tallest in the city. In

1905, the Chelsea became a hotel and has continued ever since to attract a devoted clientele of creative people, among them O. Henry, Thomas Wolfe, Dylan Thomas, and Sarah Bernhardt. As a hotel, the Victorian Gothic–style Chelsea has seen better days, but its exterior has been restored and the cast-iron balconies, dormers, and gables still evoke the period in which it was built.

## LADIES' MILE

In the Gilded Age before the turn of the century, the city's most fashionable restaurants, hotels, theaters, office buildings, shops, and department stores were clustered from 8th to 23rd streets along Broadway and adjacent Fifth and Sixth avenues. W. and J. Sloane and Arnold Constable erected monumental emporiums on Broadway, R. H. Macy opened a store on 14th Street, and B. Altman on Sixth Avenue. Many were designed by the most prominent architects of the day, who also had offices on or near Ladies' Mile. The grand era lasted until 1914 when Lord & Taylor left its extravagant Second Empire–style building, **901 Broadway at 20th**

*A typical scene at Union Square: A soap-box orator gives his views.*

Street—which, with its exuberant cast-iron facade, was in itself a tourist attraction—and moved north to its present location on Fifth Avenue at 38th Street. Other establishments followed, until Ladies' Mile became a district of architectural classics the rest of the city forgot. A few of the buildings were demolished, but a remarkable number—for this day and age—have survived.

A landmark of the beginning of Ladies' Mile, the huge cast-iron Wanamaker store at Broadway and 10th Street was destroyed by fire in 1956 after the store had closed. Across Broadway is the beautiful Gothic Revival **Grace Church** (1846), the first commission of James Renwick, Jr., who later designed St. Patrick's Cathedral and many other notable buildings. Marble for the exterior was quarried by prisoners from the notorious penitentiary Sing Sing up the Hudson River.

**Union Square,** a park bounded by Broadway, Park Avenue South, 14th Street, and 17th Street, has been restored and relandscaped by the Parks Commission. The Park was laid out in 1831 by Samuel B. Ruggles, who also designed nearby Gramercy Park; in 1937 it was raised above street level to accommodate the underground subway station. After fashionable New York moved uptown, the Park became a center for political protest and demonstrations. Union Square Park contains some of the best statuary in the city. An equestrian statue of *George Washington* (1856), Henry Kirke Brown's masterpiece, depicts Washington's return to New York on Evacuation Day. Frédéric Auguste Bartholdi, sculptor of the Statue of Liberty, did the statue of the *Marquis de Lafayette* in 1876.

North of the Park, 881–887 Broadway at 19th Street, Griffith Thomas's **Arnold Constable Dry Goods Store building** (1877), has an imposing mansard roof; extensions pushed the building west to Fifth Avenue, where Thomas duplicated the Broadway marble facade in cast iron.

On Sixth Avenue between 18th and 19th streets, the 1896 building that housed the **Siegel-Cooper and Company** department store still stands. The store billed itself as "The Big Store—A City In Itself." Richard Upjohn's 1846 **Church of the Holy Communion** (Sixth Avenue and 20th Street) has been converted into a theater. At the triangle formed where Broadway crosses Fifth Avenue at 23rd Street stands the famous **Flatiron Building,** the head of Ladies' Mile. The ornate, intricately detailed building of rusticated limestone, designed by D. H. Burnham, was the world's tallest—300 feet—when completed in 1902.

OPPOSITE: *The Flatiron Building, one of the city's earliest skyscrapers.*

North of 23rd Street, **Madison Square Park,** named after President James Madison, opened in 1847. It was already in use by baseball players, who drew up official rules and, in 1842, formed the first baseball team. The once-fashionable park's statuary includes one of the best pieces in the city, the 1881 *Admiral Farragut Monument* by Augustus Saint-Gaudens; Stanford White designed the base. White's beautiful and much-lamented Madison Square Garden, which was topped by a controversial statue of a nude Diana by Saint-Gaudens, stood from 1890 to 1925 on the east side of the Park where the Cass Gilbert–designed **New York Life Insurance Building** (1928) is now. In 1906, White was shot to death in the building's roof garden by a jealous husband, Harry K. Thaw—one of the most sensational crimes in the city's history.

On the southeast corner of Madison Avenue and 24th Street is the **Metropolitan Life Tower,** built in 1909 by Napoleon Le Brun. At 700 feet, it superseded the Flatiron Building as the tallest building in the world and remained so until the Woolworth Building was built in 1913.

## GRAMERCY PARK

Developer Samuel B. Ruggles laid out sixty-six building lots around the city's only private residential park in 1831. He named the street running north Lexington Avenue, after the Battle of Lexington, and the street going south Irving Place, after his friend Washington Irving. The sanctity of the park, which is restricted to area residents who pay a maintenance fee, has been violated only once—during the Draft Riots of 1863 when troops camped inside the fence.

Even those outside the gates, however, can see the famous **statue of actor Edwin Booth,** in the role of Hamlet. Booth purchased the 1845 house at 15 Gramercy Park South and, in 1888, had Stanford White remodel it as a club for actors, **The Players,** which it is today. Next door, at number 14–15, is another private club, also built in 1845, the **National Arts Club.** It was purchased and remodeled in 1874 by Samuel J. Tilden, New York's reform governor and unsuccessful presidential candidate in 1876. Tilden's improvements included an escape tunnel to 19th Street. The traditional "mayor's lanterns" stand in front of **4 Gramercy Park West,** the home of Mayor James Harper, a founder of the publishing house now known as HarperCollins.

OPPOSITE: *The sumptuous interior of New York's Appellate Court, at Madison Avenue and 25th Street, built in 1900.*

*"Mayor's Lanterns" mark the vine-covered Gramercy Park home of James Harper, mayor of the city from 1844 to 1845.*

Built in 1883, **34 Gramercy Park East,** an imposing red-brick building, was the city's first cooperative apartment house. The austere, Italianate **Friends' Meeting House** (1860) at 144 East 20th Street, was saved from demolition and is now a synagogue. The well-known public relations counsel Benjamin Sonnenberg purchased the 1845 house at **19 Gramercy Park South** in 1931 and lived there in splendor until his death in 1978. In the 1880s, financier Stuyvesant Fish had owned the house and entertained New York society there.

South of the park the ca. 1845 **47 Irving Place** is often thought, incorrectly, to be Washington Irving's home because of a misleading plaque on the building's East 17th Street side; an 1885 **bust of Washington Irving** is directly across the street outside of Washington Irving High School. At the turn of the century number 47 was the home—and salon—of the famous interior designer Elsie de Wolfe. According to legend, William Sydney Porter (O. Henry) wrote his well-known short story "The Gift of the Magi" in **Pete's Tavern** (in the second booth on the right), one of the city's oldest saloons, at 66 Irving Place. In 1903, Porter moved into 55 Irving Place; his parlor is now occupied by Sal Anthony's restaurant.

## THEODORE ROOSEVELT BIRTHPLACE

The house where Theodore Roosevelt was born on October 27, 1858, and spent his childhood was demolished in 1916, but after he died in 1919 the Woman's Roosevelt Memorial Association purchased the site and built this exact replica.

The interior includes the library, which Roosevelt described as a room of "gloomy respectability." Some of the Victorian horsehair furniture, which, Roosevelt recalled, "scratched the bare legs of the children when they sat on them," and other furnishings are from the original house. Roosevelt's christening dress and a replica of his 1906 Nobel prize are among the memorabilia on display.

LOCATION: 28 East 20th Street. HOURS: 9–5 Wednesday-Sunday. FEE: Yes. TELEPHONE: 212–260–1616.

*The reconstructed Theodore Roosevelt Birthplace displays a mounted statue of the Rough Rider president.*

# MURRAY HILL AND THE THIRTIES

Murray Hill—extending roughly from Lexington to Fifth avenues and from 34th to 42nd streets—is today an undistinguished but pleasant area of commercial buildings, Park Avenue apartment houses, and a few surviving brownstone residences on the side streets. In the mid-nineteenth century, Murray Hill was home for a brief time to the city's wealthiest and most socially prominent families. On the southeast corner of Madison Avenue and 37th Street, the freestanding Italianate brownstone at **231 Madison Avenue** was built in 1852 for J. P. Morgan, Jr. The residence has been purchased from the Lutheran Church by its neighbor, the world-famous Morgan Library, for their offices. Another Murray Hill landmark, at 23 Park Avenue, the former **Advertising Club** (1898), now converted to apartments, was designed by McKim, Mead & White as a Renaissance palazzo for J. Hampton Robb. Just beyond Murray Hill's southern border, **Two Park Avenue** (1927), between 32nd and 33rd streets, is one of the best Art Deco office buildings in the city.

*The New York City skyline at sunset.*

Murray Hill is also the architectural and historic high point of the generally nondescript East and West Thirties, a ten-block slice of New York that includes the still-vital Garment District (Seventh Avenue to Broadway, 34th to 42nd streets); Herald Square, really a three-block-long intersection formed by the crossing of Broadway and Sixth Avenue; and to the west on Eighth Avenue, between 31st and 33rd streets, the McKim, Mead & White **General Post Office** (1913), an immense public building set back from the street by an expanse of stairs. The entire building, particularly its set of Corinthian columns, is reminiscent of the much-lamented former Pennsylvania Station across the street, McKim, Mead & White's masterpiece that was torn down in 1963.

On the northeast corner of 34th Street and Fifth Avenue stands the former **B. Altman & Co.** department store (1906), now occupied by a branch of the New York Public Library. Benjamin Altman knew that the avenue's wealthy residents would be upset by this commercial intrusion, so the building was designed — by the firm of Trowbridge & Livingston — in a restrained Renaissance style to blend in with the neighborhood. Three blocks north,

on the southeast corner of 37th Street, the **former Tiffany & Co. Building** (409 Fifth Avenue) was modeled after the Palazzo Grimani in Venice by McKim, Mead & White in 1906.

## EMPIRE STATE BUILDING

Completed in 1931, the Empire State Building, wrote essayist E. B. White, "managed to reach the highest point in the sky at the lowest moment of the depression." No longer the tallest building in the world, it has been surpassed by the Sears, Roebuck Building in Chicago and by the World Trade Center in Lower Manhattan. Still, with its limestone facing, setbacks, and glistening steel spire, it remains the grandest and the tallest of the old-time skyscrapers. Designed by the firm of Shreve, Lamb, and Harmon, the building is on the site of the old Waldorf-Astoria Hotel. Its height was increased from 1,250 to 1,472 feet by a TV tower added in 1951. The famed observatories are on the 86th and 102nd floors. In the 1933 movie classic *King Kong*, the cinematic ape fights off planes while clinging to the tower. On a foggy night in 1945, an Army B-25 bomber crashed into the 79th floor, killing fourteen people.

LOCATION: 350 Fifth Avenue at 34th Street. HOURS: 9:30 AM–Midnight Daily. FEE: Yes. TELEPHONE: 212–736–3100.

## PIERPONT MORGAN LIBRARY

Since Pierpont Morgan was paying for it, no expense was spared in the construction of the museum's original building in 1906. McKim, Mead & White built it from marble blocks held together without mortar, as were buildings from antiquity. The museum, which opened in 1924, has been described as "among [the] most luxuriously appointed private museums in the world." The present main entrance is in the annex built by Morgan's son in 1928. The library contains sculpture, paintings, prints, illuminated manuscripts, and rare books, including three Gutenberg Bibles, one of which is on display in the historic East Room of the library.

LOCATION: 29 East 36th Street. HOURS: 10:30–5 Tuesday–Friday, 10:30–6 Saturday, 12–6 Sunday. FEE: Yes. TELEPHONE: 212–685–0610.

To the east of Murray Hill is **Kips Bay,** where the British under General Howe landed during the Revolution on September 15,

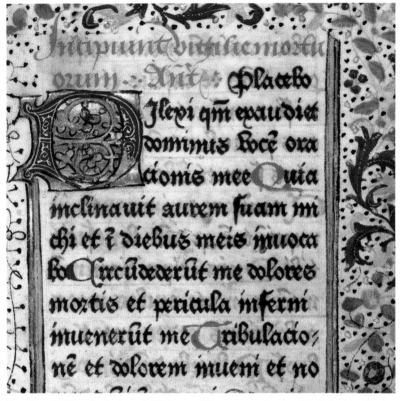

*Page from William Caxton's ca. 1476* Sarum Hours, *an early printed book, in the collection of the Morgan Library (detail).*

1776. At the time, Kips Bay, which has since been filled in, was a cove that reached almost to Second Avenue between today's 32nd and 38th streets. When Washington's inexperienced troops fled before the invaders, the angry commander-in-chief exclaimed in frustration, "Are these the men with whom I am to defend America?" Why the British didn't keep moving and cut off some five thousand American soldiers still on the southern part of the island is one of the unanswered questions of the war. It was here that lovely Mrs. John Murray, whose house lay in the path of the British advance, kept General Howe and his officers lingering over tea, while the Americans escaped up the West Side to Harlem Heights. The location of the Murray farm is marked by a plaque on the southwest corner of Park Avenue and 35th Street.

GRAND CENTRAL
TERMINAL

# NEW YORK CITY:
# MIDTOWN
## TO THE
# CLOISTERS

OPPOSITE: *Jules-Alexis Coutan's sculptural grouping,* Transportation, *adorns the south side of Grand Central Terminal.*

John Jay Chapman once wrote that "the present in New York is so powerful that the past is lost." Nowhere is this truer than in midtown Manhattan, an area of the city that shows little respect for history. There are few indications, for example, that New York high society lived along Fifth Avenue at the turn of the century, or that "Boss" Tweed had a house built for him at city expense at Fifth Avenue and 42nd Street, or that, in the 1920s, brothels, speakeasies, and dingy rooming houses occupied the land where Rockefeller Center and its satellite office towers are now.

This chapter travels north from 42nd Street to Central Park South, along the Upper East Side, through Central Park to the Upper West Side, and along the Hudson to Washington Heights.

## FORTY-SECOND STREET

This is the city's premier crosstown street, home of many of its major landmarks and southern boundary of Times Square. In addition to the New York City Public Library, the Chrysler Building, and Grand Central Terminal, the street is distinguished, near its western end, by the former **McGraw-Hill Building** (330 West 42nd Street), Raymond Hood's 1931 masterpiece noted for its blue-green terra-cotta sheathing and Art Deco lobby. One of the world's most famous blocks, 42nd Street between Seventh and Eighth avenues, which had deteriorated into a dangerous corridor of cheap movies and pornography operations, began to experience an extravagant revival in the late 1990s, as magnificent old theaters were restored and reopened, and new family-oriented enterprises began to materialize from drawing boards.

## TIMES SQUARE

This historic and much-celebrated triangle, formed by the intersection of Broadway and Seventh Avenue, is the center of New York's theater district, the most brightly lit spot in town, and still called by many the Crossroads of the World. Oscar Hammerstein, the cigarmaker-turned-composer and impresario, is often given credit for bringing theaters to what was then known as Longacre Square. At that time the area was devoted mostly to equine needs—stables, carriage factories, and blacksmith shops.

The first electric advertising sign on the Square was put up about 1895, and in 1901 an advertising man named O. J. Gude supposedly declared it "The Great White Way." Memorable signs that followed included the smoker who blew immense smoke rings

*Dancing in the streets at Times Square, World War II.*

for Camel cigarettes. The waterfall on the Wrigley sign, reputedly the largest in the world, was a gigantic aquatic scene seventy-five feet high and two hundred feet long with glowing colored fish and a Wrigley boy fishing from a boat. The sign was inspired by a Wrigley family member's passion for tropical fish.

The Square's name changed from Longacre to Times when the *New York Times* moved from Park Row into the trapezoid-shaped Times Tower in 1904. The first New Year's Eve celebration in Times Square, now an annual event, was held that year. In 1964 the building was stripped to its original steel frame, totally refurbished, and reclad in white marble. The building, which has passed through many owners, is now called **One Times Square.**

The 1927 **Paramount Building** (1501 Broadway between West 43rd and West 44th streets), is the best architectural survivor of Times Square's better days, although the palatial Paramount Theater has been closed. The building has fourteen setbacks and an illuminated bulb on top.

Of the surviving legitimate theaters, the 1907 **Belasco The atre** (111 West 44th Street) and the 1913 **Shubert Theatre** (225 West 44th Street) bear famous theatrical names and evoke memories of many famous productions.

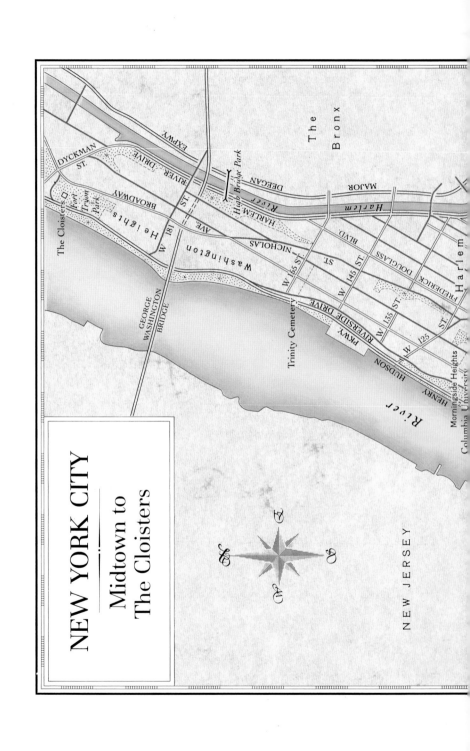

NEW YORK CITY
— · —
Midtown to
The Cloisters

The Bronx

The Cloisters

Fort
Tryon
Park

DYCKMAN
ST.

BROADWAY

W Heights

181 ST.

RIVER DRIVE

EXPWY

MAJOR

DEEGAN

Hugh Bridge Park

Harlem River

Washington

NICHOLAS

W 155 ST.

ST.

BLVD

Harlem

FREDERICK DOUGLASS

W 145 ST.

W 135 ST.

W 125 ST.

AVE

GEORGE
WASHINGTON
BRIDGE

Trinity Cemetery

RIVERSIDE DRIVE

PKWY

HUDSON

HENRY

Morningside Heights
Columbia University

Hudson River

NEW JERSEY

Queens

TRIBOROUGH BRIDGE

125 ST.

Marcus Garvey Park

Morningside Park

CATHEDRAL PKWY.

Riverside Park

Hudson

Upper West Side

Central Park

Upper East Side

East River

Gracie Mansion

Carl Schurz Park

ROOSEVELT ISLAND

QUEENSBORO BRIDGE

Metropolitan Museum of Art

E. 96 ST.

E. 86 ST.

E. 79 ST.

E. 72 ST.

E. 57 ST.

E. 42 ST.

NORTH PARK

WEST PARK

W. 96 ST.

W. 86 ST.

W. 79 ST.

W. 72 ST.

W. 67 ST.

W. 42 ST.

AMSTERDAM AVE.

WEST END AVE.

CENTRAL PARK WEST

FIFTH AVE.

MADISON AVE.

PARK AVE.

LEXINGTON AVE.

THIRD AVE.

SECOND AVE.

FIRST AVE.

YORK AVE.

FDR DRIVE

CENTRAL PARK SOUTH

Grand Army Plaza

THE AMERICAS AVE. OF

BROADWAY

Times Square

Bryant Park

NY Public Library

Columbus Circle

Lincoln Center

American Museum of Natural History

St. Patricks Cathedral

Rockefeller Center

Grand Central Terminal

Turtle Bay

United Nations Headquarters

QUEENS-MIDTOWN TUNNEL

LINCOLN TUNNEL

0          1 Mi.

# THE NEW YORK PUBLIC LIBRARY: CENTER FOR THE HUMANITIES

This Beaux-Arts landmark, guarded night and day by E. C. Potter's beloved sculptured lions, was completed on the site of the old Croton Reservoir in 1911 at a cost of $9 million. Carrère & Hastings designed the building, including the long forecourt along Fifth Avenue, today a popular gathering place for New Yorkers in all their diversity. The interior, with its grand staircase, vaulted ceilings, murals, white marble walls, and paneled reading rooms is one of the great public spaces in the city and in the country.

The building houses the New York Public Library's research collection for the humanities, formed in 1895 from the Lenox and Astor libraries plus funds from the trust of ex-governor Samuel J. Tilden. Its literary treasures rival those of the Library of Congress. The research collection includes 30,000 linear feet of manuscript archives, 11,500 recordings on disk and tape, 100,000 views of New York City streets, 11,000 atlases, and 10,000 telephone directories. The Rare Books Division includes a Bay Psalm Book, the first book printed in America (Cambridge, Massachusetts, 1640).

The 9.6-acre **Bryant Park,** once a potter's field, stretches from the library to Sixth Avenue. Restored in the 1990s, the park is a warm-weather delight, with white lawn chairs scattered on a vast expanse of green grass. Entertainment includes musical programs, comedians during the lunch hour, and films at sunset.

LOCATION: Fifth Avenue at 42nd Street. HOURS: 10–6 Monday, Thursday–Saturday, 11–6 Tuesday, Wednesday. FEE: None. TELE-PHONE: 212–221–7676.

Although the Met Life building just to its north overwhelms the Grand Central building, the terminal—New Yorkers call it Grand Central Station—is still one of the city's great landmarks. The splendid **Main Concourse** measures 120 by 375 feet; its 125-foot-high, vaulted blue ceiling is decorated by an illuminated zodiac. Outside, facing 42nd Street, are statues by Jules-Alexis Coutan showing Minerva, Hercules, and Mercury grouped over a thirteen-foot-wide clock. A bronze statue of "Commodore" Vanderbilt, who died in 1877 after consolidating New York City's three railroads into one line in 1872, is directly below.

OPPOSITE: *The DeWitt Wallace Periodical Room at the New York Public Library, with murals by Richard Haas.*

Grand Central was the work of two architectural firms, Warren & Wetmore and Reed & Stem; the latter is credited with the plan for diverting Park Avenue around the building and over 42nd Street on a raised roadway. The original Grand Central Depot, completed at the same location in 1871, was anything but central; 42nd Street was then far north of the actual city. Its facilities included a segregated waiting room for immigrants, so other passengers wouldn't have to mingle with them. By 1903, the city had caught up to the station, and ordered the line, then called the New York Central & Hudson River Railroad, either to electrify or move to the outskirts. At that point, the Vanderbilt interests put underground the line running along Park Avenue, electrified the trains as far as the Bronx, and built a new terminal. The present building, one of the world's magnificent terminals, was completed in 1913.

LOCATION: Park Avenue and 42nd Street.

## CHRYSLER BUILDING

New Yorkers love this building for its Art Deco kitsch—gargoyles modeled after hood ornaments, for example—for its soaring lines, and for the enduring imprint it makes on the city's skyline. The structure is topped by a tower made of stainless steel, a material only the likes of Walter Chrysler could afford. The building also has one of the city's most beautiful lobbies, with a veneer of African marble and Art Deco murals, and panelled elevators.

In 1930, it looked as if the Chrysler Building would lose the race to become the world's tallest to the Bank of Manhattan at 40 Wall Street. When the work stopped, as planned, on the Chrysler Building at 925 feet, the rival builders on Wall Street confidently topped theirs off at 927 feet, unaware that the Chrysler's architect, William Van Alen, had designed a 123-foot stainless-steel tower that was being assembled in secret inside the building. With that hoisted into place, the Chrysler Building became the world's tallest at 1,048 feet, outstripping even the 984-foot Eiffel Tower, until then the world's tallest structure. But the glory was short-lived: The next year the Empire State Building reached 1,250 feet.

LOCATION: 405 Lexington Avenue at 42nd Street.

Across from Grand Central Terminal, at 110 East 42nd Street, is the **Bowery Savings Bank,** a Romanesque palace with a highly ornamented central banking room with a mosaic tile floor. Nearby

OPPOSITE: *The Art Deco elevator doors of the Chrysler Building.*

are the 1929 **Chanin Building** (122 East 42nd Street), an Art Deco masterpiece with terra-cotta ornamentation on its base and an elaborate lobby of bronze and marble, and the 1930 **Daily News Building** (220 East 42nd Street).

# TURTLE BAY

Before the Revolution, the land around Turtle Bay—now the East Forties—belonged to Admiral Peter Warren of the British Navy, who had married into New York's De Lancey family. In one of the more provocative pre–Revolutionary War incidents, the Sons of Liberty raided the military stores on the Warren farm and sailed them to Boston. Once the home of Horace Greeley and Edgar Allan Poe, Turtle Bay, which may be named for the turtles that once swam the East River, is today dominated by the United Nations.

## *United Nations Headquarters*

John D. Rockefeller, Jr., gave eighteen acres on the East River for this complex of four main buildings—the glass·and marble **Secretariat Building** (1950), the **General Assembly** and **Conference** buildings (1951), and the **Dag Hammarskjöld Library** (1961)— designed by an international team of architects. There are many notable artworks in the complex, including a bronze sculpture by Barbara Hepworth in the outdoor pool; a mural, *Brotherhood,* by Rufino Tamayo in the General Assembly Building; and stained-glass windows in the **Dag Hammarskjöld Chapel** by Marc Chagall. Sessions of the General Assembly are open to the public; so is the Delegates' Dining Room.

> LOCATION: First Avenue between 42nd and 48th streets. HOURS: 9:15–4:55 Daily; tours every twenty minutes from main lobby of the General Assembly Building. FEE: None. TELEPHONE: 212–963–7713.

The intricately designed **Queensboro Bridge** (1909), a 1,182-foot span, connects Manhattan with Long Island City in Queens. Long Island City had wanted a bridge for over fifty years to aid tourism and commercial enterprises, among them the fifteen cemeteries located in Queens. As a cantilevered structure, the bridge's criss-crosses and angles make it look old-fashioned, especially when compared with the graceful simplicity of a suspension bridge. The look appeals to many, but architect Henry Hornbostel supposedly said, on seeing the completed bridge, "My God, it's a blacksmith shop!" The lilting "59th Street Bridge Song" salutes the span.

# FIFTH AVENUE

Although Fifth Avenue extends from Washington Square Park to 138th Street, it is the midtown section, anchored by Rockefeller Center and St. Patrick's Cathedral, that epitomizes New York City for many. At the end of the nineteenth century, Fifth Avenue was largely residential. In a memoir, author Edith Wharton recalled brownstone houses "in an orderly procession like a young ladies' boarding school taking its daily exercise" that lined the Avenue up to 57th Street. The arrival on the Avenue of B. Altman's at 34th Street in 1906 and Lord & Taylor at 38th Street in 1914 signaled the beginning of the end of this residential area.

Some important buildings from the turn of the century can still be found on the side streets west of Fifth Avenue: the 1891 **Century Association** (7 West 43rd Street), a club primarily for painters or, officially, "authors, artists, and patrons of the arts." Founded by forty-two members, led by Asher B. Durand and Ginlian C. Verplanck and including William Cullen Bryant, the Century was the first of many clubs designed by McKim, Mead & White in the Renaissance palazzo style that became one of the

*Manhattanites in their Easter finery parade along Fifth Avenue near St. Patrick's Cathedral ca. 1910.*

firm's trademarks. One block north at 27 West 44th Street, the **Harvard Club** (1894; additions in 1905 and 1915) is another McKim, Mead & White building, designed in a restrained Neo-Georgian style as if transplanted from Harvard Yard. Its neighbor to the west, the **New York Yacht Club** (37 West 44th Street), opened in 1901 its frivolous but immensely appealing Beaux-Arts building festooned with nautical carvings, including three bay windows shaped like the sterns of sailing ships. At the end of the street, the 1902 **Algonquin Hotel** (59 West 44th Street) has a respectable exterior and a panelled lobby that is one of the most comfortable and intimate in New York City. But the hotel is more of a literary landmark than an architectural one. Here the members of the famous Round Table—Dorothy Parker, Robert Benchley, and George S. Kaufman among them—met regularly in the 1920s to share literary insights, barbed witticisms, and gossip.

## ST. PATRICK'S CATHEDRAL

In 1850, when Archbishop John Hughes released his plan to build St. Patrick's—a church "worthy of God, worthy of the Catholic religion, and an honor to this great city"—New York City was mostly Protestant. Construction began in 1858, and the cathedral was dedicated on May 25, 1879. Architect James Renwick, Jr., based the floor plan on that of the cathedral in Cologne, Germany, but borrowed liberally from other European churches. The result was a standard cruciform layout of nave, transepts, and choir, with stained glass imported from Chartres and Nantes in France.

LOCATION: Fifth Avenue at 50th Street. HOURS: 6:30 A.M.–8:45 P.M. Daily; tours by appointment. TELEPHONE: 212–753–2261.

## ROCKEFELLER CENTER

There has probably never been a more successful urban development than Rockefeller Center. Architecturally and commercially, it fulfills the hopes of John D. Rockefeller, Jr., for a development "as beautiful as possible consistent with maximum income."

Rockefeller Center leased the land on which it was built from Columbia University until 1985, when it purchased the Columbia leasehold for $400 million. Originally the site of the famed Elgin Botanic Gardens, developed by physician and educator Dr. David

OPPOSITE: *The nave of St. Patrick's Cathedral.* OVERLEAF: *Executed by Paul Manship in bronze and covered with gold leaf, Prometheus, the founder of civilization, presides over the Lower Plaza at Rockefeller Center.*

Hosack, the then little-valued land was given to Columbia by New York State when the university appealed for funds in 1814. (The university had hoped to receive the revenues from a state lottery.) Rockefeller had planned to develop the land around a new Metropolitan Opera House, but, when the stock market crash of 1929 forced the Metropolitan to pull out, he did it alone. Between 1931 and 1940, fourteen buildings were constructed, providing jobs for 75,000 workers during the Depression.

The 850-foot, seventy-story **30 Rockefeller Plaza,** completed in 1933, was built to house Rockefeller Center's major tenant, the Radio Corporation of America, and for many years the development was popularly called "Radio City." The world-famous, 5,784-seat **Radio City Music Hall** is the largest theater in the country and an Art Deco masterpiece. The Music Hall almost closed in 1978, but after a public protest, it was refurbished and reopened in 1979 for special programs and events.

Many of the artworks in Rockefeller Center illustrate humanity's progress, an ironically positive theme considering most were commissioned during the Great Depression. Two of the best known are Paul Manship's imposing gilded bronze statue of *Prome-*

*Details from the facade of Rockefeller Center. The murals emphasize the mastery of man over his universe.*

*theus,* installed in the Lower Plaza in 1934, and Lee Lawrie's much-photographed statue of *Atlas,* who is supporting a celestial sphere twenty-one feet in diameter, in front of the **International Building** on Fifth Avenue. A limestone screen, also by Lawrie, over the building's West 50th Street entrance traces human history beginning with the four races of mankind. Isamu Noguchi's stainless-steel panel, titled *News,* showing reporters at work, is over the Rockefeller Plaza entrance to the **Associated Press Building.** What might have been the Center's best work, a mural in 30 Rockefeller Plaza by Diego Rivera, was destroyed because it included a portrait of Lenin. But many fine murals remain, symbolizing man's progress throughout time, mastering his universe.

Today the twenty-two-acre "city within a city" has expanded to the west side of Sixth Avenue to include modern office towers, all connected by more than two miles of underground promenades with entrances to shops, restaurants, and subways. Tours of the Center leave from the main floor of 30 Rockefeller Plaza.

LOCATION: Fifth and Sixth avenues between 49th and 52nd streets. HOURS: Tours Monday–Saturday; call for times. FEE: Yes, for tours. TELEPHONE: 212–664–7174.

## MUSEUM OF MODERN ART

When the museum opened in 1929 as "a modest experiment" to gauge New Yorkers' interest in modern art, the newly appointed director, Alfred H. Barr, Jr., predicted it could "easily become the greatest of its kind in the world." This prophecy has been fully realized; the Museum of Modern Art—or MoMA, as it is popularly called—quickly became the leading institution in the field. Today the museum's comprehensive collection contains work from the Impressionist period to the present, including more than 3,500 paintings and sculptures, 6,000 drawings, 40,000 prints, 20,000 photographs, as well as film, architecture, and design collections. Among the works are such masterpieces as Picasso's *Les Demoiselles d'Avignon,* Rousseau's *The Sleeping Gypsy,* van Gogh's *Starry Night,* Monet's *Water Lilies,* and Cézanne's *The Bather.* About one-third of the collection was done by American artists since 1945—Bearden, Feininger, Motherwell, O'Keeffe, Oldenburg, Wyeth, Calder, Rothko, Shahn, among others. The outdoor sculpture garden is an oasis of beauty and tranquility in busy midtown Manhattan.

The decision to organize a gallery for exhibits of modern art came from a meeting in 1929 of Mrs. John D. Rockefeller, Jr., Miss

*Vincent Van Gogh's* The Starry Night *(1889), from the collection of the Museum of Modern Art (Oil on canvas, 29" x 36¼").*

Lillie P. Bliss, and Mrs. Cornelius J. Sullivan. "The Ladies," as they were known, formed a committee that included A. Conger Good-year and Frank Crowninshield and appointed Barr director. The opening exhibit—Cézanne, Gaugin, Seurat, van Gogh—attracted 48,000 visitors, but it was the immensely popular van Gogh show of 1935, a writer later observed, that woke New Yorkers up to the fact that "art can attract as many people as a prize fight."

> LOCATION: 11 West 53rd Street. HOURS: 11–6 Saturday–Tuesday, 12–8:30 Thursday, Friday. FEE: Yes. TELEPHONE: 212–708–9480 (special exhibitions); 212–708–9490 (films); 212–708–9400 (other information).

Fifth Avenue between Rockefeller Center and Central Park South includes several outstanding buildings, most notably **St. Thomas Church** (1913), the work of the partners Ralph Adams Cram, who later redesigned the Cathedral of St. John the Divine, and Bertram Goodhue, architect of St. Bartholomew's Church. Located on the northwest corner of 53rd Street and Fifth Avenue, the Gothic church has two asymmetrical towers and an exterior of Kentucky limestone. The centerpiece of the interior is the eighty-foot stone reredos, designed by Goodhue and sculpted by Lee Lawrie.

On the side streets in this area are—or will be—three interesting museums. The **Museum of Television & Radio** (25 West 52nd Street, 212–621–6800), founded by broadcasting pioneer William S. Paley in 1975, collects, preserves, and interprets TV and radio programming. Its collection includes news and public-affairs programs, sports, and comedy and variety shows. Visitors may watch or listen to their selections at consoles. The **American Craft Museum** (40 West 53rd Street, 212–956–3535) was founded in the 1940s to recognize contemporary crafts. Its collection of glass and fabrics is particularly noteworthy. The **Museum of American Folk Art** (Columbus Avenue between 65th and 66th streets, 212–595–9533) is to move, ca. 2000, to West 53rd Street. It has a fine collection of paintings, quilts, weathervanes, and whirligigs.

The **University Club** (1 West 54th Street) was designed in 1899 by Charles McKim. Shields of American universities are among the details on the granite exterior of the Renaissance building. The opulent interior is not open to the public.

The **St. Regis–Sheraton Hotel** on the southeast corner of Fifth Avenue and 55th Street was built in 1904 by John Jacob Astor IV when the neighborhood was still largely residential. The hotel's King Cole Room, now a restaurant, takes its name from Maxfield Parrish's famous mural on the wall.

Two of New York City's most elegant stores stand catercorner at 57th Street and Fifth Avenue. **Tiffany & Co.** moved to the southeast corner in 1940; the store was founded by Charles Tiffany, father of the glass and jewelry designer, Louis Comfort Tiffany. On the west side of the avenue, **Bergdorf Goodman** extends the entire block from 57th Street to Grand Army Plaza. The store has been here since 1928; the site was once occupied by Cornelius Vanderbilt's 137-room mansion.

# PARK AVENUE

When the railroad tracks running up Park Avenue to 96th Street were covered in 1903–1913, this street began assuming its dignified air. It was once lined with mansions, apartment houses, and hotels, but south of 57th Street it is now mostly boxlike office buildings.

In 1952, **Lever House** (390 Park Avenue between 53rd and 54th streets) was the first steel-and-glass structure to appear among the avenue's masonry buildings. Although the sight of this glass box by Skidmore, Owings & Merrill was a shock at the time, it is now often praised for its open, ground-level courtyard and delicate proportions—delicate when compared to the monolithic boxes that surround it today. Ludwig Mies van der Rohe's **Seagram Building** (between 52nd and 53rd streets) is Park Avenue's contemporary masterpiece. Faced with glass and bronze, the building is set back ninety feet, providing a spacious public plaza, a layout since imitated less successfully by other builders.

Among the few pre–World War II buildings remaining on Park Avenue south of 57th Street are the Grand Central Building (1929), now the **Helmsley Building,** which faces north up the avenue from 46th Street; the still-elegant and exclusive 1931 **Waldorf-Astoria Hotel** (between 49th and 50th streets), with its landmark Art Deco interior; McKim, Mead & White's 1918 **Racquet and Tennis Club** (370 Park Avenue), a private club derived from the Palazzo Antinori in Florence; and St. Bartholomew's Church.

# ST. BARTHOLOMEW'S CHURCH

This Byzantine masterpiece was designed by Bertram Grosvenor Goodhue for an Episcopal congregation that began in 1835 on the then-fashionable Bowery and moved uptown with the city. The portico was designed by Stanford White in 1902 for the previous St. Bart's, as it is called, on Madison and 44th Street. The mosaics on the ceiling of the apse and the narthex are by Hildreth Meiere.

LOCATION: 109 East 50th Street at Park Avenue. HOURS: 8–6 Daily. TELEPHONE: 212–751–1616.

Midtown Manhattan really has two northern boundaries: busy 57th Street, a traffic-clogged main artery that runs east–west from river to river, and, two blocks to the north, Central Park South, which affords the open space and vistas so lacking elsewhere in the city. This elegant boulevard, which runs from Fifth Avenue to Columbus Circle, is bordered by elegant hotels and apartment buildings on its south side and by Central Park on its north.

On the far western edge of this area, the **Consolidated Edison Power Plant,** between Eleventh and Twelfth avenues and West 58th and 59th streets, was built in 1904 to provide power for New York's first subway. However, its architects—McKim, Mead & White—designed it to look more like one of their finer Renaissance

*Built in 1919, Byzantine St. Bartholomew's Church stands on a site that was once a brewery.*

palaces than the industrial building it still is today. At the corner of Eighth Avenue and West 57th Street, the unusual **Hearst Magazine Building** (1928) reflects the talents and background of its architect, the well-known theatrical artist, Joseph Urban, set designer for Ziegfeld's Follies and several of Marion Davies's movies. Davies was a former Ziegfeld showgirl whose movies were produced by William Randolph Hearst. A block east is the 1892 **American Fine Arts Society building** (215 West 57th Street), which houses the Art Students League of New York in the French Renaissance style by Henry J. Hardenburgh, architect of the Plaza Hotel and the Dakota Apartments. The exterior of the 1909 apartment building, **Alwyn Court** (180 West 58th Street), is an eyecatching pattern of terra-cotta detail.

## CARNEGIE HALL

The building's crowning glory is not its design but rather its 2,804-seat auditorium's exceptional acoustics. Andrew Carnegie built the theater as the first music hall in New York specifically for orchestral and choral music. William B. Tuthill's design includes a tower for rent-producing apartments, studios, and offices. Tchaikovsky conducted here the first week it was open in 1891, and virtually every important musician and orchestra in the world has played here since. In the 1960s violinist Isaac Stern led a successful fight to save Carnegie Hall from demolition. The auditorium was restored and reopened in early 1987; it and the smaller Weill Recital Hall are open only for performances and guided tours.

LOCATION: 154 West 57th Street at Seventh Avenue. TELEPHONE: 212–247–7800.

The *Intrepid* **Sea-Air-Space Museum** (West 46th Street at 12th Avenue, 212–245–2533) is on the aircraft carrier *Intrepid* at Pier 86. The carrier served in World War II and Vietnam.

## COLUMBUS CIRCLE

Central Park South's western terminus, Columbus Circle, is one of the city's least successful open spaces. The poor pedestrian who has to cross against its relentless traffic flow will hardly have time to notice the **statue of Columbus** on top of a seventy-seven-foot pillar in the middle of the square. The monument was erected in 1892 to commemorate the quadricentennial of Columbus's voyage to the New World. The *Maine* **Memorial** (1913), a granite pedestal with statuaries at the entrance to Central Park is the circle's most notable feature. It memorializes the sinking of the battleship *Maine* on February 15, 1898.

## PLAZA HOTEL

The hotel, with its stately mansard roof and French Renaissance–style facade richly festooned with architectural detail, was designed by Henry J. Hardenburgh, who also did the Dakota Apartments. Its interior has suffered from renovations, but the **Edwardian Room,** the **Palm Court,** and the panelled **Oak Room** remain three of the best public rooms in the city. The official name of the open square in front of the hotel is the **Grand Army Plaza.** During the Roaring Twenties, Scott and Zelda Fitzgerald cavorted in its **Pulitzer Fountain,** a gift of the publisher, which was designed by Carrère & Hastings in 1916. It is topped by Karl Bitter's statue of Pomona, the goddess of fruits.

OPPOSITE: *Highly polished lanterns and window boxes, elegant touches on the exterior of the Plaza Hotel.*

# THE  UPPER  EAST  SIDE

While the Upper East Side—from 57th to 96th streets—is today known as an expensive residential district, it was once an area of considerable ethnic and cultural diversity. Late in the eighteenth century the section now known as Yorkville was the site of farms and estates settled by well-to-do German families. As Central Park developed in the mid-nineteenth century, Fifth Avenue was transformed from a squalid area inhabited by squatters into the city's most elegant residential thoroughfare; many of these grand mansions are today museums along the stretch known as "Museum Mile." Park Avenue became a boulevard of the city's best apartment houses after Grand Central was built in 1913 and the railroad tracks north to 96th Street were covered over.

**Temple Emanu-el** (Fifth Avenue and 65th Street, 212–744–1400), a Reform congregation, was founded in 1845. This sanctuary (1927) is one of the largest Jewish places of worship anywhere.

## ABIGAIL ADAMS SMITH MUSEUM

Originally constructed in 1799 as an elaborate stone carriage house for Abigail Adams Smith, daughter of President John Adams, and her husband, Colonel William Stephens Smith, it subsequently became a hotel known for soup made from turtles caught in the East River. From 1833 to 1924 the building was also the private residence of the Towles family and the offices of the Standard Gas Light Company. The Colonial Dames of America opened it to the public during the 1939 New York World's Fair, and they continue to exhibit decorative arts from the Federal and Empire periods.

LOCATION: 421 East 61st Street. HOURS: September through July: 11–4 Tuesday–Sunday; June through July: 11–9 Tuesday. FEE: Yes. TELEPHONE: 212–838–6878.

## THE FRICK COLLECTION

Like other millionaires of the Gilded Age, the Pittsburgh-based steel magnate Henry Clay Frick had a taste for the masterpieces of European art. When pollution in Pittsburgh began to endanger his collection, and he became attracted to New York, he commissioned

*Henry Clay Frick built this Fifth Avenue mansion in 1913-14; it became a museum for his collection in 1935.*

Carrère & Hastings to build a French-style mansion around a garden court at 70th Street and Fifth Avenue. He moved his artworks there in 1914. In 1935, it was renovated by architect John Russell Pope, and, as Frick had planned, opened to the public.

The museum contains an outstanding collection of painting, sculpture, furniture, and other decorative arts dating from the Renaissance to the end of the nineteenth century. The building also retains the opulent atmosphere of an early twentieth-century mansion with Chinese porcelains and Renaissance bronzes in the library; paintings by Titian, El Greco, and Bellini in the living hall; and eighteenth-century English portraits in the dining room.

LOCATION: One East 70th Street. HOURS: 10–6 Tuesday–Saturday, 1–6 Sunday; closed August. FEE: Yes. TELEPHONE: 212–288–0700.

# WHITNEY MUSEUM OF AMERICAN ART

In 1907, Gertrude Vanderbilt Whitney, socialite, collector, and sculptor, began showing the work of young American artists in her studio in Greenwich Village while purchasing many paintings for her own collection. Her Studio Club evolved into the Whitney Museum and moved to 8th Street in 1931, then to the Museum of Modern Art in 1954, and to its own building—Marcel Breuer's controversial structure with three cantilevered tiers and a moat—in 1966. The museum, located amid the art galleries of Madison Avenue, includes every recognized major American artist of the twentieth century, and has become known for innovative exhibits.

LOCATION: 945 Madison Avenue at 75th Street. HOURS: 11–6 Wednesday, 1–8 Thursday, 11–6 Friday–Sunday. FEE: Yes. TELEPHONE: 212–570–3676.

# YORKVILLE

East 86th Street from Third Avenue to the East River used to be the main thoroughfare of Yorkville, one of the city's most famous ethnic communities. First settled by wealthy German farmers and estate owners in the late eighteenth century, Yorkville was later taken over by German immigrants and thrived as a working-class neighborhood until the Third Avenue Elevated was torn down and the area was transformed by high-rise apartment buildings.

On Yorkville's eastern edge is **Carl Schurz Park**—from East End Avenue to the East River, between East 84th and 90th streets—named after the nineteenth-century German-American who was a hero of the German revolutionary movement of 1848, and, after migrating to the United States, Civil War general, secretary of the interior, and New York editor. At the north end of the park is **Gracie Mansion** (212–570–4751), the official residence of the mayor of New York City since Mayor Fiorello La Guardia in 1942. The elegant villa, originally built in 1799 as the country home of the prosperous merchant Archibald Gracie, is surrounded by a fence and trees and is open to the public by appointment.

# MUSEUM MILE

The ten important museums in the mile between 82nd and 103rd streets along Fifth Avenue include **El Museo del Barrio** (1230 Fifth Avenue at 104th Street, 212–831–7272), devoted to the culture of

Puerto Rico and Latin America. The **International Center of Photography** (1130 Fifth Avenue at 94th Street, 212–860–1777), founded in 1974 as a showcase for major twentieth-century photographers, is housed in a 1915 Neo-Georgian landmark building. The **Jewish Museum** (1109 Fifth Avenue at 92nd Street, 212–423–3200) preserves and interprets four thousand years of Jewish culture to the general public with changing exhibitions and educational programs. The **National Academy of Design** (1083 Fifth Avenue at 89th Street, 212–369–4880) was founded in 1825 by Samuel F. B. Morse, Rembrandt Peale, Ithiel Town, and others as an association of established artists. The Academy houses a collection of over two thousand paintings and sculptures in a 1914 townhouse donated by the husband of sculptor Anna Hyatt Huntington.

*View of Oyster Bay, created in 1905 by Tiffany Studios, now in the collection of the Metropolitan Museum of Art.*

## Metropolitan Museum of Art

By far the largest art museum in the Western Hemisphere, with nearly 3 million works of art in its collection, the Metropolitan was founded in 1870 by civic leaders, philanthropists, and art collectors as a "national gallery and museum . . . for the benefit of the people at large." The museum has also employed some of the country's best architects. The first building, which opened in Central Park in 1880, was designed by Calvert Vaux and Jacob Wrey Mould. A portion of this building is visible from the rear in the **Robert Lehman Collection.** The Fifth Avenue facade, built in 1902, was designed by Richard Morris Hunt; McKim, Mead & White did the north and south wings in 1911 and 1913. The 1982 **Michael C. Rockefeller Wing,** displaying primitive art of Africa, the Americas, and Pacific Islands, including Eskimo and Indian art, and other additions since 1970 were designed by Roche, Dinkeloo & Associates. In January 1987, the museum opened the **Lila Acheson Wallace Wing** for the display of twentieth-century art.

American art and decoration were largely overlooked in the museum's early days. An important collection of American furniture was purchased in 1913 and, in November 1924, the first American wing opened with twenty-five period rooms and the facade of New York City's United States Assay Office (1824), which had stood on Wall Street until it was demolished in 1914. The new **American Wing,** which opened in 1980, literally enveloped the old wing. The Assay Office facade—along with a loggia by Louis Comfort Tiffany and sculpture by Gutzon Borglum, Frederick Mac-Monnies, George Grey Barnard, and Paul Manship—graces the glass-covered **Charles Engelhard Court.**

The wing includes the **Richmond Room** with Duncan Phyfe furniture, **Van Rensselaer Hall** from the manor house built by Stephen Van Rensselaer II, ca 1765, and the **Richmond Room** from an 1810 Richmond, Virginia, mansion. Fine examples of American furniture are in the period rooms as well as in such displays as the **Federal Gallery,** which has furniture from Boston, New York, Philadelphia, and Baltimore. Highlights of American decorative arts include silver pieces by the colonial silversmith Paul Revere,

OPPOSITE: *The glass-enclosed Engelhard Court of the Metropolitan Museum's American Wing. The facade of the United States Assay Office is in the background.*

Pennsylvania-German red earthenware, and Louis Comfort Tiffany's Favrile glass. American paintings and sculpture are exhibited chronologically in the Joan Whitney Payson Galleries. Emanuel Leutze's monumental *Washington Crossing the Delaware* (1851) is a drawing card, but the collections also include such masterpieces as George Caleb Bingham's *Fur Traders Descending the Missouri,* John Singer Sargent's *Madame X,* and William Glackens's *Central Park in Winter,* as well as sculpture by Augustus Saint-Gaudens, Daniel Chester French, and John Quincy Adams Ward.

> LOCATION: Fifth Avenue at 82nd Street. HOURS: 9:30–8:45 Friday-Saturday, 9:30–5:15 Tuesday–Thursday and Sunday. FEE: Yes. TELEPHONE: 212–535–7710; 212–744–9120 (concerts and lectures).

## Guggenheim Museum

The Guggenheim is the only major New York building designed by Frank Lloyd Wright, who asserted that he detested the city. The building was considered provocative when it was completed in 1959; some regard it, today, as a masterpiece. Only a fraction of the

*The curvilinear interior ramp of Frank Lloyd Wright's Guggenheim Museum.*

works in the collection, which ranges from the Impressionist period to the present, can be displayed along the quarter-mile-long ramp that spirals up the inside walls. The museum and its holdings are the legacy of the millionaire Solomon Guggenheim, who began compiling his superb collection in 1927.

LOCATION: 1071 Fifth Avenue at 88th Street. HOURS: 10–6 Sunday–Wednesday, 10–8 Friday–Saturday. FEE: Yes. TELEPHONE: 212–423–3500.

## Cooper-Hewitt National Design Museum

The museum was founded in 1897 by the granddaughters of the manufacturer and philanthropist Peter Cooper. The collections were transferred to the Smithsonian Institution in 1968 and moved in 1976 to their new home, after the Carnegie Corporation donated the 1902 Georgian Revival mansion once owned by the industrialist Andrew Carnegie. The rambling sixty-four room mansion was the first house in the city with a steel frame structure and a rudimentary air conditioning system. Today, the Cooper-Hewitt explores the processes and products of design, as revealed in many ways—in kitchen utensils, in antiques, or in a city neighborhood. The museum studies how a range of objects influence our daily lives, and concerns itself with urban planning, architecture, landscape design, interior design, textiles, advertising, and graphic arts.

LOCATION: 2 East 91st Street at Fifth Avenue. HOURS: 10–9 Tuesday, 10–5 Wednesday–Saturday, 12–5 Sunday. FEE: Yes. TELEPHONE: 212–860–6868.

## Museum of the City of New York

The museum was founded in 1923 as a tribute to New York City's varied past, and the city's museum-goers regard its collection of historical and cultural artifacts with proprietary affection. The Georgian Colonial building, completed in 1932, was designed for the museum by Joseph H. Friedlander. It contains period rooms from the seventeenth through the twentieth centuries, including two from the John D. Rockefeller mansion and a stained-glass window by Richard Morris Hunt; a toy gallery; exhibits on the Dutch and English colonial periods, including a detailed model of New Amsterdam in 1660; and antique firefighting equipment.

LOCATION: Fifth Avenue at 103rd Street. HOURS: 10–5 Tuesday–Saturday, 1–5 Sunday. FEE: Yes. TELEPHONE: 212–534–1672.

# C E N T R A L        P A R K

The Park's 843 acres (between Central Park South and 110th Street, and Central Park West and Fifth Avenue) constitute the largest open space in Manhattan, and one of the great parks of the world. The Park is entered through eighteen gates—all with names, although only three are marked; inside, a scenic winding road runs around the entire Park, while sunken crossroads unobtrusively carry traffic across. There are also endless paths, playgrounds, a bridle trail, a running track around the Reservoir, attractions such as the **Carousel** and the **Central Park Wildlife Conservation Center,** and areas for activities such as the **Skating Rink,** the **Chess and Checkers House,** the **Delacorte Shakespeare Theater,** and the **Naumberg Bandshell,** whose admirers saved it for restoration rather than demolition. Central Park's most important asset, however, is its extraordinary variety of scenery and terrain (212–360–3444).

The long process that brought Central Park to completion began in 1844, when William Cullen Bryant, poet, newspaper editor, and nature lover, persuaded the city to acquire the tract for five million dollars. Some considered this an outrageous amount because the land, a swampy part of which was described at the time as a "pestilential spot where rank vegetation and miasmic odors taint every breath of air," was then mostly occupied by squatters' shanties. In 1858 Frederick Law Olmsted, a journalist who was to become America's first professional landscape architect, submitted the winning design with his partner, the architect Calvert Vaux. Called the Greensward Plan, it emphasized the natural features of the park. Olmsted envisioned the Park as "a democratic development of the highest significance" and insisted that it be open to all classes, at the time a somewhat radical concept.

Together Olmsted and Vaux supervised the construction and landscaping, an effort that lasted twenty years, employed thousands of workmen, and involved carting in a half million cubic yards of topsoil. According to their plan, the southern end of the Park is formally landscaped and includes the popular **Bethesda Fountain,** its statue, *Angel of the Waters* by Emma Stebbins, and the **Mall,** the stately, tree-lined promenade intended to be the only repository of statuary. (Statues have since appeared throughout the park.) With the exception of the formal five-acre **Conservatory**

OPPOSITE: *Skaters in Central Park, with the Dakota Apartments in the background.*

**Gardens** (entered through the **Vanderbilt Gate** at Fifth Avenue and 105th Street)—with its trimmed hedges, arbors, and rows of flowering crabapples—the northern end was designed to keep a natural and wild look in accordance with the landscaping trend of the late nineteenth century.

One of the Park's largest structures, the **Arsenal** at East 64th Street and Fifth Avenue was built in 1847 to house the city's armaments and is older than the Park itself. For a while, the American Museum of Natural History was housed in the building; today it is headquarters for the city's departments of Parks and Recreation and Cultural Affairs. Another imposing structure, the 1869 **Belvedere Castle,** was used as a weather station. On a much smaller scale is one of the Park's most delightful buildings, the **Dairy.** Designed as a refreshment stand in 1870 by Calvert Vaux, it is now an information center. Among Vaux's other legacies are the designs for the Park's many noteworthy bridges.

On the northeastern end of the Park are the **sites of Fort Clinton and Fort Fish,** which guard a gully known as McGowan's Pass, through which Colonel William Smallwood's Marylanders retreated after the British landing at Kips Bay during the Revolutionary War. The forts were reinforced and reactivated briefly during the War of 1812 to protect the city against possible invasion by the British from the north.

Central Park is also the repository of some of the best outdoor sculpture in the city, some fifty-odd figures of soldiers, politicians, writers, to say nothing of animals and literary characters such as Jose de Creeft's *Alice in Wonderland,* a popular climbing spot for children. On the Park's southeast corner, near Fifth Avenue, is Augustus Saint-Gaudens's majestic equestrian statue of *General Sherman;* nearby is Henry Moore's abstract *Two Piece Reclining Figure: Points.* The prolific John Quincy Adams Ward did three outstanding statues: the *Indian Hunter* (1867), showing a brave with a dog; the *Pilgrim* (1885), above the 72nd Street transverse; and his brooding figure of *William Shakespeare* (1872), commissioned for the Bard's tricentennial by a group including the actor William Booth. In the animal domain, Edward Kemenys's startlingly realistic evocation of a mountain lion, titled *Still Hunt,* appears poised to pounce on traffic and joggers on the Park's East Drive; *Balto,* by Frederick George Richard Roth, depicts the heroic malamute that led the dog sled team carrying desperately needed diphtheria serum to Nome, Alaska, in 1925.

The park displays a notable curiosity from the far-distant past.

The Khedive of Egypt gave **Cleopatra's Needle,** a soaring Egyptian obelisk, to the United States in 1881. Its inscriptions, translated for visitors, contain a stirring account of ancient adventure.

# THE UPPER WEST SIDE

Described as a "sweet rural valley" by Washington Irving in his history of the city, the Upper West Side today manages to be as diverse as any other large section of the city while retaining an independence of mind and character that distinguishes it and its residents from the rest of New York City. Stretching from Central Park West to the Hudson River (57th to 110th streets), the area consists of two hundred blocks, many nearly twice as large as those on the East Side, containing many buildings of historical interest.

Throughout the city's history, the West Side has lagged behind the East in development. The grid system adopted in 1811 failed to take into account the Upper West Side's hilly terrain. The area's main thoroughfare, the Albany Post Road (later to be called Bloomingdale Road, then The Boulevard, then Broadway), carried much less traffic than the Boston Post Road that ran the length of the East Side. Even when Central Park opened in 1876, the Upper West Side was still an undeveloped area of dirt roads, shanties, slaughterhouses, and breweries. When work began on the American Museum of Natural History in 1874, most New Yorkers regarded its location on Central Park West as the city's far outskirts.

However, public transportation spurred a real estate boom. Opulent apartment buildings were built, with grand mansions along Riverside Drive, but the West Side never rivaled the East Side in wealth. Foreign-born and first-generation Jewish residents transformed the area into a center of artistic and intellectual activity. Since the 1960s the West Side has experienced a resurgence in popularity and gentrification. The **Lincoln Center for the Performing Arts** (62nd to 66th streets, 212–875–5350), is a 14-acre complex of buildings that is home to New York's Metropolitan Opera and Philharmonic Orchestra.

## DAKOTA APARTMENTS

This massive eight-story apartment house is today one of the West Side's finest buildings and its most prestigious address. But when

OVERLEAF: *The apartments of Central Park West: The towers of the Majestic (left) and the San Remo (right) grew to surround the Dakota (second from left), the area's first "high-rise."*

its developer, Singer Sewing Machine heir Edward Clark, announced plans to build it, a detractor quipped that the building was so far uptown as to be in Dakota Territory. Clark, who must have had a sense of humor, adopted the name for his building and had a bas-relief of an Indian placed above the main entrance. Henry J. Hardenburgh, architect of the Plaza Hotel, designed the Dakota in a wildly eclectic style with oriel windows, turrets, and towers, and even a New York City version of a moat. When built, the Dakota was the largest multi-family dwelling ever constructed in the United States, surpassing in size the prehistoric Pueblo Bonito in northwestern New Mexico. On December 8, 1980, former Beatle John Lennon, a resident, was shot and killed at the entrance.

LOCATION: 1 West 72nd Street at Central Park West.

Although Central Park West never became as fashionable as Fifth Avenue across the park, it eventually attracted other important apartment buildings, such as the **Majestic Apartments** (115 Central Park West), a twin-tower Art Deco building put up in 1930 that replaced a hotel of the same name. At 1 West 67th Street, the **Hotel des Artistes** (1915), built by and for artists, was home to Isadora Duncan, Rudolf Valentino, Noel Coward, and Norman Rockwell. The **Cafe des Artistes** on the ground floor has murals of frolicking nymphs painted by Howard Chandler Christy, another resident. The **San Remo Apartments** (145–146 Central Park West between 74th and 75th streets), another ornate building with twin towers, was erected in 1930 by Emery Roth, a self-taught architect born in Hungary. Roth built many of the city's finest apartment buildings, including, on Central Park West, the 1929 three-towered **Beresford** (number 211, on the corner of 81st Street) and in 1931 the Art Deco **Ardsley** (number 320 at 92nd Street).

The Classic Revival **Spanish and Portuguese Synagogue** (Central Park West at 70th Street) is an important landmark. It was built in 1897 for Congregation Shearith Israel, the oldest Jewish congregation in North America, dating from 1654.

# NEW-YORK HISTORICAL SOCIETY

The city's name was originally hyphenated, and the New-York Historical Society, founded in 1804, retains that spelling. There are four floors of galleries and an immense research library in its present building, which was completed in 1908. The collection concentrates on New York but includes a wide range of Americana, including over four hundred original Audubon watercolors from his *Birds of America* series. Other highlights include the Bella C. Landauer Advertising Collection's colorful display of early advertising posters and the Pech collection of photographs of important New Yorkers taken between 1867 and 1937. The Portrait Gallery on the fourth floor has such portraits of distinguished Americans as John Trumbull's *Alexander Hamilton;* Charles Willson Peale's *George Washington;* and John Vanderlyn's *Aaron and Theodosia Burr.*

Their comprehensive collection of Tiffany lamps and windows is displayed in a dramatically lighted exhibit. The Society is also known for its large holdings of paintings by the Hudson River Valley School, which included such artists as Asher B. Durand, Thomas Cole, and Frederic Church.

LOCATION: 170 Central Park West at 77th Street. HOURS: 12–5 Wednesday–Sunday (Museum); 12–5 Friday–Sunday (Library). FEE: Yes. TELEPHONE: 212–873–3400.

# AMERICAN MUSEUM OF NATURAL HISTORY

Scientific curiosity stimulated by the discoveries of Charles Darwin and other naturalists led to the founding of this institution by a group of wealthy New Yorkers in 1869. The original collection, purchased in France and consisting mostly of stuffed birds, was soon augmented by the thousands of specimens that Prince Maximilian of Neuwied collected in Brazil. The museum's first public home was in the Arsenal, a fortresslike building in Central Park. The present building, begun in 1874, was designed by Jacob Wrey Mould and Calvert Vaux, a designer of Central Park. There have been so many additions since, that the original building can only be glimpsed from the Columbus Avenue side. The collection today has more than 36 million items, including 16 million insects and 8.5 million fossil invertebrates. The museum's dinosaur displays, its dioramas of animals in the wild, and its exhibits of minerals and gems are world-famous. The museum is also a working scientific research institution, employing some two hundred scientists and their assistants. The **Hayden Planetarium,** built in 1935 on West 81st Street, has an interior dome seventy-five feet in diameter.

LOCATION: Central Park West at 79th Street. HOURS: 10–5:45 Monday, Tuesday, Thursday, Sunday; 10–9 Wednesday, Friday, Saturday. FEE: Yes. TELEPHONE: 212–769–5100.

Some of the city's best **rowhouses** are found on West 71st and 76th
streets just off Central Park West. The one-family dwellings on
West 71st Street are typical New York City brownstones, with high
stoops, recessed basements, and corniced tops. Faced with sandstone containing iron ore, which gives them their characteristic
brown color, typically they were built in small groups, each house
being a fraction of a standard city building lot. Some of the turn-of-
the-century facades are unusually well decorated. The rowhouses
on 76th Street between Central Park West and Columbus Avenue
were built between 1887 and 1889 and present a harmonious front
to the street, although their styles differ from house to house.

Between Central Park West and the Upper West Side's elegant
western boundary, Riverside Drive, the **subway entrance** at the
intersection of Broadway and Amsterdam Avenue at 72nd Street is
a Neo–Dutch Colonial structure designed in 1904 by Heins &
LaFarge. Its site, a triangular piece of land, is called **Sherman
Square** after General William Tecumseh Sherman.

## ANSONIA HOTEL

This sixteen-story residential landmark (2109 Broadway between
73rd and 74th streets) was built in the Beaux-Arts style with unusually rich detailing, corner turrets, ornate balconies, and terra-cotta
trim. Thick walls and heavy construction—originally for fireproof-
ing—make the apartments virtually soundproof; for this reason
the Ansonia has been popular with singers and musicians—Enrico
Caruso, Yehudi Menuhin, Ezio Pinza, Igor Stravinsky, and Arturo
Toscanini—ever since it was completed in 1904. The Ansonia was
built by William Earl Dodge Stokes, heir to the Phelps Dodge
Copper and Ansonia Brass and Copper fortunes, who actually was
responsible for its fanciful design. Originally, live seals cavorted in
a fountain in the lobby. Stokes kept goats, chickens, and other
animals on the roof and sold eggs to the tenants.

## RIVERSIDE DRIVE AND PARK

Riverside Drive today is one of New York's most pleasant avenues,
combining river views, the bucolic pleasures of Frederick Law
Olmsted's Riverside Park, and some of New York City's most genteel apartment houses. When the drive and park opened in 1880,
however, the neighborhood "was still a wasteland of asylums, athletic fields, breweries, grain elevators, rocky promontories, swamps,

*City Transportation on Riverside Drive ca. 1897.*

and slaughterhouses," writes James Trager in *West of Fifth,* an illustrated history of the area. The first apartment house on the Drive, the Turrets (84th Street), wasn't built for another twenty years. In 1904, a subway servicing the area opened, precipitating a building boom. That same year the seventy-five-room chateau on the block between 73rd and 74th streets, built by Charles M. Schwab of the Bethlehem Steel Company, was ready for occupancy. Still, despite such architectural extravaganzas, Riverside Drive never attained the social cachet enjoyed by the East Side.

At the southwest corner of Riverside Drive and West 89th Street, the **Residence of Isaac L. Rice,** now the Yeshiva Chofetz Chaim, is one of the Drive's few mansions still standing. Between 105th and 106th are a row of Beaux-Arts houses built between 1899 and 1902, part of a small historic district including many row-houses on 105th Street. Overlooking the park at West 93rd Street is the *Joan of Arc Memorial Statue,* done by the well-known New York sculptor Anna Hyatt Huntington to commemorate the five-hundred-year anniversary of the saint's birth in 1412. The marble Civil War memorial at the corner of West 89th Street, *The Soldiers' and Sailors' Monument,* executed in 1902 by sculptor Paul M. Duboy, is another of the area's artistic treasures.

# MORNINGSIDE HEIGHTS

The isolation of this once-rural area was ended in 1880 when Riverside Drive and the Ninth Avenue El both entered the vicinity. Today the boundaries of the heights are roughly 110th Street, or Cathedral Parkway, on the south, Morningside Park on the east, and 125th Street on the north. Columbia University, St. Luke's Hospital, and the Cathedral of St. John the Divine were built here at the end of the century. Frederick Law Olmsted designed both **Morningside Park** on the east side of the Heights and Riverside Park and Drive on the west.

## CATHEDRAL CHURCH OF ST. JOHN THE DIVINE

Although work on the cathedral, begun in 1892, has been proceeding for more than a century, it is not yet finished. Already very large, its two towers will be 291 feet tall when completed. In 1911, after nearly twenty years of construction, Ralph Adams Cram took over the project and radically changed the design from Romanesque to Gothic. J. P. Morgan was an early contributor, giving half a million dollars for the excavation, and John D. Rockefeller donated the same amount in 1924.

Inside, the cathedral is a dramatic expanse of open space—the nave alone is 248 feet long (total cathedral length: 601 feet), 146 feet wide, and 177 feet high—and a treasure house of carvings and other artwork. The pulpit in the crossing is carved from Tennessee marble; the seventeenth-century Barberini Tapestries, also displayed here, depict Biblical scenes; the stalls in the choir were designed by Heins & LaFarge, the cathedral's original architects. The forty-foot-wide rose window is made from more than ten thousand pieces of glass. The cathedral was conceived as "a place of worship for all people"; its Chapels of Tongues are dedicated to countries and faiths around the world. In the north ambulatory, St. Columba's Chapel (1911) contains statues by Gutzon Borglum of English church personages; the Chapel of St. Martin of Tours has a statue of Joan of Arc by Anna Hyatt Huntington. On the grounds is a Biblical Garden, which only has plants mentioned in the Bible.

LOCATION: Amsterdam Avenue at 112th Street. HOURS: 7–5 Daily.

OPPOSITE: *Details of the exterior of the Cathedral Church of St. John the Divine.*

**Columbia University** is the leading institution of higher learning in a city noted for educational facilities. Since 1983, the undergradgraduate school has been open to women, although the university is still affiliated with Barnard College. Known for its graduate schools, among them a medical school dating from 1767 and a law school established in 1858, its large School of General Studies was a pioneer in the field of adult education.

Columbia began in 1754 as King's College. Among its earliest graduates were such national figures as Alexander Hamilton (1778), Gouverneur Morris (1768), John Jay (1764), and De Witt Clinton (1786). It changed its name to Columbia after the Revolution, moved to Madison Avenue between 49th and 50th streets in 1857, and to the campus on Morningside Heights in 1879.

Charles Follen McKim of the architectural firm of McKim, Mead & White drew up plans for a campus built as a series of small courtyards around a narrow quadrangle, but only one courtyard was actually built. The firm's **Low Memorial Library** (1897), majestically placed at the top of three flights of stairs and derived from the Pantheon in Rome, now houses administrative offices. On its steps is Daniel Chester French's famous statue, *Alma Mater*. The

*Daniel Chester French's* Alma Mater *on the steps of Columbia University's Low Library. The statue was damaged by a bomb during student riots in 1970.*

university's other notable building is the brick and limestone **St. Paul's Chapel** (1907) with a dome ninety-one feet high.

Despite widespread opposition from students, faculty, and trustees, Columbia's enlightened president, Frederick A. P. Barnard, managed in 1883 to establish a separate but equivalent course of study for women. This led to the founding in 1889 of **Barnard College,** an independent women's college affiliated with the university. Barnard is located on the west side of Broadway between 116th and 120th streets, on the site of the **Battle of Harlem Heights.** Here, on September 16, 1776, Washington and his troops fought the British for several hours in a buckwheat field and forced them to retreat. The British had badly beaten the Americans the previous day at Kips Bay so the Harlem Heights victory, though minor in history, bolstered American morale. A plaque on Barnard's Mathematics Building commemorates the battle.

LOCATION: Broadway at 116th Street. HOURS: Tours of Barnard and Columbia: 11 and 2 Monday–Friday, or by appointment. FEE: None. TELEPHONE: 212–854–4900.

## RIVERSIDE CHURCH

Overlooking the Hudson River at 120th Street, the church was criticized after its completion in 1930 for its "bewildered eclecticism." Notable woodwork, stone carving, stained glass, and a 392-foot steeple are among its many attributes. John D. Rockefeller, Jr., a parishioner, gave the **Laura Spelman Rockefeller Memorial Carillon** in memory of his mother; its seventy-four bells include the heaviest—twenty tons—tuned bell in the world.

## GENERAL GRANT NATIONAL MEMORIAL

Ulysses S. Grant, victorious Civil War general and president of the United States, is entombed in the imposing granite tomb with his wife, Julia Dent Grant. Completed in 1897 by John H. Duncan, its interior is a copy of Napoleon's tomb in Paris. Grant's words—"Let us have peace"—are engraved on the parapet along the south facade. The murals depicting Grant's famous victories were done by Allyn Cox in 1966.

LOCATION: 122nd Street and Riverside Drive. HOURS: 9–5 Daily. FEE: None. telephone: 212–666–1640.

# HARLEM AND WASHINGTON HEIGHTS

Harlem was first settled by Dutch farmers in the mid-seventeenth century. In 1672, these landholders put their slaves to work building a road from Nieuw Haarlem, as it was called, to New Amsterdam ten miles to the south. The area continued to attract farmers and wealthy merchants, who built country estates there, but it was the coming of the railroad in 1837—a line running up Park Avenue to the Harlem River—that truly opened up the area for development. The Third and Second Avenue Els followed in 1879 and 1880. The railroads also split the area: East Harlem became a place of tenements for newly arrived European immigrants; West Harlem a residential area for the rich. Oscar Hammerstein, Henry Morgenthau, and William B. Astor were among those who built homes there. Some of these can still be seen on the west side (particularly along 119th and 123rd streets) of **Marcus Garvey Memorial Park,** named after the black leader who advocated the emigration of blacks to Africa.

The best rowhouses in the entire city are found in West Harlem's **St. Nicholas Historic District** (138th and 139th streets between Seventh and Eighth avenues). They were built in 1891 by a developer who hired three prominent architectural firms to do different sides of the two streets in varying but harmonious styles. The ubiquitous McKim, Mead & White did the dark-brick, Neo-Renaissance-style houses along the north side of 139th Street.

A financial panic in 1904 was an important turning point for West Harlem, forcing many well-to-do property owners to sell out. In the meantime, blacks in search of better housing were gravitating to the area and succeeding in breaking down racial barriers. Blacks were first allowed to buy in the St. Nicholas district in 1919, for example, and its many prominent residents since have included musicians W. C. Handy and Eubie Blake. Another resident, Abram Hill, founder of the American Negro Theater, wrote a play about the district, *On Striver's Row,* and it has been known by that name ever since. During the 1920s, the black population of Harlem more than doubled to over two hundred thousand. This was a period of optimism, ferment, and creativity for blacks.

The **Schomburg Center for Research in Black Culture** (515 Malcolm X Boulevard, 212–862–4000), part of the New York Public Library, has the world's largest collection of documents about the history and literature of black people, and the **Studio Museum in**

*The distinguished row houses of the St. Nicholas Historic District in Harlem, home to many prominent black Americans.*

**Harlem** (144 West 125th Street, 212–864–4500) exhibits the work of black artists and includes the works of Romare Bearden and the photographer James Van Der Zee in its permanent collection.

**Hamilton Heights Historic District,** an outstanding group of rowhouses (Convent Avenue between West 141st and West 145th streets), includes Alexander Hamilton's country home, **Hamilton Grange** (212–283–5154), now located at 287 Convent Avenue, about one hundred yards away from its original location. The badly deteriorated house, designed in 1801 by John McComb, Jr., was closed by the National Park Service in the late 1990s for structural work and planned relocation. Hamilton enjoyed his garden— "a very usual refuge for a disappointed politician." He lived there a short time before he was killed in a duel with Aaron Burr in 1804.

The development of Jumel Terrace, the short street running between West 160th and West 162nd streets, in the northern part of Harlem, took place between 1890 and 1902, and many of these substantial middle-class houses remain with few changes. The historic Morris-Jumel Mansion is also part of the **Jumel Terrace Historic District** and the only building left from the time when Harlem was a place of large homes and estates.

*A New York couple, photographed in 1932 by James Van Der Zee.*

## MORRIS-JUMEL MANSION

One of the few pre-Revolutionary houses left in the city, the mansion was built as a summer home in 1765 by Lieutenant Colonel Roger Morris, George Washington's friend and comrade-in-arms during the French and Indian War. Washington retreated to the house after the British landing at Kips Bay and headquartered here until his retreat out of the city a month later. Morris, a loyalist, had fled to England the previous year. Stephen Jumel, a rich French wine merchant, died in 1832 and left the house to his socially ambitious widow, the former Betsy Bowen of Providence. Madame Jumel, who had already scandalized New York with her extramarital affairs, married the elderly Aaron Burr about a year later, but they soon separated. Madame died in the house in 1865 at age ninety-three. The city purchased the house in 1903 and opened it as a museum under the care of the Daughters of the American Revolution in 1907. It contains furniture from the Jumel and pre-Revolutionary eras. The front parlor is decorated with a copy of the wallpaper Jumel brought from France.

LOCATION: Edgecombe Avenue at West 160th Street. HOURS: 10–4 Wednesday–Sunday. FEE: Yes. TELEPHONE: 212–923–8008.

# AUDUBON TERRACE

In 1841, after publishing the financially successful *Birds of America,* John James Audubon purchased the twenty-four acres along the Hudson River on which he built an estate and maintained a game preserve. The museum complex at Audubon Terrace now occupies the site, between 155th and 156th streets, west of Broadway. The handsome Beaux Arts buildings, which surround a paved brick courtyard, were built by the scholarly philanthropist Archer Milton Huntington, son of the railroad magnate Collis P. Huntington. Anna Hyatt Huntington, wife of Archer Huntington and a well-known sculptor, created *El Cid Campeador,* the statue of the legendary Spanish hero that dominates the plaza.

Archer Huntington had a special interest in Hispanic culture. His cousin, Charles Pratt Huntington, designed most of the complex, including the **Hispanic Society of America** (212–926– 2234). Archer Huntington's acquisitions provide the nucleus of the museum's collection, which includes unique examples of the fine and decorative arts of the Iberian Peninsula from prehistory to the present. The library contains thousands of manuscripts and more than two hundred thousand early and modern books. Goya and El Greco are among the masters represented in the collection.

The **American Academy of Arts and Letters** (212–368–5900) has a membership of 250 preeminent American writers, composers, painters, sculptors, and architects. Primarily through the granting of awards, the academy seeks to promote achievement in literature, music, and the fine arts. The academy occupies two limestone buildings in the Audubon complex, one designed by McKim, Mead, and White, the other by Cass Gilbert.

The Manhattan campus of **Boricua College** (212–694–1000) is at Audubon Terrace. Boricua was the first post-secondary educational institution in the United States specifically designed to meet the educational needs of Puerto Ricans and other Spanish-speaking people.

The **American Numismatic Society** (212–234–3130) at Audubon Terrace is an international center for the preservation and study of coins, tokens, medals, and paper money spanning twenty-five hundred years. The museum houses nearly one million objects and the world's most comprehensive library of numismatic literature. The designs on American coins and paper money from the late eighteenth century on reflect the nation's love of liberty and its growth to preeminent world power.

*An 1800 silver dollar, and a 1907 twenty-dollar gold coin designed by Augustus Saint-Gaudens, from the collection of the American Numismatic Society.*

Across 155th Street at the corner of Broadway is the 1914 Gothic **Church of the Intercession,** designed by Bertram Grosvenor Goodhue, architect of St. Bartholomew's Church in midtown, who is buried here. The church is on the grounds of **Trinity Cemetery,** which extends south to 153rd Street and from Riverside Drive to Amsterdam Avenue. The cemetery was established by Trinity Parish in 1846 when space ran short in its downtown burying ground. John James Audubon is buried here, as are John Jacob Astor, Madame Jumel of the Morris-Jumel Mansion, Philip Livingston, a signer of the Declaration of Independence, and Clement Clarke Moore, developer of Chelsea and author of *A Visit from St. Nicholas.*

Two handsome bridges leave Manhattan from Washington Heights. The **Washington Bridge,** built in 1888, crosses the Harlem River at 181st Street. A double steel arch and viaducts connect it with the heights on both sides, making it a striking sight, especially from the river. The bridge should not be confused, however, with its newer, more famous neighbor almost directly across town on the Hudson side, the 3,500-foot **George Washington Bridge,** one of the most beautiful spans in the world. Two boys on roller skates were the first to cross it on opening day in 1931; at that time it was twice the length of any other suspension bridge. The bridge was built by the Swiss-American engineer Othmar Hermann Ammann with Cass Gilbert as consulting architect. Fortunately, Gilbert's plan to cover the open framework with granite and concrete was never carried out.

The two rocky ridges that run through Manhattan—and support its skyscrapers—rise to a peak in Washington Heights, the strategically important high ground George Washington occupied but failed to hold in the latter days of 1776. Manhattan's highest point—267 feet—is at **Bennett Park** (between 183rd and 185th streets, Fort Washington and Pinehurst avenues), once the estate of *New York Herald* publisher James Gordon Bennett. Here paving stones mark the outline of **Fort Washington.**

The British launched a three-pronged attack, involving eight thousand men, on the fort on the morning of November 16, 1776. The day before, Washington, arriving from Fort Lee across the Hudson, had inspected the fortification and been assured by its commander that he could hold it against the British. In fact, the five-sided earthen fort was poorly built for defense and before nightfall the Americans had surrendered to Baron von Knyphausen, who had attacked with three thousand Hessian soldiers from the north. The cost of the battle to the Americans was high: 54 dead and 2,800 of Washington's best troops captured.

The **Dyckman House Museum and Park** (4881 Broadway at 204th Street, 212–304–9422), a Dutch Colonial farmhouse with a gambrel roof and spring eaves, is a short distance from Fort Tryon Park. Burned by the British during the Revolution, it was rebuilt with fieldstone, brick, and wood by the Dyckman family in 1783. Their three-hundred-acre farm, one of the largest in the city, was worked until 1868. In 1915, Dyckman descendants purchased the house and, after restoring it and furnishing it with period furniture, cooking utensils, toys, and heirlooms, donated it to the city.

## FORT TRYON PARK

This sixty-six-acre park, with its landscaped terraces, gardens, fort site, and dramatic views of the Hudson, was designed by Frederick Law Olmsted, Jr., son of the Central Park architect. In 1930, John D. Rockefeller, Jr., gave the city the land in trade for the property on the East River where Rockefeller Institute is now located. Fort

Tryon, of which the site remains, was an outwork of Fort Washington. It fell early on November 16, 1776, to the same force of Hessians who scaled the ridge from the north and east and later forced the surrender of the garrison at Fort Washington. The British named it Fort Tryon after the last British governor of the colony. The battle produced a heroine, Margaret Cochran Corbin, known as "Captain Molly," who took over her husband's gun when he was killed and fought with spirit until she was wounded. The roadway and plaza south of Fort Tryon Park are named for her.

## THE CLOISTERS

This enchanting reconstruction captures the style and spirit of a medieval cloister without actually being a copy of one. The Cloisters has been one of New York City's main cultural attractions ever

*The Cloisters, a branch of the Metropolitan Museum of Art.*

since it opened on this bluff overlooking the Hudson River in 1938. Designed by Charles Collens, the building incorporates architectural treasures from abandoned monasteries and churches in France that the eccentric collector and sculptor, George Grey Barnard, assembled in the years before World War I. In 1925 John D. Rockefeller, Jr., purchased Barnard's collection for the Metropolitan Museum. The exterior is of hand-quarried Connecticut granite; the courtyards paved with pavement stones taken from old New York City streets; the gardens based on those found in medieval works of art. The medieval collection is highlighted by the seven Unicorn Tapestries dating from 1499, a Rockefeller gift.

LOCATION: Fort Tryon Park. HOURS: March through October: 9:30–5:15 Tuesday–Sunday; November through February: 9:30–4:45 Tuesday–Sunday. FEE: Yes. TELEPHONE: 212–923–3700.

# GREATER NEW YORK
# AND
# LONG ISLAND

OPPOSITE: *The Brooklyn Bridge, an engineering and aesthetic triumph, designed by John A. Roebling and completed in 1883.*

The Bronx, Staten Island, Brooklyn, and Queens—New York City's outer boroughs—gave up their independent status in 1898 under the Greater New York Charter. Too often overlooked, they are in themselves rich in historic sites, and each has its own parks, shops, and ethnic neighborhoods to contradict its image as a mere urban extension of Manhattan. Nassau and Suffolk counties, the two suburban counties on Long Island, preserve many historic buildings. This chapter circles Manhattan, beginning with the Bronx to the north, moving south to Staten Island, and then east to Long Island.

# T  H  E    B  R  O  N  X

The Bronx was first settled in 1639 by Jonas Bronck, a Swedish commercial sea captain in the service of the Dutch; his Dutch wife; and a few indentured servants. The land he purchased, today only a small portion in the southwestern part of the borough on the Harlem River, was called Broncksland, and the nearby waterway on its eastern boundary Bronck's (Bronx) River. The borough was eventually named after the river, hence its use of the definite article, *the* Bronx. Bronck's settlement disbanded with his death in 1643.

The next settlers were led by the religious dissenter Anne Hutchinson, exiled from Boston by the Puritans, and John Throckmorton, an outcast Anabaptist. They both settled with small bands of followers in the reaches of the East Bronx in 1644. Hutchinson's colony was killed by Indians, and Throckmorton and his band were driven back to the safety of New Amsterdam. Their names are remembered today by two familiar Bronx landmarks, the Hutchinson River and Throg's Neck.

The borough grew slowly as an area of country estates and farms until the 1840s when Irish and German railroad workers began to settle there. In a pattern that occurred over and over again in New York City, they were displaced by other immigrants— by more Germans at midcentury, then by Italians, Jews, Poles, and Greeks. The borough of the Bronx—forty-two square miles—was officially created by the Greater New York charter in 1898. For the next half-century, the Bronx developed into a series of tightly knit and stable ethnic neighborhoods. This was an era that produced the well-known "raspberry" (the Bronx cheer) and saw the glory days of the Bronx Bombers (the New York Yankees). In the last half of the twentieth century, poorer minorities occupied much of

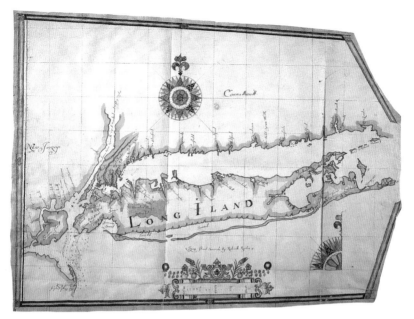

*A 1678 map of New York City and Long Island.* PAGES 128–129: *Wave Hill, a public garden, with the Hudson River and New Jersey Palisades in the distance.*

the Bronx. The borough bore more than its share of urban stress. Some areas were abandoned, but many residents showed determination to rebuild and restore their neighborhoods.

## RIVERDALE

This enclave of prosperity stretches along the Hudson River from Spuyten Duyvil to Westchester County. **Wave Hill** (675 West 252nd Avenue, 718–549–3200), a public garden and cultural center, was given to the city in 1960 by the daughter of George F. Perkins, a Wall Street financier and conservationist. In 1903, Perkins acquired the fieldstone Wave Hill Manor, originally built in 1844 with later additions, and added greenhouses, gardens, and stables. Wave Hill was Theodore Roosevelt's boyhood home. Samuel Clemens lived there at the height of his success in 1901, and Arturo Toscanini rented the manor in the mid-1940s.

James Renwick, Jr., designed the Gothic Revival **Greystone Conference Center of Teachers College** (690 West 247th Street) in 1864 for the copper magnate William E. Dodge when Riverdale

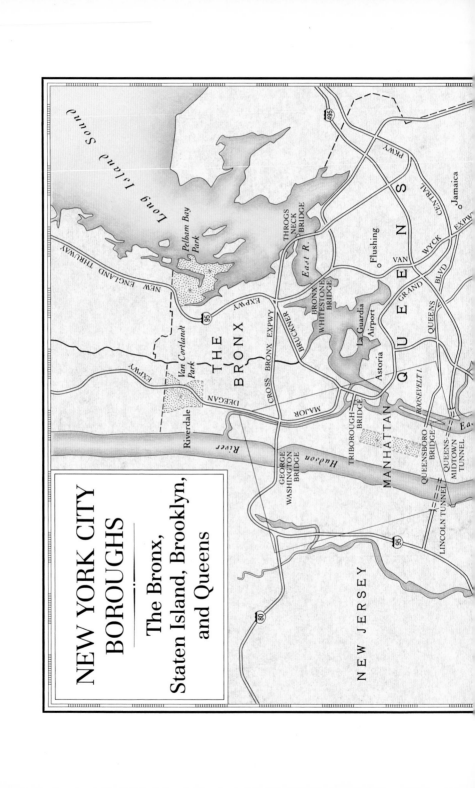

NEW YORK CITY
BOROUGHS

The Bronx,
Staten Island, Brooklyn,
and Queens

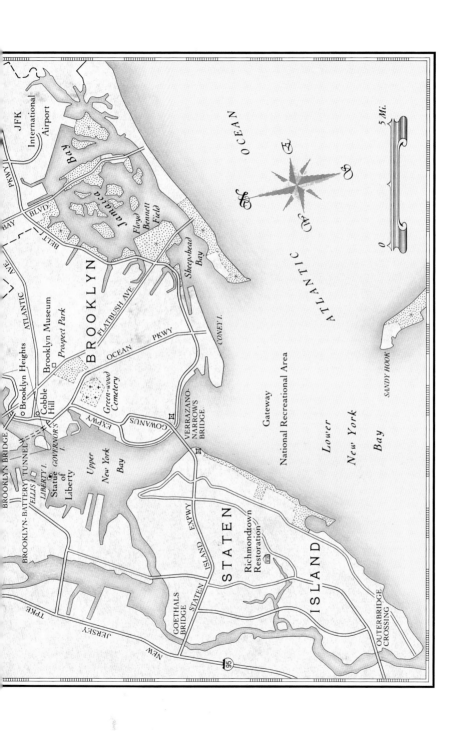

was still sparsely populated. His daughter, Grace Dodge, helped found Columbia Teachers College; her nephew eventually bequeathed the mansion to that institution.

## Van Cortlandt Mansion

George Washington briefly used the Van Cortlandt Mansion as a headquarters during the Revolution, and on July 21, 1781, dined with his French ally Rochambeau prior to the march from New York to Yorktown and the battle that would end the Revolution. The rubblestone house, which is located in Van Cortlandt Park on land that belonged to the Van Cortlandt family until 1889, was built by Frederick Van Cortlandt about 1748. The family has been prominent in New York since Oloff Stevenszen Van Cortlandt arrived from Holland in 1638. The dining room contains a portrait of John Jacob Astor by Gilbert Stuart, the Astors being just one of many important New York families related to the Van Cortlandts by marriage. The house is furnished with English, Dutch, and colonial antiques. In the east parlor there is a portrait of Augustus Van Cortlandt by John Wesley Jarvis. Augustus, who was city clerk during the Revolution, hid municipal records in the family cemetery.

LOCATION: Broadway at West 246th Street. HOURS: 10–4:30 Wednesday–Saturday, 12–4:30 Sunday. FEE: Yes. TELEPHONE: 212–543-3344.

Van Cortlandt Park abuts the well-landscaped **Woodlawn Cemetery** (212–920–0500) on the east, where more than a quarter-million people—some in splendiferous Victorian tombs and mausoleums—have been buried since 1865. Among Woodlawn's interred are financier Jay Gould, Herman Melville, F. W. Woolworth, Fiorello La Guardia—one of the city's more colorful mayors—Joseph Pulitzer, W. C. Handy, and Duke Ellington. The Cemetery, and its series of special events, is open to the public.

Nearby is the 1812 **Edgar Allan Poe Cottage** (Grand Concourse and Kingsbridge Road, 212–881–8900), a modest dwelling where Poe moved with his ailing wife in 1846. She died the first winter. Before he left in 1849 for Baltimore, he wrote "Ulalume" and "The Bells" here. The white frame farmhouse contains period furniture and Poe memorabilia.

The **Valentine-Varian House** is also in the northern Bronx. The 1758 fieldstone house was occupied by British and Hessian

OPPOSITE: *The Bartow-Pell mansion, built between 1836 and 1842, was restored in 1914 by the International Garden Club. It is noted for its gardens and view of Long Island Sound.*

troops during the Revolution. It is now the **Museum of Bronx History** (3266 Bainbridge Avenue, 718–881–8900), with many artifacts, including an outstanding research collection.

## THE BRONX ZOO

Officially called the Wildlife Conservation Park, the 262-acre Bronx Zoo is the largest urban zoo in the country. The architectural firm of Morris Ketchum, Jr. & Associates designed the innovative buildings, the **World of Birds** and the **World of Darkness,** where nocturnal animals can be seen at low light levels. Sculptor Paul Manship created the **Rainey Memorial Gate** with twenty-two full-sized animals in 1934; Anna Hyatt Huntington, whose work graces so much of New York, sculpted the **stone jaguars** near the stairs in 1937, using an actual cat in the zoo as a model.

LOCATION: Off the Bronx River Parkway. HOURS: 10–5 Daily. FEE: Yes. TELEPHONE: 718–367–1010.

## NEW YORK BOTANICAL GARDEN

The 250-acre Botanical Garden was once the estate of the Lorillard family of tobacco fame and it includes several original buildings, including the 1840 **Snuff Mill,** which was used for grinding tobacco. Founded in 1891, the Garden is a world-famous educational and research institution with gardens, conservatory, arboretum, and a forty-acre hemlock forest. The **Enid A. Haupt Conservatory** was built in 1902 and renamed in 1978 after Ms. Haupt gave $5 million for its restoration. The building has eleven galleries, including the Hanging Garden, Palm Court, and Fern Forest.

LOCATION: Off the Bronx River Parkway. HOURS: April through October: 10–6 Tuesday–Sunday; November through March: 10–4 Tuesday–Sunday. FEE: Yes. TELEPHONE: 718–817–8700.

Anne Hutchinson is believed to have settled near the present-day **Pelham Bay Park,** 2,118 acres of varied terrain and recreational facilities on the borough's eastern shore. While the city was still under Dutch rule, an Englishman, Thomas Pell, bought this land from the Siwanoy Indians. One of his descendants, Robert Bartow, completed the **Bartow-Pell Mansion** in 1842. The house is furnished with American Empire furniture and other period pieces,

OPPOSITE: *The recently-restored Enid A. Haupt Conservatory at the New York Botanical Garden.*

and surrounded by lovely gardens with views of Long Island Sound; both house and garden were restored in 1914 and are open to the public (718–885–1461). A bridge from the park leads to **City Island,** a small, picturesque maritime community whose history of shipbuilding and sailmaking is shown in the **City Island Historical Nautical Museum** (190 Fordham Street, 718–885–1600).

# S T A T E N   I S L A N D

Although to a great extent covered with suburban housing, Staten Island is still an area of considerable natural beauty and historical importance, with parts almost rural in character—at least when compared with the rest of New York City. Covering just over sixty square miles, the island is the city's third-largest borough in area but still the least populated. (The county's official name is Richmond despite occasional efforts to change it to Staten Island.) Pristine oceanfront has been preserved in the **Gateway National Recreation Area,** and expanses of salt marsh, open fields, and woods have managed—so far—to resist the pressures of development. Staten Island also has a rich legacy of architecture dating from colonial times; there are lovely views of the enveloping waters from the hills on which many wealthy New Yorkers built homes during the nineteenth century.

Todt Hill, at 409 feet the highest point in New York City or on the Atlantic seaboard south of Maine, is part of a rocky ridge dividing the island. The pinnacle (historians have never been able to explain the name, which translates as "Death Hill") obviously caught Henry Hudson's eye when he sailed into New York Harbor in 1609; he named the island Staten Island after the Dutch governing body, the States General. French and Dutch farmers settled here in 1661 in Oude Dorp (Old Town) near where Fort Wadsworth is today. In the next century, Staten Island developed as an important agricultural, fishing, and shipbuilding center.

During the Revolution, Staten Island became a staging area for British troops. In September 1776, Lord Richard Howe conferred with Benjamin Franklin, John Adams, and Edward Rutledge in an attempt to end the war. The meeting took place in the Conference House in Tottenville, now restored. The federal government fortified the strategically important island during the War of 1812 and in 1825 a Staten Islander, Cornelius Vanderbilt, became an early operator of regular ferry service to Manhattan.

*Children at play on the shore of Staten Island. The early photograph was taken by Alice Austen, a life-long Staten Island resident.*

Vanderbilt went on to compile one of the country's largest fortunes in finance, shipping, and railroads; at fifty cents a ride, the famed **Staten Island Ferry** endures as one of the great bargains in transportation and one of the most scenic rides anywhere.

## CONFERENCE HOUSE

Built about 1675 by Captain Christopher Billopp and still called the Billopp House, the steep-roofed stone manor house with high end chimneys was built with rubblestone and sits on an ancient Indian campground. The conference between the American delegates—Benjamin Franklin, John Adams, and Edward Rutledge—and Vice-Admiral Lord Richard Howe took place on September 11, 1776, and set the course of American history. The American delegation was ferried over by the British under a safe conduct pass from Perth Amboy to the beach in front of the house. At the conference, Lord Howe's offer of clemency to "all repentant rebels who would lay down their arms and return to their allegiance to the King" was rejected, because, Franklin pointed out, the Americans had already declared independence. At that time the house was occupied by the builder's grandson, Christopher Billopp II, a Loyalist, who fled to Nova Scotia at the end of the war.

LOCATION: 7455 Hylan Boulevard, Tottenville. HOURS: March through December: 1–4 Wednesday–Sunday. FEE: Yes. TELEPHONE: 718–984–6046.

Staten Island became part of New York City in 1898, but has developed more slowly than the city's other boroughs. Between 1928 and 1931, three bridges were built connecting it to its nearest neighbor—New Jersey. In 1964, the graceful Verrazano-Narrows Bridge to Brooklyn was completed, causing a major land boom that changed the small-town character of the island. Near the bridge is Fort Wadsworth, in Gateway National Recreation Area. It encompasses two forts—Battery Weed and Fort Tompkins. The former, one of only a few four-tiered granite forts in the United States, could aim one hundred cannons on the entrance to New York Harbor. The "officers' row" has well-preserved homes dating to the 1870s.

Near the terminus of the bridge, in the community known as Rosebank, is the Alice Austen House and the **Garibaldi-Meucci Museum** (420 Tompkins Avenue, 718–442–1608), a frame house where the exiled Italian liberator Giuseppe Garibaldi lived with his friend Antonio Meucci in 1850. Garibaldi returned to Italy in 1854—and eventually unified the peninsula. Meucci went on to invent a prototype of the telephone several years before Alexander Graham Bell produced his. The museum tells their story.

## ALICE AUSTEN HOUSE

This Victorian Gothic Revival house, built in 1691, has been restored and contains works by the remarkable photographer Alice Austen. Her collection of glass negatives, taken between 1880 and 1930, is now held by the Staten Island Historical Society. The house, which has magnificent views of Upper New York Bay, was acquired as a summer home in 1844 by Alice Austen's grandfather John Austen, a wealthy New Yorker. He added the Gothic Revival details and peaked dormer windows and named the house "Clear Comfort." When Alice was two years old, her father deserted the family; her mother resumed her maiden name and moved into Clear Comfort. Alice, who took up photography as a young woman, lived here until she was seventy-nine, when, ill and destitute,

OPPOSITE: *View of Manhattan from the Alice Austen house, now restored.*

she was forced to move to a city nursing home. A 1951 *Life* magazine article gave her work, at last, the recognition it deserved. Since
then her photography has been widely published and exhibited.

LOCATION: 2 Hylan Boulevard. HOURS: 12–5 Thursday–Sunday.
FEE: Yes. TELEPHONE: 718–816–4506.

Nearby is a magnificent row of Greek Revival buildings now known
as the **Snug Harbor Cultural Center** (1000 Richmond Terrace,
Livingston, 718–448–2500). Designed by Minard Lafever, these
buildings are the centerpiece of a twenty-eight-building complex
featuring architecture ranging from Greek Revival to Italianate
and Victorian to Beaux-Arts, located on eighty acres of parkland.
Sailors Snug Harbor began in 1831 as a retirement home for sailors
and when the home moved to North Carolina to cut costs, the city
began restoring the buildings to save them from demolition. Snug
Harbor presents concerts in a landmarked recital hall, adapted
from the 1855 Chapel. At the Music Hall (1882), New York's oldest
extant theater, classical and popular programs, as well as dramatic
performances and entertainment for children, are presented. The
Newhouse Center for Contemporary Art offers exhibitions in four
galleries in the sailors' dining rooms. Also at Snug Harbor are the
**Staten Island Botanical Gardens** (718–273–8200) and the **Staten
Island Children's Museum** (718–273–2060).

In central Staten Island, one of the island's oldest buildings,
the **Billiou-Stillwell-Perine House** (1476 Richmond Road, private), was built as a small Dutch farmhouse by Pierre Billiou in
1662, with later additions by the Stillwell and Perine families. It is
located in the affluent residential area known as Dongan Hills,
once the site of large estates.

Like Dongan Hills, Todt Hill is a former seventeenth-century
mining area. The **Vanderbilt Family Mausoleum,** designed in
1886 by Richard Morris Hunt, is located in the **Moravian Cemetery**
at Todt Hill and Richmond roads. The first Cornelius Vanderbilt
and several other family members are buried here. At 209 Flagg
Place, off Todt Hill Road, the **Ernest Flagg Residence** (private) is
the home that the architect of New York City's Singer and Scribner
buildings designed for himself in 1898. The thirty-two-room mansion has a two-story colonnade porch, large twin chimneys, and a
curious observation deck protruding from the gambrel roof.

## HISTORIC RICHMOND TOWN

The oldest elementary school in the country, the ca. 1696 **Voor-lezer's House,** and the ca. 1700 **Treasure House,** where $5,000 in gold coins was found behind a wall, are two of the more than thirty seventeenth- to nineteenth-century buildings in this outdoor museum. The Staten Island Historical Society began the restoration in 1936 and today the complex includes a **museum,** a **Carpenter's Shop** with an exhibit of antique tools, and a ca. 1870 **Grocery Store** that has been converted to an old printing shop. With its gambrel roof and springing eaves, the **Guyon-Lake-Tysen House** (ca. 1740) is a fine example of Dutch Colonial architecture.

> LOCATION: 441 Clarke Avenue, Richmondtown. HOURS: Most of the year: Wednesday–Sunday; call to confirm. FEE: Yes. TELE-PHONE: 718-351-1611.

# B  R  O  O  K  L  Y  N

Brooklyn, with seventy-eight square miles and a population of several million, is, more than any of the other three outlying boroughs, a self-contained city with its own parks, museums, historic sites, and independent state of mind. It was settled in the mid-seventeenth century, when the Dutch chartered six villages on land purchased from the Indians. One of these they called Breukelen, meaning "Broken Land," after a village in Holland. Among the early settlers was an indentured servant named Pieter Claesen, who, after becoming a free man in 1643, lived in the **Pieter Claesen Wyckoff House** (718-629-5400) at Clarendon Road and Ralph Avenue in the Flatlands section. Built around 1652 (with some sections possibly earlier), it is the city's oldest house.

In 1642, Cornelis Dircksen began a rowboat service across the East River to a low-lying landing just north of Brooklyn Heights that came to be known as "Old Ferry." This is the same landing from which Washington, on the night of August 29, 1776, craftily evacuated his men to Manhattan after the disastrous Battle of Long Island. Seven days earlier General Howe, debarking with 20,000 men from Staten Island, had landed at Gravesend. He quickly captured the American outposts and struck at Washington's main position on Brooklyn Heights. But instead of pressing his advantage—and probably capturing the entire force of 10,000 men—Howe settled in for a siege. This gave Washington time to evacuate

his troops in boats manned by former fishermen from Massachusetts. The area, designated the Fulton Ferry Historic District, was
renamed after Robert Fulton, who established steamboat ferry
service in 1814.

## BROOKLYN BRIDGE

From the promenade that crosses the 1,595-foot Brooklyn Bridge
pedestrians see some of the most spectacular views in the city—of
Lower Manhattan, Brooklyn Heights, the East River, and New
York Harbor. When it opened to great fanfare on May 24, 1883, it
was the longest suspension bridge ever built and one of the engineering wonders of the world. At the time, only the spire on Trinity
Church (280 feet) was higher than the bridge's 276-foot towers. Its
design was the inspiration of John A. Roebling, who had invented
the wire rope cables that made the bridge possible, but he died
before construction started. His son, Washington Roebling, took
over as chief engineer and completed the project, even though he
was crippled by caisson disease, or "the bends," in the course of the
job. A week after the bridge's opening throngs of pedestrians,
panicked by the delusion that the bridge was collapsing, rushed to
get off the span, killing twelve persons and injuring scores more in
the stampede. The next year, P. T. Barnum paraded twelve ele-
phants over the bridge to prove its solidity. The bridge opened up
sections of Brooklyn to development, most notably the gracious
residential district known as Park Slope, west of Prospect Park.

The bridge, with its granite arched towers and gracefully curv-
ing cables, gives contrasting impressions of immense strength and
infinite delicacy. A source of inspiration to poets and artists—"How
could mere toil align thy choiring strings!" Hart Crane wrote in
1930—to some it is still the most beautiful bridge in the world.

In 1898, Brooklyn joined the rest of the boroughs and voted to
become part of Greater New York; its ensuing growth was stimulated by immigration, commerce, the subways, and the bridges. A
well-known landmark, the **Brooklyn Navy Yard** (private), was purchased by the Navy in 1801 and built some of the nation's most
famous fighting ships, including the *Maine*, sunk in Havana Harbor in 1898. The 1966 closing of the Yard, which had employed as
many as 70,000 during World War II, was a devastating economic
blow to Brooklyn, although probably not as damaging to its reputation as when its famed baseball team, the Brooklyn Dodgers, de-

*Terra cotta detail from the entrance of the Brooklyn Historical Society.*

parted for Los Angeles in l957. Today Brooklyn Heights and Park Slope are rich in history. The **Cobble Hill Historic District,** an extension of Brooklyn Heights, contains the city's best ironwork, including a row of six outstanding Greek Revival houses at 228–238 Warren Street.

## BROOKLYN HEIGHTS

Since it was built in 1951, the **Esplanade,** a promenade along Brooklyn's heights on land once occupied by the Canarsie Indians, has offered pedestrians open space, salt-air breezes, and spectacular views of New York Harbor, Lower Manhattan, and the East River. This was the water Robert Fulton's ferry crossed in 1814, encouraging landowners to break up their land into building lots, thereby opening up Brooklyn Heights as New York's first suburb. By 1847, when Henry Ward Beecher began preaching against slavery at the **Plymouth Church of the Pilgrims** (75 Hicks Street)—once driving home his point by auctioning off a slave girl during a service—Brooklyn Heights had become an area of elegance and upper-middle-class respectability. It has also been home

*William Bennett's 1836 "New York from Brooklyn Heights" shows heavy traffic on the East River and church steeples towering above buildings in Manhattan (detail).*

to a number of literary figures such as Walt Whitman, and, in more recent times, writers Arthur Miller and Norman Mailer. It underwent extensive restoration starting in the 1950s, and in 1965 was declared Brooklyn's first historic district.

The collection of the **Brooklyn Historical Society** (128 Pierrepont Street, 718–624–0890) is housed in an eclectic 1878 building, designed by George B. Post in a synthesis of architectural styles — Neo-Grec, Queen Anne, and Renaissance among them. It was the city's first building to make extensive use of terra cotta in its exterior design. Inside is the recently (1988) opened **Museum of Brooklyn History/Shellens Gallery,** which interprets the borough's past according to five themes: Brooklyn's Bridge, Dodgers, Navy Yard, Coney Island, and People. Upstairs, the second-floor library contains a portion of the Society's thousands of photographs, paintings, manuscripts, books, newspapers, and periodicals, among carved wooden stacks.

*The Esplanade today, Brooklyn Heights. One of the city's best views from Manhattan's original suburb.*

Many streets in the district are named after prominent families, and five have horticultural names—Pineapple, Orange, Cranberry, Poplar, and Willow. Legend has it that these were named by a Miss Middagh, who, in a fit of pique, tore down street names honoring families she didn't like. True or not, her own surname survives, and **24 Middagh Street** is an 1824 clapboard house in a fine state of preservation.

## PROSPECT PARK

Landscape architects Calvert Vaux and Frederick Law Olmsted considered the design of Prospect Park their best work, better even than Central Park in Manhattan, their first commission. After the Civil War halted construction on an earlier plan, they took over in 1866 and worked on it until 1873. Their oval **Grand Army Plaza,** where Prospect Park West and Flatbush Avenue intersect, features

*A bronze* Victory, *created by Frederick W. MacMonnies, rides in a chariot atop the triumphal arch in Brooklyn's Grand Army Plaza.*

an eighty-foot **triumphal arch** honoring Union soldiers in the Civil War, topped by a bronze statue of *Victory* sculpted in 1898 by Frederick W. MacMonnies. The Plaza entrance leads directly to one of the Park's most spectacular features, the seventy-five-acre **Long Meadow** of open space and grass. **Concert Grove** in the southeast section has an arrangement of statues of classical composers and a statue of *Abraham Lincoln* by Henry Kirke Brown.

A marker indicates an opening in the hilly terrain known as **Battle Pass,** where General John Sullivan's troops fled at the approach of a numerically superior force of Hessians during the Battle of Brooklyn Heights on August 27, 1776. Sullivan was captured and later returned in an exchange of prisoners. The **Maryland Monument** at the foot of Lookout Hill commemorates a more valiant performance that day by the indomitable Maryland Regiment, commanded by Colonel William Smallwood. Their steadfastness under British assaults caused Washington to exclaim, "Good God, what my dear boys must suffer today!" The regiment's heroic stand saved the American army. The 250 Marylanders who fell that day are buried in a mass grave (unmarked) at Third Avenue between 7th and 8th streets, under an auto repair shop.

Daniel Chester French sculpted the ten-foot bronze *Lafayette Memorial,* with General Lafayette in high relief wearing an American uniform, near the 9th Street entrance to the park. Interesting buildings in the park include the **Lefferts Homestead** (718–965–8988), a Dutch farmhouse rebuilt in 1783 after the Americans burned it during the Revolution. The **Litchfield Villa,** which is used by the Parks Department, was built in 1857 by architect Alexander Jackson Davis, who with partner Ithiel Town did the Federal Hall National Memorial in Manhattan. The turreted Italian Renaissance mansion was built for Edwin C. Litchfield, a railroad financier and builder.

# PARK SLOPE

The **Park Slope Historic District** encompasses a large part of the area from the western edge of Prospect Park to Sixth Avenue. The district has over 1,900 buildings, with excellent examples of the

*Rowhouses of Park Slope, some of the city's best examples of this architecture.*

many styles that appeared between the Civil War and World War I—late Italianate, French Second Empire, Neo-Grec, Victorian Gothic, and Queen Anne, among others. Building in the area accelerated after the Brooklyn Bridge opened in 1883, particularly along Prospect Park West, known as the "Gold Coast" because of its many fine buildings. **The Montauk Club,** an unusual building at 25 Eighth Avenue, was the gathering place of Brooklyn's elite from the time it was built in 1891 to World War II. Its facade was inspired by a Venetian palazzo but also incorporates the history of Long Island's Montauk Indians in its terra-cotta frieze.

Two noteworthy side streets off Prospect Park West are **Montgomery Place,** which has many architecturally interesting houses designed by Charles P. H. Gilbert, and **Carroll Street** to Eighth Avenue, which contains houses by such prominent nineteenth-century architects as Gilbert (numbers 838–846), William B. Tubby (numbers 864–872), and Napoleon Le Brun & Sons (number 863).

*The exterior of The Montauk Club, 1891, is a mixture of Venetian architectural elements and American Indian motifs.*

*A ca. 1400 b.c. portrait of "Lady Thepu" from Thebes, left, and a Kongo power figure from Zaire, right, both from the collection of the Brooklyn Museum.*

# INSTITUTE PARK

Located on the triangle created by Flatbush Avenue, Eastern Parkway, and Washington Avenue, the Park contains Brooklyn's three premier cultural institutions—the Brooklyn Museum, the Central Library, and the Botanic Garden.

The **Brooklyn Museum** (718–638–5000) was founded in 1823 as a library "to shield young men from evil associations" and became the Brooklyn Institute of Arts and Sciences twenty years later. The museum today is housed in a monumental Neo-classical building (1897) by McKim, Mead & White. World famous for its Egyptian collection, it also contains one of the country's foremost collections of Americana, including Indian art in the Hall of the Americas and American paintings from early colonial times to the present. Notable among the period rooms, recently reinterpreted and redone, are the entire interior of the two-room Jan Martense Schenck House (ca. 1675) from the Flatlands section of Brooklyn and the Moorish Room from John D. Rockefeller's townhouse on West 54th Street in Manhattan.

The main entrance to the museum on the Eastern Parkway side is flanked by statues of *Manhattan* and *Brooklyn* (1916) by Daniel Chester French. They were moved here from the Manhattan Bridge when the bridge's ramps were widened in 1963.

The **Brooklyn Botanic Garden** (718–622–4433), founded in 1910 as part of the Brooklyn Institute of Arts and Sciences, is fifty acres of more than 13,000 species grouped in thirteen specialized gardens. The Cherry Walk and Cherry Esplanade are spectacular in early May when the Kwanzan cherry trees are blooming. The Cranford Rose Garden has more than nine hundred varieties of roses, and the Local Flora Section features plants and trees found within a one-hundred-mile radius. The Fragrance Garden for the Blind has raised beds for easy touching and signs in Braille. The 1941 **Central Branch of the Brooklyn Public Library,** a well-designed Beaux-Arts building, also houses a photography collection of more than 25,000 images of Brooklyn as far back as 1870.

## GREEN-WOOD CEMETERY

This 478-acre cemetery, which opened in 1840 and includes Brooklyn's highest point (216.5 feet), has over twenty miles of winding paths as well as ponds and hills in its elaborate landscaping. In its size and grandeur, it represents a departure from the way Americans had been buried—mostly in small church burying grounds or family plots. Green-Wood and the other large cemeteries that would follow became popular places for strolling and other sedate outings during the Victorian era. The **Main Gate** was executed in the Gothic Revival style in 1861 by Richard Upjohn, architect of Trinity Church. Made of brownstone, the gate and adjoining gatehouse and chapel are intricate assemblages of spires, turrets, finials, crockets, and portals topped by traciered gables. Buried here are such eminent New Yorkers and Brooklynites as Henry Ward Beecher, Peter Cooper, Horace Greeley, James Gordon Bennett, Samuel F. B. Morse, Boss Tweed, and Lola Montez.

LOCATION: Fifth Avenue at 25th Street (Main Gate). HOURS: 8–4 Daily.

## CONEY ISLAND

The words "Coney Island" have such gaudy connotations that their derivation from the Dutch *Konijn Eiland,* meaning Rabbit Island, is seldom recalled. The Island, long since connected with Brooklyn itself, today harbors forlorn vestiges of a once-fabulous entertainment complex that thrived from the time George C. Tillyou opened Steeplechase Park in 1897 until World War II. The two-and-a-half-mile **Boardwalk,** which opened in 1921 shortly after the subway arrived, still remains. The awesome **Cyclone,** once the ultimate in roller-coaster rides, still operates, although the Parachute Jump, moved to Coney Island from the 1939 World's Fair, is an abandoned tower. The **New York Aquarium** (Surf Avenue and West 8th Street, 718–265–3400) was founded in 1896 in Manhattan's Battery Park and moved here in 1957.

## FORT HAMILTON

Since the early European settlement of New York, the land on which Fort Hamilton is located has served as a military installation. Around 1660 the Dutch maintained a blockhouse here, but surrendered it in 1664 when the English seized the colony. On July 4, 1776 a group of Patriots fired on HMS *Asia* from this point in an effort to damage the invading British fleet. In August of that year, British troops landed nearby at the start of the Battle of Long Island. During the War of 1812 Fort Lewis, an earth and timber fort on the site, joined its companion forts on Staten Island to prevent British blockaders from attacking the Navy Yard and New York City. The cornerstone of Fort Hamilton, the first granite fort in the harbor, was laid in 1825. It has since housed, trained, and processed troops and officers including Robert E. Lee, Thomas "Stonewall" Jackson, and Abner Doubleday. World War I saw Fort Hamilton used as a training and embarkation center. The Narrows were then guarded against submarines by a steel cable net stretched between the fort and Staten Island. During World War II, the fort again trained troops and sent them overseas.

The **Harbor Defense Museum,** housed in part of the original nineteenth-century fort structure, recounts the variety of methods used in defending the harbor and provides maps for a walking tour of Fort Hamilton. **Battery Weed** and **Fort Tompkins,** two nineteenth-century companion battlements, are visible across the Narrows on Staten Island.

LOCATION: 101 Street, at the foot of the Verrazano-Narrows Bridge. HOURS: 1–4 Monday–Friday. FEE: None. TELEPHONE: 718–630–4349.

# Q   U   E   E   N   S

Queens, like the city's other outlying boroughs, was settled by the Dutch in the 1640s. In 1683 the British controlled the city and organized the scattered villages into Queens County, named in honor of Catherine of Braganza, queen of Charles II. But unlike its neighbors, it was slow to grow. When it became part of Greater New York in 1898, Queens was still a fairly rural area with a population that scarcely exceeded 150,000.

From 1919, Queens was briefly a movie capital, producing films starring Gloria Swanson, the Marx Brothers, and Rudolf Valentino. Until taken over by Paramount Pictures, Astoria Studio (34th–38th streets on 35th Avenue) was run by the Famous Players Corp. In World War II the studios made training films. At that site, the **American Museum of the Moving Image** (718–784–0077) presents the art, history, and technology of film and digital media.

Because it is the city's largest and flattest borough with more than 118 square miles, Queens has attracted airports—both La Guardia and JFK International are within its boundaries—and

*The* Unisphere, *symbol of the 1964–1965 World's Fair.*

world's fairs; both the World's Fairs of 1939–40 and 1964–65 were in **Flushing Meadows-Corona Park,** and remnants of each remain, such as the U.S. Steel Corporation's global *Unisphere,* 120 feet in diameter. **The Queens Museum** (718–592–9700), which has items of local history and a 19,000-square-foot panoramic model of the city, is in the Fair's New York City Building, and the **Hall of Science** is on the fairgrounds as well.

The borough is also a popular burying ground with a stretch of cemeteries, known humorously as "the terminal moraine," that runs east from Brooklyn along the Interborough Parkway.

Queens remains an area of distinct communities, as it was after the Dutch and the English settled it in the seventeenth century. Flushing, for example, is derived from the Dutch town of Vlissingen. John Bowne, who built the **Bowne House** (37-01 Bowne Street, 718–359–0528), in 1661 was a Quaker convert deported by Peter Stuyvesant for opening his house to services. His eventual acquittal by the Dutch West India Company was an important victory in the struggle for religious freedom in the colonies. The house, which is furnished with Bowne family furniture, was owned by nine generations of Bownes until opened to the public in 1947.

Nearby is the **Kingsland House** (143–35 37th Avenue, west of Parsons Boulevard, 718–939–0647), moved to that location to save it from demolition. The house was built about 1785 by Charles Doughty, supposedly the first Quaker in the area to free a slave, and named after his son-in-law, Joseph King. King's daughter Mary married Lindley Murray of the family that gave its name to Murray Hill in Manhattan. Kingsland House is now the headquarters of the Queens Historical Society.

John Bowne and other prominent Quakers are buried in the graveyard of Flushing's **Friends' Meeting House** (137-16 Northern Boulevard), one of the oldest houses of worship in the country. The gray-shingled building with the steep hipped roof has been in continuous use—except for a period during the Revolution when occupied by the British Army—since it was built in 1694.

Jamaica, home to JFK International Airport, Aqueduct Race Track, and King Manor, was originally a Dutch settlement called Rustdorp. The **King Manor** (153rd Street and Jamaica Avenue, 718-206-0545) was built about 1730 and from 1805 to 1827 was the home of Rufus King, a member of the Continental Congress, an important representative (then from Massachusetts) at the Constitutional Convention, and, after the Revolution, an able ambassador to England. Guided neighborhood walking tours are available.

# L O N G         I S L A N D

The native population of Long Island was small, and in early colonial days, the land was claimed by both the Dutch, who moved in from Manhattan, and the English, who came from New England and settled on the eastern end beginning in 1640. English and Dutch claims to their respective ends of the island were recognized by a 1650 treaty that drew a line from Oyster Bay south to the ocean.

The Revolution divided Long Island; the eastern end supported the American cause, while the western end, like the rest of the area around New York City, tended to side with the Crown. Once General Howe had chased General Washington off the island in the battle of Long Island in the early days of the Revolution, Long Island remained in British hands for the duration, though one rebel raid led by Lieutenant Colonel Return J. Meigs destroyed a British supply depot at Sag Harbor and returned to Connecticut with ninety British prisoners.

After the War of 1812, whaling, begun much earlier by the Indians and Dutch, became an important industry, bringing prosperity to towns like Sag Harbor and Greenport. With the important New York market so close, agriculture prospered, particularly potatoes, cauliflower, and poultry, including the famed Long Island duckling, oysters and clams.

The Long Island Rail Road, chartered in 1834, was originally part of the rail route to Boston, with passengers crossing Long Island Sound by boat from Greenport. In 1910 rail service via a tunnel to Pennsylvania Station in Manhattan began a real-estate boom on Long Island that still persists. Millionaires settling on the island in the late 1800s and early 1900s turned the north shore into the "Gold Coast," a concentration of great estates in towns like Old Westbury, Locust Valley, and Oyster Bay, some of which still remain in private hands. In 1927—about the same time that F. Scott Fitzgerald was writing *The Great Gatsby*, immortalizing the lifestyle of the Island's Gold Coast—Charles A. Lindbergh took off from Roosevelt field in Garden City to begin the first nonstop flight between New York and Paris in history. After World War II, veterans settled in low-cost housing developments on the western end of the island, turning it into an unbroken expanse of densely populated suburbs. Long Island is divided into four counties: Kings (the borough of Brooklyn), Queens, Nassau, and Suffolk.

The first two became part of Greater New York City in 1898, leaving the latter two independent. They remain an incongruous mixture of farms and estates, rimmed by beautiful beaches.

Eastern Long Island ends in two pincerlike spits of land, the North Fork and the South Fork. The North Fork, flat and fertile with seemingly endless expanses of fields and occasional vineyards, is still predominantly agricultural. In fact, Suffolk County, comprising roughly the eastern half of the island, is the state's most productive farm region. In Great Peconic Bay, the body of water between the forks, there is Shelter Island, a summer retreat. The South Fork begins with the famous resort town of Southampton and ends at the busy fishing village of Montauk.

One hundred and twenty miles long and twenty-three miles wide at its widest point, Long Island has a remarkable concentration of historic sites, mostly along its coastline. This itinerary proceeds from Port Washington eastward to Montauk. On its western end, Long Island is easily reached by several bridges from New York City and the mainland. At mid-island there is a ferry from Bridgeport, Connecticut, to Port Jefferson. The eastern end is accessible by ferry from New London, Connecticut, landing at Orient Point on the tip of the North Fork.

## GARDEN CITY

After the Civil War, the New York merchant Alexander Turney Stewart laid out the village's wide streets and parks as a model town for people of moderate income—eventually it became one of the wealthiest residential communities in the country. Garden City has an important place in the history of aviation: Glenn Hammond Curtiss, an early flyer and inventor of airplanes, did much of his pioneering work from 1909 through the 1920s here at **Roosevelt Field, Mitchel Field,** and his own **Curtiss Field.** In 1923, the first nonstop transcontinental flight to San Diego took off from Mitchel Field and, a year later, transcontinental airmail service was initiated between Garden City and San Francisco. In 1927, Charles A. Lindbergh flew to Paris from Roosevelt Field. The sister ship to Lindbergh's *Spirit of St. Louis* and other vintage aircraft and aviation artifacts are on display at the **Cradle of Aviation Museum** (Mitchel Field, 516–572–0410, closed for renovation until late 1999).

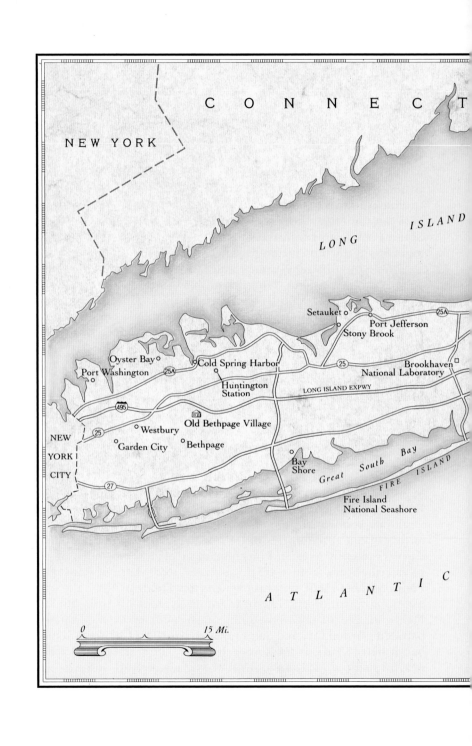

CONNECT

ISLAND

NEW YORK

LONG

Setauket ○                         25A
Port Jefferson
Stony Brook

Oyster Bay ○         ○ Cold Spring Harbor        25            Brookhaven
Port Washington      25A                                      National Laboratory
                                  Huntington        LONG ISLAND EXPWY
                                  Station

                         Old Bethpage Village
                         495

NEW           ○ Westbury
YORK          ○ Garden City      ○ Bethpage
CITY          25                              ○ Bay      Great  South  Bay
                                               Shore                    FIRE  ISLAND
              27                                         Fire Island
                                                         National Seashore

                                                                      ATLANTIC

0                    15 Mi.

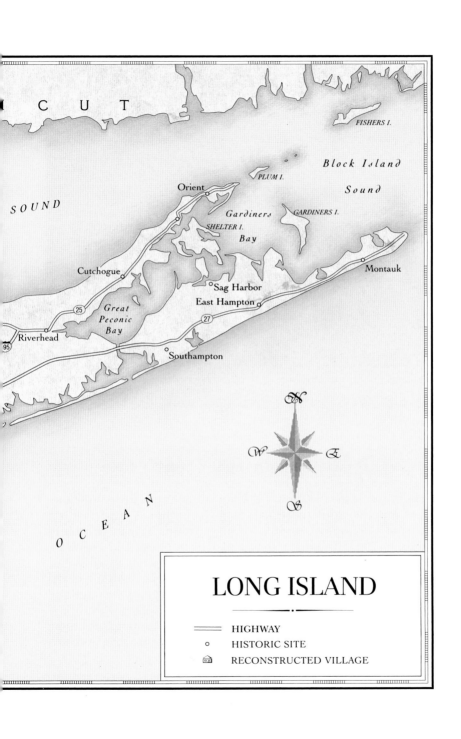

C U T

SOUND

FISHERS I.

Block Island

PLUM I.

Orient

Gardiners

Sound

GARDINERS I.

SHELTER I.

Bay

Cutchogue

Montauk

Sag Harbor

25

East Hampton

Great
Peconic
Bay

27

Riverhead

95

Southampton

N

W    E

S

O C E A N

## LONG ISLAND

⸺ ⸺ •|• ⸺ ⸺

═════  HIGHWAY

○  HISTORIC SITE

⌂  RECONSTRUCTED VILLAGE

OPPOSITE: *Westbury House, the red brick Phipps estate, is one of Long Island's grandest. Old Westbury Gardens (above) has one hundred acres of plantings.*

## OLD WESTBURY GARDENS

Here in the heart of country dominated by the estates of million-aires, financier and sportsman John S. Phipps, son of Andrew Carnegie's longtime partner, Henry Phipps, began **Westbury House** in 1903. Today the spectacular plantings of **Old Westbury Gardens** are the estate's main attractions, including a walled garden containing the longest expanse of herbaceous borders in the country, a formal Rose Garden, a thatched children's cottage and garden, lakes, and tree-lined vistas. Both the house, with its fine eighteenth-century furniture and over seventy paintings, including works by Raeburn, Reynolds, Gainsborough, Constable, and Sargent, and the gardens are open to the public.

LOCATION: 71 Old Westbury Road, Old Westbury. HOURS: April through mid-December: 10–5 Wednesday–Monday. FEE: Yes. TELE-PHONE: 516–333–0048.

# OLD BETHPAGE VILLAGE RESTORATION

This site recreates an early nineteenth-century farming village of the type, now vanished, that dotted the island in the period before the Civil War. The mid-eighteenth-century **Powell Farmhouse** is original to the location, but the complex's other forty-nine buildings were moved here. The village includes a blacksmith shop, country store, tavern, church, and a working farm.

> LOCATION: Round Swamp Road, Old Bethpage. HOURS: March through October: 10–5 Wednesday–Sunday; November through December: 10–4 Wednesday–Sunday. FEE: Yes. TELEPHONE: 516–572–8400.

*Old Bethpage Village, a 19th-century restoration, is also a working historic farm. Most of the buildings were moved here from other parts of Long Island.*

# SANDS POINT PRESERVE

The estate of industrialists Daniel and Harry Guggenheim is now preserved as a 216-acre reservation that includes **Falaise,** where Captain Harry Guggenheim, an early backer of aviation, entertained Charles Lindbergh and other important fliers. Also known for his many philanthropies, Daniel Guggenheim expanded the worldwide activities of the American Smelting and Refining Company. In addition, he founded the Daniel Guggenheim Fund for the Promotion of Aeronautics, which encouraged the development of air passenger service. The estate was originally owned by the railroad heir Howard Gould, who built in 1902 **Castlegould** (an equestrian-parade stable and carriage/automobile house) and, in 1912, the Tudor-style **Hempstead House,** the main residence.

> LOCATION: Middleneck Road, Port Washington. HOURS: Mid-March through Labor Day: 10–5 Tuesday–Sunday; otherwise, times vary. FEE: Yes. TELEPHONE: 516–571–7900.

# OYSTER BAY

Legend has it that because the English and Dutch, who settled Oyster Bay in the mid-seventeenth century, rarely agreed on anything, they established the town's two main streets a block apart. During the American Revolution, **Raynham Hall** (20 West Main Street, 516–922–6808), home of the Townsend family, was headquarters for the Queen's Rangers and the scene of intrigue when Robert Townsend, a spy for General George Washington, spread information about the British attempt to take command of West Point. Almost a century later Solomon Townsend II, a wealthy merchant, added a Victorian Gothic Revival wing to the house. Five colonial and five Victorian period rooms are restored and open.

    **Planting Fields Arboretum** (Planting Fields Road, 516–922–9201), estate of the British financier William Robertson Coe, includes large collections of rhododendrons and azaleas and two greenhouses. **Coe Hall,** the large Tudor Revival mansion he built in 1920, is on the estate, restored and open to the public.

## Sagamore Hill National Historic Site

Not long after he graduated from Harvard, from 1884 to 1885 Theodore Roosevelt helped design the three-story, twenty-three-room Sagamore Hill. It was his main residence for the rest of his

*Sagamore Hill in the snow. Theodore Roosevelt's 23-room home was built in 1884 and added to in 1905.*

life and served as the summer White House during his terms as president. "At Sagamore Hill," he wrote, "we love a great many things—birds and trees, and books . . . and horses and rifles, and children and hard work and the joy of life." In 1905 Roosevelt met here with envoys of Russia and Japan to forge an agreement that would end the Russo-Japanese War, an effort for which he became the first American to be awarded the Nobel Peace Prize.

The first two floors—including Roosevelt's study and the north room, which he added in 1905 to hold his many hunting trophies—are furnished largely with original artifacts. In 1938 Roosevelt's son, General Theodore Roosevelt, Jr., built what is now the **Old Orchard Home,** with exhibits about Roosevelt's career and the lives of his six children, and a documentary film.

LOCATION: 20 Sagamore Hill Road. HOURS: 9:30–5 Daily. FEE: Yes. TELEPHONE: 516–922–4788.

# COLD SPRING HARBOR

So many sailors speaking foreign tongues came to this important whaling town in the mid-nineteenth century that its main street was popularly called "Bedlam Street." The **Whaling Museum** (Main Street, 516–367–3418) has a whaleboat, ship models, and a large scrimshaw collection.

# HUNTINGTON STATION

The poet Walt Whitman was born here on May 31, 1819, in a two-story shingle house built about a decade earlier from hand-hewn beams and wooden pegs. Now administered by the state as the **Walt Whitman Birthplace State Historic Site** (246 Old Walt Whitman Road, 516–427–5240), the house has been restored as it was when he was a boy. Upstairs is a museum with exhibits on his life and work. Whitman left school when he was thirteen and spent the next fifteen years doing odd jobs and writing. In 1838 and 1839 he edited and published the *Long Islander* in Huntington Village. In 1889 the Long Islander Building (still standing) was constructed and remained the newspaper's offices for a century before the paper moved across the street. His family had farmed in the area for generations; in *Specimen Days* (1882), he describes the family homestead in Huntington, which no longer stands.

The Huntington Historical Society (516–427–7045) owns and operates two house museums. The **David Conklin Farmhouse** (2 High Street) is furnished to reflect the various stages of its con-struction—pre-Revolutionary, federal, and Victorian—and in-cludes furniture used by George Washington on his 1790 tour, Huntington-made silver, samplers, and quilts. The **Kissam House** (434 Park Avenue), built in 1795 as a gentleman's townhouse, is unique in Huntington. The Society has its offices in the 1905 **Trade School** (209 Main Street), with a research library and exhibit gallery.

# BAY SHORE

Founded in 1708 but not developed to any extent until after 1840, Bay Shore is located on Great South Bay at its widest point. **Sagti-kos Manor** (Route 27-A, 516–665–0093) was British General Hen-ry Clinton's headquarters during the Revolution. President George Washington spent the night here on April 23, 1790. The frame house was built by Stephanus Van Cortlandt, a mayor of New York City, in the 1690s.

# FIRE ISLAND NATIONAL SEASHORE

Almost the entire length of Long Island's south shore—from Coney Island within the precincts of New York City to Southampton Beach on the east—is protected from the ocean by a stretch of narrow barrier beaches. The longest of these, Fire Island, is thirty-two miles long and accessible by bridge and ferry. The island has the only designated federal wilderness area in New York State. There are a number of private communities on Fire Island, beautiful public beaches, and nature trails. Across Great South Bay from Smith Point County Park is the **William Floyd Estate** (Floyd Parkway to Neighborhood Road, 516–399–2030), centering upon a white frame Georgian building built about 1729. General William Floyd (1734-1821), a signer of the Declaration of Independence and a member of the Continental Congress, was born in the house, which remained in the family for 250 years.

# STONY BROOK

Originally settled in the seventeenth century by colonists from Boston, this port town became a shipbuilding center in the 1800s.

## *The Museums at Stony Brook*

Founded in 1939 to preserve and exhibit collections of American history and art with special focus on nineteenth-century Long Island, this multi-building complex is the largest privately-supported history museum on Long Island. It is particularly noted for its carriage collection, housed in twelve galleries. The centerpiece of the **Carriage Museum** is its largest vehicle, the twenty-three-foot-long omnibus, Grace Darling, which has landscapes, still lifes, people, and animals painted on its panels. One permanent exhibit in the building explains how the Carriage Museum grew from the collection of the industrialist and philanthropist Ward Melville.

The nine-acre museum complex includes the 1725 Hawkins Mount House (private), home of William Sidney Mount, born in nearby Setauket in 1807, who portrayed Long Island life in his genre paintings. Stony Brook's **Art Museum** has three-quarters of Mount's work. The **History Museum,** housed in a restored lumber

OPPOSITE: *Lighthouse on Fire Island National Seashore along Long Island's south side—a true island of solitude near New York City.*

*One of more than three hundred carriages and other horse-drawn vehicles in the collection of the Carriage Museum at Stony Brook.*

mill, has collections of textiles, costumes, and antique decoys, most of them locally made. There is also a late-eighteenth-century barn, a blacksmith shop, and a one-room schoolhouse.

> LOCATION: Route 25-A and Main Street. HOURS: January through June and September through November: 10–5 Wednesday–Saturday, 12–5 Sunday; July, August, December: 10–5 Monday–Saturday, 12–5 Sunday. FEE: Yes. TELEPHONE: 516–751–0066.

## SETAUKET

During the Revolution, the minister of the Anglican church here chastised British officers for allowing their men to plunder the town while the people were in church. The noted Long Island historian Benjamin Thompson was born in Setauket. The ca. 1700 **Thompson House** (North Country Road, 516–941–9444) was the family home until 1887 and now displays fine antique furniture and an herb garden. The ca. 1730 **Sherwood-Jayne House** (Old Post Road, 516–941–9444) belonged to Howard Sherwood, who founded the Society for the Preservation of Long Island Antiquities.

# CUTCHOGUE

The **Old House** on the village green, built in 1649, is one of the most important examples of English colonial architecture in the country. Inside the two-and-a-half-story house exposed sections reveal construction techniques; it is furnished with seventeenth- and eighteenth-century antiques. Also on the green are the 1840 **Old Schoolhouse** and the 1700 **Wickham Farmhouse,** both restored and open to the public.

# ORIENT

More than one hundred buildings in the **Orient Historic District** reflect the agricultural and seafaring tradition of this settlement on Gardiners Bay. The town was once a center for agricultural products bound by sea for Connecticut, and by land for New York City. The town's **Museums of the Oysterponds Historical Society** (Village Lane, 516–323–2480) operates seven historic buildings open to the public, including exhibits, period room settings, an 1870s barn, and the ca. 1780 **Webb House.** A ferry to New London, Connecticut, departs from nearby **Orient Point,** which is also the entrance to **Orient Beach State Park,** where the North Fork of Long Island peters out in a stretch of beach and glacial moraine.

# SOUTHAMPTON

Southampton is one of the oldest towns on Long Island; English settlers from Lynn, Massachusetts came here in 1640. Built in 1648, the restored saltbox **Halsey Homestead** (South Main Street, 516–283–3527) may be the oldest frame house in the state. Southampton's rural atmosphere and unspoiled beaches began to attract vacationing New Yorkers in the mid-nineteenth century, and the summer influx increased greatly when the railroad arrived in 1870. Although it has kept some historic buildings, Southampton has become better known as a chic resort. It is especially attractive to affluent young professionals, best-selling literati, and jet-setters. Writers abound from Montauk to Fire Island.

The **Southampton Historical Museum and Colonial Society** (17 Meeting House Lane, 516–283–2494) is a complex of twelve buildings, including the 1843 Captain Rogers Homestead, a carpenter's shop, drugstore, and country store. The **Parrish Art Museum** (516–283–2118), founded in 1898, has a collection of nine-teenth- and twentieth-century American art, including works by

*Detail of a Shinnecock landscape, painted by William Merrit Chase about 1892.* OPPOSITE:
*The Greek Revival Whaling and Historical Museum, once a Masonic Temple, Sag Harbor.*

William Merritt Chase and Fairfield Porter. It is located at 25 Job's
Lane, Job Sayre being the original settler. The **Water Mill Museum**
(516–726–4625), just east of Southampton, has a working 1644
gristmill. The **Shinnecock Reservation,** inhabited by descendants
of Indians who lived in the Southampton area, is adjacent to town
off Route 27-A. It is open to the public only during the annual
Shinnecock Powwow in early September.

## SAG HARBOR

Settled in 1707, the town became Long Island's principal whaling
port and, in the 1800s, one of the busiest in the world. During the
Revolution, the British used Sag Harbor as a supply depot. On May
23, 1777, Lieutenant Colonel Return J. Meigs led 234 Americans in
a flotilla of thirteen whaleboats across Long Island Sound from
Guilford, Connecticut, took the depot by surprise, destroyed it,
and returned with ninety British prisoners.

In 1789 Congress created two ports of entry for the United
States; the first was Sag Harbor, the other New York City. The
**Custom House** (Main and Garden Streets, 516–941–9444) dates

from that year. It is now a museum furnished with family pieces belonging to Henry Packer Dering, the first customs master. James Fenimore Cooper visited Sag Harbor several times between 1819 and 1823 and supposedly worked on his first novel, *Precaution* (1820), here. The whaling industry declined in the second half of the nineteenth century, as petroleum replaced whale oil as fuel, and the last whaling ship, the *Myra,* sailed out of Sag Harbor in 1871 under Captain Henry Babcock, never to return to port.

Despite its transformation into a summer resort, Sag Harbor has held on to some of its seafaring heritage. For years the steeple, shaped like a spyglass, on the **Whalers Presbyterian Church** (Union Street) was a landmark for ships; the steeple blew down in the hurricane of 1938. Minard Lafever, who was also noted for his work in the Gothic Revival style, designed the Egyptian-Greek church, and, it is believed, the Greek Revival–style **Benjamin Huntting House** on Main Street, now the **Sag Harbor Whaling and Historical Museum** (516–725–0770), which has a full-size whale-boat in its collection.

# EAST HAMPTON

Until New Yorkers discovered its charms in the late nineteenth century, East Hampton was a farming community, with numerous windmills. The nineteenth-century dramatist, actor, and poet John Howard Payne, who wrote the sentimental "Home Sweet Home," was born in 1791 in the late-seventeenth-century house at 14 James Lane. Now called the **Home Sweet Home Museum** (516–324–0713), it contains period antiques, the Gustav Buek Collection of American furniture and English ceramics, and, on the grounds, a nineteenth-century windmill. The East Hampton Historical Society (516–324–6850) operates four historic buildings on Main Street: The 1680 **Mulford House** is a museum of eighteenth-century architecture, interior design, and building techniques; **Clinton Academy,** built in 1784 as the state's first preparatory school, is now a museum with artifacts from the early days of the town and school; the ca. 1725 **Osborn-Jackson House** hosts changing exhibits and public programs; and the ca. 1731 **Town House** contains early school furnishings. On North Main Street, the **Hook Mill** is an 1806 windmill offering guided tours.

Lion Gardiner, the first proprietor of Gardiners Island in Gardiners Bay, was buried in East Hampton in 1663. The island,

*The village of East Hampton, on Long Island's southern shore.*

which became part of East Hampton in 1683, remains privately owned by the Gardiner family to this day. In 1699 Lion's grandson, John Gardiner, entertained the pirate Captain Kidd, who was then in partnership with the governor of New York and the Livingston family. He supposedly left treasure hidden on the island—a claim made by scores of other islands from Maine to Florida.

Buried in East Hampton are such prominent artists as Childe Hassam (1859–1935), Thomas Moran (1837–1926), Jackson Pollock (1912–1956), and Stuart Davis (1894–1964).

## MONTAUK

Named after the Indian tribe that once lived on eastern Long Island, the town is now a busy commercial and sportfishing port at the tip of the South Fork. In 1797 President George Washington authorized the construction of the **Montauk Point Lighthouse,** on Montauk Point east of town. The octagonal stone structure is still an important landmark for oceangoing vessels.

# CHAPTER FOUR

# THE
# HUDSON
# RIVER VALLEY

OPPOSITE: *The Hudson River Valley.*

Few regions in America have a richer store of natural beauty, history, and legend than the Hudson River valley. It evokes superlatives. Henry James wrote that the Hudson—"mountain-guarded and dim"—has a place "in the geography of the ideal." Another nineteenth-century American writer proclaimed it "nature's greatest panorama."

From its source high in the Adirondack Mountains, at the romantically named Lake Tear of the Clouds, the Hudson flows 315 miles to its mouth at New York harbor. For part of its course the Hudson is an estuary—the Atlantic tides are felt up to Troy.

During the Ice Age the Hudson's course was 120 miles longer than it is today because the level of the Atlantic was lower. When melting ice raised the level of the oceans, the Atlantic began to flow up the Hudson, "drowning" it. The first settlers on the Hudson were Algonquian Indians, who migrated to this bountiful source of shad, striped bass, and oysters from homelands to the west. Their discovery of the river fulfilled a prophecy, which had foretold that the tribe would live "by water that flows two ways." The first European to discover the Hudson was Giovanni da Verrazano, in 1524, flying the flag of Francois I of France. But Verrazano ventured only a short distance beyond the mouth of the river, and correct credit for the first true exploration of the river goes to Henry Hudson. On the *Half Moon,* Hudson, in search of a northwest passage to Asia for the Dutch West India Company, sailed as far north as the site of Albany in 1609; a few of his sailors, in a longboat, reached the site of Troy.

The Dutch began settling the river in the 1620s, maintaining remarkably good relations with the Indians. Their treaties with each other called upon both sides "to keep the Great Chain of Friendship polished bright." Even though the English gained control of New York in the 1660s, the Dutch put their permanent stamp on the region's architecture, place names (Catskill, Claverack, Kinderhook), and language. Dutch was spoken in the valley well into the 1820s, and there were a few native Dutch speakers into the 1940s. Two of the most pleasant concepts expressed in American English—*Santa Claus* and *cookie*—are Dutch words, as is one of the least pleasant, *boss.*

In the Revolutionary War, control of the Hudson was the strategic focus of both sides. Had the British gained control of the river, they could have split New England from the rest of the colonies and, having divided the rebels, conquered them piecemeal. No one understood this more clearly than George Washing-

*Pavel Petrovich Svinin's painting of one of Fulton's Hudson River steamboats,* Deck Life on the Paragon. *Fort Putnam and West Point are in the background.*

ton. Maintaining the Hudson as an American river was the core of his planning, and as a result, some of the Revolution's most desperate and dramatic battles took place on or near the river. Saratoga and Stony Point are places that will always figure prominently in the annals of American arms. And one of the most tragic episodes of the Revolution was also enacted on the Hudson—the treason of Benedict Arnold, who sought to deliver West Point, "the key to America," to the British.

The Hudson played a large role in the history of American commerce. In the early 1800s Robert Livingston had cannily obtained a monopoly on steam-powered transport on the Hudson—a coup he was able to carry off because no one thought steam power was feasible. He contracted with Robert Fulton to build him such a boat, and Fulton obliged with the *Clermont,* which made its debut in 1807, steaming from New York to Albany in thirty-two hours. It was not the world's first steam-powered boat, as is often asserted, but it was the first to be commercially successful.

The opening of the Erie Canal in 1825 linked the Hudson with the Great Lakes and made the river America's most important avenue of commerce. With the manufactures of the nation and the world steaming to its piers, New York City became the country's

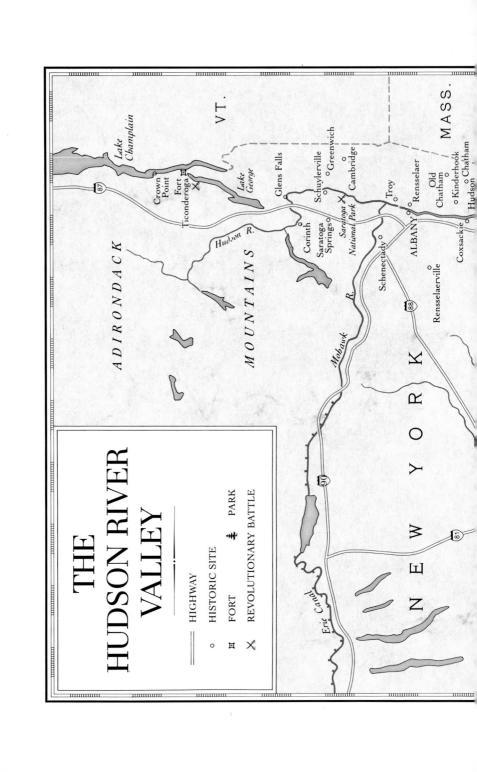

THE
HUDSON RIVER
VALLEY

═══ HIGHWAY

○ HISTORIC SITE

Ħ FORT ♣ PARK

✕ REVOLUTIONARY BATTLE

premier business center, and to the north, the great mansions of the commercial barons rose along the east bank of the Hudson.

In the same era, when commerce boomed, the art of painting flourished along the Hudson. The river inspired America's first school of painters, the Hudson River School. Thomas Cole, Asher Durand, Thomas Doughty, and others were lured by the mountainscapes and placid expanses of blue water. Their lyrical paintings set a style for capturing the grandeur of the American scene.

In literature, Washington Irving presented the Hudson as a realm of legend, where the spirits of the old Dutch sailors still governed the affairs of men. Irving wrote one of the finest descriptions of the Hudson in his tale of the man who slept for twenty years, capturing the view that Rip Van Winkle had of the river before his long nap: "He saw at a distance the lordly Hudson, far, far below him, moving on its silent but majestic course, with the reflection of a purple cloud, or the sail of a lagging bark here and there sleeping on its glassy bosom, and at last losing itself in the blue highlands." Today the Hudson Valley retains much of its eighteenth- and nineteenth-century flavor, and for long stretches the river looks much as it did when Henry Hudson explored it. The most dramatic scenery can be found in the Hudson Highlands, a fifteen-mile-long gorge that extends roughly from Stony Point to Newburgh. Many towns along the river—Cold Spring, Rhinebeck, and Hudson, for example—still have the ambience of a century or two ago.

This chapter covers sites on both banks of the river, beginning at Yonkers and proceeding north to Fort Ticonderoga.

# PHILIPSE MANOR HALL

This broad, two-and-a-half-story brick house was the country residence of the Philipse family until the Revolution, when Frederick Philipse III, a Loyalist, was put into prison for his politics. The founder of the family was Frederick Philipse I, who arrived in New York from Holland in the 1640s or 1650s and made a fortune in shipping and the slave trade. He established the mill preserved in Tarrytown (Philipsburg Manor) and acquired a large tract of land covering about one-fifth of modern Westchester County. His property was given manor status by a royal patent in 1693.

The manor house was built in the first half of the eighteenth century by Frederick Philipse II. His son, Frederick III, inherited the property in 1751 and lived a life of rural ease, supported by the rents of his tenant farmers, until the Revolution dislodged him. After spending six months in prison he took refuge in New York City, which was controlled by the British. After the Revolution he left for England and his lands were sold in lots to farmers. The house (Yonkers' city hall from 1868 to 1908) has not been restored, but some decorative woodwork and plaster dating to the 1750s may be seen, along with a small museum and art collection.

> LOCATION: Warburton Avenue and Dock Street, Yonkers. HOURS: Early April through early October: 11–2 Wednesday–Thursday, 2–5 Sunday. FEE: None. TELEPHONE: 914–965–4027.

# TARRYTOWN

Tarrytown was probably derived from a corruption of the Dutch word for wheat, *tarwe,* although one of its prominent inhabitants, Washington Irving, claimed that the area's Dutch wives named it for their husbands' habit of tarrying at the village tavern after dropping off their wheat at the ferry. Tarrytown is where the British spy Major André was caught with the plans for West Point in his boot. The Historical Society of the Tarrytowns maintains two buildings. The **Museum Headquarters** (1 Grove Street, 914–631–8374), an Italianate house built in 1848, holds eight rooms of furniture, household implements, dolls, toys, Indian artifacts, weapons from the Revolution to World War II, and exhibits about the capture of Major André. The **Education and Research Center** (19 Grove Street) contains the society's map room, with seven hundred maps and atlases of the Tarrytown area and the Hudson Valley, archaeological laboratory, and library.

## Sunnyside

Although it is not on the same order of magnificence as the estates upriver, Sunnyside is one of the most pleasant places to visit along the Hudson. It was the home of Washington Irving, America's first internationally successful author. In 1836 Irving purchased a stone cottage set in a drowsy nook only fifty yards or so from the river's edge. He rebuilt it, adding a tower inspired by a Spanish monastery and stepped gables in the Dutch style. The result, in Irving's own words, is "a little, old-fashioned stone mansion all made up of gabled ends, and as full of angles and corners as an old cocked hat." Wisteria planted by Irving in 1842 now covers the facade over the entrance. The interior is modest but quite comfortable, and some of Irving's original furnishings have been preserved. The

*A footbridge across a millpond leads to Philipsburg Manor, the restored home, farm, and mill of the Philipse family.*

most notable room is the writer's ground-floor study, where he wrote his biography of George Washington.

> LOCATION: Off Route 9 in Tarrytown. HOURS: April through December: 10–5 Wednesday–Monday. FEE: Yes. TELEPHONE: 914–631–8200.

## Lyndhurst

Perhaps the finest surviving example of Gothic Revival style in America, Lyndhurst was the summer home of the financier and railroad magnate Jay Gould from 1880 until his death. The house was built, in two stages, for earlier owners by the noted architect Alexander Jackson Davis. Gould purchased Lyndhurst and its furnishings from the second owner, George Merritt. The enormous stone house, with its tower, spires, battlements, and relentlessly Gothic interior, might appear to modern eyes as an unduly ostentatious display of wealth, but in the nineteenth century the Gothic, or "English Collegiate," style was regarded as the embodiment of the picturesque. Alexander Jackson Davis strove to create a mansion with an atmosphere of romance and rural ease, not a gaudy show-

place. He was most successful on the second floor, where he created a magnificent yet comfortable billiard room and art gallery
with a lofty ceiling and tall windows. One of Gould's daughters
occupied the mansion until 1961 and preserved its remarkable
furnishings intact. Among the interesting details of life there are
the daily menus, now displayed in the basement kitchen. The
property was acquired in 1964 by the National Trust for Historic
Preservation.

> LOCATION: Off Route 9 in Tarrytown. HOURS: May through Octo-
> ber: 10–5 Tuesday–Sunday; November through April: 10–5 Saturday–
> Sunday. FEE: Yes. TELEPHONE: 914–631–4481.

**Philipsburg Manor** (Route 9 in North Tarrytown), the restored
farming and milling center of the Philipse family, ably re-creates
the tenor of daily life in the early eighteenth century. The manor
includes the Philipse house, a working farm with livestock, and a
functioning mill. Guides explain how the huge millstones were
made and set into place, and then give a demonstration of milling,
with power provided, just as it was 250 years ago, by the Pocantico
River. At the visitor center, an excellent short film traces the
history of the family and shows the country life of the period.

**Van Cortlandt Manor** (off Route 9 in Croton-on-Hudson), was the
home of the Van Cortlandt family from the early 1700s until 1945.
Many of the family's furnishings from the eighteenth and nineteenth centuries have been preserved, and the house offers a
history of changing tastes and styles. The Ferry House on the
manor's grounds is a restored eighteenth-century inn.

Van Cortlandt Manor is one of the five Historic Hudson Valley sites, along with Sunnyside, Philipsburg Manor, Union Church,
and Montgomery Place. Single or combined tickets are available
(914–631–8200).

# OLD CROTON DAM AND
# AQUEDUCT TRAILWAY

One of the great engineering achievements of the first half of the
nineteenth century, the 33-mile-long Croton Aqueduct brought
drinking water from Westchester County into New York City. The
construction of the system was prompted by uncontrollable fires
and a cholera epidemic in the city in the 1830s. The project was
supervised by John Jervis, born in Rome, New York, who had

learned the basic skills of surveying and engineering as a young helper on the Erie Canal project. Construction began in 1837 and the first water reached the city in 1842. Along with the water the city received a now-familiar urban pest, the cockroach, which migrates along water lines. New Yorkers of the 1840s called it the Croton bug. A continuous portion of the aqueduct's right-of-way has been preserved as a trail from the Croton Dam to Van Cortlandt Park in the Bronx. The path runs over the underground waterway, but walkers can see masonry ventilator shafts. For information on the self-guided walking tour, call 914–889–4100. The most impressive sight is the Croton Dam (Croton Dam Road, off route 129 in Cortlandt), a sturdy and handsome work of granite. In Ossining, a weir chamber for waste water is occasionally open for viewing (914–941–3189).

## STONY POINT BATTLEFIELD

Just after midnight on July 16, 1779, General Anthony Wayne led 1,200 light infantry in a surprise attack against British fortifications here. Wayne captured the fort with only a few casualties, winning

*The United States Military Academy sits high on a bluff overlooking the Hudson River.*

him a gold medal from Congress and earning international acclaim for the American army. A British publication reported that the attack "would have done honor to the most veteran soldiers." The site includes a museum and a self-guided walking tour.

> LOCATION: Park Road, off Route 9-W in Stony Point. HOURS: Mid-April through October: 10–5 Wednesday–Saturday, 1–5 Sunday. FEE: None. TELEPHONE: 914–786–2521.

Built around 1804 by States Morris Dyckman, **Boscobel** (Route 9-D, 8 miles north of Bear Mountain Bridge, 914–265–3638) is one of the finest restored mansions in America. The house features superb examples of New York Federal furniture, including pieces by Duncan Phyfe, and English silver and china.

# WEST POINT

From the early days of the Revolution the Americans recognized the crucial strategic importance of the Hudson—Washington himself said that the area was "the key to America"—and the need to fortify it, at some point, in order to control it. The Highlands were

*The Battle Monument, West Point.*

the natural place to erect fortifications, as they overlooked the river from a great height, and cannon on a promontory could command the river. The plateau was so high that cannon fire could not reach it from ships below, and because the river turns sharply here, ships had to slow down, making them better targets for the point's guns.

In 1778 Washington put Colonel Thaddeus Kosciusko in charge of designing and building the fortifications, which included numerous forts and a system of redoubts to prevent flanking maneuvers. As an additional safeguard the Americans stretched an enormous chain, on floats, across the river from West Point to Constitution Island. Known as the Great Chain, this iron barrier was never tested: The British did not venture that far up the Hudson again—although they wanted to. In 1780 General Benedict Arnold offered to spy for General Clinton; Clinton wanted the plans for West Point and sent Major John André to collect them from Arnold. On his way back André was stopped at a checkpoint just north of Tarrytown, searched, and the plans were found in his boot. He was hanged (not without regret—his courage after his capture won the admiration and sympathy of American officers), but Arnold escaped capture. His treason did not pay; he spent the rest of his life in England, penniless and an object of scorn.

The United States Military Academy was established at West Point in 1802, and underwent a sweeping reorganization under Superintendent Sylvanus Thayer from 1817 to 1833. Many Civil War commanders on both sides were trained here, including Ulysses S. Grant (who hated the Academy), Robert E. Lee (who excelled), Stonewall Jackson, William Tecumseh Sherman, George Armstrong Custer, Philip Sheridan, Jefferson Davis, and Jeb Stuart. Perhaps the least happy cadet of this era was Edgar Allan Poe, who did not graduate. Dwight D. Eisenhower, Douglas MacArthur, George Patton, and Omar Bradley were among the World War II generals who graduated from the Academy.

The **West Point Museum,** which is one of the finest military museums in the country, has an enormous and fascinating collection of weapons, art, uniforms, and military memorabilia, including dioramas of important battles in world history, a mural of Omaha Beach on D-Day, and the casing of an early atomic bomb. One of the forts built by Kosciusko, **Fort Putnam,** has been restored, and offers a spectacular view of the Hudson, 450 feet below. By the **Plain,** the academy's drill field, are the few remnants of **Fort Clinton,** a mound and some stones. Also near the Plain are

a few links of the Great Chain. The fortress-like, Neo-Gothic architecture of the Academy was the work of Bertram Grosvenor Goodhue. Goodhue's **Cadet Chapel** was built in 1910. The Greek Revival
**Old Cadet Chapel** dates to 1836.

LOCATION: West Point. HOURS: 10:30–4:15 Daily. FEE: None.
TELEPHONE: 914–938–2203.

## COLD SPRING

This pleasant riverside town was supposedly named after a spring
where ships stopped to take on water. During the Civil War a
foundry here manufactured Parrott guns, and Lincoln visited for a
demonstration of their firepower. The test coincided with the
president's lunch hour, and after the inventor, Colonel Robert
Parrott, had discharged a shell across the river Lincoln said, "I'm
confident you can hit that mountain over there, so suppose we get
something to eat." The views from the river bank are excellent,
with West Point to the south and Storm King to the north. In a cave
on Crow's Nest, near Storm King, Captain Kidd is said to have
hidden part of his pirate loot.

*The West Point foundry at Cold Spring produced over three thousand cannon for the Union
during the Civil War. John Ferguson Weir painted* Forging the Shaft *(shown above, detail)
there between 1874 and 1877.*

One of the river's oddest landmarks, **Bannerman's Castle** on Polle-
pel Island was a combination of country house and arsenal, built
between 1905 and 1918 by Francis Bannerman, a wealthy arms
merchant. An explosion in 1920 severely damaged the castle,
which was in use as a munitions depot until 1967. It remains in
hazardous condition. The island is now the property of New York
State, but there are no facilities for visitors.

## STORM KING MOUNTAIN

Storm King (just north of West Point via Route 218) is one of the
most spectacular of the Hudson's natural wonders—a massive
dome of granite overlooking the river. The mountain is best
viewed from across the river in the area of Cold Spring, but Route
218 traverses Storm King and affords dramatic views at several
stopping points. Route 218 also leads to the **Museum of the Hudson Highlands,** a wildlife museum in Cornwall-on-Hudson housing indigenous animals (914–534–7781).

## NEWBURGH

George Washington had a headquarters here during the Revolution at **Jonathan Hasbrouck House** (Liberty and Washington
streets, 914–562–1195), a small stone dwelling that has been preserved. There is an adjacent museum devoted to Revolutionary
history. The Historical Society of Newburgh Bay and the Highlands has its headquarters in the **Crawford House** (189 Montgomery Street, 914–561–2585), a handsome 1830 mansion with period
furnishings and exhibits on local history. Hudson River School
paintings and ship models are displayed.

The site of the Continental army's last encampment, **New
Windsor Cantonment,** is located six miles south of Newburgh in
**Vails Gate** (Route 300, 914–561–1765). There is a visitor center
with exhibits, and, from mid-April through late October, musket
and artillery, blacksmith, and living history demonstrations. **General Henry Knox's Headquarters** (Route 94, southwest of Newburgh, 914–561–5498) has displays of period furnishings and the
portable camp equipment officers used.

## BEACON

Named for Mount Beacon, where Patriots lit signal fires during the
Revolution to warn of British troop movements, Beacon is the site

of the **Madame Brett Homestead** (50 Van Nydeck Avenue, 914–831–6533), a Dutch-style house built in 1709. It was owned and occupied by seven generations of the same family until 1954, and the house displays the family's furnishings, dating from the 1600s to the early 1900s, in twelve restored rooms. Baron von Steuben used **Mount Gulian** (145 Sterling Street, 914–831–8172) as his headquarters, and the Society of the Cincinnati, a fraternal organization of Revolutionary officers, was founded here in June 1783. This fieldstone house, built in the 1730s by Gulian Verplanck, has the gambrel roof and curved overhang above the veranda typical of the valley's Dutch houses. It was reconstructed in the 1970s.

# FISHKILL

During the Revolutionary War Fishkill was an important supply depot and the site of a military encampment commanded by General Israel Putnam. The **Dutch Reformed Church** on Main Street was a holding prison for Tories and the meeting place for the New York Provincial Congress while delegates were writing a state constitution in 1776 and 1777. **Trinity Episcopal Church,** also on Main Street, served as a hospital. Some scenes in James Fenimore Cooper's novel *The Spy* were set at the **Van Wyck House** (routes 9 and 84, 914–896–9560), now a museum.

# POUGHKEEPSIE

An important industrial and commercial center in the nineteenth century, Poughkeepsie is the site of **Vassar College** (Raymond Avenue, 914–437–7000), founded in 1861. The main building was designed by James Renwick, Jr. The Vassar College Art Gallery offers changing exhibits. **Clinton House** (Main and North White streets, 914–471–1630) is a museum maintained by the Dutchess County Historical Society, displaying furniture, books, and maps.

## *Locust Grove*

Originally built in 1830, Locust Grove was purchased in 1847 by the inventor and painter, Samuel F. B. Morse. He hired Alexander Jackson Davis to assist him in remodeling the house in the manner of a Tuscan villa. The writer Benson Lossing visited Morse in the 1860s and found him a congenial host, who "dispenses generous hospitality to friends and strangers and . . . delights all who enter

the charmed circle of Locust Grove." The house displays furniture
and china gathered by a subsequent owner, Martha Innis Young.

LOCATION: Route 9, two miles south of the Mid-Hudson Bridge.
HOURS: May through October: 10–5 Monday and Wednesday–
Sunday; March, April, November, December: By appointment.
FEE: Yes. TELEPHONE: 914–454–4500.

## NEW PALTZ

In 1677 twelve French Huguenots purchased more than thirty-
nine thousand acres of land from the Esopus Indians and founded
the town of New Paltz along the Wallkill River. Today six houses
built by the first settlers survive on **Huguenot Street,** the oldest
street with its original houses in the country. The 1717 **French
Church** was reconstructed in the 1970s. The Huguenot Historical
Society, located in **Deyo Hall** (914–255–1660), offers tours of the
houses, which are furnished with period items. The society also
administers two historic houses in nearby **Gardiner,** four miles
south of New Paltz (914–255–1660). The first, built in 1814 ·by
Josiah Hasbrouck, is **Locust Lawn,** a fine example of rural New
York Federal architecture. The three-story mansion displays the
Hasbrouck family furniture, china, clothing, toys, and portraits by
Ammi Phillips and John Vanderlyn. The 1738 **Terwilliger House,**
on the same site, is a more modest stone house in the Dutch style.

## FRANKLIN D. ROOSEVELT
## HOME AND MUSEUM

Franklin D. Roosevelt was born in this house on January 30, 1882,
the only child of James and Sara Delano Roosevelt. The house is
furnished in a comfortable, well-worn mid- to late-Victorian style
with furnishings and memorabilia belonging to the president and
his family. Roosevelt often used the house as his Election Day
headquarters and as a summer White House. The adjacent **Museum of the Franklin D. Roosevelt Library** displays a fascinating
collection of items that illuminate FDR's life and the events of his
long tenure in office—the Great Depression, World War II, and
the development of the atomic bomb. On display are his "Day of
Infamy" message to Congress asking for a declaration of war
against Japan; the letter Albert Einstein wrote to him urging development of the atomic bomb; his White House desk, cluttered with
knickknacks and smoking paraphernalia; and the specially designed car, with hand controls, in which he drove guests around

the estate. A separate gallery is devoted to Eleanor Roosevelt's distinguished career in public service.

LOCATION: Route 9 in Hyde Park, six miles north of Poughkeepsie. HOURS: 9–5 Thursday–Monday. FEE: Yes. TELEPHONE: 914–229–9115.

## Eleanor Roosevelt National Historic Site

This retreat originated in Eleanor Roosevelt's desire for freedom from her overbearing mother-in-law, who had her way at Hyde Park. Eleanor and two friends had a small fieldstone house built here, named for a nearby stream, in 1925. In the 1920s and 1930s the women also maintained a furniture, weaving, and pewter factory, to provide jobs for unemployed local workers. Eleanor Roosevelt lived here until her death, welcoming John Kennedy, Khrushchev, Tito, and Nehru, among other dignitaries.

LOCATION: Two miles east of the Roosevelt Home. HOURS: May through October: 9–5 Daily; November, December, March, and April: 9–5 Saturday–Sunday. FEE: For shuttle bus from Roosevelt Home. TELEPHONE: 914–229–9115.

## VANDERBILT MANSION

For sheer splendor, no house on the Hudson rivals the Vanderbilt Mansion, an Italian Renaissance–style palace built for Frederick W. Vanderbilt by McKim, Mead & White. Completed in 1899, the mansion took almost four years to build at a cost of over $2 million. To create a suitably sumptuous atmosphere for their country retreat the Vanderbilts furnished the mansion with French furniture, art, tapestries, mantels, columns, and ceilings (some of the architectural elements and furnishings were taken from another of Vanderbilt's houses—a chateau near Paris that was once occupied by Napoleon).

LOCATION: Off Route 9, north of Poughkeepsie. HOURS: 9–5 Thursday–Monday. FEE: Yes. TELEPHONE: 914–229–9115.

## MILLS MANSION

Ruth Livingston Mills and her husband, Ogden, hired Stanford White to design this opulent, sixty-five-room Beaux Arts mansion around an earlier house, built by her grandfather, Morgan Lewis, in the 1840s. Ogden Mills was the heir to a substantial fortune

OVERLEAF: *The 18th-century Hasbrouck House, on Huguenot Street, New Paltz.*

Herb
arden

amassed in California by his father, a banker. In 1938 their descendants gave the house to the state. The interior is elaborately decorated with molded plaster, marble, oak panelling, and gilded wood. The original furnishings and decorative objects remain, such as the Flemish tapestries hanging on the marble walls of the dining room. The mansion may have been the inspiration for the Bellomont estate in Edith Wharton's 1905 novel, *The House of Mirth*.

> LOCATION: Route 9 in Staatsburg. HOURS: May through Labor Day: 10–5 Wednesday–Saturday, 1–5 Sunday; Labor Day through late October: 12–5 Wednesday–Saturday, 1–5 Sunday. FEE: None. TELEPHONE: 914–889–8851.

Southwest of Kingston in **High Falls,** the small **Canal Museum of the D & H Canal Historical Society** (Mohonk Road, 914–687–9311) displays old photographs and models of canalboats. Nearby are several locks built from 1847 to 1852, when the canal was improved.

# HURLEY

Settled in 1662, Hurley preserves twenty-five eighteenth-century stone houses (private), ten of them along Main Street. Many are open to the public on the second Saturday in July; but only the **Hurley Patentee Manor** (914–331–5414) is regularly open. Hurley was the state capital for one month in 1777, when the legislature, burned out of Kingston by the British, sought refuge in the town and convened at the **Jan Van Deusen House** (11 Main Street, 914–331–8852).

# RHINEBECK

Rhinebeck has long been a favorite country retreat for New York's wealthy families. To the east are numerous horse farms and orchards. The well-preserved nineteenth-century town retains some fine examples of Victorian architecture, including the Gothic-style, gingerbread-encrusted **Delamater House** (now an inn), built in 1844 and designed by Alexander Jackson Davis. Rhinebeck also has the country's oldest hotel still in operation, the **Beekman Arms,** which was started in 1766 and sheltered George Washington, Aaron Burr, and Franklin D. Roosevelt, among others.

The **Old Rhinebeck Aerodrome** (Stone Church Road off Route 9, 914–758–8610) displays a world-famous collection of

OPPOSITE: *The Hudson River Valley, as seen from the Vanderbilt Mansion, a fifty-room palace designed by McKim, Mead & White.*

vintage airplanes, dating from the early 1900s to 1937. Pilots reenact World War I dogfights, and, for a fee, will take visitors for flights in open-cockpit biplanes. Just south of Rhinebeck on Route 9, Mill Road leads to the **Sixteen-Mile District,** the location of nearly forty country houses built by the Beekman and Livingston families. The district is one of the most picturesque along the Hudson—it was landscaped in the Romantic style over a century ago. Although many of the houses are not visible from the road, they announce their presence with monumental gates and gatehouses. Property lines are marked by old stone walls. From the district, Fishing Ground Road leads north to the hamlet of **Rhinecliff,** a ferry stop from the early 1700s to 1957 with fine views of the Hudson.

## MONTGOMERY PLACE

The house, located in Annandale-on-Hudson, was built by Janet Livingston Montgomery, the widow of General Richard Montgomery, who was killed during the Revolution at Quebec in 1775. Mrs. Montgomery was in her fifties when she purchased the land and began work on the house, which was completed in 1805. Her niece, Coralie Barton, inherited the house and hired Alexander Jackson Davis to enlarge it and Andrew Jackson Downing to landscape the grounds, which now encompass 434 acres.

Montgomery Place remained in the family until 1986, when the house and its contents—an invaluable collection of furniture, artworks, decorative arts, toys, games, and clothing—were acquired by Historic Hudson Valley. The portrait collection includes works by Gilbert Stuart and John Wesley Jarvis. The restoration of the house reflects all periods of its occupancy from the early 1800s to the 1960s and is unusually authentic because the family had saved, in a trunk left in the attic, samples of all the wallpapers used in the house, as well as moldings, balusters, and other pieces of woodwork. Such modern additions as concrete steps and a refrigerator have been preserved to show the development of the house.

LOCATION: River Road, north of Rhinebeck off Route 9-G. HOURS: Mid-April through October: 10–5 Wednesday–Monday; November, December, March: 10–5 Saturday–Sunday. FEE: Yes. TELEPHONE: 914–758–5461.

OPPOSITE: *Montgomery Place; a portrait of the Revolutionary War general hangs over the mantel.*

# KINGSTON

Founded in 1652 by the Dutch, who called their settlement Wiltwyck, Kingston became one of the important transportation centers on the Hudson in the early nineteenth century. It was the eastern terminus of the 107-mile-long Delaware and Hudson Canal (opened in 1828) on which anthracite coal was barged to eastern markets from the Pennsylvania mines. The city was home port for both freighters and the fastest and most luxurious passenger steamers of their time on the Hudson.

During the Revolutionary War, Kingston became New York State's first capital, and was the site of the completion and presentation of New York State's first constitution in 1777. The first New York State senators met at merchant Abraham Van Gaasbeek's home (now called the Senate House) for about six weeks in 1777, until word of the advancing British army forced the evacuation of the fledgling government and community before the town was burned. The **Senate House State Historic Site** (312 Fair Street, 914–338–2786) houses exhibits about eighteenth-century life and government in New York as well as an extensive collection of eighteenth- and nineteenth-century paintings by John Vanderlyn and other Hudson Valley artists.

The **Stockade District** encompasses some of the city's fine historic buildings, including the **Urban Cultural Park Visitor Center** (914–331–7517), which provides information about the history, architecture, and attractions within Kingston. The **Old Dutch Church** (Wall and Main streets, 914–338–6759) is a lovely, eclectic building dating to 1852, with an 1891 Tiffany window behind the pulpit. The **Kingston Volunteer Fireman's Museum** (914–331–0866) is also located in the Stockade District, and is open seasonally. At the waterfront at the southern end of town are the **Hudson River Maritime Museum** (914–338–0071) and the **Trolley Museum of New York** (914–331–3399), featuring rides on vintage trolleys.

# CLERMONT

Clermont, the home of Robert R. Livingston, was rebuilt in 1778 after its destruction, in October 1777, by the British. The house has not been restored to a specific period, but reflects seven generations of Livingston family occupancy (until 1962). The architecture of the house possesses the understated elegance of the late Georgian period, despite the steeply pitched roof that was added in 1874. Livingston served in the Continental Congress, was a member of the drafting committee for the Declaration of Independence, and negotiated the Louisiana Purchase. As chancellor of the state of New York, he swore in George Washington at the first presidential inauguration. He was a partner with Robert Fulton in the development of commercial steamboat service on the Hudson. The river's first steamboat was named *Clermont.*

> LOCATION: Off Route 9-G, four miles south of Germantown. HOURS: Mid-April through Labor Day: 11–5 Tuesday–Sunday; Labor Day through October: 12–4 Tuesday–Sunday; November through mid-December: 12–4 Saturday, Sunday. FEE: Yes. TELEPHONE: 518–537–4240.

## CATSKILL

The shipping business brought prosperity to Catskill in the eighteenth and nineteenth centuries, and many houses and commercial buildings survive from that era. **Cedar Grove** (218 Spring Street, 518–943–6533) was the home of Thomas Cole, the landscape painter, from 1836 to 1848. The house displays a small collection of works by Cole and other painters of the Hudson River School.

## OLANA

Olana was the home of the landscape painter Frederic E. Church, one of the greatest of the Hudson River School painters. Situated on the top of a 460-foot hill, Olana occupies a beautiful spot overlooking the Hudson. Church wrote, "About an hour this side of Albany is the center of the world. I own it." He conceived the house as a living landscape painting, with large windows and doorways to frame views of the river valley. The house is an eclectic blend of Middle Eastern styles that Church labeled "personal Persian." He began construction in 1870 and moved into the partially completed house two years later. The painter designed an extraordinarily rich decorative scheme, with gilded doorways, stenciled walls, and meticulously contrived color schemes—in the sitting room, for example, the delicate rose color that predominates in the painting over the mantel matches the stone of the fireplace. The estate's 250 acres are crossed by miles of carriage roads.

> LOCATION: Route 9-G, one mile south of Rip Van Winkle Bridge. HOURS: Mid-April through Labor Day: 10–4 Wednesday–Saturday, 12–4 Sunday; Labor Day through October: 12–4 Wednesday–Sunday. FEE: Yes. TELEPHONE: 518–828–0135.

# HUDSON

The town of Hudson was one of several ports along the river founded after the Revolution by New England merchants who recognized the business opportunities of this developing region. Some also retained Loyalist sympathies and did not want to expose themselves any longer to reprisals in fiercely patriotic New England. Hudson, settled by families from Nantucket and Martha's Vineyard, was a remarkably successful commercial venture from the outset. In the 1830s, the town's businessmen started a whale fishery that flourished until 1845. The town's rich expressions of Greek Revival architecture reflect their success. Hudson also preserves a variety of later architectural styles. The 1811 **Robert Jenkins House** (113 Warren Street, 518–851–9049) is operated by the Daughters of the American Revolution as a museum of local history and whaling. The **American Museum of Fire Fighting** (Harry Howard Avenue, 518–828–7695) has the oldest and most comprehensive collection of firefighting equipment in the country.

# COXSACKIE

Settled in the late seventeenth century by Dutch farmers, Coxsackie derived its name from the Indian word meaning "hoot of an owl." In January 1775 the local farmers signed their own declaration of independence from England, stating their grievances over "arbitrary and oppressive" acts of Parliament. Fine examples of Dutch architecture are preserved at the **Bronck Museum** (Route 9-W, 518–731–8862), a complex of restored houses and barns occupied by the Bronck family for nine generations. Two houses, a stone house built in 1663 and a brick house built in 1738, display furnishings from the eighteenth and nineteenth centuries.

# KINDERHOOK

A Dutch word meaning "children's corner," Kinderhook was the birthplace of President Martin Van Buren. His home, **Lindenwald** (2 miles south on Route 9-H, 518–758–9689) was renovated and enlarged for him by Richard Upjohn in 1849. The **Vanderpoel House** (16 Broad Street, 518–758–9625) is a beautiful, Federal-style building containing a collection of furniture and paintings.

OPPOSITE: *Olana, a flamboyant confection of Middle Eastern styles, was designed by its owner, the landscape painter Frederic E. Church.*

The **Van Alen House** (Route 9-H, 518–758–9625), built in 1737, is an important example of early Dutch architecture. This brick house is representative of a form of northern European architecture once very common in the region, and it is the only house that has been restored and furnished to the early Dutch period.

## THE SHAKER MUSEUM

This Shaker Museum has a beautiful collection of Shaker furniture and other items, perhaps the finest collection anywhere. The museum's eight buildings, which were moved here from other locations, include several built by Shakers. There are working blacksmith, cabinetmaking, and weaving shops and a chair factory, as well as displays that explain the Shaker religious beliefs and way of life.

LOCATION: Shaker Museum Road, Old Chatham. HOURS: May through October 10–5 daily. FEE: Yes. TELEPHONE: 518–794–9100.

## NEW LEBANON

Located minutes away from the Shaker Museum in Old Chatham, Mount Lebanon Shaker Village—once one of the largest Shaker

*The attic of the Shaker Meetinghouse at New Lebanon. The complex framing and barrel roof allowed builders to leave the entire first floor open for meetings.*

communities and the intellectual spiritual center of this sect—is a showplace of Shaker architecture. The twenty-five buildings and the grounds were sold to the Darrow School in the 1930s, when the Shaker community had nearly expired. The school has converted many of the buildings to its own use. The visitor center offers a walking tour, slide show, and a glimpse inside some of the buildings.

LOCATION: Route 20, southeast of Albany. HOURS: Memorial Day through Columbus Day: 9:30–5 Daily. FEE: Yes. TELEPHONE: 518–794–9500.

# RENSSELAER

The town was named for one of the Hudson's wealthiest Dutch families, the Van Rensselaers. **Crailo** (9½ Riverside Avenue, 518–463–8738), a reconstruction of a brick house occupied by the family in the early 1700s, is now a museum of Dutch life and culture.

# ALBANY

When Henry Hudson reached the end of the river's navigable water at the future site of Albany he found a thriving community of Mohican Indians, their well-cultivated fields, and an excellent supply of furs. Just five years later, in 1614, Dutch fur traders set up a post that burned, followed in 1624 by Fort Orange, a permanent trading settlement established by the Dutch West India Company. Kiliaen Van Rensselaer, an Amsterdam merchant, obtained a large land grant from the company, and dispatched farming families to settle it in 1630. The site was called Beverwyck from 1652 to 1664, when the English gained control of the valley and named the town Albany. By the 1680s there were about two thousand inhabitants. The town prospered as a trading center for the valley's farmers, and as the residence of the owners of the sloops that carried produce along the river and down to the West Indies.

Albany grew slowly in the eighteenth century (there were only 3,500 citizens in 1790), but rapidly after the Revolution, when it was a gateway and supply center for New Englanders heading west. In 1797 Albany was selected as the state capital. Transportation, banking, iron manufacturing, and lumber trading enriched Albany throughout the nineteenth century—it was a hub of the region's turnpikes, canals, and railroads. In 1853 two Albany men, Erastus

Corning and J. V. L. Pruyn, combined ten lines and created the New York Central Railroad. In the late 1800s, dwindling yields of iron ore and lumber in the Adirondacks led to a decline of Albany's industries. In the twentieth century, state government was the city's chief activity. The catalyst of the downtown renovation was the complex of government buildings completed in 1978—the Nelson A. Rockefeller Empire State Plaza, also called the Mall.

The city's **visitor center** (25 Quackenbush Square, 518–434–6311) has exhibits and a film about Albany's history and provides information about walking tours and children's programs. The **Historic Albany Foundation** (44 Central Avenue, 518–463–0622) also provides information about self-guided walking tours of historical and architectural sites.

## New York State Capitol

Thirty years of construction (1867–1898), five architects (including Henry Hobson Richardson), and $25 million created this architecturally strange but endearing combination of styles— Italian and French Renaissance, and Romanesque. The interior, restored in the 1980s, is a grand expression of the stoneworker's craft, with three beautifully ornamented stairways with soaring arches. Richardson's handsome Senate Chamber is embellished with red granite, yellow and pink marble, stained glass, onyx, and mahogany.

LOCATION: Empire State Plaza. HOURS: Guided tours: 9–4 Monday–Friday, 12–4 Saturday, Sunday. FEE: None. TELEPHONE: 518–474–2418.

## New York State Museum

The museum features permanent exhibitions on the Adirondack Wilderness; the Ice Age in New York, with dioramas of Indian life in that era; the New York Metropolis, focusing on the daily life of the city; the birds of New York; the story of Jewish refugees from Nazi-held Europe who came to New York during World War II; gems; and antique fire-fighting equipment. The museum also has changing exhibits on a variety of historical and cultural subjects.

LOCATION: Empire State Plaza. HOURS: 10–5 Daily. FEE: None. TELEPHONE: 518–474–5877.

*The New York State Capitol, Albany, built over thirty years by a succession of architects.*

## Albany Institute of History & Art

With its lineage going back to organizations founded in the late 1700s and the nineteenth century, the Institute has a superb collection of art and historical items. It houses important collections of paintings by the Hudson River School and eighteenth-century portraits of Dutch inhabitants of the region; a re-creation of a colonial Dutch room; regional folk art; and outstanding exhibits of furniture and silver.

LOCATION: 125 Washington Avenue. HOURS: 12–5 Wednesday–Sunday. FEE: Yes. TELEPHONE: 518–463–4478.

## Schuyler Mansion

Among the finest American houses of its period, the mansion was built in 1726 for Philip Schuyler, then twenty-nine years old, whose mother was a Van Cortlandt and wife a Van Rensselaer. A successful businessman and the heir to large landholdings (he owned about 125,000 acres), Schuyler served with distinction in the Revolution as a major general, although his contributions are not well remembered. It was Schuyler who organized the ox-train by which Henry Knox carried Fort Ticonderoga's cannon to Boston. When General Burgoyne was making his way south to invade the Hudson Valley, Schuyler skillfully impeded the British advance south of Whitehall. Political maneuvering put Horatio Gates in command at Saratoga instead of Schuyler, but he had the pleasure of being keeper of the captured Burgoyne at his house. His daughter Betsy married Alexander Hamilton in the drawing room in 1780. The two-and-a-half story house, of rose red bricks with a balustraded roof, displays Schuyler family items, colonial and Federal furniture, porcelain, and glassware.

LOCATION: 32 Catherine Street. HOURS: Mid-April through October: 10–5 Wednesday–Saturday, 1–5 Sunday. FEE: Yes. TELEPHONE: 518–434–0834.

**Historic Cherry Hill,** (523½ South Pearl Street, 518–434–4791), a gambrel-roofed house built in 1787 for Philip and Maria Sanders Van Rensselaer, was occupied by their descendants until 1963. The house contains the furnishings of five generations of the family. It is Albany's only house museum showing three centuries of continuous family living. **Ten Broeck Mansion** (Ten Broeck Place, 518–436–9826) is a 1798 brick mansion with an excellent collection of period furniture. Its builder, Abraham Ten Broeck, commanded troops at Saratoga.

The works of the Watervliet Arsenal, which has manufactured guns, ammunition, and large-caliber weapons for the U.S. Army since 1813, are on display at the **Watervliet Arsenal Museum** (321 Broadway, 518–266–5805). The museum is housed in a rare cast-iron warehouse that is one of the few remaining examples of this building type. The building parts were cast in New York City, shipped up the Hudson River, and assembled at the site in 1859.

# TROY

Dutch farmers were settling in this region in the late 1600s, but it was not until the 1780s that the streets of the early town, named Vanderhayden, were laid out. The name was changed to Troy in 1789. The area developed as a manufacturing center in the nineteenth century because of readily available water power and cheap river transportation. The Bessemer process for making steel, developed in England, was first put to use in America here, in 1865.

Sam Wilson, a local meatpacker, supplied beef to the Army during the War of 1812. Soldiers joked about the government stamp, "U.S. Beef," saying it meant "Uncle Sam's Beef," and thus was born the legend of Uncle Sam, who became a symbol for the country. **Uncle Sam's Tablet** marks his grave in Oakwood Cemetery.

The **Hart-Cluett Mansion** (59 Second Street, 518–272–7232), owned by the Rensselaer County Historical Society, is a restored townhouse built in 1827. There are thirteen rooms displaying the furnishings, arts, and decorative items of the period. The Italian Renaissance **Troy Public Library** (100 Second Street, 518–274–7071), built in 1897, has a signed Tiffany memorial window.

# SARATOGA SPRINGS

"Society, sport, and sin," as the writer John Reed put it, were the ingredients that made Saratoga Springs America's premier resort in the nineteenth century. Supposedly, people came to take the waters, widely believed to have curative powers, that bubbled from the town's springs. Indeed, many sufferers came to Saratoga seeking relief from jaundice, dyspepsia, constipation, and other ailments. But for other visitors, after one ceremonial sip of the foul elixir, the drink of choice was champagne, and the order of the day was not exercise but gambling and socializing.

From 1802, when an entrepreneur put up the first hotel, Saratoga Springs attracted the social elite from all over the country. Before the Civil War, the resort was a particular favorite of Southern plantation owners. The Springs reached the height of glamour after the Civil War, attracting such notables as Boss Tweed, Commodore Vanderbilt, Diamond Jim Brady, who once arrived in a silver-plated railroad car, and Brady's constant companion, Lillian Russell. Broadway was lined with great hotels.

Visitors can taste the waters that made Saratoga famous in **Congress Park,** where the town's information center is located. The park also holds **Canfield Casino** (518–584–6920), one of Saratoga's original gambling establishments. The elegant club was built in 1870 by John Morrissey, a former boxer and onetime enforcer for Tammany Hall in New York. The casino now houses a museum devoted to the history of the town, with displays of Victorian clothing, furniture, and gambling paraphernalia, and an exhibit explaining the geological forces that created the springs.

Saratoga Springs is a showplace of American architecture, in styles including Greek Revival, Gothic Revival, and Queen Anne. Nine hundred of the town's buildings are listed on the National Register of Historic Places. The best places to view the town's architecture are North Broadway, Union Avenue, Lake Avenue, and Circular Street, the location of the Victorian **Batcheller Mansion** (private), possibly the town's finest building.

During the Civil War three millionaires built **Saratoga Race Track** and sponsored the first running of the Travers Cup, America's oldest racing event. The original grandstand, with its exuberant peaks and gables, is still in use—August is the racing season at Saratoga. The **National Museum of Racing** (518–584–0400), across the avenue from the racetrack, contains artworks and racing memorabilia, such as the gavel used to auction Man o' War.

## SARATOGA BATTLEFIELD

Saratoga National Battlefield Park looks much the same today as it did in the autumn of 1777, when Burgoyne's army of nine thousand British regulars, Hessians, and Indians clashed with American forces led by General Horatio Gates.

Saratoga may have been the decisive battle of the Revolutionary War. In 1777 the British launched a vast, three-pronged

OPPOSITE: *The Batcheller Mansion, a splendid Victorian mansion in Saratoga Springs.*

*The Saratoga Battlefield, where Americans under General Gates defeated the British in one of*

attack, aimed at the Hudson. Barry St. Leger advanced on the Hudson from the west, along the Mohawk Valley; Sir William Howe was to sail north from New York; and General John "Gentleman Johnny" Burgoyne marched south from Canada along Lake Champlain. Their goal was to join forces at Albany, thus taking control of the river and dividing the colonies. Burgoyne crossed the Hudson and landed near Saratoga on September 13, 1777. But the Americans had taken up strong positions at Bemis Heights, blocking the river road to Albany, and also threatened the British rear. Burgoyne tried to break out in two battles, at Freeman's Farm on September 19, and at Bemis Heights on October 7. The American commanders Benedict Arnold, Daniel Morgan, and Horatio Gates stymied both attempts. Surrounded and outnumbered, Burgoyne surrendered on October 17. The victory at Saratoga had profound consequences. The patriots dispatched messengers to Boston, where a fast ship left for France on November 1. On December 4, Benjamin Franklin was handed a note in Paris telling him of Burgoyne's surrender. The news electrified Europe, and in two days King Louis XVI declared France in alliance with the American rebellion.

The park's visitor center displays artifacts unearthed at the site, along with maps and a short film that outline the ebb and flow of the battles of September and October 1777. A road loops

*the most important battles of the American Revolution.*

through the battlefield, punctuated with ten stopping points, each with a plaque and a map explaining what happened at that site.

LOCATION: U.S. Route 4 and State Route 32, at the river, south of Schuylerville. HOURS: 9–5 Daily. FEE: None. TELEPHONE: 518–664–9821.

## SCHUYLERVILLE

Schuylerville was originally named Saratoga, and the battle took place closer to this town than to modern Saratoga Springs. The British surrender took place here at a spot known as the Field of Grounded Arms. The town was incorporated in 1831; it was named Schuylerville after General Philip Schuyler, whose restored summer house, **Schuyler Mansion,** is at the edge of town (Route 4). The British burned the original mansion, and the house seen today was constructed immediately after the Battle of Saratoga, in thirty days. Atop a three-hundred-foot hill in the town, on the site of Burgoyne's last encampment, is the 1883 **Saratoga Battle Monument,** a 155-foot-high granite tower. At the base are niches holding statues of generals Schuyler and Gates and Colonel Daniel Morgan; the fourth niche, where a statue of Benedict Arnold would have stood, is empty. The views from the top are spectacular.

# UPSTATE NEW YORK

As he was touring the state after the Revolution, General George Washington remarked to Governor George Clinton that New York had the potential to become "the seat of Empire." It took a man of some vision to see the possibilities, for at the time New York ranked seventh in population and was having trouble attracting new settlers, who saw better opportunity elsewhere.

The colony's beginnings were unpromising as well. For the century and a half after Samuel de Champlain and Henry Hudson both explored the state in 1609, New York was the stage for a struggle for control—the Dutch, the French, and the English contending, in varying combinations, with varying combinations of Indians.

The Dutch got the first toehold in the state in 1614 when they built a fort on Castle Island, south of where Albany is today. In 1625 the Dutch West India Company offered large estates, called patroonships, to any member who would put fifty settlers on the land. The patroons were generally unsuccessful in doing so, but the British also divided the Hudson Valley into huge proprietorships—now called "manors"—after they seized the Dutch colony in the 1670s. Since there was plenty of other land around, settlers were reluctant to subject themselves, as mere tenants, to either patroons or manor lords. Therefore, New York was less attractive than other colonies to settlers.

Starting in 1689 with King William's War and ending in 1760, the British and the French fought four world wars, of which local conflicts, for control of territory and trade, were sideshows. When the final "French and Indian War" began in 1754, New York was in the middle of it. British defeats at Niagara, Crown Point, Oswego, and Fort William Henry were followed by a series of victories. Lord Jeffrey Amherst captured Ticonderoga and Crown Point in July 1759, while Sir William Johnson, the influential Indian agent, took Fort Niagara and reoccupied Oswego at about the same time.

New York's strategic importance was even clearer during the American Revolution. The war in northern New York went well for the colonists at the start, with Ethan Allen taking Ticonderoga and Seth Warren capturing Crown Point in the spring of 1775. In October of 1776 Benedict Arnold's improvised fleet lost the Battle of Valcour Bay on Lake Champlain but succeeded in halting the enemy's southward thrust. However, General William Howe was driving Washington from New York City and forced his retreat

*The Erie Canal, ca. 1830, by J. W. Hill.*

into New Jersey after the Battle of White Plains on the twenty-eighth of the same month.

British strategy in 1777 was to conquer New York—and thereby divide the rebellious colonies, north from south—with a three-pronged attack converging on Albany. The plan was dealt a blow when Britain's Colonel Barry St. Leger was forced to turn back after failing to take Fort Stanwix, and it collapsed completely when General John Burgoyne met defeat at Saratoga.

Raids on frontier settlements provoked the punitive Sullivan-Clinton campaign of 1779, and the Tories and Indians were routed at Newtown, near present-day Elmira. The Mohawk Valley was the site of the final battle on New York soil. On October 25, 1781, six days after Lord Cornwallis surrendered at Yorktown, the Americans under Marinus Willett defeated a combination of British, Tories, and Indians at the Battle of Johnstown.

The postwar period brought intensified land speculation on the frontier; many shares were sold abroad and most of western New York ended up in the hands of the Holland Land Company.

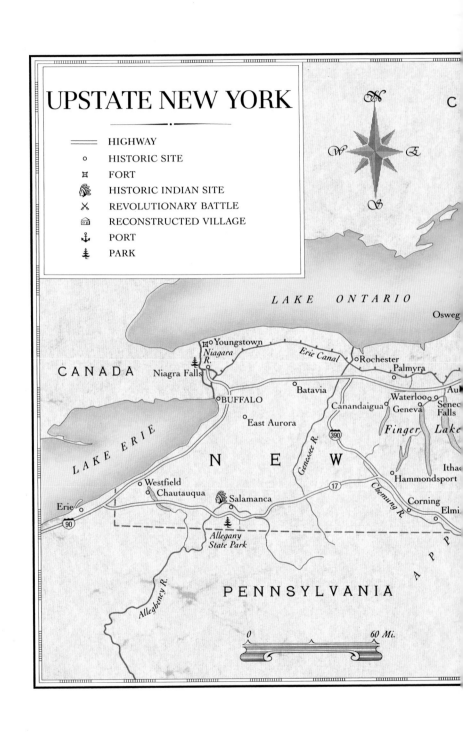

# UPSTATE NEW YORK

═══ HIGHWAY
○ HISTORIC SITE
⊞ FORT
 HISTORIC INDIAN SITE
✕ REVOLUTIONARY BATTLE
 RECONSTRUCTED VILLAGE
⚓ PORT
⚐ PARK

CANADA

LAKE ONTARIO

Oswego

⊞○ Youngstown
*Niagara R.*
Niagra Falls

Erie Canal
○ Rochester
Palmyra ○

○ BUFFALO

○ Batavia

Canandaigua ○
Waterloo ○ ○ Au
Geneva ○
Seneca
Falls

CANADA

East Aurora ○

*Genesee R.*

390

*Finger Lake*

N   E   W

Ithac
Hammondsport ○

○ Westfield
○ Chautauqua
 Salamanca

17
*Chemung R.*
Corning ○
Elmi

Erie ○
90

⚐
*Allegany State Park*

PENNSYLVANIA

A P P

*Allegheny R.*

0          60 Mi.

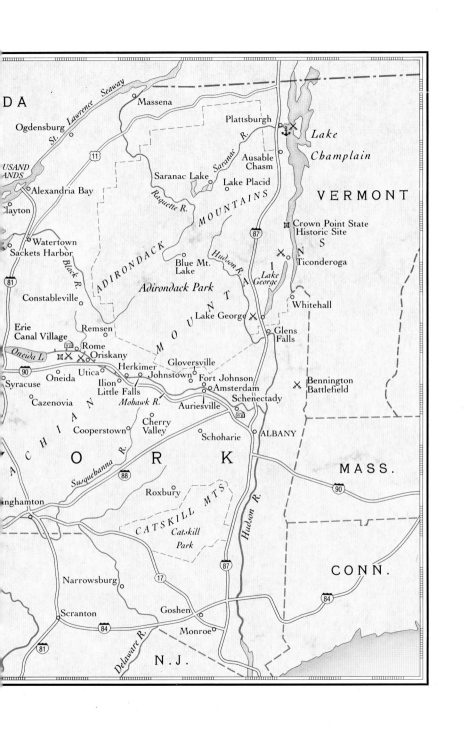

In 1801 the company opened a land office in Batavia with Joseph Ellicott, founder of Buffalo, as agent. The availability of rich land attracted a rush of new settlers—by 1820 New York was the country's most populous state, having overtaken Virginia.

The War of 1812 was not popular in New York, although the state sent 77,000 men to battle and bore the brunt of much of the fighting. As the war shifted back and forth across the Niagara River, the British succeeded in capturing Fort Niagara on December 13, 1813, and burned several settlements, including Buffalo. The Americans put on a good showing at Chippawa and Lundy's Lane, and in the taking of Fort Erie, all on the Canadian side of the river.

On the eastern end of Lake Ontario, the British attacked the important American naval base and shipbuilding yard at Sackets Harbor on May 29, 1813. But they were beaten back. A turning point came when Lieutenant Thomas Macdonough outmaneuvered and defeated a British fleet on Lake Champlain near Plattsburgh on September 11, 1814. Victory on water ensured victory ashore; on the same day General Alexander Macomb defeated a much larger force of British veterans invading from Montreal at the Battle of Plattsburgh. The two defeats weakened the enemy's will and ended Britain's hopes for total dominion over the Great Lakes.

After the war, farsighted New Yorkers like DeWitt Clinton moved to open the way to the west. In 1817, the same year he was elected governor, Clinton pushed through a bill authorizing construction of a canal—"Clinton's Ditch," it was derisively called by the plan's many opponents—connecting Lake Erie to New York City via the Mohawk and Hudson rivers. In 1825 the 363-mile, 4-foot deep, $7 million canal with 83 locks opened with Clinton leading a procession of canalboats from Buffalo to New York City. On arrival, he poured a kegful of Lake Erie water into the Hudson.

The Erie Canal, one of the great engineering feats in history, united the state. It opened western New York and the entire Great Lakes region to settlement and development, and brought produce and goods flowing east. Soon New York City would be the nation's leading port. The cost of shipping a ton of freight from Buffalo to New York City dropped from $120 to $14, and in its first year, the canal earned nearly a million dollars.

Since the 1680s, tenants on the manorial estates had resisted efforts to collect back rents and fees on transfers from one lessee to another. In the 1830s, these disturbances spread and secret antirent societies sprang up; on occasion, members would tar and feather lawmen who tried to evict leaseholders. Finally, the anachronism of the system was recognized in the state constitution of 1846, which ended the regime of the patroons and manor lords.

Antislavery sentiment among the new settlers made New York a center of abolitionism; at the same time, religious fervor produced many new sects, several long-lasting, such as Mormons and Seventh Day Adventists. New York was an important center of the women's rights movement, which was founded in Seneca Falls, and the temperance movement. Intolerance of Catholics and immigrants grew also; the appropriately-named Know-Nothing party, opponent of all things "foreign," was founded here in 1849.

Agriculture and dairying remained important in New York, but by 1859 the state also produced 23 percent of the country's manufactured goods. The Civil War only increased New York's lead over the other states. Uniforms were produced in Elmira, boots in Rochester, while Troy made the plates for the ironclad *Monitor*. Many of the industries that sprang up in the nineteenth century are still strong today—glass in Corning, photographic equipment in Rochester, silver plate in Oneida. The last, which began as part of a utopian experiment in 1848, continued to thrive after the community disbanded over thirty years later.

Although the state is best known for New York City, it has much more to offer. Buffalo has buildings by such noted architects as Louis Sullivan and Frank Lloyd Wright, and parks by Frederick Law Olmsted; Rochester is known for its museums and schools. Central New York contains scores of Greek Revival villages, superb reliquaries of the culture of the antebellum period. Saratoga has its racetrack and buildings of the later nineteenth century. Cooperstown, boyhood home of James Fenimore Cooper and the place where, it is said, Abner Doubleday invented modern baseball in a cow pasture in 1839, is the location of the manorial Hyde Hall.

Heavy industry in New York State began declining soon after the Civil War. In agriculture it lost its predominance to the Midwest; in textiles, to the South. New York's population took second place to California's with the census of 1970. Still, New York remains the Empire State. If any other state aspires to challenge it for that title, it has yet to step forward and make itself known.

OVERLEAF: *Schoharie Crossing north of Auriesville, where the Erie Canal crossed Schoharie Creek.*

# C E N T R A L    N E W    Y O R K

The central New York region illustrates well the influence of geography on history. In colonial times, the rugged Catskill Mountains were inhospitable to European settlers and travelers, and of little economic or strategic value. Consequently, these mountains saw few of the momentous events of European-American history, and there are correspondingly few historic sites in the area arising from that tradition. Today, the Catskills are cherished for their scenic beauty. Sportsmen also honor the area as the birthplace of American fly-fishing.

The Mohawk River Valley, by contrast, is a cauldron of history. Since prehistoric times, the river that runs west to east into the Hudson along the northern part of Central New York has been a corridor through the Appalachian chain of mountains and an important link in the passage from the Great Lakes to the Hudson River. The strategic importance of this route first pitted Indian tribes against each other, then the French against the English, and finally, the English against the Americans in the Revolution.

After the fighting was over, settlers began moving west through the valley, replacing the Iroquois, who were confined to reservations or driven into Canada. In 1825 the Erie Canal from Buffalo to the Hudson was completed, and the railroad soon followed. Together they carried settlers, commerce, and industry to the frontier and brought western products back to city markets. Today the New York State Barge Canal, which replaced the Erie, and an interstate highway run the length of the valley past many historic sites and monuments.

The tour of the region that follows starts in Schenectady and moves west through the valley, then reverses itself south through Cooperstown and Schoharie. From there it moves south in a swing around the Catskills, picking up the relatively few historic attractions but much of the scenery that those mountains have to offer.

## SCHENECTADY

As the western end of the portage between the Hudson and the Mohawk rivers, Schenectady was at first a much beleaguered frontier town and later the gateway to the west. On the night of February 8, 1690, a French and Indian raiding party, retaliating against raids by the British and their Indian allies, burned the small

*A fine example of the Hudson River School of painting is William Guy Wall's* Cauterskill Falls on the Catskill Mountains.

settlement, killed sixty inhabitants, and took twenty-seven captives to Canada. "The cruelties committed at sd. Place no Penn can write nor Tongue expresse," the mayor of Albany wrote a few days later, preferring not to consider, either, the cruelties committed by his own compatriots. Today the **Stockade Historic District** borders on the Mohawk River and contains more than sixty of the town's earliest buildings.

The campus of **Union College,** chartered in 1795, was designed by a French architect, Joseph Jacques Ramée. The unusual sixteen-sided **Nott Memorial** constructed from 1858 to 1876—with sixteen interior chimneys and a sixteen-sided cupola—was designed by a Union graduate, Edward Tuckerman Potter, who was a pupil of Richard Upjohn. (Another of Potter's notable works is the Mark Twain House in Hartford, Connecticut). William Seward, a native upstate New Yorker who became Lincoln's secretary of state, and President Chester A. Arthur are among the college's prominent graduates.

# AMSTERDAM

This important carpet-manufacturing center is the site of the stone Georgian manor of Guy Johnson (1740–1788), nephew and successor in office of Sir William Johnson (1715–1774), the influential superintendent of Indian affairs. Johnson built the house in 1773 but, as a Loyalist, had to abandon it when the Revolution began two years later. The village adopted its present name in 1804 because the ancestors of most early residents had come from the Netherlands. It grew in economic importance after the Erie Canal was opened in 1825.

# FORT JOHNSON

Sir William Johnson, land baron, Indian agent, and soldier, built this two-story Georgian residence in 1749 and lived here until 1763. During this time he had ample opportunity to exercise his skills as a negotiator; as many as one thousand Indians camped here during the many Indian councils held at the fort. Johnson was

*Johnson Hall, now a state historic site, was built by the influential Indian agent and soldier, Sir William Johnson.*

knighted after his victory at the Battle of Lake George and made superintendent of Indian affairs. His restored home, **Old Fort Johnson** (Route 5, 518–843–0300) contains a decorative arts collection and items of local history.

## AURIESVILLE

On October 18, 1646, a French missionary, Father Isaac Jogues, and his companions were killed in the Indian village of Ossernenon. Father Jogues, who demonstrated extraordinary devotion to his flock, and his group were later canonized by the Roman Catholic church as martyrs. The **National Shrine of North American Martyrs** (Route 5-S, 518–853–3033) marks the place where they were executed. Auriesville is the 1656 birthplace of Blessed Kateri Tekakwitha, a Mohawk woman beatified in 1980, and in process of being canonized based on reports of miraculous cures.

## JOHNSTOWN

Like its neighbor, Gloversville, Johnstown was once an important glove-making center. Sir William Johnson built **Johnson Hall State Historic Site** (Hall Avenue, 518–762–8712) in 1763 and lived here until he died in 1774. The large frame house covered with wide clapboards cut to resemble stone blocks contains period furnishings. Johnson's son, Sir John Johnson, was a leader of the Loyalist forces during the Revolution. He inherited the house, but it was confiscated. Sir William also built the **Fulton County Court House,** North William Street, in 1772. It is the oldest colonial courthouse in the state and the oldest in the nation still in use.

The feminist leader Elizabeth Cady Stanton was born in Johnstown in 1815. Although her birthplace (Main and Market streets), where she lived until 1842, is now a bank, the **Johnstown Historical Society** (17 North William Street, 518–762–7076) has exhibits on her life and work, as well as artifacts of early Johnstown history.

## LITTLE FALLS

Mortally wounded at the Battle of Oriskany, August 6, 1777, General Nicholas Herkimer is remembered for his heroic effort in that bloody conflict. His ca. 1760 Dutch Colonial home, **Herkimer Home State Historic Site** (Route 169, 315–823–0398), now a museum, exhibits many of his personal furnishings and belongings.

*Detail of Maurice Prendergast's* Landscape with Figures, *from the collection of the Munson-Williams-Proctor Institute, Utica.*

# HERKIMER

Settled in 1723, this small industrial center was renamed after the slain General Herkimer, whose fatal march to the Battle of Oriskany began here. The **Herkimer County Historical Society** (400 North Main Street, 315–866–6413), housed in an 1884 Queen Anne building, displays items of local history. The building stands on the site of Fort Dayton, attacked in 1778 by Indians under Chief Joseph Brant. Adam Helmer's run for reinforcements was vividly depicted in Walter Edmonds's 1936 novel, *Drums Along the Mohawk*.

Another famous novel, Theodore Dreiser's 1925 *An American Tragedy,* was inspired by the murder trial of Chester Gillette, which took place in the Romanesque Revival–style **Herkimer County Courthouse** (320 North Main). Across the street, an 1834 jail is open for tours (315–866–6413).

# ILION

After Eliphalet Remington, Jr., made a rifle barrel at his father's forge, there were so many orders from neighbors that the father and son, who moved here from Connecticut in 1800, began producing rifles full-time. In 1873, after decades of astounding growth, the Remington Arms Company produced the first successful commercial typewriter. The **Remington Firearms Museum** (14 Hoefler Avenue, 315–895–3200) displays their products.

# UTICA

Located at the site of the area's only ford across the Mohawk River, Utica was established after the Revolution as an Indian trading post. Although Utica's industries prospered during the nineteenth century, the city is also known for an important failure, that of the first five-and-ten store that Frank Woolworth, a native of Watertown, established on Bleecker Street in 1879. (Several other Woolworth ventures also failed before he finally succeeded with a store in Lancaster, Pennsylvania.)

**Fountain Elms** (318 Genesee Street, 315–797–0000), an 1850 Italianate mansion, once the home of the prominent Williams-Proctor family, is owned by the **Munson-Williams-Proctor Institute** and houses their Museum of Art's decorative collection in four period rooms and displays changing exhibits. Their museum next door, designed by contemporary architect Philip Johnson, houses a fine collection of American and European paintings, including the original version of Thomas Cole's series, *The Voyage of Life*.

# REMSEN

When the Continental Army's drillmaster, General Friedrich Wilhelm Augustus von Steuben, retired after the Revolution, the state of New York granted him 16,000 acres in the Mohawk Valley in gratitude for his success in turning the army into an effective fighting force. A replica of his cabin, the **Steuben Memorial State Historic Site** (Starr Hill Road, 315–492–1756), contains some period furnishings. The landscape designed for von Steuben by a French architect, Pierre Pharoux, was the earliest executed on a large scale in New York.

# ORISKANY BATTLEFIELD

As he was marching to relieve the siege of Fort Stanwix on August 6, 1777, General Nicholas Herkimer halted his force of Americans near this town to await a prearranged signal from the fort's defenders for a coordinated attack on St. Leger's force. Herkimer's officers, however, protested the delay and Herkimer proceeded, against his judgment. At the place now commemorated by the

Oriskany Battlefield State Historic Site, Herkimer and his men were ambushed by Tories and Indians as they entered a ravine. In the battle that followed—one of the bloodiest of the Revolution— Herkimer was wounded in the leg and his horse killed, but he directed the battle propped up against a tree in his saddle. The enemy retreated when reinforcements came from Fort Stanwix. Ten days later Herkimer died of his wounds.

Although the Battle of Oriskany was not a clear-cut victory for the Americans, it contributed to the British disaster at Saratoga. Because he was unable to take Fort Stanwix after the battle, St. Leger was forced to retreat to Oswego and could not aid Burgoyne in his subsequent encounter with the Americans at Saratoga.

The Battlefield (two miles west of town on Route 69) has a visitor center, tours, self-guided paths, and interpretive signs.

> LOCATION: Route 69, two miles west of Oriskany. HOURS: May through October: 9–5 Monday, Wednesday–Saturday, 1–5 Sunday. FEE: None. TELEPHONE: 315–492–1756.

# ROME

Rome, settled in 1786 under the aegis of another Irish-American (like Johnson and William Constable), Dominick Lynch of Galway, is located on the plain near the Indian portage between Wood Creek and the Mohawk River, which were connected by a canal as early as 1797. In 1768 Sir William Johnson, who came with twenty boatloads of presents, met with two thousand Indians here to draw up the Treaty of Fort Stanwix, after which the Indians relinquished vast territories to European settlement.

In 1851 Jesse Williams established the country's first cheese factory in Rome. Rome was also the home of Francis Bellamy (1855–1931), who authored the Pledge of Allegiance for the four hundredth anniversary of the landing of Columbus. Once a prosperous copper- and wire-manufacturing center, the town lost thousands of factory jobs when plants closed in the 1950s.

## Fort Stanwix National Monument

According to legend, the Stars and Stripes, hastily sewn up from garments, flew for the first time in battle during the siege of Fort Stanwix in 1777, when a garrison of 550 Americans commanded by

OPPOSITE: *Fort Stanwix, where Americans withstood a British assault during the Revolution, has been reconstructed in Rome, New York.*

Colonel Peter Gansevoort withstood a siege by Colonel Barry St. Leger's force of 1,400 British, Hessians, Tories, and Indians. Upon receiving a written demand for surrender after the Battle of Oriskany, Gansevoort announced his "determined resolution, with the forces under my command, to defend this fort at every hazard, to the last extremity, in behalf of the United American States, who have placed me here to defend it against all their enemies." The fort has been carefully reconstructed and exhibits some of the over one hundred thousand historical artifacts found on the site.

LOCATION: 112 East Park Street. HOURS: April through December: 9–5 Daily. FEE: Yes. TELEPHONE: 315–336–2090.

There is also a **Rome Historical Society Museum** (200 Church Street, 315–336–5870) with exhibits and audiovisual presentations. The nearby **Tomb of the Unknown Soldiers of the American Revolution,** 1977, was designed by Lorimer Rich, who did the 1931 Tomb of the Unknowns in the Arlington National Cemetery.

## ERIE CANAL VILLAGE

This reconstructed 1840s village is located near where ground was first broken for the Erie Canal. A mule-drawn packet boat offers

*Erie Canal Village, a historic restoration re-creating the era when the canal was the economic lifeline of the entire region.* OVERLEAF: *Cooperstown, on the shores of Otsego Lake.*

rides along a restored section of the Enlarged Erie, which was widened in the 1840s to incorporate double locks. Original buildings, including a tavern, schoolhouse, and ice house, have been moved from within a fifty-mile radius to create the village. The **Canal Museum** portrays the history of the canal through paintings, models, and photographs. There is also a reconstruction of a packet-boat interior. The **New York State Museum of Cheese,** located at the village, has exhibits on the history and manufacturing of cheese.

LOCATION: Route 49-W. HOURS: Early May through late October: 9:30–5 Daily. FEE: Yes. TELEPHONE: 315-337-3999.

# ONEIDA

John Humphrey Noyes, a visionary with a flair for leadership, organization, and business, established the Oneida Community in 1848. Noyes believed that man could overcome sin and thus attain spiritual perfection. His followers, known as Bible Communists or Perfectionists, practiced plural marriage, birth control, selective breeding, and communal ownership of property. The community prospered when it began to manufacture animal traps. However, in 1880 opposition outside and discontent within the community forced it to dissolve as a religious and social experiment. Ownership was distributed as stock among the members, and the resulting corporation continues to thrive on one of the Community's later endeavors—manufacturing stainless steel flatware. The four-hundred-room **Mansion House** built by the Oneida Community in the 1860s is open by appointment (Kenwood Avenue, 315–361–3671).

**Cottage Lawn** (435 Main Street, 315–363–4136) is a fine example of the work of Alexander Jackson Davis, architect of Lyndhurst in Tarrytown, New York, and many other Gothic Revival and Greek Revival villas and mansions. Cottage Lawn, now the museum of the Madison County Historical Society, features decorative arts, furniture, tools, and textiles. The collection also includes an 1862 stagecoach, 1850s bank vaults, and the Oneida Indian Gallery.

# COOPERSTOWN

Cooperstown was founded in 1786 by Judge William Cooper. Cooper was agent for the manorial Clarke family, whose once-magnificent mansion, Hyde Hall, is located in the nearby Glimmerglass State Park (607–547–8662). In 1790 he brought his family, including his infant son, the future novelist James Fenimore Cooper,

here from New Jersey to live. Young Cooper drew from his youthful knowledge of the wilderness and his acquaintance with the frontiersmen for his books, especially the widely acclaimed series, The Leatherstocking Tales. Cooperstown is located on nine-mile-long Otsego Lake, which is called Glimmerglass in Cooper's stories; markers show the location of other sites he wrote about. **Fenimore House** (Lake Road, 607-547-1400), the museum of the New York State Historical Association, exhibits Cooper memorabilia and has one of the finest collections of American folk art in the country.

The town, which calls itself the "Village of Museums," is much blessed by architecture, location, and history. Located far from major cities, Cooperstown became a popular summer resort but never developed industrially. Therefore, much of the village remains unchanged from its early days. For years it was popularly believed that Abner Doubleday invented the modern game of baseball in Cooperstown, although debunkers today claim he made no significant changes in the game.

## Farmers' Museum and Village Crossroads

A re-creation of an early nineteenth-century village, this museum has a dozen commercial and residential buildings, including a

ABOVE AND OPPOSITE: *Some of the early tools and other implements on display at the Farmers' Museum in Cooperstown.*

country store, lawyer's and doctor's offices, smithy, printshop, farmhouse, church, and tavern. The museum features a notable collection of farming, kitchen, and crafts tools and gives demonstrations of their use. Among the artifacts displayed is the famous Cardiff Giant, which was unearthed in 1869 on the farm of William Newell in Cardiff, New York. The ten-foot-tall figure, thought to be a petrified prehistoric man, was exhibited widely, until it was discovered that it had been carved from gypsum in Chicago. The fact that it was a hoax, however, didn't stop P. T. Barnum from displaying a replica of the figure.

> LOCATION: Lake Road. HOURS: June through Labor Day: 9–5 Daily. FEE: Yes. TELEPHONE: 607–547–1450.

### National Baseball Hall of Fame and Museum

Among the attractions of this shrine to the national pastime are rooms called Great Moments, Ballparks, World Series, and Baseball Today. There are also exhibits on each of the players immortalized by election to the Hall of Fame and memorabilia, films, and a research library relating to the game.

> LOCATION: Main Street. HOURS: May through September: 9–9 Daily; October through April: 9–5 Daily. FEE: Yes. TELEPHONE: 607–547–7200.

## GOSHEN

The fertile land around this town inspired its early eighteenth-century settlers to name it after the Biblical land of Goshen. For well over a century, the town's main attraction has been the **Historic Track,** where trotting-horse competition began in 1838, making it the oldest track for trotters in the country. The **Trotting Horse Museum,** home of the Hall of Fame of the Trotter (240 Main Street, 914–294–6330), is housed in a 1913 stable and has original Currier & Ives trotting prints and paintings, as well as exhibits on famous trotting and pacing horses.

## SCHOHARIE

To protect itself from raids during the Revolution, the valley fortified its limestone church and on October 17, 1780, withstood an attack of Indians and Tories. The **Old Stone Fort Museum Complex** (North Main Street, 518–295–7192) has exhibits on the Schoharie Valley and the Revolution. The annex, **Badgley Museum and**

**Carriage House Complex,** has a diverse collection of artifacts, including farm tools, old fire engines, and a 1902 Rambler.

## ROXBURY

When Jay Gould (1836–1892), the railroad tycoon and financier, and John Burroughs (1837–1921), the naturalist and writer, were friends in school here, Gould wrote a poem for the writer-to-be to save him from staying after school, and Burroughs once bought some books from Gould when the future millionaire was broke, or so the story goes. The **Burroughs Memorial State Historic Site** (off Hardscrabble Road, 315–492–1756) is the site of the naturalist's "boyhood rock," which now marks his grave. Burroughs, a respected sage in his day and a friend of such leading figures as Theodore Roosevelt, accompanied Henry Ford, Harvey Firestone, and Thomas Edison on several well-publicized camping trips. A prolific author, he established nature writing as a branch of literature.

## MUSEUM VILLAGE IN ORANGE COUNTY

A collection of more than thirty buildings—among them a one-room schoolhouse, general store, blacksmith shop, apothecary—this village demonstrates the crafts and early industrial technology of the nineteenth century. There are also collections of glassware, farm machinery, wagons, and hand tools in this re-creation of a nineteenth-century town. The museum sponsors education programs and family workshops.

> LOCATION: Route 17-M, Monroe. HOURS: May through December: 12–5 Saturday, Sunday; May, June, and September through November: 10–2 Wednesday–Friday; July, August: 10–5 Wednesday–Friday. FEE: Yes. TELEPHONE: 914–782–8247.

## L A K E   G E O R G E   A R E A

The Jesuit missionary Father Isaac Jogues named the thirty-two-mile-long lake in the foothills of the Adirondacks Lac du Sacrement when he reached it in 1646. The lake became an important link in the Hudson–Lake Champlain route to Canada and the scene of many battles of the French and Indian War and the Revolution. The first resort hotel was built in 1800. Lake George had its heyday as a fashionable year-round resort in the first half of the twentieth century, although the grand hotels of that era have disappeared. Today, the beauty of the lake clashes with the motels and tourist attractions of the highly commercialized village. A local-history museum, the **Lake George Historic Museum** (Canada Street, 518–668–5044), with paintings, photos, and artifacts is located in the **Old Warren County Courthouse Complex,** a group of five attached brick structures, including an 1845 courthouse, judges' chambers, and jail.

## Lake George Village

After successfully defending a fortification south of the village against Baron Dieskau and his force of 1,700 French and Indians on September 8, 1755, the British forces under Sir William Johnson took the offensive, pursued the retreating enemy, and took many prisoners, including Dieskau. The ruins of the fort can be seen at the **Lake George Battlefield Picnic Area** off Route 9. Earlier in the day, in a clash with Dieskau, Colonel Ephraim Williams was killed. Thirty years later Williams's estate was used to endow Williams College.

In 1756 Johnson built Fort William Henry to defend the strategic passage between Lake George and the Hudson. In August 1757 the French commander Montcalm took the fort and razed it. Although he had promised safe conduct to the inhabitants of the fort, the Indians massacred large numbers of men, women, and children and took others into captivity. The **Fort William Henry Museum** (Canada Street, 518–668–5471) has been reconstructed from original plans of the fort and displays artifacts—some found on the site—and documents from the French and Indian War and the early days of the region. There are also demonstrations of bullet molding, musket and cannon firing, and military drilling.

# WALLOOMSAC

Overextended and short of supplies on his march from Canada to the Hudson Valley, British General John Burgoyne sent Lieutenant Colonel Friedrich Baum to raid storehouses at Bennington, Vermont. On their way, on August 16, 1777, Baum and his eight hundred men were attacked at Walloomsac, just two miles from the Vermont border, and defeated in a two-hour battle that the American leader, Brigadier General John Stark, would later describe as "one continuous clap of thunder." Baum and two hundred of his

OPPOSITE: *Detail from* A Perspective Plan of the Battle Fought near Lake George, *between the English and French and their Indian allies.*

*Lake George, at the foothills of the Adirondacks.*

men were killed in the fighting; the rest were captured. A late-arriving column of reinforcements was routed by the Americans. The loss further weakened Burgoyne and contributed to his defeat at Saratoga. At the **Bennington Battlefield** (Route 67, 518–686–7109), relief maps and markers explain the battle.

# L A K E    C H A M P L A I N

Lake Champlain, which separates the states of New York and Vermont, begins just beyond the Canadian border in the north and stretches 125 miles southward, ending in a riverlike extension near Whitehall, New York. The history of this lovely region until 1815 was one of almost continual conflict and bloodshed. Samuel de Champlain, who discovered the lake in 1609, described it as a no-man's-land between warring Indians. The French began fortifying the northern end of the lake as early as 1640 and built Fort Saint Frédéric at Crown Point in 1731 and Fort Carillon at the southern end in 1756. Driving the French out became a prime British objective, but they were unsuccessful until Lord Jeffery Amherst's victories at Ticonderoga and Crown Point. The lake lost none of its strategic importance during the American Revolution and the War of 1812; only the combatants changed. Actions at Ticonderoga, Crown Point, and Plattsburgh were important in both wars.

# WHITEHALL

The town of Whitehall considers itself the birthplace of the American Navy, since Benedict Arnold assembled his hastily constructed fleet here in the early days of the Revolution. Arnold's flotilla, manned by soldiers and sailors, was overwhelmed in the Battle of Valcour Bay on October 11, 1776, but prevented the British from moving south on Lake Champlain that year. This early chapter in naval history is memorialized at the **Skenesborough Museum** (Route 22, 518–499–0716), which displays models of the first naval yard, the ships being built, and the hull of the USS *Ticonderoga,* War of 1812, which was raised from Lake Champlain in 1958. Although the U.S. Navy acknowledges the importance of the Battle of Valcour, it does not officially recognize Whitehall as its "birthplace." Arnold's fleet was under army command. The Navy was officially "born" in Philadelphia on October 13, 1775, when Congress authorized the purchase of warships.

# TICONDEROGA

The Liberty Monument erected at Moses Circle—depicting a French soldier, an Indian, a Royal Highlander, and a Green Mountain Boy—reflects the complex, war-torn history of this area on the portage route between Lake George and Lake Champlain. The now partially restored **Mount Hope Battery** (Burgoyne Road, 518–585–2821), erected in 1758, guarded the passage. A graphite mine and the easy availability of lumber made Ticonderoga a graphite-producing center for lead pencils from 1840 until the end of the century. The town continues to produce paper today.

## Fort Ticonderoga

This strategic point on the southern end of Lake Champlain—gateway to both the Hudson and Canada—was hotly contested from the time the French fortified it in 1755 through the Revolution. In 1758 French General Montcalm's troops, outnumbered almost five to one, met the British, under James Abercromby, on the field northwest of the fort; in the bloody debacle that followed,

*From the mid-18th century through the American Revolution, Fort Ticonderoga was a prize in the struggle for control of the Lake Champlain region.*

Abercromby lost 1,944 men and was forced to retreat. The next year Sir Jeffrey Amherst took the fort for the British, who held it until Ethan Allen and his Green Mountain Boys, together with Colonel Benedict Arnold, took it in a surprise attack on the morning of May 10, 1775. Allen demanded the fort's surrender "in the name of the Great Jehovah and the Continental Congress" or, according to a popular version, with the command: "Come out, you damned old rat."

In 1777 Burgoyne forced the Americans, under General Arthur St. Clair, to abandon the fort by dragging cannon up nearby Mount Defiance. When the news of St. Clair's retreat reached England, George III rejoiced prematurely, "I have beat them! I have beat all the Americans!" The British abandoned Fort Ticonderoga after Burgoyne's surrender at Saratoga.

The fort, restored according to early plans, encompasses a museum with a collection of weapons, paintings, and uniforms; a restored blockhouse; and barracks. Activities include drills, fife and drum corps performances, and cannon firings.

LOCATION: Two miles east of town on Route 74. HOURS: Mid-May through mid-October: 9–5 Daily. FEE: Yes. TELEPHONE: 518–585–2821.

# CROWN POINT

This strategic point dominates the narrows of Lake Champlain. French control of the point, which started when they built Fort Saint Frédéric in 1734, was a "sharp Thorne" to the British, but their attempts to oust the French were unsuccessful until Sir Jeffrey Amherst dislodged them on August 4, 1759. Amherst then built the largest British fort in the colonies; the main fortification burned in 1773.

Seth Warner and a detachment of the Green Mountain Boys took the fort from its small British garrison on May 11, 1775. The evocative ruins at the **Crown Point State Historic Site** include remains of the moat, stonework, bastions, and barracks. There is also a visitor's center with historical exhibits.

LOCATION: Bridge Road, Route 903. HOURS: May through October: 10–5 Wednesday–Saturday, 1–5 Sunday. FEE: Yes. TELEPHONE: 518–597–3666.

*Built by the French in 1734 and seized by the British in 1759, the fortification at Crown Point was taken by the Green Mountain Boys in 1775.*

# PLATTSBURGH

First settled in 1785, Plattsburgh is located on Lake Champlain at the mouth of the Saranac River on which the city's mills—at first corn and lumber, later pulp and paper—are located. The Battle of Valcour Bay, in which Benedict Arnold with a makeshift fleet stopped the British southerly advance on Lake Champlain, took place off Plattsburgh on October 11, 1776. The military—now represented by the U.S. Air Force—has been established in town ever since a base was opened on the Lake shore six months after the Battle of Plattsburgh, an important American naval victory in the War of 1812.

The Battle of Plattsburgh was fought on September 11, 1814, near Crab Island in Lake Champlain, just offshore from the city. Credit for the victory goes to the American commander, Lieutenant Thomas Macdonough, aboard the flagship *Saratoga*. After a British broadside disabled his port battery, Macdonough swung his ship around to fire from his starboard side by means of a cable running from his bow to an anchor astern. (According to legend, after a British cannonball destroyed a chicken coop aboard the *Saratoga,* a rooster flew up into the rigging and crowed for the rest of the battle. This favorable omen supposedly inspired the cocks on the weather vanes that were popular in the region.)

While Macdonough, whose fleet was guarding the entrance to Cumberland Bay, was beating the British on water, the Americans under General Alexander Macomb were dug in south of the Saranac River and holding off a vastly superior force of British veterans from Canada in the Battle of Plattsburgh. When the British lost their naval support, they retreated. The dual American victory that day hastened the end of the War of 1812. One hundred forty-three Americans and some British who died in the battle are believed to be buried on Crab Island.

Both Plattsburgh's **City Hall** (City Hall Place), a 1917 two-story classical building with a Doric portico, and the nearby **Macdonough Monument** commemorating the 1814 naval victory were designed by the New York City architect John Russell Pope, who also did the Jefferson Memorial in Washington, DC. City Hall is now the home of the **Clinton County Historical Museum** (518–561–0340), which tells the history of the area through artifacts, paintings, documents, and military items. The museum also maintains the 1871 **Valcour Island Lighthouse.** Macomb's contribution is memorialized by the **Macomb Reservation State Park** southwest of town. The restored **Kent-Delord House** (17 Cumberland Avenue, 518–561–1035) was used as headquarters by the British during the Battle of Plattsburgh. Built in 1797, it contains period furnishings and War of 1812 documents and artifacts.

# THE ADIRONDACKS

The Adirondacks were named by Ebenezer Emmons, a Williams College professor, in the mistaken belief that it was the name of "a well-known tribe of Indians who once hunted here." Actually, the word is an Iroquois term of derision meaning "bark eaters." Until Emmons, who conducted a survey of the region in 1837, discovered that Mount Marcy was more than a mile high, the then better-known Catskill Mountains were thought to be the state's highest.

The Adirondacks, including extensive foothills, encompass 11,000 square miles—almost one-fourth of the state—although the tall peaks are concentrated in 1,200 square miles of the range's east-central region. Of the 2,500 mountains in the range, forty-three are over four thousand feet tall, the two tallest being Mount

*White birches line the shore of Cascade Lake in Keene, N.Y., one of the many lakes in Adirondack Park.*

*A view of Blue Mountain Lake from a gazebo on the grounds of the Adirondack Museum. This structure is a replica of the rustic gazebos built a century ago in the Adirondack camps.*

Marcy (5,344 feet) and Algonquin Peak (5,114 feet). The region has some 2,800 lakes and ponds, including Lake Tear of the Clouds, source of the Hudson River. There are 1,200 miles of streams but only 1,100 miles of highways through the park.

The Adirondacks were the first forest preserve in the United States; in 1894 the 40 percent owned by New York State was declared "forever wild," although by this time much of the area had been scarred by lumbering. The **Adirondack Park** today consists of almost six million acres, about half of it wilderness. Vestiges of the days when the park included the elegant although rustic "camps" of millionaires can be seen at the Adirondack Museum in Blue Mountain Lake; although many of the "camps" survive, only one or two are open to the public as inns. For natural beauty Adirondack Park, which takes in Lake George and descends to the western shore of Lake Champlain, is unsurpassed. On its fringes there took place some of the fiercest fighting of this country's early days.

The few roads through the Adirondacks all eventually converge on Lake Placid, the touristic center of the park, and all afford splendid scenery. The historic attractions, however, are modest in scale and are generally on private lands.

# CONSTABLE HALL

William Constable, Jr., a merchant at home in Paris, New York, and Constableville, built this villa from 1810 to 1819. It brings a touch of sophistication to an area still sparsely settled. Notable for its double-bowed front united by a portico, the house contains original furnishings and objects belonging to seven generations of the family. William Constable, Sr., was a land speculator who, with his partner Alexander Macomb, acquired the nearly four-million-acre tract known as the Macomb Purchase from the state in 1791.

LOCATION: Route 26, Constableville. HOURS: June through mid-October: 10–4:30 Tuesday-Saturday, 1–4:30 Sunday. FEE: Yes. TELEPHONE: 315–397–2323.

# ADIRONDACK MUSEUM

Overlooking Blue Mountain Lake, the museum's 22 exhibit buildings capture some of the atmosphere of the great Adirondack camps of millionaires. There are also displays of Adirondack furniture, the often elaborate constructions of logs and bent saplings, and exhibits on logging, ice-harvesting, and transportation, including the graceful wooden Adirondack guide boat, a craft indigenous to the region. This section of the Adirondacks was developed by Dr. Thomas Clark Durant, a financier who helped organize the Union Pacific Railroad, and his son. Dr. Durant built a railroad from Saratoga to Blue Mountain Lake and with his son constructed elaborate "camps" that he sold to the likes of J. P. Morgan, Alfred G. Vanderbilt, and Collis P. Huntington.

LOCATION: Routes 28-N and 30, Blue Mountain Lake. HOURS: Memorial Day through mid-October: 9:30–5:30 Daily. FEE: Yes. TELEPHONE: 518–352–7311.

# SARANAC LAKE

Weakened by tuberculosis that had not responded to climate therapy elsewhere, Dr. Edward Livingston Trudeau, a New York physician, came to beautiful Saranac Lake, at that time a primitive camp of guides and lumbermen, in 1876. His unexpected improvement—he lived until 1915—inspired him to establish a sanatorium and research laboratory here in 1884, in hopes that other victims of the disease would also benefit from the clear mountain air. Robert

Louis Stevenson, the Scottish writer, was Trudeau's most famous patient. Stevenson lived here the winter of 1887–88, when he conceived *The Master of Ballantrae*. The **Robert Louis Stevenson Memorial Cottage** (11 Stevenson Lane, 518–891–1990) is a museum with mementoes of his life. Christopher "Christy" Mathewson, the legendary New York Giants pitcher who died in 1925, was also treated for tuberculosis here toward the end of his life.

## LAKE PLACID

This world famous resort area on Mirror Lake in the heart of the Adirondack Mountains, scene of the 1932 and 1980 Winter Olympics, was also the home of the abolitionist John Brown. Brown's son-in-law built a clapboard farmhouse for him in 1855, and he lived there off and on until his execution on December 2, 1859, for his raid on Harpers Ferry the previous October. The **John Brown Farm Historic Site** (John Brown Road, 518–523–3900) contains some original furnishings. Brown, his two sons, and ten followers who died at Harpers Ferry are buried in the nearby graveyard.

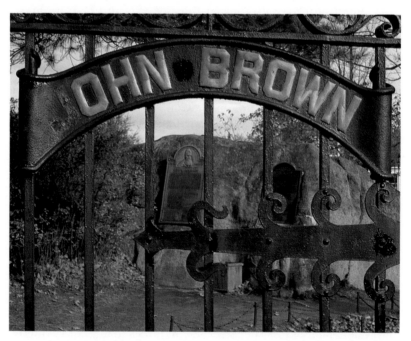

*The gate to the Lake Placid graveyard where John Brown and some of his followers are buried.*

# OGDENSBURG

In 1837 Ogdensburg was the base for American supporters of a brief, abortive effort to free Canada from England known as the Patriots' War. The noted western artist and sculptor, Frederic Remington, was born in nearby Canton in 1861 and lived as a boy at 218 Hamilton Street in Ogdensburg. The finest collection of his works, including bronzes, oils, watercolors, pen-and-ink sketches, and archival material, is housed in the **Frederic Remington Art Museum** (303 Washington Street, 315–393–2425). His Ridgefield, Connecticut studio has also been meticulously re-created in a villa, now much remodeled, that was once the residence of David Parish, one of the financiers of the War of 1812 and the Second Bank of the United States.

# T H O U S A N D      I S L A N D S

Although seventeenth-century French explorers first called them the Thousand Islands (*les milles îles*), there are actually 1,753 or so of them, ranging in size from several square feet to twenty miles square. Two-thirds of the islands scattered in the region where the

*The farm where John Brown lived before his raid on Harpers Ferry.*

St. Lawrence River and Lake Ontario join are owned by Canada. Control of the St. Lawrence River was an important objective in the colonial wars, the American Revolution, and the War of 1812. The **St. Lawrence Seaway** is a Canadian-American system of locks, dams, and canals that opened in 1959. Two important locks of the sort that made the river navigable for large vessels can be seen at Massena. **Alexandria Bay** is named for the daughter of James Leroy de Chaumont, "neighbor" of David Parish and once owner of 400,000 acres of this portion of New York. The Alexandria Township Historical Society operates the **Cornwall Store** (Market Street, 315–482–4586), an 1850s-era heritage center located on what was once the main pier catering to Alexandria Bay's waterfront trade.

## Boldt Castle

George C. Boldt, a Prussian immigrant, began his career as a hotel dishwasher and ended up owning an entire chain, including the Waldorf–Astoria in New York City and the Bellevue–Stratford in Philadelphia. His wife died before he finished building Boldt Castle on Heart Island in the St. Lawrence River as a present for her, and he never finished the job. The construction of the six-story stone extravaganza cost nearly $2.5 million.

> LOCATION: Heart Island. HOURS: Mid-May through mid-October: 10–6 Daily. FEE: Yes. TELEPHONE: 800–8-ISLAND.

## SACKETS HARBOR

Because of its strategic location at the head of Lake Ontario, Sackets Harbor was an important shipbuilding base and staging area for the invasion of Canada during the War of 1812. On July 19, 1812, an American thirty-two-pound cannon supposedly fired the first shot of the war at a British squadron attacking the harbor. When the Americans recovered a British cannonball, a sergeant loaded it into the cannon, crying, "We've caught them out now, boys, send it back!" The British soon withdrew after a short bombardment that did no serious damage.

The battle of Sackets Harbor on May 29, 1813, lasted from dawn to late afternoon. When the British troops landed, the New York militia fled, but they were rallied by General Jacob Brown. Together with the regulars, they drove the British back to their ships. Losses were about equal on both sides. This is the battle that is commemorated at the **Sackets Harbor Battlefield State Historic Site** (West Washington Street, 315–646–3634), where there is a visitor center with five rooms of interpretive exhibits in the restored 1817 Union Hotel, as well as the restored naval yard.

# WATERTOWN

Founded in 1800 by five New Englanders who built the first of the town's many mills, Watertown is divided by the Black River. Frank W. Woolworth was a clerk in a general store in 1878 when he set out a table at a country fair with a sign, "Any Article 5¢." The quick sellout inspired him to open his first five-and-ten store in Utica.

The 1876 high-Victorian mansion that is the headquarters of the **Jefferson County Historical Society** (228 Washington Street, 315–782–3491) was custom-built by local businessman Edwin Paddock with attention to architectural detail. Along with the period rooms and Victorian gardens, the house has a display of water turbines of the sort used in town to harness the Black River for industry. The **Roswell P. Flower Memorial Library** (229 Washington Street, 315–788–2359) was given in memory of the governor of New York at the end of the nineteenth century and contains a doll collection and murals of local history. John Foster Dulles, secretary of state under President Eisenhower, lived at the Presbyterian parsonage at 162 Clinton Street as a boy and later said, "I will always look upon Watertown as my real home."

# OSWEGO

In 1756 the Marquis de Montcalm captured and destroyed three British forts near the mouth of the Oswego River that had contested the French and Huron control of the western fur-trading routes. In 1759 the British rebuilt one of them—Fort Ontario—and in 1766 the Ottawa chieftain, Pontiac, signed a peace treaty with Great Britain at the fort.

During the War of 1812, a fleet of small boats left Oswego bound for Sackets Harbor with guns and supplies. The Americans were forced ashore by British men-of-war at Sandy Creek, where they drove off a British landing party. From there, the cargo, including a four-ton cable that needed a hundred soldiers to carry it, was transported by land to Sackets Harbor.

Midshipman James Fenimore Cooper was stationed in Oswego in 1808–9; his novel *The Pathfinder* is set in the Oswego Valley. The physician and feminist Mary Edward Walker was born there in 1832. Today the **Fort Ontario State Historic Site** (East 7th Street, 315–343–4711) is open to the public and includes a museum of military items and hosts military drills in summer. The pentagonal fort, the third on this site, was built in 1839 to cool the ardor of the would-be Patriots of the abortive Patriot's War of 1837–38, who wanted to free Canada from Britain. Action by both the American and Canadian governments effectively quelled the undisciplined alliance of farmers, adventurers, and unemployed artisans, who lived along the Canadian border from Vermont to Michigan. From 1944 to 1946 the fort was the only emergency refugee shelter in North America for victims of the Nazi Holocaust.

Local history, including exhibits relating to shipping on Lake Ontario, is on display at the Oswego County Historical Society, located in the **Richardson-Bates House** (135 East Third Street, 315–343–1342). Built for Maxwell Richardson, attorney, real-estate and insurance broker, and two-term mayor of Oswego, the building was done in two stages between 1867 and 1890 in a style now known as Italian Villa. Period rooms arranged according to photographs taken in the house around 1890 display the society's collection of furnishings.

# F  I  N  G  E  R    L  A  K  E  S

The eleven lakes were scooped out by glaciers in prehistoric times or, as the Indians believed, the Great Spirit placed his hand on the region, creating the reaches of silver water. Lake Cayuga, the longest, stretches for forty miles. Lake Seneca is the deepest at 630 feet. Before white settlers came, the Finger Lakes region, which reaches from the shores of Lake Ontario south to the Pennsylvania border, was the abundant hunting and fishing ground of the Five Nations of the Iroquois. Indian control of the region was weakened during the Revolution by the punitive Sullivan-Clinton campaign of 1779, and after the war the Indians were induced to relinquish their land to the government, which, in turn, set much of it aside for veterans of the Revolution. Settlement and land speculation intensified with the opening of the Erie Canal in 1825.

The region attracted and produced a remarkable collection of Americans of every stripe—industrialists, dreamers, reformers, inventors, writers, visionaries, and politicians. Such important movements as abolitionism and feminism, the Mormon church, and the Republican party had their start in the area. Today the Finger

Lakes remain a lovely, historically rich region of vineyards, hills, idyllic lake towns, and waterways. Although the sights can be seen in any order—and any random route would traverse scenery of great beauty—the tour outlined below starts in the area's major city, Rochester, and proceeds south, tracing a zigzag route through the lakes.

# ROCHESTER

This prosperous, business- and culture-oriented city was named after Colonel Nathaniel Rochester of Maryland, who purchased the tract on the Genesee River in 1803. After the Erie Canal came through in 1823, so many flour mills were built along the river to process farmers' wheat that Rochester became known as the Flour City. (When the nursery business began to flourish in the 1840s, the city was then called the Flower City.) The Vacuum Oil Company, which would become Mobil, was founded in Rochester in 1866. But today the city is best known for George Eastman's Kodak camera. While working as a bank clerk in 1880, Eastman began making photographic dry plates. In 1888 he marketed the first Kodak and the next year developed flexible film for Edison's motion-picture camera. Eastman's philanthropy sustained the city's cultural institutions, including the Eastman School of Music and the University of Rochester.

## *The George Eastman House*

George Eastman (1854–1932), who put photography within reach of the masses, built this ivy-covered forty-nine-room Georgian mansion in 1905. It was designed from photographs he had taken of other houses. Eastman left the house to the University of Rochester, and it has been expanded to include the **International Museum of Photography.** The museum's massive collection includes some 600,000 prints and negatives, 15,000 films, 3 million movie stills, 11,000 cameras, and a large research library. Interactive exhibitions and a theater interpret the history of more than 130 years of photography.

LOCATION: 900 East Avenue. HOURS: 10–4:30 Tuesday–Saturday, 1–4:30 Sunday. FEE: Yes. TELEPHONE: 716–271–3361.

The Eastman House is located in the **East Avenue Historic District,** where the city's manufacturers and businessmen built their

*The 49-room house that George Eastman built in 1905 is now the International Museum of Photography.*

new homes after the Civil War in styles—Greek Revival, Roman-esque, Gothic Revival—popular in the period. The Rochester His-torical Society has its headquarters in **Woodside** (485 East Avenue, 716–271–2705), an 1839 Greek Revival house that was owned by several important Rochester families.

## The Strong Museum

The only child of wealthy parents, Margaret Woodbury Strong grew up to become one of the most single-minded collectors ever, sometimes acquiring items by the freight-car load. When she died she endowed a museum on the condition that her collection be displayed. After years spent sorting and winnowing the collection down to some three hundred thousand items, the museum of nineteenth- and early twentieth-century Americana—decorative arts, toys, dolls, dollhouses, furniture, and kitchen utensils—opened in 1982 and has become a primary intellectual center for the study and display of nineteenth-century history. The collection includes the greatest single collection of works by the painter and architect Harvey Ellis.

LOCATION: One Manhattan Square. HOURS: 10–5 Monday–Satur-day, 1–5 Sunday. FEE: Yes. TELEPHONE: 716–263–2700.

Next to Eastman, Susan B. Anthony (1820–1906) is Rochester's best-remembered citizen. She lived in the two-story brick house at 17 Madison Street, now the **Susan B. Anthony Memorial** (716–235–6124), for the last forty years of her life. As a reformer, she was involved in many causes, especially women's suffrage, the abolition of slavery, and temperance. The house contains original furnishings, photos, and documents relating to her work. Frederick Douglass, the escaped slave who became an abolitionist orator and publisher, also lived in Rochester until his house was burned down—he suspected arson—in 1872. Governor Theodore Roosevelt dedicated a monument to him in 1899.

Jennie Jerome, Winston Churchill's mother, lived in a house, no longer standing, in what is now the **Third Ward Historic District,** or **Cornhill,** the city's most exclusive area in the mid-nineteenth century. Of the many fine residences that remain, the **Campbell-Whittlesey House** (123 Fitzhugh Street, 716–546–7034) has been restored with magnificent interiors in the Greek Revival style.

# PALMYRA

In 1820, fourteen-year-old farm boy Joseph Smith had a vision while praying in the woods that led to the founding ten years later, on April 6, 1830, of the Church of Jesus Christ of Latter-day Saints, better known as the Mormon church. On **Hill Cumorah** Joseph Smith received from a heavenly messenger, the angel Moroni, golden plates on which the *Book of Mormon* was engraved. Using special instruments, Smith translated the book, which is the story of the predecessors of the Indians and Polynesians in North America who migrated from the Middle East, according to Mormon belief. There is a **monument** to the angel on the hill. The restored **Joseph Smith Home** (Stafford Road), where he lived as a boy, is a few miles away. Nearby is the **Sacred Grove** where he had his first vision. Each site has a visitor center, and the main **Bureau of Information** is located at Hill Cumorah.

The **Martin Harris Farm,** a mile and a half north, was home of a witness to the golden plates. The first edition of the *Book of Mormon* was printed, beginning in June 1829, at the **E. B. Grandin Print Shop** on Main Street, Palmyra. In addition to the town's sites related to the early Mormons, there are the three museums of Historic Palmyra, Inc. (315–597–4794): the **Alling Coverlet**

*A view of Sonnenberg Gardens with the mansion built by Frederick Ferris Thompson in the background.*

**Museum** (122 William Street), which displays the largest collection of nineteenth-century coverlets in the United States; the 1826 **William Phelps Store Museum** (140 Market Street), which remained under Phelps family ownership from 1868 to 1976; and the **Palmyra Historical Museum** (132 Market Street), which exhibits local artifacts.

LOCATION: Hill Cumorah, four miles south of Palmyra on Route 21. HOURS: 9–7 Daily. FEE: None. TELEPHONE: 315–597–5851.

## CANANDAIGUA

The first land-sales office in America was set up in Canandaigua in 1789 on territory that New York purchased from Massachusetts. The **Granger Homestead and Carriage Museum** (295 North Main Street, 716–394–1472) was built in 1816 by Gideon Granger, postmaster general under presidents Jefferson and Madison. Its design was influenced (or possibly produced) by Joseph-Jacques Ramée. The house displays nineteenth-century decorative arts. The fifty-acre **Sonnenberg Gardens** (151 Charlotte Street, 716–394–2192), on the estate of Frederick Ferris Thompson were landscaped by Ernest Bowditch between 1900 and 1907. Nine gardens, including a colonial flower garden, and restored rooms in the mansion are open to the public.

# GENEVA

This pleasant location at the foot of Seneca Lake was once the site of an Indian village burned by the Sullivan-Clinton campaigners in 1779. The town was established shortly after the Revolution. In Victorian times it attracted so many retired ministers and spinsters that it was known as "The Saints' Retreat and Old Maids' Paradise." **Hobart College** (Routes 5 and 20, 315–789–5500) was founded in 1822. The college **chapel** was designed by Richard Upjohn in 1860; Upjohn, the leading practitioner of the Gothic Revival style, also designed Trinity Church in New York City. Elizabeth Blackwell, the country's first woman physician, graduated from Geneva Medical College in 1849.

There are many historic homes in the **South Main Street Historic District,** built between the end of the eighteenth century and the beginning of the twentieth. The 1829 **Prouty-Chew House** (543 South Main, 315–789–5151) is a brick, federal-style residence

*Trompe l'oeil walls inside Rose Hill, a magnificent Greek Revival estate on Lake Seneca.*

that has been restored with furnishings from other Geneva homes of the same period. It also houses the **Geneva Historical Society Museum.**

Beautifully sited on Seneca Lake three miles east of town is one of the greatest Greek Revival homes in the nation, **Rose Hill** (Route 96-A, 315–789–3848). The restoration is decorated in the Empire style, with paint colors, wallpaper, and textiles appropriate to the tastes of General William K. Strong, who built the house in 1839, and Robert Swan, a pioneer in agricultural research who purchased it in 1850.

# WATERLOO

Joseph Smith and five followers organized the Church of Jesus Christ of Latter-day Saints on the **Peter Whitmer Farm** (south of town off Route 96, 315–539–2552) on April 6, 1830. Smith also directed missionary work from this log farmhouse, which the Mormon church has reconstructed. There is also an 1830s chapel on the site, as well as a visitor center with exhibits relating to the early history of the church.

# SENECA FALLS

On July 19 and 20, 1848, the modern women's rights movement was born at the Seneca Falls Convention, which was called by Lucretia Mott and Elizabeth Cady Stanton. At the gathering Stanton read a *Declaration of Sentiments,* an outline of the grievances that formed the basis of the women's suffrage movement. Seneca Falls was also the home of Amelia Jenks Bloomer, a feminist pioneer who gave her name to the garment.

The **Women's Rights National Historic Park** (136 Fall Street, 315–568–2991) has exhibits on the history of the women's movement and on the lives of its founders. A facsimile of the *Declaration of Sentiments* is also on display. The park provides a slide presentation and information on the homes it is restoring, such as the **Elizabeth Cady Stanton House** (32 Washington Street), which is open to the public.

The **National Women's Hall of Fame** (76 Fall Street, 315–568–8060) honors famous American women in art, athletics, business, education, government, humanities, philanthropy, and science, and serves as an education and information center for women's issues. The **Seneca Falls Historical Society Museum** (55

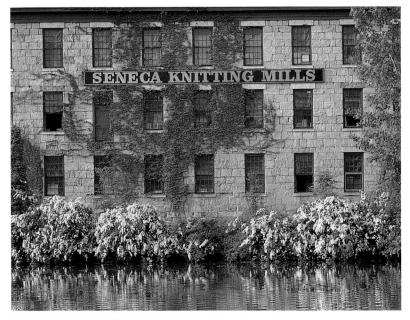

*Seneca Knitting Mills, a reminder of an industry that once flourished in the region.*

Cayuga Street, 315–568–8412) contains Victorian period rooms, local history exhibits, a library, and archives, including material on the area's role in the women's movement.

# AUBURN

A founder of the Republican party and Lincoln's secretary of state, William H. Seward settled in Auburn in 1824 and turned the town on the northern end of Lake Owasco into a center of political activity. The 1817 brick two-and-a-half story **Seward House** (33 South Street, 315–252–1283) contains original furniture and memorabilia of his career, including documents on the 1867 purchase of Alaska, disparagingly called "Seward's Folly" by the opposition. In 1857, when he was United States senator, Seward sold Harriet Tubman the white clapboard house on twenty-six acres at 180 South Street. Tubman, an escaped slave herself, helped at least three hundred slaves escape to Canada and, before she died, gave the house as a home for indigent elderly blacks. The **Harriet Tubman Home** (315–252–2081) now displays her furnishings and other items, among them a huge Bible.

# ITHACA

In addition to being a famous college town, Ithaca, which was settled by veterans after the Revolution, is an attractive city in its own right. The **De Witt Park Historic District,** bounded roughly by East Buffalo, East Court, North Cayuga, and North Tioga streets, includes private residences; a park named after Simeon De Witt, the New York State surveyor-general from 1784 to 1834; and the 1867 **Boardman House** (120 East Buffalo Street), a two-and-a-half-story brick home with a hip roof and central cupola, now converted to offices. Beginning in 1914 Ithaca was, briefly, a movie-making center; the *Exploits of Elaine,* with Lionel Barrymore and Pearl White, was one of the films made here.

## *Cornell University*

Cornell University was chartered in 1865 as an institution, in the words of founders Ezra Cornell and Andrew Dickson White, "where any person can find instruction in any study." This included what were then called the "useful arts" as well as the classics. The university was innovative for its time in that it was coeducational and nonsectarian.

The cofounders, both state legislators, sponsored a bill that gave the university the land that the state had received for agriculture and mechanical arts from the Morrill Act of 1862. The four-story stone building, **Morrill Hall** (1866–68), the second oldest on campus, honors Justin Morrill of Vermont, the author of the bill. Cornell, who made a fortune when his telegraph companies were incorporated within Western Union, guided the university's growth and was chairman of the board of trustees until he died in 1874. White, a historian, was the university's first president. The **Andrew Dickson White House** was built by him in 1871 on the university's original faculty row. The campus is beautifully located on East Hill overlooking Lake Cayuga.

# ELMIRA

After the Erie Railroad reached Elmira in 1849, and a canal connecting Chemung Canal in Elmira with the north branch of the Susquehanna River was completed in 1854, the city grew rapidly as a wool-, lumber-, and iron-producing center. According to legend,

OPPOSITE: *The Uris Library at Cornell University overlooking Lake Cayuga.*

the city was named in 1808 after Elmira Teall, the daughter of an early settler. The girl's mother used to summon her in an unusually shrill voice that could be heard all over town, so when it came time to pick a new name for the settlement, originally called Newtown, Elmira seemed a natural choice.

In 1870 Samuel Langhorne Clemens married Olivia Langdon of Elmira; under his pen name, Mark Twain, he wrote most of *The Adventures of Tom Sawyer* and other books while summering at Quarry Farm, the Langdon summer home, which he did from 1874 to 1903. The **Mark Twain Study,** now at Elmira College (607–735–1941), is in the shape of an octagon. It was originally located in the Langdon's orchard, where, Twain wrote, "it sits perched in complete isolation on the very top of an elevation that commands leagues of valley and city and retreating ranges of distant blue hills."

There are also Mark Twain items among the exhibits at the **Chemung County Historical Society** (415 East Water Street, 607–734–4167). The author is buried with his wife and children in the Langdon family plot in **Woodlawn Cemetery** (Walnut Street), as is his son-in-law, Ossip Gabrilowitsch, the well-known musician who married Clara Clemens in 1909. The cemetery is adjacent to the **Woodlawn National Cemetery,** where nearly three thousand Confederate prisoners are buried. They were brought to the overcrowded and unsanitary prison camp in Elmira in 1864 and 1865. The Italianate **Chemung County Courthouse,** an 1861 two-story brick building with a three-story corner tower, is the center of a complex of landmark municipal buildings (210–228 Lake Street) built in the same style.

Elmira is also a popular gliding center. The history of the sport is depicted in exhibits at the **National Soaring Museum** (Harris Hill Soaring Site, 607–734–3128).

Six miles southeast of Elmira, the **Newtown Battlefield Reservation** is the site of the only pitched battle of the Sullivan-Clinton campaign of 1779. Here General John Sullivan defeated a band of Indians and Tories on August 29, 1779. The Sullivan-Clinton campaign was ordered by General Washington to deter further Indian and Tory attacks on frontier settlements, such as the "Wyoming Massacre" in Pennsylvania's Wyoming Valley in July 1778. On June 18, 1779, Sullivan left Easton, Pennsylvania, with 2,500 men and proceeded through Wyoming to Tioga, New York, where he was joined by General James Clinton, who had been moving westward along the Mohawk Valley with 1,500 men. The combined force moved on to Elmira, where the Battle of Newtown occurred. The army then proceeded toward Niagara, into the territory of the Seneca and Cayuga, burning villages and crops.

# CORNING

Erastus Corning of Albany purchased land here in 1833 with the idea of building a railroad to transport anthracite from Pennsylvania to the just-completed Chemung Canal. More important to the town's future, however, was the decision of the Flint Glass Company of Brooklyn to move to Corning. It sold two-fifths of its stock to local residents and became the Corning Glass Works in 1875.

The restored **Benjamin Patterson Inn** (59 West Pulteney Street, 607–962–5281) was built in 1796 "to encourage settlement in the Genesee Country." Its period rooms include a ladies' parlor, kitchen, and ballroom. A ca. 1800 log cabin and an 1878 one-room schoolhouse are also on the grounds. The **Rockwell Museum** (Cedar Street at Denison Parkway, 607–937–5386), located in Corning's restored 1893 city hall, displays an extensive collection of American western paintings and bronzes, Indian artifacts, Steuben glass, and turn-of-the-century toys.

## *Corning Glass Center*

There are three touring areas in the Glass Center complex: The modern **Corning Museum of Glass** displays the world's most comprehensive glass collection in attractively designed general galleries and special study collections; the **Hall of Science and Industry** demonstrates the technology of fiber optics and the many uses of glass; and Corning's famous art glass can be seen in the making at the **Steuben Glass Factory.**

LOCATION: On Centerway. HOURS: 9–5 Daily. FEE: Yes. TELEPHONE: 607–974–2000.

# HAMMONDSPORT

This town on the southern tip of Keuka Lake is in the center of the winegrowing region, and several of the large local vineyards offer tours of their wineries. The town was the birthplace of Glenn Hammond Curtiss, the inventive aviation pioneer. On June 4, 1908, Curtiss flew "a practical aerodrome driven by its own motive power and carrying a man" a distance of two thousand yards on nearby Stony Brook Farm. The **Glenn H. Curtiss Museum of Local History** (south on Route 54, 607–569–2160) tells the story of Curtiss's many contributions to early aviation and has exhibits on the history of the region.

# SYRACUSE

Pioneers Comfort Tyler and Asa Danforth first extracted salt from naturally occurring brine springs near the head of Onondaga Lake in 1788, thereby starting an industry that would thrive for almost one hundred years. Manufacturing also had an early start; in 1793 Thomas Wiard began making wooden plows, a business that would soon be a success, and the city prospered after the Erie Canal arrived in the 1820s.

In 1851 a famous incident in the history of abolition—the Jerry Rescue—occurred in Syracuse when a band of abolitionists forcibly freed an escaped slave from jail and smuggled him to Canada. Jerry had been free for over thirty years when his former master tried to reclaim him.

*A reconstruction of a Jesuit mission, Sainte Marie de Gannentaha, is located in Liverpool, a suburb of Syracuse.*

*Syracuse's Clinton Square, named for the New York governor who built the Erie Canal. The city prospered after the canal opened.*

There were other milestones in the city's history: Horace Greeley and Thurlow Weed met in Syracuse in 1854 to discuss forming the Republican party. In 1869 Charles Dickens came to town and described Syracuse as "a most wonderful out-of-the-world place, which looks as if it had begun to be built yesterday, and were going to be imperfectly knocked together with a nail or two the day after tomorrow. I am in the worst inn that was ever seen. . . ."

In the Syracuse of today, canal history is on display in the **Erie Canal Museum** (318 Erie Boulevard East, 315–471–0593). The museum is located in the 1850 **Weighlock Building,** the only structure of its kind, where canalboats were once weighed. Another aspect of the city's early history is covered by a reconstructed boiling salt block, and exhibits on local geology and history are on display at the **Salt Museum** in Onondaga Lake Park in the suburb of Liverpool (315–453–6767). **Sainte Marie among the Iroquois,** a recreation of a French Jesuit mission built in 1656 and abandoned two years later, is also in the park. The Onondaga Historical Association's **Museum and Research Center** (311 and 321 Montgomery Street, 315–428–1864) interprets the region's history through thematic exhibits drawn from their collection of over one million items relating to central New York state.

The **Everson Museum of Art** (401 Harrison Street, 315–474–6064) has a collection of American paintings and the most comprehensive collection of American ceramics in the country. **Syracuse University** (315–423–1870), founded in 1870 with forty-one students, today is a major private institution with approximately 15,000 men and women enrolled. The university's **Crouse College,** a three-and-a-half story sandstone building designed by Archimedes Russell, was completed in 1884 as a fine arts center, one of the first at a university in the country.

# W E S T E R N    N E W    Y O R K

The Marquis de Lafayette, visiting Niagara County in 1825, remarked that it offered "the greatest natural and artificial wonders, second only to the wonders of freedom and equal rights." A tour of the territory would logically start in Niagara Falls—with a side trip to Youngstown and a visit to the much fought-over fortification at Old Fort Niagara State Park—and then proceed south through Buffalo to Allegany and Chautauqua country. Here, vineyards and orchards cover the Erie Plain; Dunkirk calls itself the "Concord Grape Capital of the World." In contrast to these bucolic attractions, oil pumps can still be seen along Route 17 between Wellsville and Olean. The first well in Wellsville, Triangle No. 1, began producing in 1879.

## NIAGARA FALLS

"The Universe does not afford its Parallel," wrote Father Louis Hennepin in 1678. A missionary with LaSalle, he was the first European to see and describe the Falls at length. "The Waters which fall from this horrible Precipice do foam and boyl after the most hideous manner imaginable." Father Hennepin guessed that the Falls were six hundred feet high. They are actually only 176 feet tall, but **American** and **Luna falls** on the United States side and **Horseshoe Falls** on the Canadian side extend for 3,600 feet and afford one of the most spectacular sights in the world. More than ten million visitors come to gaze at the expanse of cataracts each year.

Control of the fourteen-mile portage around the east side of the Falls was an important prize in the struggle between the French

OPPOSITE: *The immense power of Niagara Falls.*

and the British in the region during colonial times. The French built three forts to back up Fort Niagara at the mouth of the Niagara River in 1669, 1687, and 1726. The last, still standing, was captured by the British on July 25, 1759. The British received full rights to the "Carrying Place of Niagara," as the portage was called, by a treaty with the Seneca Indians in 1764.

During the War of 1812, the British burned the manufacturing community that Augustus Porter had established at the Falls about 1806 to exploit the water power. A canal between the upper and lower rivers was completed in the 1850s, and the first basic electric generator began operating in 1881. Eventually an extensive industrial complex grew up around the Falls, attracting large numbers of laborers. Today the Niagara Project is one of the largest hydroelectric developments in the western world. The hydroelectric operation is explained by exhibits at the **Niagara Power Project Visitor Center** (716–285–3211), four-and-a-half miles north of the Falls on Route 104. The center also has a **mural** by Thomas Hart Benton showing Father Hennepin viewing the falls.

Niagara Falls presents a natural challenge to the thrill-seeker and daredevil. In 1859 a Frenchman known as "the Great Blondin" became the first to cross the Niagara gorge on a tightrope; once he made a trip carrying his manager on his back. In 1901 a schoolteacher named Annie Edson Taylor was the first woman to go over the Falls in a barrel—she lived. The Falls got its start as a spot for honeymooners when Jerome Bonaparte, Napoleon's nephew, visited with his bride in 1803.

The traditions, art, and history of the Indians of the region have been preserved in the **Native American Center for the Living Arts** (25 Rainbow Boulevard, 716–284–2427), a structure overlooking the Falls known as "the Turtle" for its shape. In Iroquois mythology, the earth was created on a turtle's back.

## Niagara Reservation State Park

Frederick Law Olmsted was a main advocate of the idea of turning the Falls into a park, and after many setbacks, Governor Grover Cleveland signed the bill creating the reservation, the first state park in the country.

The park includes the 282-foot **Prospect Point Observation Tower,** which rises one hundred feet above the cliffs. The excursion boat *Maid of the Mist,* which passes directly in front of the Falls, leaves from a dock on Prospect Point. **Goat Island,** separating the

American from the Canadian falls, has drives and walks with excellent views. **Cave of the Winds,** behind American Falls, is reached by elevator from Goat Island; visitors protected by rain gear follow walkways through the Falls' mist.

A **Viewmobile** travels around the entire reservation by six scenic vistas. The **Schoellkopf Geological Museum** (716–278–1780) tells the story of 12,000 years of natural history and reviews the technological aspects of Niagara Falls through exhibits and audiovisual presentations.

LOCATION: End of Robert Moses Parkway. HOURS: Open Daily, call for specific times. FEE: None. TELEPHONE: 716–278–1796.

## FORT NIAGARA STATE PARK

Located at the mouth of the Niagara River, the 504-acre state park includes **Old Fort Niagara,** a strategically important fortification from the time it was first built by LaSalle in 1679 through the War of 1812. The main structure, the Castle, survives today. It was built by the French in 1725–26 to look like a manor house to fool the Indians.

Sir William Johnson captured the fort for England in 1759. Local tradition says that during the Revolution the British paid the Indians allied with them eight dollars for every American scalp they brought in (it is unrecorded how much was paid to the allies of the independence forces for British scalps). The Americans, who took over the fort after the Revolution, lost it to the British during the War of 1812 but got it back in 1815 after the Treaty of Ghent was signed.

The fort was restored between 1927 and 1934 and includes ramparts, a parade ground, the Castle, a moat, a drawbridge, blockhouses, and a museum displaying equipment and uniforms.

LOCATION: North of Youngstown on Route 18. HOURS: 9–dusk Daily. FEE: Yes. TELEPHONE: 716–745–7611.

## BUFFALO

When Joseph Ellicott of the Holland Land Company laid out Buffalo, he called it New Amsterdam in deference to his employers. However, the name taken from nearby Buffalo Creek was the one that stuck. Ellicott based his plans on those for Washington, DC on which his brother, Andrew, worked as a surveyor for Major

Pierre Charles L'Enfant. The town was burned by the British during the War of 1812 but quickly rebuilt. The first steamboat on the Great Lakes, *Walk-on-the-Water,* was launched here in 1816. The opening of the Erie Canal in 1825 brought growth and prosperity; as the canal's western terminus, Buffalo became the center through which east-west trade and immigration flowed.

Buffalo also became a major manufacturing city; in 1829 John Hibbard began building steam engines here, and Joseph Dart invented a steam-powered grain elevator here in 1843. As the canal lost importance, the city became a railroad center, and the Civil War, which cut off more southerly routes to the West, increased the city's commercial importance. Grover Cleveland first received national attention as Buffalo's mayor in 1881.

A major event contributing to the city's growth and the spread of its name was the Pan-American Exposition of 1901, designed to show a century of progress in the hemisphere. The only surviving building is the Parthenon-like **New York State Pavilion** (25 Nottingham Court, 716–873–9644), which now houses the **Buffalo and Erie County Historical Society** and its extensive display of artifacts from the Niagara frontier. President William McKinley was shot by the anarchist Leon F. Czolgosz after delivering the speech opening the exposition on September 6 in the Temple of Music. The president is memorialized by the 1907 **McKinley Monument,** with its crouching lions, in Niagara Square. The monument was designed by the New York City architects Carrère & Hastings and sculpted by A. Phimister Proctor.

## Theodore Roosevelt Inaugural

For a while after President McKinley was shot on September 6, it looked as if he would recover; Vice President Theodore Roosevelt, who had been summoned to Buffalo with the cabinet, therefore left town, only to be called back when the president took a turn for the worse. After McKinley died, on September 14, Roosevelt took the oath of office at the home of a friend, Ansley Wilcox. Roosevelt rose to the occasion as if he had anticipated it all along: "Here is the task, and I have got to do it to the best of my ability and that is all there is about it."

Built about 1838, the brick Wilcox mansion was originally part of an Army post. Wilcox enlarged it when he purchased the house in the late 1880s, and the mansion stayed in the family until the

1930s. In the 1960s preservationists fought successfully to save it. It is now a National Historic Site, administered by the National Park Service. Exhibits highlight the events of nine dramatic days in Buffalo in September 1901.

LOCATION: 641 Delaware Avenue. HOURS: 9–5 Monday–Friday, 12–5 Saturday–Sunday. FEE: Yes. TELEPHONE: 716–884–0095.

Although Buffalo was built in a hurry—"everything has an air of great pretensions," Frances Trollope wrote in 1828—today the city is noted for its architecture. The thirteen-story, steel-framed **Guaranty Building,** which opened on the corner of Church and Pearl streets on March 1, 1896, was designed by the partners Louis Sullivan and Dankmar Adler and illustrated to near-perfection Sullivan's conception of a skyscraper as a "proud and soaring thing." The Guaranty was the last building Sullivan built with Adler before their partnership was dissolved. Across the street is **St. Paul's Episcopal Cathedral,** a Gothic Revival sandstone edifice designed by the prominent architect Richard Upjohn.

Nine of the buildings Henry Hobson Richardson designed for the **Buffalo State Hospital** (now the Buffalo Psychiatric Center, 400 Forest Avenue) have survived since the complex was opened in 1880. (Frederick Law Olmsted designed the grounds.) Both Sullivan and Frank Lloyd Wright, who is also well represented in Buffalo, admired and were influenced by Richardson. Wright's Prairie-style 1904 **Darwin Martin House** (125 Jewett Parkway, 716–831–2406) is a particularly fine example of Wright's philosophy of "organic architecture" that is designed to adapt to specific environments, materials, and conditions. The floor plan of the house has been restored and many of the original furnishings are in place. Two other houses (private) that were part of the Martin complex are the brick **Barton House** (118 Summit Avenue) and the stuccoed frame **Gardener's Cottage** (285 Woodward Avenue). The **Davidson House** (57 Tillinghast Place) and the **Heath House** (76 Soldier's Place), both private, were also designed by Wright.

The **Albright-Knox Art Gallery** (1285 Elmwood Avenue, 716–882–8700) is housed in a 1905 Greek Revival building that has side porches adorned with caryatids by Augustus Saint-Gaudens. The gallery's collection, which includes cycladic sculpture dating back to 3000 B.C., has notable nineteenth- and twentieth-century American paintings, among them works by Gilbert Stuart, George

Bellows, George Inness, Jackson Pollock, Clyfford Still, Frank Stella, and watercolorist Charles E. Burchfield. Burchfield moved to Buffalo in 1921 to become head designer in a wallpaper factory. He left the company in 1929 to devote himself full-time to his art, but he made extensive use of western New York's industrial areas, docks, and bridges as subject matter. The **Burchfield-Penney Art Center** (716–878–6011) at Buffalo State College has the largest public collection of his works and items related to his life.

## EAST AURORA

After he met with William Morris, leader of the Arts and Crafts movement in England, in 1894, Elbert Hubbard set up an artistic community in East Aurora dedicated to Morris's principle, "not how cheap, but how good." He called the community Roycroft from the old French, meaning "craft of kings." Hubbard started with a printing press; other crafts such as furniture-making, sculpture, and bookbinding soon followed. In 1899 he published his famous "Message to Garcia," an inspirational tract for businessmen that has sold millions of copies over the years. At one time, the campus, as the complex was called, employed over one thousand craftspeople in nine buildings. The **Roycroft Campus,** a complex of buildings with crenelated towers and stone and shingled exteriors, includes the **Roycroft Inn.** The Roycroft crafts program has undergone a modest revival in recent years. Examples of Roycroft crafts are on display at the **Elbert Hubbard Museum** (363 Oakwood Avenue, 716–652–4735).

Millard Fillmore, who became president on the death of Zachary Taylor in 1850, built the small frame cottage at 24 Shearer Avenue for his wife in 1825. It now houses the **Millard Fillmore Museum** (716–652–4228) and includes a replica of Fillmore's law office and a period rose and herb garden. The museum is run by the Aurora Historical Society and has undertaken the arduous task of refurbishing the reputation of one of the country's least-known chief executives, a northern man of southern sentiments.

## BATAVIA

In a transaction called the Holland Land Purchase, Robert Morris sold 3.3 million acres—practically all of New York state west of the

OPPOSITE: A Glimpse of Notre Dame in the Late Afternoon, *(1902), by Henri Matisse, one of many notable paintings in the Albright-Knox Art Gallery.*

Genesee River—to a group of Dutch capitalists in 1793. In 1801 the company agent, Joseph Ellicott, opened an office in Batavia that did so well that it gave rise to the expression, "doing a land office business." In 1815 Ellicott built the graceful building that today houses the **Holland Land Office Museum** (131 West Main Street, 716–343–4727) and its collection of early Genesee County artifacts. Ellicott also surveyed the territory and founded many towns, including Buffalo. He remained particularly attached to Batavia, however, once saying, "I intend to do all I can for Batavia, because the Almighty will look out for Buffalo."

## CHAUTAUQUA

The Chautauqua Institution was founded in 1874 as a training camp for Methodist Sunday school teachers at a camp meeting ground on Lake Chautauqua and quickly grew into an extensive

*The 1886 Old Pier Building at Chautauqua, where steamboats once docked hourly.*

ecumenical system of adult education and home study. In its first period of popularity, as many as 25,000 people a year took courses in such diverse and secular fields as language, arts and crafts, and mathematics. In addition, local "Chautauquas" appeared in hundreds of communities in the next few decades, and in 1900 a traveling Chautauqua started, moving from town to town offering lectures, concerts, and recitals. William Jennings Bryan appeared frequently on the Chautauqua circuit to give repeat performances of his famous "Cross of Gold" speech.

As the movement grew, so did the lakeshore meeting ground, now designated as the **Chautauqua Institution Historic District.** Lewis Miller, an Ohio businessman who founded the institution with John Heyl Vincent, a Methodist minister, designed the 6,000-seat **Amphitheater** in 1893. Miller entertained President Ulysses S. Grant and other notables in his residence, the **Lewis Miller Cottage. Palestine Park** is a walk-through model of the Holy Land that Vincent devised to teach Bible stories. The rambling 1873 **Atheneum Hotel,** with its high ceilings, wide porches, and wicker outdoor furniture is another landmark on the 856-acre grounds.

The Chautauqua Institution (716–357–6200) was described by Theodore Roosevelt as "typical of America at its best." A very successful nine-week summer program of concerts, classes, workshops, exhibits, and other educational and spiritual pursuits amid the lovely, parklike surroundings and Victorian gingerbread buildings and cottages provides an opportunity to experience a resurgence of the wholesome living, spiritual uplift, and intellectual excitement that characterized the Chautauqua movement in its heyday.

In the area, from **Fredonia** to **Asheville** and **Jamestown,** there are many beautiful Greek Revival villages.

# SALAMANCA

Salamanca claims to be the only city in the country located on an Indian reservation, in this case the Allegany Indian Reservation. The **Seneca-Iroquois National Museum** (Broad Street, 716–945–1738) has exhibits on the history of the Seneca Nation and contemporary arts and crafts. Three major railroad lines once converged here. The **Salamanca Rail Museum** (170 Main Street, 716–945–3133), in a restored 1912 passenger depot, recalls those days.

# NEW JERSEY

OPPOSITE: *A view of Morristown National Historical Park, where Washington and his army spent two winters during the American Revolution.*

N[ew Jersey was once the bountiful land of the peaceful Lenni Lenape Indians, but after Swedish and Dutch traders arrived from Europe in the early seventeenth century, the colony was rent by confusion over land grants, conflicting claims to territory, shifting allegiances, and resistance to authority. The Swedes were soon driven out by the Dutch, who, in turn, ceded the land to the English. In 1664 the Duke of York created "Nova Caesarea," or New Jersey, after the Isle of Jersey. On July 1, 1676, some order was imposed on the colony's affairs when it was divided into East and West Jersey. The boundary was a line extending from just north of the Delaware Water Gap to Little Egg Harbor on the Atlantic coast north of Atlantic City.

The division was the doing of William Penn, who had established his first Quaker settlement in the western sector. Officially the separation lasted only six years—in 1682 Penn and his associates purchased East Jersey, too—but the boundary reflected cultural, economic, and geographic differences that still exist today.

West Jersey was settled largely by Quakers fleeing persecution. Its territory included the navigable southern end of the Delaware River and the flat, fertile coastal plain today called South Jersey. Despite the long coastline, ports never flourished as they did elsewhere. Whalers from New England settled in South Jersey ports like Cape May at the end of the seventeenth century, and Tuckertown on the Atlantic coast became an important shipbuilding town, but farming soon became the predominant way of life. To this day, the southern region, which includes coastal marshes, cranberry bogs, and wild pine barrens, is mostly agricultural.

East Jersey, by contrast, was settled by Puritans from New England and Long Island, who put their own austere stamp on life there. The rugged Kittatinny Mountains, an extension of the Appalachians that sweeps across the northwestern part of the state, contained the iron that gave New Jersey its first industry. On the north, New Jersey shares a fifty-mile land border with New York; otherwise it is an island cut off from other states by the Hudson and Delaware rivers.

In 1911, when he was governor of New Jersey, Woodrow Wilson accurately observed that "we have always been inconvenienced by New York on the one hand and Philadelphia on the other." Even in William Penn's day, the state was dominated by these cities, with East Jersey gravitating toward New York City, and West Jersey toward Philadelphia. After the Revolution, their influ-

*Detail of the* Battle of Princeton *by William Mercer.*

ence was so strong New Jersey was described as "a keg tapped at both ends."

On the other hand, New Jersey prospered as a conduit between the two growing cities, providing transportation for goods and passengers. The nation's first stagecoach service began in New Jersey in the early eighteenth century, and soon entrepreneurs in the state were busy building canals and railroads. When New Jerseyans were unable to decide which was the better form of transportation in the early nineteenth century, they built both—a canal and a railroad—along the same route. And to accommodate the automobile, New Jersey naturally created the country's first cloverleaf interchange in 1929.

Philadelphia and New York City also provided markets for New Jersey's goods and services, financing for its industry, and residents for its towns. When the George Washington Bridge was built across the Hudson in 1931, the towns of New Jersey's Bergen County changed almost overnight from rural communities to heavily populated suburbs.

Its geography turned New Jersey into a battleground during the American Revolution. The prize was control of the Hudson

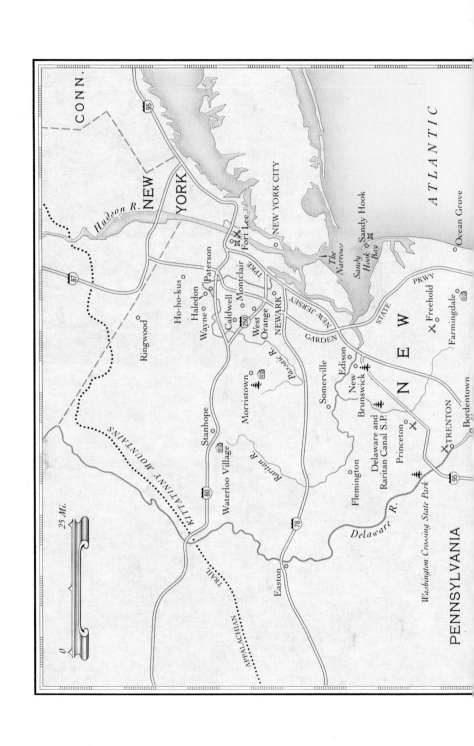

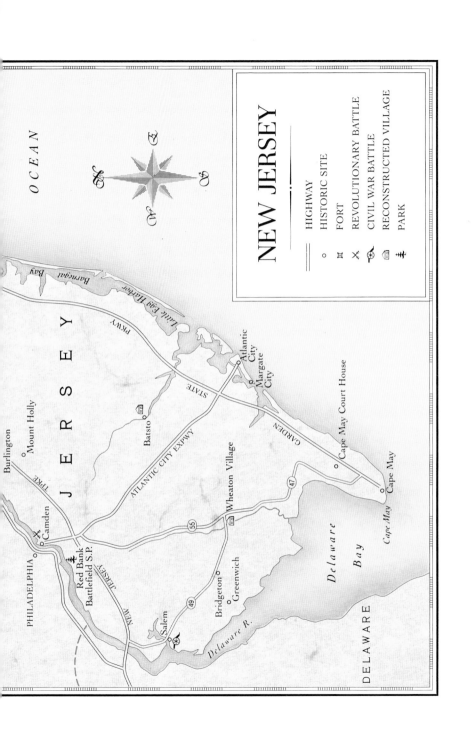

# NEW JERSEY

— — HIGHWAY
○ HISTORIC SITE
⊟ FORT
✕ REVOLUTIONARY BATTLE
⚜ CIVIL WAR BATTLE
🏚 RECONSTRUCTED VILLAGE
🎋 PARK

OCEAN

Barnegat Bay

Little Egg Harbor

PKWY

STATE

J E R S E Y

Burlington

Mount Holly

Atlantic City

Margate City

Batsto

ATLANTIC CITY EXPWY

GARDEN

Cape May Court House

TPKE

Camden

Wheaton Village

55

47

Cape May

PHILADELPHIA

Red Bank Battlefield S.P.

NEW JERSEY

49

Bridgeton

Greenwich

Salem

Delaware R.

Delaware Bay

Cape May

DELAWARE

and Delaware valleys. General George Washington spent one-quarter of his time as commander-in-chief shuttling back and forth across the state; the victories he won at Trenton, Princeton, and Monmouth were critical to the American cause. The Continental Army also spent two winters at Morristown in cold and suffering worse than any they experienced at Valley Forge.

At the Constitutional Convention of 1787, the New Jersey delegation, led by William Paterson, spoke for the smaller states when it proposed a one-chamber legislature with equal representation for each state. The so-called New Jersey Plan was defeated, but in the end, each small state did receive a vote in the U.S. Senate equal to that of each large one. On December 18, 1787, New Jersey became the third state to ratify the new Constitution.

After the war, New Jersey turned its attention to industry and transportation. In 1791, Alexander Hamilton founded Paterson, a planned industrial community on the Great Falls of the Passaic River; three years later Hamilton's Society for Establishing Useful Manufactures opened a calico factory there. Meanwhile, leather industry was developing at Newark, pottery at Trenton, and banking and insurance became established in the state. New Jersey's growth was aided by some inventive minds. The genial inventor Seth Boyden of Newark devised methods for producing both patent leather and malleable iron. By 1810 New Jersey was the third-largest iron producer in the country.

The genius of another native, John Stevens, helped make the state a leader in transportation. In 1804, Stevens's twin-propeller steamboat, *Little Juliana,* began making trips between Hoboken and New York City, and in 1825 he built the first American-made "steam waggon," which ran on a circular track around his Hoboken estate, all to prove that railroads were feasible. When Stevens's inventive son, Robert, obtained the charter for the Camden and Amboy Railroad to strengthen the link between New York City and Philadelphia, he imported an English locomotive, the John Bull, the first engine to have a cowcatcher. In 1831, with Robert Stevens at the throttle, the line opened. The line came to dominate the state's political and economic life, and New Jersey was sometimes disparagingly called "the state of the Camden and Amboy."

New Jersey found itself on both sides of the slavery issue as the Civil War approached. Slavery had existed since colonial times on the farms of southern Jersey, as it had in New York. Even today life in the area has a southern cast—if the Mason-Dixon Line were extended across New Jersey, it would cut the state practically in half. But the state supported the Union cause in the Civil War with $23 million and 80,000 troops, including the first uniformed soldiers sent to Washington, DC.

In the postwar era, New Jersey opened its doors to further development—shipbuilding in Camden, silk processing in Paterson, oil products in Bayonne. The state's lenient attitude toward incorporation encouraged trusts and monopolies to form there. Muckraker Lincoln Steffens derided the state as "The Mother of Trusts," and reformers managed to elect Woodrow Wilson governor in 1910. Wilson saw the state as "the fighting center of the most important social questions of our time," and he managed to pass laws restraining monopolies before he became president in 1913. The laws, however, were repealed and diluted soon after he left the governorship.

Although New Jersey remains in the shadow of New York City and Philadelphia, it has made important contributions to the nation's cultural life. In colonial times, it was the only colony to have two institutions of higher learning—at Princeton and New Brunswick. Early writers included the Quaker preacher John Woolman (1720–1772), the revolutionary pamphleteer, poet, and journalist Philip Freneau, and Thomas Paine, who wrote "These are the times that try men's souls" in Newark. When he went to France after the Revolution, Paine so missed his home that he wrote: "I would rather see my horse, Button, eating the grass of Bordentown, than see all the show and pomp of Europe." Walt Whitman, who died in 1892, lived the last twenty years of his life in Camden. More recently, William Carlos Williams wrote poetry and practiced medicine in Rutherford, New Jersey, until he died in 1963.

The fourth-smallest state in the Union, New Jersey is richly endowed with destinations of historic interest. Most of the state's Revolutionary War sites, including a large number of places where George Washington supposedly slept, are found in the so-called M counties—Middlesex, Mercer, Monmouth, and Morris. But historic sites are everywhere throughout its 7,468 square miles.

The one sure way *not* to find them, however, is to stay on the New Jersey Turnpike or one of the many other major highways that crisscross the state. Travelers can't see much from these roads except the industrial sprawl and overdevelopment that give so many outsiders a false impression of New Jersey. But visitors who leave the beaten track to seek out the state's rich history will surely find, as did an officer aboard Henry Hudson's *Half Moon* in 1609, "a very good land to fall with, and a pleasant land to see."

The tour of North Jersey starts with Newark and proceeds north through the metropolitan area toward the New York State border, then follows a zigzag southerly course down the Delaware to Trenton. The final leg is east across the state to the Atlantic and back in the direction of New York City.

In South Jersey, the tour starts in Camden across from Philadelphia and swings south to Cape May. It then heads north through Atlantic City and cuts northwest across the state to Bordentown on the Delaware. From there it is a fairly short but interesting jaunt back to the Camden area.

# N  O  R  T  H     J  E  R  S  E  Y

## NEWARK

Arriving from Connecticut in 1666, settlers led by Robert Treat "purchased" Newark on the Passaic River—and most of what is now Essex and Union counties—from the Indians for little more than "20 hoes, two ankers of liquor . . . and three trooper's coats." The settlement was named Newark after a town in England, and its gristmills and tanneries, and, after the Revolution, leather and shoemaking were important industries. Aaron Burr, the wily Revolutionary War soldier and vice-president under Thomas Jefferson, was born here in 1756; his father, the Reverend Aaron Burr, Sr., a Presbyterian clergyman, was president of the College of New Jersey, which eventually became Princeton University.

Early in the nineteenth century, Newark became a transportation center; the ninety-mile Morris Canal, cutting through Newark from New York Harbor to the mouth of the Lehigh River, was finished in 1832. The New Jersey Railroad and Transportation Company ran a line from Newark to Jersey City beginning in 1834. Newark's industry boomed during the Civil War; after the war, the manufacture of celluloid also became important. Prosperous Newark attracted banks and insurance companies.

In the early twentieth century Newark attracted business and wealth from New York City as well as many of its most recent

*Essex County Court House in Newark, designed in 1907 by the well-known architect Cass Gilbert.*

immigrants, including Jews from Eastern Europe and blacks from the South. Such urban problems as overcrowded housing, unemployment, and poverty followed and intensified after World War II, as Newark became increasingly overshadowed by New York City. Still, it is New Jersey's largest and most important city, retaining many sites of historic and cultural interest that are conveniently located close together in the downtown area.

The **New Jersey Historical Society** (230 Broadway, 201–483–3939) has dioramas of state history, original plans of Robert Fulton's steam engine, and the Gilbert Stuart portrait of Newark-born Aaron Burr, as well as period rooms and nine galleries of historical artifacts. The famous architect Cass Gilbert designed the monumental marble-and-brick **Essex County Court House** (470 Martin Luther King, Jr., Boulevard) in 1904–1907. Gutzon Borglum, carver of Mount Rushmore, did the bronze statue of *Abraham*

*Lincoln* in the courtyard about 1911. Borglum also created *The Wars of America,* a bronze group of forty-two soldiers from previous conflicts, located in **Military Park** (Park Place and Market Street), which was used as a drillfield in colonial times. Jacques Lipchitz's bust of *John F. Kennedy* is also in the park.

The early-eighteenth-century **Old Plume House** (407 Broad Street, 201–483–8202) is probably Newark's oldest building. During the Revolution, Ann Van Wagenen Plume locked a Hessian soldier in her icehouse before turning him over to the Americans. The knocker on the door is supposed to have been forged of metal taken from the soldier's hat. The house is now the rectory of the Gothic Revival **House of Prayer Episcopal Church** (1849), which is noted for the quatrefoil clerestory windows in the nave.

The **Sacred Heart Cathedral** (89 Ridge Street) is modeled after the cathedral at Rheims, France. Started in 1898 and more than forty years in the building, it has two towers 232 feet high.

## Newark Museum

Its fine American paintings and decorative arts, the Shaeffer Collection of ancient glass, the Sculpture Garden, Tibetan Collection, and Fire Museum make this seven-building complex one of the country's leading museums. John Cotton Dana, who founded it in 1909, believed museums should be useful to the community. The museum also operates the adjacent 1885 **Ballantine House,** the opulent late Neo-Renaissance home of the wealthy brewing family.

LOCATION: 49 Washington Street. HOURS: 12–5 Wednesday–Sunday. FEE: None. TELEPHONE: 201–596–6550.

# EDISON NATIONAL HISTORIC SITE

Thomas Alva Edison opened his West Orange "Invention Factory" in 1887. Here he developed the phonograph, motion-picture camera, fluoroscope, ore-milling machinery, electric storage battery, and other products of his inventive mind. The Historic Site's **Laboratory Complex** includes his chemistry lab and library, demonstrations of early phonographs, and a replica of "The Black Maria," the world's first motion-picture studio, where movies were made in the 1890s. Edison's home, **Glenmont,** is located one-half mile from his

OPPOSITE: *From the the Newark Museum: Wooden dance helmet from the Ivory Coast (top); 20th-century Hopi bowl (bottom).* OVERLEAF: *Springtime at the Reeves-Reed Arboretum, a beautiful mix of native woodlands and formal gardens, in Summit.*

*Edison's laboratory at the Edison National Historic Site, West Orange.* OPPOSITE: *The Edison light bulb.*

laboratory. The 1880 Victorian mansion was home to Edison from 1886 until his death in 1931. It is restored with original furnishings and family possessions.

LOCATION: *Laboratory:* Main Street and Lakeside Avenue, West Orange. *Glenmont:* Llewellyn Park West. HOURS: *Visitor Center:* 9–5 Daily. *Laboratory:* Tours 10:30–3:30 Daily. *Glenmont:* 11–4 Wednesday–Sunday; Reservations required for groups. FEE: Yes. TELEPHONE: 201–736–0550.

# MONTCLAIR

Originally called Cranetown, then Speertown, Montclair was founded by Connecticut Puritans who landed in Newark in 1666. The writer Stephen Crane was descended from one of Cranetown's founders; so was the prosperous manufacturer who built the **Israel Crane House** (110 Orange Road, 201–744–1796) in 1796. Now restored, the Federal style house with an Empire parlor offers demonstrations of crafts and open-hearth cooking.

The **Montclair Art Museum** (3 South Mountain Avenue, 201–746–5555) has a notable collection of American art, an American Indian gallery, and space for changing exhibits. Its permanent collection includes works by two famous Montclair artists: the landscape painter George Inness and the sculptor Thomas Ball, whose statues are in New York's Central Park and Boston's Public Garden.

# FORT LEE

George Washington ordered Fort Lee erected to defend New York City and to prevent the British from sailing up the Hudson River. Here, on November 16, 1776, he watched Fort Washington fall to the British across the river in northern Manhattan. Several days later, the British invaded New Jersey and attacked Fort Lee, then commanded by General Nathanael Greene, forcing the Americans to abandon it and begin their retreat across New Jersey into Pennsylvania. Now called **Fort Lee Historic Park** (Palisades Interstate Park just south of the George Washington Bridge, 201–461–1776), the complex includes reconstructed cannon batteries and a visitor center with exhibits on the Revolutionary War.

Fort Lee today is a residential community spread out around the approaches to the George Washington Bridge, but in the early twentieth century it was a center of the fledgling movie industry. The cliffs above the Hudson River were a convenient setting for the silent film series *The Perils of Pauline* and many others.

# CALDWELL

Grover Cleveland, president of the United States for two nonconsecutive terms (1885–1889 and 1893–1897), was born in the three-story white clapboard house at 207 Bloomfield Avenue on March 18, 1837. When he was four, his family moved to Fayetteville, New York. Cleveland returned to New Jersey after his second term as president and died in Princeton in 1908. The **Grover Cleveland Birthplace State Historic Site** (207 Bloomfield Avenue, 201–226–1810) contains period furnishings and personal mementoes.

# PATERSON

Paterson, America's first planned industrial community, was founded in 1791 by Alexander Hamilton's Society for the Establishment for Useful Manufactures. Hamilton chose the site for the energy potential of the Great Falls on the Passaic River. Major Pierre Charles L'Enfant, designer of Washington, DC, built the raceways to harness the energy. Early industries included cotton and silk mills; in 1836 Samuel Colt began manufacturing repeating revolvers in Paterson, and America's first locomotive, the Sandusky, was built here in 1837. A walkout of cottonworkers in 1828,

OPPOSITE: *A loom on view in an early spinning mill in the Great Falls Historic District, Paterson.*

America's first factory strike, and subsequent labor unrest have made Paterson important to the history of the labor movement. In his most ambitious work, *Paterson,* poet William Carlos Williams of Rutherford, New Jersey, focused on the industrial town.

The **Great Falls Historic District,** on the Passaic River between Grand Street and Ryle Avenue, preserves a number of factories, including the **Old Gun Mill** (Mill and Van Houten streets) where Samuel Colt manufactured the first successful revolvers. The area illustrates the development of industrial architecture in this country. Some plants are still operating; others are being adapted to other uses. Guided group tours and maps for self-guided tours can be obtained from the Great Falls Tour Office (65 McBride Avenue, 201–279–9587).

The **Paterson Museum** (2 Market Street, 201–881–3874) contains the hull of a submarine built by J. P. Holland, an Irish-American schoolteacher, in 1878. In 1893, the U.S. Navy purchased one of his designs, and he formed the J. P. Holland Torpedo Boat Company, which built submarines whose specifications were copied by many nations. **Lambert Castle** (Valley Road in Garret Mountain Reservation, 201–881–2761) was built overlooking the town in 1892 by Catholina Lambert, a wealthy silk manufacturer. Constructed of red and gray stone with many balconies and terraces, it now houses the **museum** of the Passaic County Historical Society, which displays eighteenth- and nineteenth-century decorative arts, paintings, and other exhibits, including a room containing the furniture of Garret A. Hobart, vice-president in the first McKinley administration from 1897 until his death in 1899.

# HALEDON

During the strike against the silk mills in nearby Paterson in 1913, workers organized by the Industrial Workers of the World held many mass meetings in Haledon, at what is now the **Botto House National Landmark** (83 Norwood Street, 201–595–7953). The strike was led by union organizer William Dudley "Big Bill" Haywood, and reported by such major journalists as John Reed and Upton Sinclair. The Paterson strike and other important moments in the American labor movement are depicted in the period rooms of the **American Labor Museum** in the Botto House.

OPPOSITE: *The Great Falls on the Passaic River in Paterson, the source of power for the early industrial town.*

# WAYNE

The **Dey Mansion** (199 Totowa Road, 201–696–1776) is an outstanding Georgian house with a brick front and sides of local brownstone. Built in 1740 for Colonel Theunis Dey, commander of the local militia, it was Washington's headquarters in July, October, and November 1780. Period rooms on the first and second floors are furnished with antiques. There is also a detached kitchen, a colonial garden, and reconstructed outbuildings.

The 1786 **Van Riper-Hopper House** (533 Berdan Avenue, 201–694–7192) is a Dutch Colonial, fieldstone farmhouse that is now operated as a museum by the town, furnished with pieces from the late eighteenth to the mid-nineteenth centuries.

# HO-HO-KUS

The Chihohokies Indians are the source of the town's unwieldy name, although in colonial times the town was known as Hoppertown, after an early settler. Aaron Burr courted his wife-to-be, the widow Theodosia Prevost, at **The Hermitage** (335 North Franklin Turnpike, 201–445–8311), built about 1760. George Washington and Lafayette both slept here. The house was rebuilt in 1845 in the Gothic Revival style complete with a fanciful exterior. It is now a state museum displaying period furniture.

# RINGWOOD STATE PARK

The mines in the Ramapo Mountains around Ringwood first began producing iron in the 1740s. In 1764 the property was bought by Peter Hasenclever for a partnership of English investors called The American Company. He improved the existing ironworks and established new ones in the area. During the Revolutionary War the Ringwood forges turned out minimal military supplies owing to the loss of skilled workers to the army. However, the ironmaster Robert Erskine served as geographer and surveyor general and made many maps for Washington.

About 1810 the original ironmaster's mansion (ca. 1740) was demolished by the new owner, Martin Ryerson, who built a small Federal style house that forms the west wing of the present **Ringwood Manor.** In 1853 the property was purchased by the Trenton Iron Company, for Abram S. Hewitt, a partner and business manager. Over twenty years. Hewitt and his wife, Amelia, expanded

*Ringwood Manor, originally built for the owner of a New Jersey iron mine.*

the house to its present size—fifty-one rooms—covered the exterior with stucco, and added decorative touches. They landscaped the grounds with statuary and architectural artifacts from Europe and America, including the stone columns from the New York Life building in New York City. In 1936, the Hewitt family donated house and grounds to the state. Twenty-one rooms have been restored and include exhibits on the iron industry.

The park also contains the forty-four-room **Skylands,** built in 1924 for millionaire Clarence McKenzie Lewis as a summer home. Skylands (not open) has superb woodwork, paneling, and stained glass from Europe. The **New Jersey State Botanical Garden at Skylands** embraces 96 acres of beautifully landscaped grounds with flowering trees from around the world.

LOCATION: Sloatsburg Road, 2 1/2 miles north of Ringwood. HOURS: 10–5 Wednesday–Sunday. FEE: Yes. TELEPHONE: 201-962-7031.

# MORRISTOWN

Reports of iron ore in the Watchung Mountains attracted settlers from Newark about 1710. By the time of the Revolution, there were some forty-five forges operating in the area to supply munitions. The importance of the iron industry in the early nineteenth century is illustrated by **Historic Speedwell** (333 Speedwell Avenue, 201–540–0211), a nine-building restoration that includes the home and factory of Stephen Vail. In 1818, Vail's Speedwell Iron Works produced the engine and parts for the SS *Savannah,* the first steam-driven vessel to cross the Atlantic. His son, Alfred, became the partner of Samuel F. B. Morse; in January 1838, they demonstrated the electromagnetic telegraph for the first time in America in the Vail factory. Tools and industrial equipment are displayed in the other buildings. The Vail House includes family furniture and a primitive central heating system.

Other Morristown landmarks include the 1760 **Schuyler-Hamilton House** (5 Olyphant Place, 201–267–4039), where Alexander Hamilton courted Elizabeth Schuyler during the winter of 1779–1780. Today it is a house museum operated by the Daughters of the American Revolution. The headquarters of the Morris County Historical Society, the Italianate Victorian **Acorn Hall** (68 Morris Avenue, 201–267–3465), is furnished from the mid-Victorian Era and has been restored. The garden has been designed with flowers and shrubs typical of nineteenth-century landscapes.

**Macculloch Hall Historical Museum** (45 Macculloch Avenue, 201–538–2404), a Federal style mansion built about 1810 by the builder of the Morris Canal, contains period furniture and a collection of drawings by political cartoonist Thomas Nast. From 1872 to 1902, Nast lived at the **Villa Fontana** (50 Macculloch Avenue, private). These two buildings are highlights of the Morristown Historic District, which includes a number of privately owned Federal, Greek Revival, and Victorian homes.

West of Morristown center, **Fosterfields Living Historical Farm** (Kahdena Road, off Route 24, 201–326–7645) is an example of a late-nineteenth-century working farm. Trails, workshops, farming demonstrations, audio-visual presentations, and a restored Gothic Revival mansion, **The Willows,** re-create life of the era.

OPPOSITE: *One of the fifty-one rooms of Ringwood Manor, in Ringwood State Park.*

## Morristown National Historical Park

This 1,600-acre site, the nation's first National Historical Park, was created by an act of Congress in 1933. Washington and his army spent two winters here, protected by mountains to the east and near the munitions-producing forges and furnaces of northern New Jersey—a good place to watch for a British attack that never came. The winter of 1779–1780 was the worst of the century in this region—there were eight blizzards in December alone. Washington had to contend with food shortages—"the soldiers ate every kind of horse food but hay," he wrote—disease, cold, desertions, and mutiny. In May 1780, the 1st Connecticut Brigade rebelled briefly, and the following winter, with the rest of the army encamped on the Hudson River, the men of the battle-weary Pennsylvania Line killed an officer and started off to confront Congress in Philadelphia with their grievances, before being persuaded to return.

General Washington spent his second winter at Morristown headquartered at the newly built Georgian home of the recently widowed Theodosia Ford. Her husband, the well-to-do owner of a mine, forge, and powder mill, had died the previous January. The house became a national shrine in 1873 when a local group purchased the landmark for $25,000 and founded the Washington Association to collect artifacts and encourage scholarship.

A tour of the Park today can start either at the visitor center at Jockey Hollow or at the **Headquarters Museum and Library** across the lawn from the Ford Mansion. A film about the winter of 1779–1780 is shown at both locations. The museum and library also contain art and artifacts from the period as well as 50,000 manuscripts and 20,000 volumes.

The **Ford Mansion** (1772–1774) has been restored to show the many ways it was used during Washington's stay. The two rooms where the general and his staff conducted military business and the second floor bedroom he occupied with his wife, have been furnished with Chippendale furniture. The kitchen and the two rooms Mrs. Ford shared with her four children are also on view.

A block of granite on the northern crest of Mount Kemble today marks the site of **Fort Nonsense,** an earthworks built to protect military supplies during the winter of 1779. Legend has it that Washington ordered the fort built simply to keep his men busy, hence its name, but historians now doubt the story.

Reconstructions of the huts the troops used during the winter of 1779–1780 have been built at **Jockey Hollow,** originally a 920-

*The Ford Mansion, Morristown, where Washington made his headquarters during the terrible winter of 1779-1780.*

acre encampment of 1,200 log huts. The **Grand Parade Field** and **Stark's Brigade** encampment are part of the Jockey Hollow area, while the **New Jersey Brigade** bivouac area, a short distance to the southwest, is reached by the **Patriot's Path.**

The **Wick House,** adjacent to the Jockey Hollow Visitor Center, was the headquarters of Major General Arthur St. Clair, commander of the Pennsylvania Line, during the winter of 1779–1780. Far less grand than the Ford Mansion, the Wick House, which is built around a central chimney, has been furnished with pieces typical of a rural household of the period.

LOCATION: Morristown Avenue and Route 287. (*Jockey Hollow:* 5 miles south of Morristown.) HOURS: 9–5 Daily. FEE: Yes. TELEPHONE: 201–539–2016.

West of Morristown on Route 24 is **Cooper Mill** (201–879–5463), a nineteenth-century working gristmill. Continuous tours show how grains such as corn and wheat were ground in the last century, with waterwheels and grinding stones.

# WATERLOO VILLAGE

The forge located here in 1763 was known for producing high-quality iron. Then called Andover Forge, the town was renamed Waterloo by its English owner to honor Wellington's victory over Napoleon in 1815. Although the forges eventually closed for lack of timber, the town became a prosperous canal port after the Morris Canal was built across the Musconetcong River at Waterloo in 1824. By the turn of the century, however, the town had begun to stagnate, and was almost totally deserted when two interior designers purchased it in 1947 and proceeded to restore it. Restored buildings open to the public today include the **Wellington House,** a restored Victorian home; the **General Store,** stocked with craft items made by local artisans, and the 1859 **Methodist Church.** Throughout the Village there are twenty-three restored homes and buildings where period furniture, art, and antiques create a living museum. Costumed guides interpret the history of each site,

*Gristmill at Historic Waterloo Village, a restoration of a forge that once produced high-grade iron.*

and craftspeople often work in the various shops, such as the **Broom and Cabinet Shop,** the **Gristmill and Sawmill,** and the **Blacksmith Shop.**

LOCATION: Off I-80, Exit 25, Stanhope. HOURS: Mid-April through September: 10–6 Wednesday–Sunday; October through December 10–5 Wednesday–Sunday. FEE: Yes. TELEPHONE: 201–347–0900.

# FLEMINGTON

Flemington, a glass- and potterymaking town, became the center of worldwide attention in 1935 as the location of the forty-day trial of Bruno Hauptmann, the accused kidnapper and murderer of Charles A. Lindbergh, Jr., infant son of the first man to fly across the Atlantic alone. More than a half-century later visitors are still attracted to the **Hunterdon County Courthouse,** an 1828 Greek Revival building on Main Street where the trial took place. The Lindbergh estate in Hopewell was divided by the Mercer County line, but since the baby was taken—in 1932—from a building on the Hunterdon side, the trial was held in Flemington. Hauptmann was found guilty, and, although he maintained his innocence to the end, was electrocuted at the State Prison in Trenton in 1936.

Flemington contains a group of handsome Greek Revival buildings by Mahlon Fisher, a local designer, and has a large Designated Historic District illustrative of many architectural styles from colonial through Art Deco.

# RAVEN ROCK

**Bull's Island** in the Delaware River, a substation of the Delaware and Raritan Canal State Park, has restored locks and picnic and camping facilities. Raven Rock was the beginning of a twenty-two-mile feeder canal that connected with the main canal in Trenton and transported Pennsylvania coal. Three miles south in Stockton, **Prallsville Mills,** a restored mill complex that includes a sawmill, gristmill, linseed oil mill, and bunkhouse, is located on Canal State Park property and run by the Delaware River Mill Society.

# WASHINGTON CROSSING STATE PARK

This 841-acre park preserves a section of the Delaware River shoreline where Washington and 2,400 men landed after crossing the ice-clogged Delaware River on Christmas night, 1776, to attack the

Hessian garrison at Trenton. Historical markers have been placed along **Continental Lane,** the beginning of Washington's route to Trenton, which stretches the length of the park. The **Ferry House** that sheltered Washington after the historic river crossing is now a museum and restored tavern. The Swan Collection of the American Revolution, housed in the visitor center, interprets critical events surrounding the Battle of Trenton.

Every Christmas Day a band of uniformed history buffs reenacts the crossing in replicas of the flat-bottomed Durham boats Washington and his men used.

LOCATION: Eight miles northwest of Trenton off Route 29, on Route 546. HOURS: *Park:* Memorial Day weekend through Labor Day: 8–8 Daily; Rest of year: 8–4:30 Daily. *Visitor Center:* 9–4 Wednesday–Sunday. *Ferry House:* 10–4 Wednesday–Saturday, 1–4 Sunday. FEE: Yes, for Ferry House. TELEPHONE: 609–737–0623.

## TRENTON

The city's motto, "Trenton Makes—The World Takes," reflects its pride in its industry. Colonial potteries grew into major industries here in the latter half of the nineteenth century; Walter Scott Lenox apprenticed in Trenton with Isaac Davis before establishing his own world-famous pottery in 1889. John A. Roebling's Trenton wire factory (est. 1848) produced steel cables for the Brooklyn Bridge. The city is named for another entrepreneur, William Trent, who turned Trenton into an important shipping point. He built the early-Georgian **William Trent House** (15 Market Street, 609–989–3027) on an estate of 800 acres five years after his arrival in 1714. Now restored, it contains period furniture contributed by the Daughters of the American Revolution.

Trenton's place in history was secured on the morning of December 26, 1776, when General George Washington, after crossing the Delaware on Christmas night, routed the Hessian garrison and captured 23 officers and 886 men. Lieutenant James Madison, a future president of the United States, was among the few Americans wounded. The battle was a crucial turning point of the Revolution; Lord Germaine, the British secretary of state for war, said that, "All our hopes were blasted by the unhappy affair at Trenton."

The battle is commemorated by the Beaux-Arts **Battle Monument** (1893). Designed by John Duncan, the 155-foot granite col-

OPPOSITE: *The icy Delaware River, where Washington crossed his army on Christmas night, 1776.*

*John Trumbull's* Capture of the Hessians at Trenton, *painted ca. 1787.*

umn  stands where Washington's artillery first fired on the enemy. On the night of the attack, some Hessians were quartered in the Trenton Barracks on Barrack Street. Now the **Old Barracks Museum** (609–396–1776), it was built during the French and Indian War so troops would no longer be lodged in private homes.

Washington returned to Trenton on January 2, 1777, where he clashed with Cornwallis, just arrived from Princeton with fresh troops. Instead of pressing his advantage, Cornwallis announced, "We'll bag the fox in the morning." But by morning the fox was gone; Washington had withdrawn his men to Princeton, where he won another important battle.

Trenton was chosen as the state capital in 1790. The **State House** (135 West State Street, 609–292–4661) is an architectural composite that has grown up around a core built in the early 1790s. John Notman of Philadelphia designed the first rotunda and portico in the 1840s. He was also the architect of the 1846 Italian Villa–style **Ellarslie Trenton City Museum** (609–989–3632). It is located in the park named for Doctor Thomas Cadwalader, Trenton's first chief burgess, who pioneered the use of inoculations against

*Trenton's Old Barracks' Museum, where Hessian troops were quartered prior to the Battle of Trenton.*

disease in the mid-eighteenth century. **Cadwalader Park** was laid out by Frederick Law Olmsted in 1891.

# PRINCETON

First called Stony Brook after a stream that ran along its borders, the town was named Prince's Town in 1724 and later Princeton. In colonial times, Princeton was an important coach stop on the New York–Philadelphia turnpike and, despite its royalist name, a hot-bed of support for the cause of independence. During the dark, early days of the Revolution, Princeton was the site of an important American victory.

After the war, the Continental Congress met in Princeton from June to November 1783. In August it summoned Washington to Nassau Hall to convey the nation's gratitude.

In more recent years, Princeton has been marked by the growth of the university and, nearby, important research institutes. Albert Einstein worked at the prestigious Institute for Advanced Study from the time it opened in the early 1930s until his death in

1955. (The Institute's imaginatively designed **Academic Building and Dining Hall** (1971), by architect Robert Geddes, is open to the public during the academic year.) In 1935, George Gallup opened his American Institute of Public Opinion to measure the likes and dislikes of Americans. RCA built a research plant there in 1942, and in 1951 the university opened its 825-acre research center, The James Forrestal Campus.

Historic buildings in Princeton include the 1727 **Stony Brook Meeting House** (Mercer Road, private), the town's first place of worship, which was rebuilt in 1757 using local fieldstone. Richard Stockton, a signer of the Declaration of Independence, is buried in the adjacent cemetery. Until 1982 Stockton's 1759 home, **Morven** (55 Stockton Street, 609–683–4495), was the New Jersey governor's official residence. During the Battle of Princeton, General Cornwallis used it as his headquarters. Stockton's grandson, Robert, a naval officer who seized California for the United States during the war with Mexico, built a stone and stucco house, **Westland** (15 Hodge Road, private), for his daughter Caroline Stockton Dod, in 1854. It is also known as the Grover Cleveland House, because Cleveland lived there from the end of his second term as president in 1897 until he died in 1908.

Information on self-guided walking tours of Princeton is available at **Bainbridge House,** headquarters of the Historical Society of Princeton (158 Nassau Street, 609–921–6748). The restored, brick-front house (ca. 1766) is the birthplace of William Bainbridge, a commander of the USS *Constitution* during the War of 1812. A museum, with exhibits on the town's history, is open to the public.

Charles Steadman, a local architect and builder, designed the central portion of **Drumthwacket** (354 Stockton Street, 609–683–0057), a magnificent Greek Revival mansion with an ornate interior, in 1835. The house, now the official governor's residence, is open Wednesdays for tours, 12–2. Steadman also built many private homes in Princeton, including those at 20 Alexander Street and 38–40 Mercer Street, and the privately owned **Woodrow Wilson House** (1836) at 73 Library Place. John Notman, the English-born Philadelphia architect, created one of his most impressive Italianate villas for the Potter family as a private residence. It is now the Princeton Faculty Club.

Many of Princeton's early settlers, as well as Cleveland and Aaron Burr, Junior and Senior, are buried at the **Princeton Cemetery** at the corner of Witherspoon and Wiggins streets.

## Princeton Battlefield

The week after his victory at Trenton Washington decided to press his advantage with another surprise attack, on the British outpost at Princeton. The Battle of Princeton began inauspiciously for the Americans: As they approached town at dawn on January 3, 1777, the advance guard under General Hugh Mercer was driven back with heavy losses by two British regiments, themselves en route to Trenton. Washington, arriving with seasoned veterans, boldly galloped into the heat of the fighting and rallied his panic-stricken troops, who dispersed the outnumbered British. American troops then captured Nassau Hall, taking several hundred prisoners. With the advance of superior British forces from Trenton, Washington headed north to Morristown to encamp for the winter. Though the Americans suffered heavy casualties, including General Mercer, the victories here and at Trenton restored the morale of the army and helped to rally support for the cause of independence.

The State Park includes the ca. 1770 **Thomas Clarke House,** a Quaker farm where General Mercer died nine days after being wounded in the battle. A grave of British and American dead is also within the Park. The victory is also commemorated by the 1922 **Princeton Battle Monument** at the junction of Mercer, Stockton, and Nassau streets. This fifty-foot block of Indiana marble, carved in high relief by the Brooklyn-born sculptor Frederick W. Mac-Monnies, depicts a figure representing Liberty rallying Washington and his troops.

LOCATION: One mile southwest from town on Mercer Street. HOURS: *Park:* Dawn–Dusk Daily. *House:* 10–4 Wednesday–Saturday, 1–4 Sunday. FEE: None. TELEPHONE: 609–921–0074.

## Princeton University

Princeton, the fourth-oldest university in the country, was founded as the College of New Jersey in 1746 to train Presbyterian teachers. In 1756, the school moved into the newly built Nassau Hall at Princeton. The Reverend John Witherspoon, a Scotsman who became president in 1768, was an ardent revolutionary and a member of the Continental Congress. After signing the Declaration of Independence, he stated that the country was "not only ripe for the measure but in danger of rotting for the want of it." Under Witherspoon the college turned out so many public figures that Woodrow Wilson later described the school as "a seminary of statesmen."

Because many students were wealthy southerners, the Civil War divided the school, with undergraduates serving on both sides during the conflict. In the postwar years 1868–1888, the size of the school doubled during the presidency of Doctor James McCosh, who deemphasized religious studies and opened a graduate school. In 1896, on the 150th anniversary of the school's founding, the name was changed to Princeton University.

Woodrow Wilson, appointed in 1902, was the first nonclergyman to head the university. His attempts to strengthen its intellectual life caused controversy, and when the trustees hindered his plan to weaken the hold of Princeton's exclusive eating clubs on campus life and to integrate the graduate school into the rest of the university, Wilson resigned. A month later he was elected governor of New Jersey.

Although the university's campus, broken up into quadrangles and crisscrossed by paths, is an outstanding example of the late-nineteenth-century style known as "Collegiate Gothic," its first building, **Nassau Hall,** is the architectural focal point. When finished in 1756, it was the largest academic building in the Colonies. The design by Robert Smith of Philadelphia—a simple dignified facade highlighted by a pedimented pavilion—influenced important buildings at other schools. Smith also designed the **President's House** in 1756 for Aaron Burr. The two-and-a-half story painted brick house is now used by the Princeton Alumni Council.

The Princeton dormitory known as **Blair Hall** (1897) is the best early example of the Collegiate Gothic style. This architectural movement, which spread to other campuses, reached, as writes architectural historian G. E. Kidder Smith, its "spiritual climax" in the **Graduate School** (1913) and **University Chapel** (1928), both by Ralph Adams Cram.

> LOCATION: For tours apply at Maclean House, 73 Nassau Street. HOURS: Tours start at 10, 11, 1, 1:30, and 3:30 Monday–Saturday, 1:30 and 3:30 Sunday; Closed mid-December to early January. FEE: None. TELEPHONE: 609–258–3603.

# ROCKINGHAM

While Congress met in nearby Princeton in 1783 to debate the peace treaty with England, General George Washington lived here, entertaining state visitors and writing his "Farewell Address to the

OPPOSITE: *An arch in the Collegiate Gothic style at Princeton University.*

Armies." The original portion of the two-story, white clapboard farmhouse was built about 1710 by Judge John Berrien. His widow, unable to sell the house because of the Revolution, willingly rented it to George and Martha Washington.

LOCATION: Route 518, Rocky Hill. HOURS: 10–12 and 1–4 Wednesday–Saturday, 1–4 Sunday. FEE: None. TELEPHONE: 609–921–8835.

## FREEHOLD

Freehold, whose original name, Monmouth Court House, was changed in 1801 to avoid confusion with other towns with similar names, was the site of the Battle of Monmouth on June 28, 1778, one of the longest and fiercest battles of the Revolution. Although the day started badly for the Americans, General George Washington rallied his retreating advance troops, who went on to defeat the British under General Henry Clinton. During the conflict, Mary Ludwig Hays, later nicknamed "Molly Pitcher," earned immortality by carrying water to the troops and then loading cannon after her husband was overcome by heat. The visitor center at the **Monmouth Battlefield** (Route 522 northwest of town, 908–462–9616) has interpretive exhibits about the battle.

During the battle, Sir Henry Clinton stayed at **Covenhoven** (1752) (150 West Main Street, 908–462–1466), now a finely restored house with period furnishings. The simply designed **Old Tennent Church** (1751) in nearby Tennent is surrounded by old gravestones. Many soldiers are buried here.

## ALLAIRE

The planned community that James P. Allaire built in the 1830s for the 500 residents of his Howell Works ironworks included homes, a school, and stagecoach service; it even issued currency for the company store. When the furnace became uncompetitive after anthracite was discovered in Pennsylvania, the town was deserted. The State of New Jersey began restoring Historic Allaire Village in Historic Allaire Village in **Allaire State Park** has been restored. Brick and iron buildings amid ancient sycamores include a bakery, blacksmith shop, carriage house, and Allaire's house. The beehive blast furnace and church are unique in the United States.

LOCATION: Route 524, Allaire. HOURS: Memorial Day through Labor Day: 10–4 Wednesday–Sunday. FEE: None. TELEPHONE: 908–938–2253.

New Brunswick tavern in 1771 as a school for Dutch Reformed ministers. (The school's actual birthplace, however, is in nearby Somerville.) The college's first and, at the time, only teacher, eighteen-year-old Frederick Frelinghuysen, became an artillery officer during the Revolution and later a U.S. senator. The college's first building, **Old Queens,** a three-story brownstone, was designed in 1809 by John McComb, Jr., who also designed New York's City Hall. It is the present-day administrative center of the university. The school was renamed after benefactor Henry Rutgers in 1825. The eighth-oldest university in the country, it is the only state university with a colonial charter. Theodore Frelinghuysen, son of the original teacher, was president of Rutgers from 1850 to 1862.

The poet Alfred Joyce Kilmer, whose most famous poem is the widely quoted "Trees," was born in the simple frame house at **17 Joyce Kilmer Avenue,** now a museum. Kilmer was killed in action during World War I and is buried in France.

## DELAWARE AND RARITAN CANAL STATE PARK

New Brunswick is the eastern terminus of the Delaware and Raritan Canal, built 1830–1834 to connect the Raritan and Delaware rivers and hence, by navigable waters, New York City and Philadelphia. The main canal extends forty-four miles from the Raritan River at New Brunswick via Trenton to Bordentown on the Delaware River. There is also a twenty-two-mile feeder canal, built to "feed" water to supply the main canal (later to transport coal from Pennsylvania), extending from Raven Rock to Trenton. In 1974 the canal, which had been disintegrating and in disrepair since it closed in 1933, was turned into the Delaware and Raritan Canal State Park (headquarters at 643 Canal Road, Somerset, west of New Brunswick (908-873-3050).

Vestiges of the canal and/or the railroad—the famous Camden and Amboy that ran along it—are at virtually every place a road crosses the canal: locks, wooden swing bridges, towpaths, canal houses, and, southwest of New Brunswick, in Griggstown, restored homes and stations for the lock and bridge tenders (private). Three miles north in Black Wells Mills is a **bridge tender's house and station.** The canal, 75 feet wide and 8 feet deep, could handle sizeable vessels in its locks, which were 24 feet wide and 220 feet long. The canal passes through twenty-four communities and close to many historic sites.

# SOMERVILLE

The **Old Dutch Parsonage** (65 Washington Place, 908–725–1015) is considered "the cradle of Rutgers University." John Frelinghuysen, a Dutch Reformed minister, established the church's first American seminary—with four students—in the Dutch brick house he built in 1751. After he died in 1754, his widow married one of the students, seventeen-year-old Jacob Rutsen Hardenbergh. (When he proposed, the startled Mrs. Frelinghuysen supposedly responded, "Why, child, what are you thinking about!") Hardenbergh went on to become the first president of Queens College (now Rutgers) when it was chartered in 1766, and his stepson Frederick became its first teacher. Now a State Historic Site, the parsonage was moved about 500 yards to its present location in 1913 and is today used for meetings and educational programs.

During the Revolution, while the main part of the American army spent the winter of 1778–1779 at the Middlebrook encampment, General Washington stayed at the **Wallace House** (38 Washington Place (908–725–1015), then a newly built clapboard house with a fieldstone foundation. The Old Dutch Parsonage was then located next door, and the Washingtons and the Hardenberghs became friends during the winter. The Wallace House is furnished with eighteenth-century period pieces.

**Duke Gardens** (Route 206, 908–722–3700) is the legacy of tobacco heiress Doris Duke. One of the twelve acres is entirely under glass, with gardens from different periods of history, including colonial America.

# S  O  U  T  H      J  E  R  S  E  Y

## CAMDEN

Camden was founded in 1681 when William Cooper set up a ferry to transport travelers across the Delaware River to Philadelphia. Although overshadowed by its neighbor, the city has some interesting sites, including **Pomona Hall,** built by William Cooper's descendants in 1726, with an addition in 1788. It is furnished with fine antiques and maintained by the Camden County Historical Society (Park Boulevard and Euclid Avenue, 609–964–3333). The Society's library and museum of regional history are adjacent.

In 1894, a Camden machinist named Eldridge R. Johnson produced the Victor Talking machine; his company was purchased by the Radio Corporation of America in 1929. Campbell Soup, another major company based in Camden, maintains a museum of more than 250 antique soup tureens, bowls, and ladles at the **Campbell Museum** (Campbell Place, 609–342–6440).

After he suffered a stroke in 1873, the poet Walt Whitman moved from Washington, DC, to Camden to live with his brother George. Although he had completed his most important work by then, he produced five revised editions of *Leaves of Grass* in Camden and in 1882–1883 prepared for publication his autobiographical recollections, *Specimen Days and Collect,* about his early life. The house where Whitman lived from 1884 until his death in 1892, now the **Walt Whitman Home State Historic Site** (330 Mickle Boulevard, 609–964–5383), has been restored and contains his furnishings, books, and mementoes. It is the only house the poet ever owned. He is buried at **Harleigh Cemetery** (Haddon Avenue and Vesper Boulevard) beneath his self-composed epitaph: "For that of me which is to die."

## RED BANK BATTLEFIELD

The **Red Bank Battlefield,** on a bluff overlooking the Delaware River (one mile from town off Route 130), is the site of Fort Mercer, which no longer stands although the location of the ramparts is well marked. Thanks to nineteen-year-old Jonas Cattell, who ran nine miles to warn the Americans of the enemy's approach, the Americans had time to reinforce the fort before a brigade of Hessians attacked on October 22, 1777. As a result, the Americans drove off the enemy, killing over five hundred. The British captured Fort Mercer a month later, but the initial victory rallied morale and encouraged the French to enter the war. There are interpretive markers on the battlefield and a museum containing relics of Fort Mercer.

## SALEM

According to legend, the English Quaker John Fenwick purchased Salem, oldest settlement on the Delaware River, from the Lenape Indians in 1675. The treaty was concluded under the **Salem Oak,** now more than 500 years old, that still stands at the entrance of the **Friends Burying Ground.**

Salem's historic district has more than sixty eighteenth-century homes and buildings. The 1721 **Alexander Grant House** (79–83

*Salt marshes of Cumberland County, South Jersey.*

Market Street, 609–935–5004), headquarters of the Salem County Historical Society, houses a twenty-one-room museum and a staffed genealogical library. The museum rooms, which include a seventeenth-century keeping room, are all furnished with period pieces. A stone barn, a 1736 octagonal law office, and a colonial garden are part of the complex. The two-and-a-half story **Friends Meeting House** (East Broadway and Walnut Street) dates from 1772. Five miles south of town is the **Hancock House** (1734), where thirty militiamen guarding a bridge were killed by three hundred British in 1778.

    **Fort Mott** (Fort Mott Road, 609–935–3218), now contained in a state park, defended Philadelphia and the Delaware River during the Civil War. More than two thousand Confederate prisoners are buried at the adjacent **Finns Point National Cemetery**.

## GREENWICH

This charming, well-preserved town is the site of New Jersey's only tea-burning party; in December 1774, a band of forty young men dressed as Indians burned a load of tea belonging to the East India Company on the town square. The spot is marked by the **Tea Burners Monument,** erected in 1908.

Maps of the extensive historic district, an interesting amalgam of colonial, Federal, and Victorian houses on either side of Ye Greate Street, are available at **The Gibbon House** (Ye Greate Street, 609–451–8454), headquarters of the Cumberland County Historical Society. Built in 1730, the house is furnished with eighteenth- and early-nineteenth-century pieces. The grounds include the ca. 1650 **Swedish Granary,** a rare example of a cedar-log structure built by early Swedish settlers.

## BRIDGETON

About 1763 the patriotic citizens of Bridgeton purchased a bell; on July 7, 1776, it rang to summon the town to hear the Declaration of Independence. Now called **The South Jersey Liberty Bell,** it is displayed in the lobby of the Cumberland County Courthouse (Brand and Fayette streets, 609–451–8000). The red-brick **Old Broad Street Church** (1792–1795) at Broad Street and West Avenue, an outstanding example of Georgian architecture, has its original high-backed pews.

Bridgeton also has the largest historic district in the state with some 2,200 homes and commercial buildings registered as landmarks. A walking-tour map is available at the **Nail House Museum** (1 Mayor Aiken Drive, 609–455–4100), an industrial museum in an early ironworks.

## WHEATON VILLAGE

This eighty-eight-acre complex is a restoration of a glassmaking community that grew up around the T. C. Wheaton Glass Company. Doctor Wheaton founded the company—to make glass for pharmaceutical purposes—after he moved to Millville in 1883. Among its fourteen buildings are period reconstructions of a one-room schoolhouse, train station, and general store. There are glassmaking demonstrations in its factory, an authentic replica of the 1888 factory building with a large cylindrical brick furnace, fueled today by natural gas instead of by coal and wood.

The seven thousand objects in the village's **Wheaton Museum of American Glass** cover the history of American glassmaking from the first glassworks in Wistarburgh, New Jersey, in 1739 to

South Jersey

the present. Located in a replica of a turn-of-the-century Cape May hotel, the museum includes a paperweight room with antique Sandwich, pinchbeck, and Steuben types. Contemporary paperweights are sold in the village shop.

The silica in the ground around Millville is ideal for glassmaking. In writing about the town in 1904, Carl Sandburg wrote of "bottles, bottles, bottles, of every tint and hue, from a brilliant crimson to the dull green that marks the death of sand and the birth of glass."

LOCATION: 10th and G streets, Millville. HOURS: April through December: 10–5 Daily; January through March: Call for hours. FEE: Yes. TELEPHONE: 609–825–6800.

# CAPE MAY

This delightful architectural treasure claims to be the oldest seaside resort in the United States. Named by the Dutch explorer Cornelius Jacobson Mey, who sailed by in 1621, the Cape was settled by whalers from New England. Although they, as William Penn wrote, "hope a considerable profit from a whalery," these hopes were never fully realized and the settlement turned to farming early in the eighteenth century. The resort era supposedly began in 1801 with an advertisement in a Philadelphia newspaper that "the subscriber has prepared himself for entertaining company who use sea bathing, and he is accommodated with extensive houseroom, with fish, oysters, crabs and good liquor." Steamships—and later a railroad—were soon bringing guests in droves.

In the resort's heyday throughout most of the nineteenth century, summering at Cape May was the height of fashion. It then had fifty-seven hotels, and was known as the "Resort of Presidents"—Buchanan, Pierce, Grant, Harrison, and Lincoln vacationed here. Many of the more ornate Victorian buildings were built after a fire destroyed thirty acres in 1877.

After a rapid decline caused by poor roads and the rise of Atlantic City to the north, Cape May was rediscovered in the 1960s and extensively restored. Today practically the entire town of more than six hundred Victorian buildings, which are painted in the subtle colors and pastels of the time, is a National Historic Landmark. Particularly fine examples of what architectural historians call "Seaside Vernacular" are along Congress Place.

OPPOSITE: *A street of Victorian days, Cape May.*

The **Victorian Museum** with furniture, toys, clothing, and other items of the era is housed in the 1879 **Emlen Physick House** (1048 Washington Street, 609–884–5404), built by the Philadelphia architect and Civil War hero Frank Furness. The Mid-Atlantic Center for the Arts operates tours and a Victorian Week in October from the house.

Cape May's many guesthouses include a former gambling house, the **Mainstay Inn** (635 Columbia Avenue, 609–884–8690), which has been painstakingly restored by its owners. The **Abbey** (Columbia Avenue and Gurney Street, 609–884–4506) was built in 1869 around a Gothic arch motif. Both bed-and-breakfast inns are furnished with period antiques and offer tours to the public.

The era of the grand resort hotel also lingers on at **The Chalfonte** (301 Howard Street, 609–884–8409). Built in 1876 and noted for the gingerbread verandas on first and second floors, it has been partially restored by guests, who stay free on certain weekends in return for labor. **Congress Hall** with its pillars and mansard roof was once President Benjamin Harrison's summer White House. Information on the town is provided by the Chamber of Commerce (The Depot, Lafayette Street, 609–884–5508) and the Welcome Center (405 Lafayette Street, 609–884–9562).

## CAPE MAY COURT HOUSE

Although overshadowed by Cape May, this town has its own notable collection of colonial and Victorian homes in the vicinity of the courthouse. As for the courthouse, there are actually two—an 1850 structure and a newer brick building. One mile north on Route 9 is the **Cape May County Historical Museum** (609–465–3535), with an eighteenth-century garden, whaling artifacts, tools, furniture, decoys, and a genealogical library.

## MARGATE CITY

This resort town was originally known as South Atlantic City; part of it was once owned by real estate developer James V. Lafferty, who wanted to sell building lots. He designed and patented a building in the shape of an elephant, completed in 1881, to attract prospective buyers. **Lucy, The Margate Elephant** has since become New Jersey's most whimsical landmark. After a checkered career as a bar, restaurant, and tourist attraction, the six-story pachyderm was taken over by the city in 1970 to ward off demolition.

# ATLANTIC CITY

When Atlantic City opted for gambling in the 1970s, it essentially turned its back on its past. Most of the once-grand hotels have been replaced with glitzy modern boxes, leaving only the Boardwalk, five miles long and sixty feet wide, and amusement piers, such as the 1898 **Steel Pier,** to link the city with its heyday in the late nineteenth century. Development of Atlantic City began in 1852, when the Camden and Atlantic Railroad reached Absecon Island. By then, the **Absecon Lighthouse** was already a few years old.

The resort's first grand hotel, the 600-room United States, was the largest in the country in 1854. Others lining the Boardwalk,

*A photograph, probably taken about the turn of the century, of the Steel Pier and the Boardwalk at Atlantic City.*

such as the Traymore, grew from smaller establishments. The Marlborough-Blenheim, the first hotel to have private baths in every room, was the ornate merger of two hotels. A room at the deluxe Hotel Rudolf at the turn of the century cost five dollars. The Claridge wasn't completed until 1930, and by then Atlantic City was in decline. Several grand hotels last made headlines in the 1970s when, in a spectacular demonstration of the art of demolition and a more-than-symbolic finale for the self-styled "Queen of Resorts," they were blown up.

## BATSTO VILLAGE

This restoration of an eighteenth- and nineteenth-century iron-making village has a gristmill, sawmill, and barns, although the original iron furnace and glassworks no longer stand. The restoration's most imposing building, the thirty-six-room **Ironmaster's House,** parts of which date from 1766, was extensively renovated in the 1870s by the Philadelphia financier Joseph Wharton, who used it as a country home. Wharton also added the five-story tower. The house is lavishly decorated with furnishings, decorative arts, and paintings from this period. There are also seventeen workers' houses—two-story structures covered with cedar clapboard. One house has been simply furnished as a typical worker's home; traditional craftspeople use the others for demonstrations. Guided tours of Wharton's house are also available.

Batsto, a bog-iron furnace founded in 1766, was an important producer of munitions during the Revolution. The ironworks and the town around it continued to thrive until the anthracite fields in Pennsylvania opened in the 1820s and 1830s. After the furnace closed, financier Joseph Wharton purchased the nearly deserted village in 1876 and added it to his estate of almost 100,000 acres. The village is now part of the Wharton State Park and has been undergoing restoration since the 1960s.

> LOCATION: Wharton State Forest, Route 542, Hammonton.
> HOURS: *Grounds:* Dawn to dusk Daily; *Visitor Center:* 9–4:30 Daily.
> FEE: Yes. TELEPHONE: 609-561-3262.

## BORDENTOWN

During the Revolution, Patriots here floated kegs loaded with gunpowder down the Delaware River into the British fleet at Philadelphia. The panic that followed was lampooned in verses by

Bordentown's remarkable Francis Hopkinson, poet, composer, revolutionary activist, and lawyer. In retaliation for the kegs and the poem, the British attacked the town in May 1778 and burned the home of Joseph Borden, the town's founder and Hopkinson's father-in-law. The **Borden House** (32 Farnsworth Avenue, private) was built by Borden's son to replace it. The 1750 **Francis Hopkinson House** at 101 Farnsworth Avenue is also privately owned.

Thomas Paine was another famous Bordentown resident. So were Stephen Girard, the Philadelphia capitalist, General Jean Victor Moreau, who was Napoleon's primary competitor to be leader of France, and Joseph Bonaparte, the exiled king of Spain and brother of Napoleon. Remnants of Bonaparte's 1,500-acre estate can be seen at **Point Breeze** (101 Park Street, 609–298–0549). The **Clara Barton School** (Crosswicks and Burlington streets) honors the founder of the American Red Cross. Miss Barton opened the school in 1852 to demonstrate her belief in free public education.

# BURLINGTON

Burlington, which became the capital of West Jersey after the colony split in 1676, was settled by Quakers in 1677. The original governing body, The Council of Proprietors, still meets each May in the one-room, eighteenth-century red-brick **Surveyor General's Office** (West Broad Street between High and Wood streets).

Despite a promising start, Burlington never developed into a major port. Therefore, many of its fine, historic buildings have survived. The 1685 **Thomas Revell House** (213 Wood Street, private) might be the oldest residence still standing in the state. It is sometimes called the "Gingerbread House," because, according to popular lore, a young printer's apprentice named Benjamin Franklin was given gingerbread here in 1723 as he passed through on his way to Philadelphia. The 1785 **Friends Meeting House** (High Street), a reminder of the town's Quaker heritage, is open by appointment and for services.

Also on High Street is the ca. 1780 **Cooper House** (609–386–4773), where author James Fenimore Cooper was born in 1789 and lived for about a year. The house, now a museum and headquarters of the Burlington County Historical Society, is open to the public and displays Cooper artifacts, dining implements, and Joseph Bonaparte objects. Next door is the **Captain James Lawrence House,** also administered by the historical society. Lawrence was

the heroic commander of the *Chesapeake* during the War of 1812, who died exhorting his comrades, "Don't give up the ship!"

With its towering 174-foot steeple and harmonious proportions, **New Saint Mary's Episcopal Church** (West Broad Street) is a masterpiece of the Gothic Revival style. Completed in 1854, it was designed by Richard Upjohn, architect of Trinity Church in New York City. Next door, the original 1703 church is the oldest Episcopal church building in the state.

## MOUNT HOLLY

The 1771 brick and frame **John Woolman Memorial** (99 Branch Street) honors the Quaker humanist and early abolitionist, who is best remembered for his reflective *Journal*. Woolman died a year after he built this house for his daughter. He perhaps taught at the **John Brainerd School** (35 Brainerd Street), founded in 1759. This historic Quaker town has many old buildings of interest along its pleasant, tree-lined streets, including a **Friends Meeting House** dating from 1775. Of architectural and historic interest are the 1810 **Burlington County Prison Museum** (128 High Street) and, across the street, the 1796 **Court House.** The Prison Museum was designed by Robert Mills, architect of many historic public buildings.

The **Relief Fire Company Building** on Pine Street is the oldest continuously active fire company in the United States, organized in 1752. The original first minutes book, leather buckets, and other memorabilia are on display. Across the street is the **Three Tuns Tavern,** built in 1723 with walls fourteen inches thick and still used as a tavern. It has changed little since Hessian troops, following decoy Continental troops, were quartered there in 1776. The ruse brought success to Washington's raid on Trenton that December. The "mountain" after which the town is named is 183 feet high.

Three miles east off Route 295 is **Smithville,** the Victorian mansion (Jacksonville Road, 609–265–5068) and village of Hezekiah B. Smith, a colorful inventor and manufacturer of bicycles and other products. Smith campaigned for Congress in a carriage drawn by a trained bull moose.

OPPOSITE: *New St. Mary's Episcopal Church in Burlington was designed in the early 1850's by Richard Upjohn, an important practitioner of the popular Gothic Revival style. Old St. Mary's, built in 1703, is nearby.*

# CHAPTER SEVEN

# PHILADELPHIA
## AND
# ENVIRONS

OPPOSITE: *A statue of Commander John Barry, a Philadelphian and a naval officer during the Revolution, in front of Independence Hall.*

Atop Philadelphia's City Hall Tower, a statue of William Penn, looking very much the proper Quaker gentleman, surveys the city from 548 feet in the air. It is a position of eminence that he well deserves, for even today Philadelphia, the fifth-largest city in the country, is this man's legacy. Before landing on these shores in 1682 Penn had planned out "a greene Countrie Towne, which will never be burnt, and allways be wholsome," not threatened by the devastating fires and plagues he had seen in Europe. As its citizens would be peaceful, Philadelphia needed no fortification against the Indians.

His commissioners purchased an undeveloped tract west of the Delaware River and the next summer Penn's surveyor-general, Captain Thomas Holme, laid out a city between what are now South and Vine streets. When Penn arrived in October 1682, he purchased land on the Schuylkill so that the city would have frontage on both rivers.

Holme's second plan of the city shows a symmetrical gridiron emanating from a central square, today the site of City Hall. The gridiron plan—although not without its drawbacks—was innovative for its day and later became the standard for American cities. Philadelphia's open spaces were unknown in metropolises of the time; High (today Market) and Broad streets were 100 feet wide; other streets were 50 feet across.

Philadelphia was well situated for a capital city. The Delaware provided an excellent port for large ships, the Schuylkill River a natural passageway to the colony's interior. The first settlers grouped along the Delaware and only slowly spread west toward the Schuylkill. Eighty houses were built the first year; by the next, Penn could report to England: "I have led the greatest colony into America that ever man did upon a private credit." In 1700, the Swedish pastor of Gloria Dei (Old Swedes') Church wrote: "If anyone were to see Philadelphia who had not been there [before], he would be astonished beyond measure that it was founded less than twenty years ago. . . . All the houses are built of brick, three or four hundred of them, and in every house a shop, so that whatever one wants at any time he can have, for money."

For all his lasting influence, Penn spent only a few short years in the colony; he left after his second trip in 1701, never to return. In his absence, his interests in the colony and the city were represented by his secretary, an Ulster-born ex-schoolmaster named

*Christ Church in William Birch's* Second Street North from Market.

James Logan. Logan held a succession of high offices, including mayor of Philadelphia, and grew wealthy in fur trading and land speculation.

Logan, who advised Penn's descendants after the founder's death in 1718, oversaw Philadelphia's development from settlement to town, but it was Benjamin Franklin who personified its growth into the preeminent American city of the eighteenth century. Franklin arrived in Philadelphia as a penniless young printer in the summer of 1723. ("I was very hungry, and my whole Stock of Cash consisted of a Dutch Dollar and about a Shilling in Copper," he wrote in his *Autobiography*.) But before long he was making his influence felt. In 1729, he took over the newspaper for which he was working, shortened its name to the *Pennsylvania Gazette*, and proceeded to produce "as agreeable and useful Entertainment as the Nature of the Thing will allow." This was followed by *Poor Richard's Almanack*, a journal soon read throughout the colonies. And, unlike the dour Logan, Franklin had wit, a liberal spirit, and

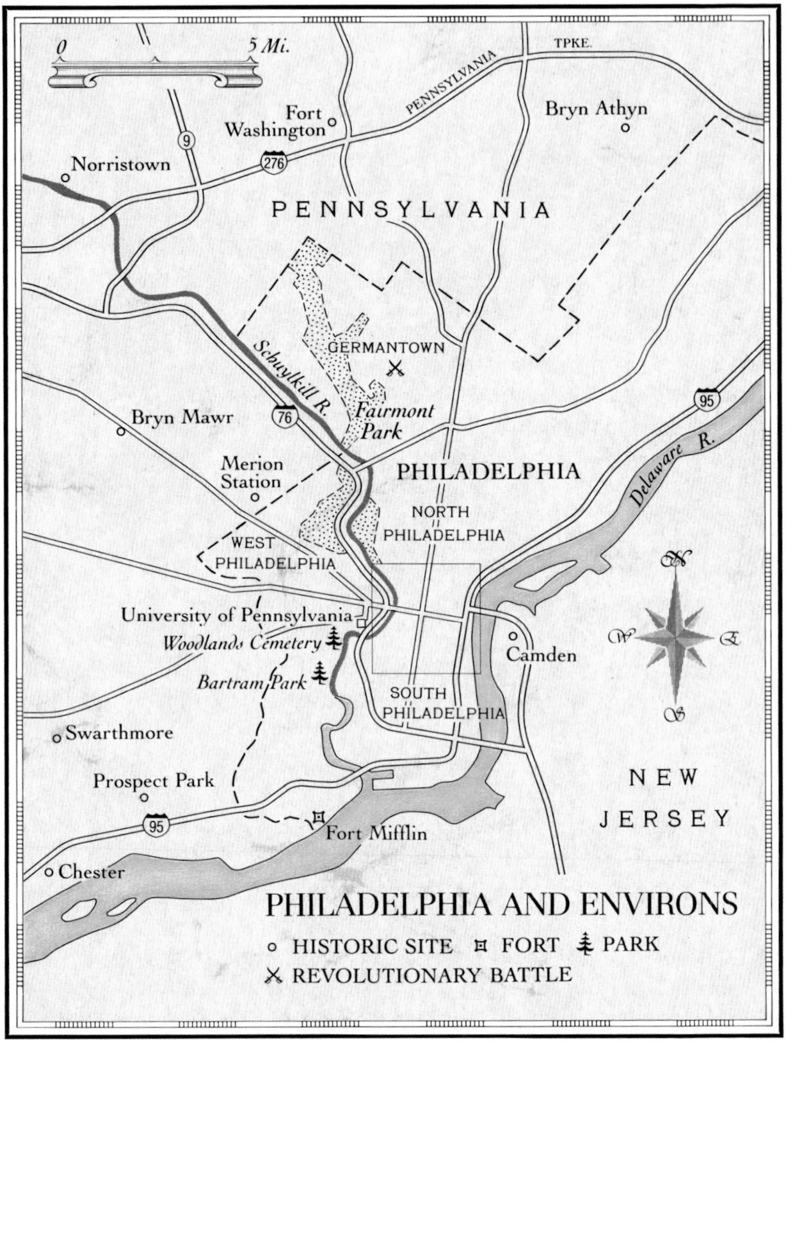

0
5 Mi.
PENNSYLVANIA TPKE.
Fort Washington
Bryn Athyn
9
276
Norristown
PENNSYLVANIA
GERMANTOWN
Schuylkill R.
Fairmont Park
76
Bryn Mawr
95
Delaware R.
Merion Station
PHILADELPHIA
NORTH PHILADELPHIA
WEST PHILADELPHIA
University of Pennsylvania
Woodlands Cemetery
Camden
Bartram Park
SOUTH PHILADELPHIA
Swarthmore
NEW JERSEY
Prospect Park
95
Fort Mifflin
Chester
PHILADELPHIA AND ENVIRONS
HISTORIC SITE
FORT
PARK
REVOLUTIONARY BATTLE

Boathouse Row

Philadelphia
Museum of Art

BENJ. FRANKLIN PKWY.

Schuylkill R.

76

N. BROAD ST.

SIXTH ST.

0          0.8 Mi.

95

LOGAN SQ.

VINE ST

MARKET    ST.

FRANKLIN SQ.

City Hall

Atwater Kent
Museum

Liberty Bell

Independence
Mall

WALNUT ST

RITTENHOUSE
SQ.

WASHINGTON
SQ.

SOUTH ST

S. BROAD ST.

SOCIETY
HILL

Independence
National
Historical Park

Penn's
Landing

Delaware R.

Thaddeus
Kosciuszko N.M.

N
W        E
S

DOWNTOWN
PHILADELPHIA

an outgoing nature that helped him overcome his humble beginnings and rise quickly in Philadelphia society.

A remarkable number of the institutions founded by Franklin
and his contemporaries are going strong today. Franklin was also
responsible for the paving, lighting, and patrolling of Philadelphia's streets, and his improvements to the postal service made the
city the communications center of the country.

Franklin left for London in 1757 to present Pennsylvania's
grievances against the Penn family to the king, and acted as an
unofficial ambassador to the Crown until 1775. On arriving home,
he was made a member of the Second Continental Congress, a
collection of notables including John Hancock, George Washington, Patrick Henry, Peyton Randolph, Richard Henry Lee, and
John and Samuel Adams.

By then an elder statesman and Philadelphia's most famous
citizen, Franklin came home to a city infused with the revolutionary
spirit. Both the Stamp Act of 1765 and the Townshend Acts of
1767 had provoked protests and boycotts. When the news of the
Boston Tea Party reached Philadelphia on Christmas Eve 1773, the
demonstrations in front of the State House (today known as Independence Hall) were so fervent that a tea ship bound for Philadelphia never even tried to land; it pulled up anchor in New Jersey
and returned to England.

In May 1774, Paul Revere rode to Philadelphia with the news
that the British had closed Boston Harbor, provoking a citywide
protest. In September 1774, the First Continental Congress convened in Carpenter's Hall and on October 14 passed the Declaration of Rights, a resolution that spelled out how colonists' rights to
"life, liberty, and property" as English citizens had been violated.

By the time the Second Continental Congress convened,
American blood had been spilled at Lexington and Concord and
the country was, in effect, at war. Philadelphia, which had already
organized its first military troop, the Light Horse of the City (a unit
that still exists), greeted the delegates with enthusiasm. Although
the Pennsylvania Assembly still opposed a break with England, the
Continental Congress was moving fast in that direction. In June,
Virginia's Richard Henry Lee presented a resolution that "all political connection" with Great Britain "is, and ought to be, totally
dissolved" and Thomas Jefferson, a young delegate from Virginia,
was assigned the task of writing a Declaration of Independence.

Jefferson composed the document in rented rooms in the
house of Jacob Graff. On July 4, 1776, Congress adopted "The

unanimous Declaration of the Thirteen United States of America."
When John Hancock, president of the Congress, urged the delegates to "hang together" in supporting the Declaration, Franklin
replied with characteristic wit and wisdom: "We must indeed all
hang together, or most assuredly we shall all hang separately."

The enthusiastic crowd that gathered on the State House
grounds to hear the Declaration read on July 8 did not represent
all Philadelphians. Some citizens were actively hostile to the cause.
The Quakers, in theory pacifists, actually split over the question;
supporters of the Revolution founded the Free Quakers. Even the
British occupation of the city after the American defeat at the
Battle of Brandywine was not unwelcome to all Philadelphia's citizens. When Major General Charles Lord Cornwallis led part of the
victorious British Army into Philadelphia on September 26, a large,
joyous crowd greeted them and, a Loyalist wrote, "the sun shone
out with a sweet serenity."

Washington's surprise attack on the British in the Battle of
Germantown on October 4 failed, and with it went American hopes
of quickly regaining the city. While the British reveled in Philadelphia, patronizing such well-known watering spots as the City Tavern, the American Army suffered through the winter at Valley
Forge. The occupation lasted until June 18, 1778, when the British
pulled out for New York. Major General Benedict Arnold was
appointed the American military commander of the city, and on
June 27, Congress left its place of exile in York and returned.

The Constitutional Convention, called to revise the Articles of
Confederation, was conducted from May to September 1787 in
total secrecy, although Washington and other delegates were highly visible at many social occasions. After a long hot summer of
debate, politics, and compromise, the delegates signed the document that, ratified, formed the basis of United States government
from 1789 to the present. Benjamin Franklin, by then eighty-one
years old and quite feeble, as usual had the last word with his now-
famous observation that the sun carved on the back of Washington's chair was indeed a good omen—a rising, not a setting sun.

Yellow-fever epidemics in the early 1790s killed more than five
thousand, a tenth of the city's population, and encouraged wealthy
Philadelphians to build more summer estates in what they per-
ceived to be the healthier air of the suburbs. Even Washington, the

OVERLEAF: *John Trumbull's famous painting,* The Declaration of Independence.

government having returned to Philadelphia in 1790, rented in Germantown a "summer White House," to escape the plague.

The Federal period (1783–1815) saw Philadelphia's preeminence begin to erode. Harrisburg replaced it as the state capital in 1799, and the federal government left for Washington, DC, in 1800. With the census of 1810 the city lost the title of the nation's largest to New York, then growing approximately twice as fast as Philadelphia. The port of New York was closer to Europe and, with the completion of the Erie Canal in 1825, acquired a direct link to the West. New York also replaced Philadelphia as the financial capital of the country after the failure of Nicholas Biddle's Second Bank of the United States in 1841, following President Andrew Jackson's successful assault on its charter. This and the subsequent failure of Biddle's state-chartered bank were blows from which Philadelphia reeled. Then, in 1844, Protestant gangs burned Catholic churches and attacked foreigners on the street in the so-called Native American riots, the worst mob violence the city had ever seen.

For the 100th anniversary of the signing of the Declaration of Independence, Philadelphia staged the famous Centennial Exposition, the first international fair in the country, on more than 450 acres in Fairmount Park. The city spent over $11 million. Although there were exhibitors from thirty-seven nations, examples of American industrial might stole the show—particularly the Corliss Engine in Machinery Hall with a flywheel thirty feet in diameter and weighing fifty-six tons; the engine supplied the power for eight hundred other machines at the fair. Alexander Graham Bell's new telephone and other technological innovations also drew tremendous crowds.

Philadelphia continued to grow into the next century, its seemingly ever-expanding suburbs prompting the cozy but uninspiring nickname "City of Homes." In the 1920s it chose for itself the dreary title of "World's Greatest Workshop," making "more items necessary for Twentieth Century living, comfort, and convenience than any other American municipality."

In the 1950s the city tore down the elevated railroad tracks, running from West Philadelphia to Broad Street Station, that had cut the city in half. The historic Society Hill district was redeveloped in a program that carefully preserved the section's many historic sites. Newer buildings, including I. M. Pei's distinguished Society Hill Towers and Town Houses, were mixed with old with unusual success.

This chapter divides the central part of Philadelphia, between the Delaware and the Schuylkill rivers, into three parts: Center Square (now Penn Square), including the area around Philadelphia City Hall; the Old Town section, focusing on Independence National Historical Park; and Society Hill, south of Old Town, today an unusual mix of urban renewal and important historical places. Fairmount Park, with its museums and historic buildings, is covered in a separate section, as is Germantown, a repository of fine country houses. The rest of the city—North, West, and South Philadelphia, and the Delaware River Corridor—is less rich historically, but has sites worth noting and visiting.

# CENTER SQUARE

William Penn's original plan for the city included an open square at its center, at the junction of Broad and Market streets. In 1800, Benjamin Henry Latrobe, the country's first well-known professional architect, designed a Center House for the water department on the location, thereafter known as Center Square. Latrobe's building was demolished in 1827 when the new Fairmount Water Works opened on the Schuylkill River. Any chance of keeping the Square open was lost when the city began building its massive City Hall in 1871 on the site, now called Penn Square.

In this guide, the Center Square area is bounded by the Schuylkill River on the west, Vine Street on the north, Ninth Street on the east, and South Street on the south. This part of the city, too large to cover in a single outing, can be toured methodically section by section or even crisscrossed at random, for any route you choose is sure to take you past historic sites. For convenience, the text will first discuss City Hall on Penn Square, then go on to the major axes, Market and Broad streets, and the sites in their vicinity, and proceed on to Logan Circle and Rittenhouse Square.

## PHILADELPHIA CITY HALL

This massive building covers five acres in the center of the old town, at the intersection of its two main streets, Broad and Market. The blocky exterior is festooned with caryatids, bas-reliefs, and statues, all designed by the Scottish-born Alexander Milne Calder, a prominent Philadelphia sculptor. Large entrance portals, mansard roofs, and columns make it the epitome of the French

OVERLEAF: *Philadelphia on a snowy evening. City Hall, right, and the PSFS sign are fixtures of the skyline. A statue of George Washington is in the foreground.*

*City Hall on Center Square. The carvings on the ornate exterior were designed by Alexander Milne Calder.*

Renaissance style so popular for public buildings after the Civil War. Construction began in 1871 under architects John McArthur, Jr., and the aged Thomas U. Walter, both of whom died before it was officially completed in 1901.

At 548 feet tall, City Hall is still a prominent Philadelphia landmark. Until recently no building was permitted to exceed it in height. It is still the tallest masonry-bearing building in the world; completely stone, it has no steel frame. City Hall is the country's largest municipal building; it was the largest building of any kind when it was built. The interior, particularly the Council Chamber and the Mayor's Reception Room, is splendid, with marble, encaustic tiles, mosaics, and carved woodwork. George Herzog, a prominent local interior designer, did much of the best inside work.

## MARKET STREET

This commercial thoroughfare has such landmarks as the Renaissance style **Reading Terminal** (Twelfth and Market streets). Built in 1893 for the Philadelphia and Reading Railway, which went bankrupt shortly thereafter, it has the largest single-span arched train shed left in the country. The Reading Terminal Market still operates on the premises.

The **John Wanamaker Store** (1330–1324 Market Street), a Renaissance Revival commercial palace, was built in three stages from 1902 to 1910 by Daniel H. Burnham & Co. of Chicago, and fills an entire block. The five-story interior court is unequaled in the city, and the Crystal Tea Room remains spacious and elegant. Both the store's massive organ and its 2,500-pound bronze eagle were acquired from the Louisiana Purchase Exposition of 1904 in St. Louis. The museum on the eighth floor includes Wanamaker's office, as it was left when he died in 1922.

In a more modern vein, the **Philadelphia Saving Fund Society Building,** known as the **PSFS Building** (corner of Market and Twelfth streets), was hailed as the "Building of the Century" by the American Institute of Architects. Designed by William Lescaze of New York City and George Howe of Philadelphia, the steel-frame

*The interior court of the John Wanamaker Store, a famed Philadelphia institution and landmark.*

building with granite and glass curtain walls was the first American office building in the International style being practiced in Europe by Walter Gropius, Mies van der Rohe, and Le Corbusier, and it is sometimes called the first modern American skyscraper. A year after the thirty-two-story building was completed in 1932, the twenty-seven-foot-high red neon PSFS sign, a classic of modern graphic design, was erected on the roof.

The twin octagonal towers of the 1822 Gothic Revival **St. Stephen's Episcopal Church** (Tenth and Market streets) are a familiar Philadelphia sight. Tiffany windows and a sanctuary of marble and glass further distinguish it, although the architect, William Strickland, is better known for his graceful Greek Revival buildings, such as the Second Bank of the United States in Philadelphia. The transept was designed by Frank Furness in 1870.

# BROAD STREET

Appropriately named, this north–south thoroughfare was originally planned to be one hundred feet wide, unprecedented for the era. It was one of North Philadelphia's most fashionable residential addresses in the latter half of the nineteenth century and, in the Center Square area, some of the city's most prestigious cultural institutions have a Broad Street address.

## *Pennsylvania Academy of the Fine Arts*

A cleaning of the exterior in 1966 and an interior restoration completed in 1976 revived the splendor of this High Victorian landmark. Built in 1876, the red brick and limestone building was designed by Frank Furness and his then-partner, George W. Hewitt, both important local architects. The interior is distinguished by a grand staircase and rich ornamentation. The Academy, founded in 1805, is the oldest art institution in the country. Its collection includes portraits of George Washington by Gilbert Stuart, Charles Willson Peale, and Rembrandt Peale, as well as works by Thomas Eakins—the director of the Academy School in the 1880s—and his contemporaries, Mary Cassatt,. Winslow Homer, William Merritt Chase, and John Singer Sargent.

LOCATION: Corner of North Broad and Cherry streets. HOURS: 10–5 Monday–Saturday, 11–5 Sunday. FEE: Yes. TELEPHONE: 215–972-7600.

# Masonic Temple

One of the world's finest masonic temples, this Romanesque Revival building was designed in 1868 by architect James H. Windrim. Construction took five years because, according to one account, "all the stone had to be cut, squared, and marked at the quarries according to Masonic tradition." The granite exterior is marked by two distinctive towers, one five and one seven stories tall. Lavish interior rooms in many exotic styles are the building's outstanding feature; the interior designer George Herzog, who worked on nearby City Hall, did the Egyptian, Ionic, and Norman halls.

LOCATION: 1 North Broad Street. HOURS: Guided tours except July and August: 10 and 11 AM, 1, 2, and 3 PM Monday–Friday; 10 and 11 Saturday. FEE: None. TELEPHONE: 215–988–1932.

# Academy of Music

This dignified Renaissance Revival palace is praised more for its acoustics, considered among the best in the world, than for its architecture. Designed by Philadelphia architect Napoleon Le Brun, the three-story hipped-roof brick building was originally to be faced with stone and marble; instead it was trimmed with sandstone. Built in 1857 and home to the Philadelphia Orchestra since its inception in 1900, it is the oldest musical auditorium still in use in the country.

LOCATION: Broad and Locust streets. HOURS: Guided tours; call for times. FEE: Yes. TELEPHONE: 215–893–1935.

Farther south is Haviland Hall, of the **University of the Arts** (South Broad Street, 215–875–4800), an 1824–1826 Greek Revival building designed by John Haviland that has retained its original aspect through many alterations and extensions.

Two exceptional troves of literary and historical research are located to the east of South Broad Street. The **Library Company of Philadelphia** (1314 Locust Street, 215–546–3181) moved from its monumental Greek Revival building in South Philadelphia, the Ridgway Branch, to this modern building in 1966. The Library Company is the nation's oldest subscription library. It was founded by Benjamin Franklin in 1731, and the library of James Logan, William Penn's secretary, was added to the collection in 1792. The Library Company constructed its own building in 1789–1790 to a

OVERLEAF: *The grand staircase of the Pennsylvania Academy of the Fine Arts, the oldest art institution in the country.*

design by Dr. William Thornton, who later won the U.S. Capitol competition. It was later torn down, but the American Philosophical Society built a replica in 1959 for its own library. The Library Company's collection includes the original bust of Franklin that appeared in a niche over the front door.

The library's neighbor, the **Historical Society of Pennsylvania** (1300 Locust Street, 215–732–6201), has 14.5 million rare documents, books, maps, prints, and genealogical records, as well as collections of antique furniture, silver, and early American paintings. They also own the portrait of a stern-looking James Logan, painted by Swedish immigrant Gustavus Hesselius, whom Logan described as "no bad hand, who generally does justice to the men, especially to their blemishes." Hesselius' portraits of Lenni Lenape Indian leaders are also at the Historical Society.

# LOGAN CIRCLE

One of the four parks in William Penn's original layout of the city, Logan Square now contains a traffic circle that bisects the Benjamin Franklin Parkway between the Philadelphia Museum of Art and Penn Square. It is named for James Logan, the prominent citizen-scholar who did so much to develop the early city. The fountain in the Circle was cast by Alexander Stirling Calder; the three classical figures spouting water represent the city's three rivers, the Delaware, Schuylkill, and Wissahickon.

Logan Circle, appropriately, is home to the **Free Library of Philadelphia** (Vine Street between 19th and 20th streets), housed in a 1927 building of French Renaissance design. The library was founded in 1891 with a bequest of $250,000 from George Pepper, a Philadelphia philanthropist. P. A. B. Widener later gave $1 million to the library; his home, at Broad and Girard streets, for years housed a branch of the Free Library. The library's Fleisher collection of about 11,000 orchestral scores is the largest in the world.

West of the Circle is the **Franklin Institute** (20th Street and Benjamin Franklin Parkway, 215–448–1200), founded in 1824 to popularize scientific knowledge and encourage quality manufacturing and craftsmanship. The Institute's original building is now the Atwater Kent Museum. Their new (ca. 1930) home houses a science museum, a planetarium, and the **Benjamin Franklin National Memorial,** which includes a statue of Franklin by James Earle Fraser.

East of the Circle, the massive brownstone **Cathedral of Saints Peter and Paul** (18th Street and the Benjamin Franklin Parkway) took twenty years (1846–1866) to build. Scottish-born John Notman, and Napoleon Le Brun were the architects. The copper dome and the entrance pavilion are credited to Notman. It was the largest of many churches built for wealthy Philadelphians moving west into this section of the city.

## RITTENHOUSE SQUARE

Another of Penn's four parks, this Square was not a fashionable residential area until the mid-nineteenth century. It bears a prominent Philadelphia name: William Rittenhouse, who emigrated to America from Prussia in 1688, built the first colonial paper mill on Wissahickon Creek, now in the city's Fairmount Park. His great-

*A detail from Alexander Stirling Calder's fountain in Logan Circle, representing the city's three rivers.*

grandson, David Rittenhouse (1732–1796), was a clockmaker, celebrated astronomer, mathematician, and Revolutionary War leader.
Once the height of elegance, Rittenhouse Square is now hemmed
in by tall buildings.

Although several important buildings on the Square have been
torn down, in 1968 preservationists saved the **Church of the Holy
Trinity** from demolition. Designed by John Notman and completed in 1859, the brownstone church is an early example of Romanesque Revival style. The three-stage, pinnacled corner tower was
added in 1868 by architect George W. Hewitt.

The streets around Rittenhouse Square still contain lovely old
mansions, examples of Philadelphia rowhouses, and other architectural highlights. The Beaux-Arts **Fell-Van Rensselaer House**
(1801–1803 Walnut Street), completed in 1898, is one of the
Square's last surviving mansions. Two blocks east, **St. Mark's Episcopal Church** (1625 Locust Street) was designed by John Notman
in 1848 in an Anglo-Catholic Gothic Revival style.

## The Rosenbach Museum and Library

This townhouse, built as the Rittenhouse Square area was developed for wealthy Philadelphians in the mid-nineteenth century,
was the home of brothers A. S. W. Rosenbach, one of the world's
leading rare-book dealers, and Philip H. Rosenbach, a noted art
dealer. Founded in 1954, the Rosenbach Museum and Library is
one of the few townhouses in the city open to the public. Major
works in the library's rare-book collection include illuminated
manuscripts of *The Canterbury Tales,* Lewis Carroll's own copy of
*Alice in Wonderland,* and the manuscript of Joyce's *Ulysses.* The
house, furnished with English, French, and American period furniture, contains collections of prints and drawings by such artists as
Daumier and Blake and some three thousand original drawings
and watercolors by Maurice Sendak. Appointed with period furniture, the house has artifacts of eras ranging from the Spanish
Explorers to World War II.

LOCATION: 2010 DeLancey Place. HOURS: 11–4 Tuesday–Sunday;
closed August. FEE: Yes. TELEPHONE: 215–732–1600.

OPPOSITE: *Rittenhouse Square, one of the four parks laid out by William Penn.*

# S O C I E T Y   H I L L

Society Hill takes its name from the Free Society of Traders, a London-based commercial company. In 1681, William Penn granted the society a charter and sold it 20,000 acres, including a strip of land between present-day Spruce and Pine streets that extended from the Delaware to the Schuylkill rivers. The boundaries of the present district are vague, but it can be roughly defined by Walnut Street on the north, South Street on the south, and the Delaware River and Ninth Street on the east and west.

Development of Society Hill was at first sporadic. Two of its earliest standing structures are the matching brick **John Palmer House** and the **Joseph Wharton House** (117 and 119 Lombard Street, private), both built about 1743, possibly by Palmer, a bricklayer. After 1750, Society Hill developed rapidly, although when the original wing of the Pennsylvania Hospital was erected in 1755–1757, its location at Eighth and Pine streets was purposely— for the health and safety of the patients—on the outskirts of the city. As well-to-do Philadelphia edged westward after the Civil War, immigrants from eastern and southern Europe moved to Society Hill, and many of the older buildings became tenements, warehouses, or factories. Deterioration of the area was finally reversed in the late 1950s with what has proven to be a very successful redevelopment project that has restored nearly eight hundred houses and turned Society Hill into an attractive and historic residential neighborhood.

This tour starts with the Pennsylvania Hospital, loops north through Washington Square, then south through Head House Square, ending at the Thaddeus Kosciusko National Memorial.

## PENNSYLVANIA HOSPITAL

Founded in 1751 by Dr. Thomas Bond, Benjamin Franklin, and other public-spirited citizens, the majestic Pennsylvania Hospital is the first hospital in the United States and, architecturally, one of the most impressive public buildings of the eighteenth century. The east wing of the original building (the Pine Building) was designed by Samuel Rhoads and completed in 1756. The west wing was finished in 1797. The center section, completed in 1804,

OPPOSITE: *Brick row houses on Society Hill, a historic neighborhood that has been redeveloped since the 1950s.*

houses the country's first surgical amphitheater. The Pennsylvania set the standard for American hospitals and helped make Philadelphia a center of medical learning.

The hospital is also a veritable museum. Among its historical documents and artworks are letters from Franklin and Benjamin West's famous *Christ Healing the Sick in the Temple,* which he painted in 1815 to help raise money for the hospital. The **statue of William Penn,** created by eighteenth-century sculptor John Cheere in 1774, on the Pine Street side was found in a London junk shop in 1804 by Penn's grandson and given to the hospital. According to legend, Penn comes down off his pedestal in the early hours of the New Year and tours the hospital grounds.

> LOCATION: Entrance on Eighth Street, between Spruce and Pine streets. HOURS: By appointment. FEE: None. TELEPHONE: 215–829–3971.

Just north of the hospital, **Mikveh Israel Cemetery** (Spruce between Eighth and Ninth streets) is the oldest Jewish burial ground in the city, dating from 1738 on land deeded to Nathan Levy by the Penn family. Haym Salomon, called the "financier of the American Revolution," and Rebecca Gratz, purportedly the model for Rebecca in Sir Walter Scott's 1820 novel *Ivanhoe,* are buried here.

**St. George's Greek Orthodox Cathedral,** the graceful Greek Revival temple at 250 South Eighth Street, was designed by John Haviland and completed in 1822 as St. Andrew's Episcopal Church. Its acquisition by the Greek Orthodox Church in 1922 reflected the area's changing ethnic character. Of all the buildings Haviland designed in Philadelphia, this was his favorite. He was a member of the original congregation and is buried beneath the church.

# WASHINGTON SQUARE

One of Penn's four original city parks, Washington Square became the city's potter's field and the place where Revolutionary War soldiers and victims of the yellow-fever epidemic of 1792 were buried. Today a lovely, shaded refuge on the edge of Society Hill, it is the site of the **Tomb of the Unknown Soldier of the American Revolution,** a simple monument with a statue of George Washington and the flags of the original thirteen colonies. The Square was landscaped in 1815 and became a fashionable residential area until after the Civil War, when law offices set up in its elegant buildings.

*Statue of George Washington on the Tomb of the Unknown Soldier of the American Revolution, Washington Square.*

On the northwest corner of Sixth and Walnut is the white marble **Curtis Publishing Company** building, from which the *Saturday Evening Post* and *Ladies' Home Journal* were once published and printed. Inside the lobby is a fifty-foot-long Tiffany glass mosaic mural based on the Maxfield Parrish painting *The Dream Garden,* and a small museum devoted to the work of Norman Rockwell, the artist and illustrator who did so many covers for the *Saturday Evening Post.*

## The Athenaeum of Philadelphia

Founded in 1814 as a "place of common resort" by literary gentlemen, the Athenaeum had its first reading room and library in Philosophical Hall. The present Renaissance Revival building was designed by John Notman and covered in 1847 with brownstone, a last-minute replacement for more costly marble. This new look influenced many other buildings in Philadelphia.

The Athenaeum is still a private library, the oldest in continuous use in the city, and lavishly decorated with antique furniture, sculpture, and paintings, including works by the well-known Philadelphia portrait painter John Neagle and chairs that once were in

the New Jersey home of Joseph Bonaparte. A carved wood staircase with cast-iron railings in the center hall leads to reading rooms
overlooking a quiet garden in the rear.

LOCATION: 219 South Sixth Street, on the east side of Washington
Square. HOURS: 9–5 Monday–Friday. FEE: None. TELEPHONE: 215–
925–2688.

The **Society Hill Synagogue** (426 Spruce Street), designed by
Thomas U. Walter, was built in 1829 as the Spruce Street Baptist
Church. The square corner towers originally supported cupolas,
removed in 1911 when the building became a synagogue.

The **Philadelphia Contributionship for the Insuring of
Houses from Loss by Fire** (212 South Fourth Street, 215–627–
1752), the oldest continuously active mutual fire insurance company in the country, was founded by Benjamin Franklin and others
in 1752. Today it includes a museum with a nineteenth-century
insurance office, boardrooms, and a collection of antique fire-
fighting equipment. The fire mark of the Contributionship, which
can still be seen about town as well as in the collection of the
museum, is believed to have been designed by Philip Syng and cast
by John Stow. The house was designed by Thomas U. Walter and
erected in 1836. The mansard roof and fourth story were added
after the Civil War.

At 225 South Third Street is the **Old St. Paul's Church,**
designed by the bricklayer John Palmer in 1760–1761. Two prominent Philadelphia architects remodeled it in 1830: William Strickland redid the exterior in a more up-to-date Greek Revival style,
while Thomas U. Walter attended to the interior. The church was
founded in 1760 by the Reverend William McClenachan, considered a radical for advocating the separation of church and state.

# PHYSICK HOUSE

This distinguished four-story brick house is the only free-standing
Federal townhouse remaining in historic Society Hill. Now a museum, it was built in 1786 for Henry Hill, a prosperous wine merchant and legislator. In 1815, Dr. Philip Syng Physick took up
residence; called the "father of American surgery," he invented the
needle forceps that advanced the science of medicine. The exterior
of the house is noteworthy for its large, graceful fanlight over the
front door. Inside, it is elegantly furnished with many pieces

*Fanlight over the door of the Physick House, now a museum, on Society Hill.*

original to the house, supplemented by loans of French and American pieces from the Philadelphia Museum of Art.

LOCATION: 321 South Fourth Street. HOURS: May through August: 12–5 Thursday–Sunday; September through April: 11–2 Thursday–Saturday; tours on the hour. FEE: Yes. TELEPHONE: 215–925–7866.

## POWEL HOUSE

In 1786 an English visitor praised this fine Georgian residence as being "of admirable Design both without and within, and might do credit to London." Built in 1765 for Charles Stedman, a merchant, the three-and-a-half-story brick house with stone string-courses was later the home of Samuel Powel, who was mayor of Philadelphia both immediately before and after the Revolution. Both George Washington and John Adams called on him here, and several Powel family artifacts are among the impressive collection of eighteenth-century family furnishings.

LOCATION: 244 South Third Street. HOURS: May through July: 10–4 Tuesday–Saturday; Rest of year: Call for hours. FEE: Yes. TELEPHONE: 215–627–0364.

At 270 South Second Street, the **Abercrombie House,** two blocks east of the Powel House and similar to it in design, was built about 1759 for a sea captain. At four and a half stories, it was one of the tallest buildings in the city. When Society Hill fell out of fashion after the Civil War, the house was gutted, and it was then used as a warehouse.

A block east toward the Delaware River is an establishment with an appealing name, **A Man Full of Trouble Tavern** (127 Spruce Street), a 1760 structure with a gambrel roof and the original cove cornice. It is one of the last surviving examples of the many seamen's taverns that once lined the waterfront. Now owned by the University of Pennsylvania, it is utilized for offices.

The tavern building also includes the adjacent **Paschall House,** operated until 1884. In 1960, it was restored by the Knauer Foundation for Historic Preservation. The basement kitchen and the barroom have many of the original utensils, cutlery, and tableware, and a large collection of English delft.

## ST. PETER'S PROTESTANT EPISCOPAL CHURCH

This beautiful brick church, designed by Dr. John Kearsley and built by Robert Smith, has marble trim, a large Palladian window on its eastern end, and a six-story-high belfry tower topped by a tall, slender steeple, the latter an 1842 addition by the architect William Strickland. The interior is highlighted by the soft colors of the stained-glass windows, the box pews, and a rectangular chancel.

George Washington and his friend Samuel Powel attended services here together, and many prominent Americans are buried in the churchyard, including William Shippen; Nicholas Biddle, the literary statesman and financier; and the artist Charles Willson Peale. A fierce-looking carved eagle is perched on a column over the grave of Commodore Stephen ("our country, right or wrong") Decatur, naval hero of the War of 1812.

LOCATION: Third and Pine streets. HOURS: 9–3 Tuesday–Saturday. FEE: None. TELEPHONE: 215–925–5968.

Across from St. Peter's is the **Thaddeus Kosciuszko National Memorial** (301 Pine Street, 215–597–9618), the 1775 house where the Polish patriot and statesman lived in exile in 1797–1798, after

OPPOSITE: *St. Peter's Protestant Episcopal Church on Society Hill.*

failing to free his native Poland from Russia. During the American Revolution. Kosciuszko fought for the Americans and rose to the rank of chief engineer of the Continental Army. The unpretentious brick house with a gable roof is administered by Independence National Historical Park.

In 1787, Richard Allen, the first ordained black minister in the country, built a church at 419 South Sixth Street and founded what is now called **Mother Bethel African Methodist Church.** The congregation included many free blacks who moved to Society Hill after the Revolution. The distinguished Romanesque Revival church (1889–1890), with its rough-hewn granite exterior, is the third church building constructed by the congregation on this site.

## HEAD HOUSE SQUARE

This splendidly restored historic square, built between 1740 and 1811, takes its name from the 1803 **Head House** at the Pine Street end, which is topped by a cupola and weathervane. The house was the residence and office of the market master, who ran the **Second Street Market,** now also restored, located just behind the Head House. The market's arcades are now used by artists and craftspeople to display their wares. Many other original eighteenth- and early nineteenth-century buildings remain, such as the 1780 **Ross House** on Lombard Street. The **Head Tavern** across the street is a reconstruction.

## O     L     D     T     O     W     N

William Penn envisioned a "greene Countrie Towne" spread out between the Delaware and the Schuylkill rivers, but the city clustered along the Delaware for over a century and a half. Thus it is the Old Town that encompasses "the most historic square mile in America," for it was the heart of Philadelphia's social, political, and cultural life when some of the most momentous events in the history of the country were taking place.

The area's main historic attraction is the remarkable cluster of buildings grouped together as Independence National Historical Park, which includes two of the nation's most popular historical shrines, Independence Hall and the Liberty Bell. In this guide, Old Town is bounded by Vine Street on the north, Walnut Street on the south, Ninth Street on the west, and the Delaware River on the east.

# ATWATER KENT MUSEUM

This Greek Revival building fronted by four square pilasters was built in 1825–1827 as the Franklin Institute, part of a movement to bring knowledge of science to the working classes. Its designer, John Haviland, also taught the first courses for would-be professional architects in the country here. In 1939, the building became a museum devoted to the history of Philadelphia and noted for its outstanding collection of toys, prints, and dioramas. It was named for Atwater Kent, a radio pioneer.

LOCATION: 15 South Seventh Street. HOURS: 10–4 Thursday–Monday. FEE: Yes. TELEPHONE: 215–922–3031.

The **Afro-American Historical and Cultural Museum** (Seventh and Arch streets, 215–574–0380) presents a broad view of black history in Philadelphia, the United States, and the entire hemisphere through paintings, sculpture, prints, and performing arts. It opened in 1976 as part of the city's Bicentennial celebration. There has been a black community in Philadelphia since its earliest days, although the Quaker concept of brotherly love did not always include blacks. William Penn himself was a slaveholder.

Near Vine Street is **St. Augustine's Catholic Church** (1848), a one-story structure of Italian Renaissance design by architect Napoleon Le Brun, designer of the Cathedral of Saints Peter and Paul. The original church was burned in the anti-Catholic riots of 1844, which were fomented by the Native American Party, who wanted to deny the vote to all but native-born Americans.

A block south at the corner of Race and Fourth streets is the 1837 **Old First Reformed Church** (215–922–4566) of the United Church of Christ. Once a German Reformed Church founded in 1727 and the center of a German settlement in the area, the building became a paint factory in 1882 and later was abandoned as the neighborhood deteriorated. In 1967, it was restored along with nearby Colonial and post-Revolutionary homes and shops.

# ELFRETH'S ALLEY

This fifteen-foot-wide passageway between Second and Front streets, bordered by thirty-three houses, is the oldest continuously inhabited street in Philadelphia. The alley was opened between 1702 and 1704, although Jeremiah Elfreth didn't acquire the property until the mid-eighteenth century. By then many of the houses

*Fifteen feet wide, Elfreth's Alley has been inhabited since 1702.*

were already built—the oldest, numbers 122 and 124, between 1725 and 1727—but a few were erected in the early nineteenth century. They range in height from two to three and a half stories and have gable or gambrel roofs. The alley is considered typical of the narrow side streets where eighteenth-century artisans lived. An early property owner was silversmith Philip Syng, who in 1752 made the silver inkstand eventually used for the signing of both the Declaration of Independence and the Constitution. Number 126 is open to the public as **Elfreth's Alley Museum** (215–574–0560) and contains period furniture and a colonial kitchen. Other houses are open on Elfreth's Alley Days, the first weekend in June.

# BETSY ROSS HOUSE

The popularity of this charming eighteenth-century house has not been diminished by the recent recognition that Betsy Ross, contrary to legend, did not make the first Stars and Stripes. Possibly she never even lived here. In numbers of visitors, the house ranks second only to the Liberty Bell. Betsy, a Quaker and a patriot, was indeed a seamstress and a flagmaker who made ships' colors during the Revolution. The quaint brick house, built ca. 1740 with a large gable roof and panelled shutters, has a basement kitchen, winding stairs, and a restored upholsterer's shop. The rooms are furnished with period pieces, some of them belonging to her. The house was restored by Atwater Kent in 1936. Betsy and her third husband, John Claypoole, are buried in the adjoining garden.

LOCATION: 239 Arch Street. HOURS: 10–5 Tuesday–Sunday. FEE: None. TELEPHONE: 215-627-5343.

Directly across Arch Street is the **Friends Meeting House** (215–627–2667), a plain but impressive example of Federal architecture, surrounded by a high brick wall. Originally the site was a burial ground given to the Religious Society of Friends—Quakers—by William Penn in 1693; the meetinghouse was constructed in 1804, the largest in the United States. The main room seats one thousand people, testimony to the dominant influence of Quakers in Pennsylvania's first 125 years. Dioramas and early Quaker artifacts are on display. In the middle of the block west of the Betsy Ross House, **Loxley Court** is where, in 1752, Benjamin Franklin flew his famous kite in a summer storm to prove lightning was electrical. The key tied to his kite string was supposedly from the door of number 2, home of carpenter Benjamin Loxley.

En route to Penn's Landing, described below, the visitor can detour to the **Philadelphia Bourse** (1893–1895, Fifth Street between Chestnut and Market streets), a monument to the city's commercial aspirations at the turn of the century. The Victorian building, with its striking inside court, covers a block and, when built, had industrial exhibitions and a grain and stock exchange.

# INDEPENDENCE SEAPORT MUSEUM

The museum, at Penn's Landing, on the Delaware River, has collections of ship models, historic small boats, figureheads, paintings, prints, drawings, weapons, and other artifacts relating to ships and the sea. Pier 34 creates the ambiance of a wharf of the early 1900s.

Magnificent ships dominate the waterfront. The four-masted *Moshulu* has been restored to the era of 1904, when she was built. The elegant art nouveau interior features Honduran mahogany, etched glass, and chandeliers. A restaurant in the ship also offers warm-weather dining on the deck. The 1883 barkantine *Gazela* is the last of the square-rigged Portuguese fishing ships. The 1904 iron *Lightship Number 79* illuminated the shipping lanes of Philadelphia for sixty-three years. The USS *Olympia* was Commodore George Dewey's flagship during the Battle of Manila Bay, May 1, 1898, a decisive American naval victory in the Spanish-American War. The USS *Becuna* is a World War II, guppy-class submarine.

> LOCATION: Penn's Landing, 211 South Columbus Boulevard at Walnut Street. HOURS: 10–5 Daily. FEE: Yes. TELEPHONE: 215–925–5439.

# INDEPENDENCE NATIONAL HISTORICAL PARK

At the heart of "the most historic square mile in America," the national historical park embraces a number of buildings and sites in 44 acres that capture the era of the nation's founding and reflects the values of the Founding Fathers with a clarity rarely found in preservation projects. The Park was founded by an act of Congress in 1948 for the preservation of Independence Hall and a few surrounding buildings. In 1950, the Park took over the preservation and administration of other structures belonging to the city of Philadelphia. Restoration began in earnest in 1951 and continued into the 1970s.

This process was marked by constant wrangling and debate. For example, many fine nineteenth-century commercial buildings were lost, despite considerable opposition, to make way for the Park's Independence Mall. (The esteemed architectural critic Lewis Mumford complained the open spaces of the Mall imposed on Independence Hall "an aesthetic burden that only a vast palace . . . could hope to pull off.") Unless otherwise noted, sites in this section are in the historical park. For information about hours, fees, and special programs, call the Visitor Center (215–597–8974).

The more distant sites are as follows: The Benjamin Franklin National Memorial inside the Franklin Institute Science Museum on Logan Circle; the Deshler-Morris House in Germantown; the Thaddeus Kosciuszko National Memorial and the Mikveh Israel Cemetery, both on Society Hill; the Edgar Allen Poe National Historic Site in North Philadelphia; and Gloria Dei (Old Swedes') Church, in South Philadelphia.

## Independence Hall

The meticulously restored and preserved centerpiece of a national historical park, Independence Hall was built as the Pennsylvania State House between the years 1732–1748. It was designed by lawyer Andrew Hamilton, an amateur architect and speaker of the Assembly. Hamilton selected a site on the western edge of the city over protests that the location was too remote.

Constructed of brick with marble trim, it is two stories tall with a balustraded gable roof. In 1753, its builder, the master carpenter Edmund Wooley, finished adding a square tower and octagonal steeple on the south side in which to hang the Liberty Bell. The steeple was removed in 1781 and in 1828 William Strickland designed a new steeple that captured the spirit of the original though it was not an exact copy.

The visit of the Marquis de Lafayette in 1824 and the fiftieth anniversary of the signing of the Declaration of Independence two years later inspired the first serious restoration of the building. Still, periods of neglect followed; when a restoration was undertaken by the city in 1871, it was found that the Assembly Room had become a storehouse for unwanted furniture and contained a huge block of marble intended for the Washington Monument in the nation's capital. Since the involvement of the National Park Service, the major rooms have been restored close to their original appearance. The tour includes the Assembly Room, where the original "rising sun" chair is displayed, and the adjacent Pennsylvania Supreme Court Chamber. On the second floor are the Governor's Council Chamber, the Long Room, and the Committee Room.

Independence Hall well deserves its status as a national shrine. The State House was the site of events on which the history of this country turned, the most important being the signing of the Declaration of Independence and the drafting of the Constitution.

LOCATION: Chestnut Street between Fifth and Sixth streets.

*The Assembly Room, Independence Hall, where on the morning of July 4th, 1776, delegates*

## Liberty Bell Pavilion

As with any icon, the Liberty Bell has a story that is part legend and part fact. Visitors are surprised to learn that the bell was not cast to commemorate the country's independence but for the fiftieth anniversary of the Charter of Privileges granted to the colony of Pennsylvania in 1701 by its founder, William Penn. A bell was cast in London, England, and sent to Philadelphia in 1752. Upon first ringing, the bell cracked beyond repair. Two local craftsmen cast a new bell that was placed in the tower of the State House and functioned daily for many years. The bell is known to have tolled on July 8, 1776, not July 4th as legend has it, to summon the citizens of Philadelphia for the first public reading of the Declaration of Independence. In the 1830s, it came to be called the Liberty Bell, and it began to crack. Abolitionists working to outlaw slavery were inspired by the inscription from the Old Testament (Leviticus 25:10) located on the bell: "Proclaim liberty throughout all the

*approved the Declaration of Independence.*

land, unto all the inhabitants thereof." The bell was adopted as their symbol of liberty, its name changed forever.

In 1846 as the bell rang in that year's celebration of George Washington's birthday the crack extended to the point that the Liberty Bell could never ring again. In 1852, the bell was placed on display in Independence Hall and, on January 1, 1976, was moved to the glass Liberty Bell Pavilion, where it can be viewed twenty-four hours a day.

LOCATION: Independence Mall between Fifth and Sixth streets.

## Carpenters' Hall

This splendid cruciform building with an octagonal cupola is still owned and operated by the Carpenters' Company, founded in 1724 by a group of masterbuilders. The First Continental Congress met here to air grievances in 1774. The hall served as a hospital for

Washington's army, and from 1791 to 1797 it served as the original offices for the First Bank of the United States. In 1857 it became a public museum and still houses exhibits relating to the building's history, including a detailed scale model of its construction.

LOCATION: 320 Chestnut Street between Third and Fourth streets. HOURS: 10–4 Tuesday–Sunday. FEE: None. TELEPHONE: 215–925–0167.

## New Hall and Pemberton Hall

Also in Carpenters' Court are two reconstructed historic buildings which line the alley leading to Carpenters' Hall. **New Hall** was erected by the Carpenters' Company in 1791 and was originally used to house the offices of the first secretary of war, Henry Knox, and his staff. The building currently houses a museum highlighting the role of the Army, Navy, and Marines from 1775 to 1800.

**Pemberton House** is a reconstruction of one built by wealthy Quaker merchant Joseph Pemberton in 1775 and is typical of the Georgian style of architecture popular during the eighteenth century. The America's National Park Museum Shop is currently housed in this building.

## Franklin Court

By using steel beams to outline the frame of the only house Benjamin Franklin ever owned, the contemporary architect Robert Venturi has evoked the spirit of the Colonial dwelling while providing an appropriate setting for a museum exhibit on Franklin's life and work. This unusual approach to historic restoration was undertaken for the nation's Bicentennial after the Park Service decided it lacked sufficient information to reconstruct the house.

Franklin, who built a three-story dwelling here in 1763–1765, once called it, "a good House contrived to my mind." For most of the next twenty years, however, he was abroad on diplomatic missions. When he returned in 1785, he added a library and two bedrooms and built a printshop for his grandson. "I hardly know how to justify building a Library at an age that will so soon oblige me to quit it," he wrote. He was then eighty.

Within the "ghost structure" are viewing tubes through which the visitor can inspect remains of the original foundation. An underground museum is entered by a ramp on the west of the house. Here Franklin is presented in his many facets—printer,

*Steel beams on Franklin Court mark the outline of the only house that Benjamin Franklin ever owned.*

inventor, thinker, writer, diplomat, innovator—through a film and other exhibits. His opinions on a variety of subjects appear on a video screen and phones can be used to call up famous figures, past and present, for their views on Franklin.

The Franklin Court complex also includes the **Market Street Houses,** three of the five structures that Franklin built as rentals in front of his own home. The exteriors of all five are now restored to their eighteenth-century appearance; number 314 is a bookstore; number 316 is a working post office and postal museum, honoring Franklin as founder of the postal service; number 318 exhibits archaeological material found in the area; and numbers 320 and 322 house a printshop, bindery, and subscription office.

LOCATION: Market Street between Third and Fourth streets. Underground museum is accessible by wheelchair.

## *Congress Hall*

Built as the Philadelphia County Court House, the exquisite red-brick building topped by a cupola and weathervane was completed in 1789, and used by Congress from 1790 to 1800. In this building,

Congress ratified the Bill of Rights (1791), signed the Jay Treaty (1794), watched Washington (for the second time) and John Adams take the presidential oath of office, and heard Washington's Farewell Address (1797). After Congress moved to Washington in 1800, the building resumed its role as a courthouse.

LOCATION: Sixth and Chestnut streets.

## Old City Hall

This building is almost a copy of Congress Hall, but smaller and less elegant in demeanor. It was built in 1790–1791 for the city government and used by the U.S. Supreme Court from 1791 to 1800. Here the court under Chief Justice John Jay asserted its independence from the other branches of government and decided cases that established the supremacy of federal over state law. The building was Philadelphia's City Hall for most of the nineteenth century. Today exhibits on the judicial phase of the building's history are on the ground floor.

LOCATION: Fifth and Chestnut streets.

Directly behind Old City Hall is **Philosophical Hall,** 1785–1789, a restrained building in the style of its neighbors. Privately owned and closed to the public, it still houses the American Philosophical Society, which Franklin founded in 1743 "for the promotion of useful knowledge among the British plantations in America." Today the society has many Nobel prizewinners among its members.

To house its library, which includes a large collection of Frankliniana, the society constructed **Library Hall** across Fifth Street in 1959. The original building, torn down in 1884, was built in 1789–1790 by the Library Company of Philadelphia. The new building is an exact copy of the original right down to the balustrade of urns along the roof line and the statue of Franklin in the niche above the door. According to legend, the statue sometimes comes down off its perch after dark and heads for the nearest saloon.

The building was designed by Dr. William Thornton, who later won the competition to design the Capitol in Washington, DC.

## Second Bank of the United States

This adaptive restoration of a majestic Greek Revival building houses "Portraits of the Capital City," an exhibit containing paintings of famous colonial and federal leaders by Charles Willson

*The Greek Revival Second Bank of the United States, designed by William Strickland, now part of the Independence National Historical Park.*

Peale and others. Peale founded the nation's first museum in Independence Hall in 1802. The bank brought architect William Strickland to prominence; it was his first large commission. The eight-columned porticoes on each end are approached by low-rising steps. The sides of the building are plain—Strickland apparently never intended them to be seen.

Chartered in 1816, the bank prospered under the leadership of Nicholas Biddle, who assumed its presidency in 1823. However, President Andrew Jackson saw it as a bastion of privilege and in 1833 ordered the removal of federal deposits and vetoed a bill to recharter the bank in 1836. From 1845 to 1935 the building was the city's Custom House.

LOCATION: 420 Chestnut Street between Fourth and Fifth streets.

## The Declaration House

This three-story, narrow brick building (Seventh and Market Streets) is a 1975 reconstruction of the house where Thomas Jefferson wrote the Declaration of Independence. He rented two

second-floor rooms in the summer of 1776 while a Virginia delegate to the Continental Congress. A reproduction of his lap desk
and swivel chair are displayed with other period pieces. The original house was built in 1775 by the bricklayer Jacob Graff, Jr.

   The **First Bank of the United States** (120 South Third Street),
with the first marble portico to be built in America, was designed by
Samuel Blodgett, Jr., probably with some help from James Hoban.
Blodgett was a talented amateur architect and merchant who made
a fortune in the China Trade. The First Bank of the United States
was created by Alexander Hamilton in 1791; until this building was
finished in 1797, the institution rented space in Carpenters' Hall.
After the bank's charter expired in 1811, the building was taken
over by a bank founded by financier Stephen Girard, which occupied it until 1926. The exterior has been restored but the building
is not open to the public.

## City Tavern

The present three-and-a-half story brick building is a faithful reconstruction of the City Tavern built in 1773 by some of the city's

*Across the street from City Tavern is Bookbinders, a popular Philadelphia restaurant since
1865.* OPPOSITE: *William Strickland's Philadelphia Exchange.*

"principal gentlemen." It became famous over the next three decades as a gathering place for notable Americans. When he arrived in Philadelphia as a delegate to the First Continental Congress—"dirty, dusty and fatigued" by the long trip from Massachusetts—John Adams wrote that "we could not resist the importunity to go to the tavern, the most genteel one in America." The tavern was also the site of Washington's farewell dinner before leaving for Boston in June 1775 as the newly elected commander of the Continental Army. The tavern hosted British officers during the occupation of Philadelphia in 1777 and 1778, but lost most of its prominent patrons after the federal government moved to Washington, DC, in 1800. The building was demolished in 1854.

City Tavern is furnished with period reproductions and serves lunch and dinner. Some of the items on its menu have been adapted from colonial dishes.

LOCATION: Second Street near Walnut. HOURS: 11:30–10 Daily. FEE: None. TELEPHONE: 215–413–1443.

Just behind City Tavern is the **Philadelphia Exchange** (later known as Merchants' Exchange). The exterior of this, William Strickland's 1834 Greek Revival masterpiece, has been restored but it is not open to the public. Here Philadelphia merchants awaited the arrival of ships, traded shares, and bought insurance. The building, with its distinctive, curved Corinthian colonnade, later housed the Maritime Exchange and the Philadelphia Stock Exchange. Its location is indicative of the city's westward movement in the first half of the nineteenth century.

## Walnut Street Houses

Through reconstruction and meticulous restoration, this block-front of brick houses on the north side of Walnut Street between Third and Fourth streets has been brought back to its original eighteenth-century appearance. The **Bishop White House** (309 Walnut Street) was built in 1787 for The Reverend Dr. William White, the first Episcopal bishop of Pennsylvania and rector of both St. Peter's Church and Christ Church. The house is an example of how upper-class Philadelphians of the period lived. White lived here until he died in 1836; many of the furnishings are his, donated by descendants.

By contrast, the **Todd House** (northeast corner of Fourth and Walnut streets) presents a picture of middle-class life after the

Revolution, specifically that of the young lawyer John Todd, who purchased the 1775 house in 1791, and his wife, Dolley Payne. Todd died of yellow fever in October 1793. In September of the following year the young, vivacious widow of twenty-three left Philadelphia to marry Congressman James Madison, the future president. Madison's friend, Senator Aaron Burr, introduced the couple. Dolley was later a renowned hostess in the national capital. Tours of the Bishop White House and the Todd House are by reservation only; reservations may be made at the national historical park's Visitor Center.

The Philadelphia Horticultural Society formerly occupied the two historic buildings at 319–325 Walnut Street.

## Christ Church

From a twentieth-century point of view, this is one of the nation's quintessential Colonial churches, rivalled chiefly by St. Michael's in Charleston and St. Paul's Chapel in New York. Designed by a physician, Dr. John Kearsley, who was evidently influenced by the London churches of Christopher Wren, and James Gibbs, it was built between 1727 and 1744. Parishioner Benjamin Franklin may have contributed to the design of the 200-foot steeple, added in 1754. There is a magnificent Venetian—sometimes called "Palladian"—window on the east end. The church preserves the pews occupied by George Washington, John Adams, and their wives; historical exhibits are located in the Tower Room. Signers of the Declaration of Independence James Wilson and Robert Morris are buried in the churchyard. Benjamin Franklin and Benjamin Rush are among the signers buried in the **Christ Church Cemetery** (Fifth and Arch streets).

LOCATION: Second Street north of Market Street.

## Free Quaker Meeting House

Now a museum operated by the Junior League of Philadelphia, the Free Quaker Meeting House was built, as a tablet in the north gable patriotically informs, "in the year / of OUR LORD 1783 / of the EMPIRE 8." The one hundred or so founders were Quakers driven from their meetings for supporting the Revolution, among them Thomas Mifflin, a Revolutionary War general and a signer of the Constitution. Betsy Ross and Lydia Darragh were also Free Quakers. Darragh became a heroine of the American Revolution when, on December 2, 1777, she overheard British officers planning a surprise attack on Washington at Whitemarsh, eight miles away, and warned the Americans.

The exterior of the building has architectural details, such as the pediment over the doorway, unusual for Quaker meetinghouses. Under the street are wine vaults, built by the Free Quakers to earn revenue.

LOCATION: Fifth and Arch streets. HOURS: Memorial Day through Labor Day: 10–4 Tuesday–Saturday, 12–4 Sunday. FEE: None. TELEPHONE: 215–923–6777.

Built in 1769, the three-story **St. George's United Methodist Church** (Fourth and New streets, 215–925–7788), with a gable roof, is distinguished for its age rather than its architecture; it is the world's oldest Methodist church still in use. An adjacent museum contains such Methodist historical items as the Bible and spectacles of Bishop Francis Asbury, the Methodist leader who preached his first American sermon here in 1771, and the chalice sent by John Wesley.

# F A I R M O U N T     P A R K

The name of this 8,700-acre expanse of parkland supposedly came from William Penn, who stood on the banks of the "Skokill" River and rhapsodized, "What a faire mount." The park grew from a five-acre plot of landscaped ground around the Fairmount Water Works, after the central pumping station was moved from Center Square in 1812. By 1889, the writer and world traveler Lafcadio Hearn could ask, "Is it possible you have never seen Fairmount Park? Believe me, then, that it is the most beautiful place of the whole civilized world. . . ."

Frederick Graff designed the **Fairmount Water Works,** built from 1812 to 1815 on a dammed section of the river, a stretch of six Greek Revival stone buildings flanked by a pavilion. The view of the waterworks from the river was a favorite of artists, while the pumping station, an engineering marvel of its age, became a source of civic pride. Visiting Philadelphia without seeing the Fairmount Water Works was like going to London and missing Westminster Abbey, natives used to say. The building, which has been restored, ceased operating as a water station in 1911; it housed the city aquarium until 1962.

North of the waterworks, near the river, **Laurel Hill Cemetery** also became a popular place for public outings and helped in the eventual formation of the Park. Begun in 1836, the cemetery was inspired by rustic cemetery plans in Paris and in Edinburgh. The Edinburgh-trained architect John Notman, Jr., designed the grounds and the **Gatehouse** with its portico supported by eight Doric columns. In 1844, the city acquired **Lemon Hill** (off Kelly and Sedgley drives; 215–232–4337), a villa of the Federal period, north of the waterworks, and forty-five acres to protect the water supply. It was opened to the public eleven years later. Lemon Hill has been joined by other mansions taken over by the city, seven of which have been restored and are open to the public as the **Fairmount Park Mansions** (215–684–7922).

The popularity of the sport of rowing, which began on the placid waters of the Schuylkill about 1835, also contributed to the development of the Park. By the 1850s there were daily races organized by the Bachelors' Barge Club, and the graceful shells on the river provided inspiration to Thomas Eakins and other artists. The ten buildings that the city's rowing clubs erected between 1860 (**Quaker City Barge Club**) and the early twentieth century are known collectively as **Boathouse Row**. With the Fairmount Water Works, the boathouses are one of the premier sights of the river, particularly the **Undine Barge Club** (1882–1883), designed by the Philadelphia architects Furness and Evans.

In 1867, the state legislature officially established Fairmount Park by setting aside—"forever"—land along the Schuylkill River. Frederick Law Olmsted and Calvert Vaux, designers of New York City's Central and Prospect Parks were consulted, but the plans of a city engineer, H. J. Schwarzmann, were eventually adopted.

Schwarzmann also planned the **Philadelphia Zoological Garden,** the country's first zoo, which opened in 1874. Today the zoo (34th Street and Girard Avenue, 215–243–1100) retains the picturesque, two-story **Entrance Pavilions** with the steep hipped roofs designed by architects Furness and Hewitt. The zoo houses more than 1,400 mammals, birds, reptiles, and rare species. Offices are located in the tiny hipped-roofed villa called **Solitude,** built in 1784–1785 for John Penn, William Penn's grandson. In Solitude, one can see some of the finest plasterworked ceilings in America.

OVERLEAF: *A popular Philadelphia view: The Schuylkill River and the Fairmount Waterworks, beneath the Philadelphia Museum of Art.*

The Centennial Exhibition of 1876, one of the great world's fairs in history, spurred the development of West Fairmount Park. **Memorial Hall,** designed by Schwarzmann with an iron-and-glass Beaux-Arts dome, still stands on the North Concourse. An art gallery during the exhibition, it was a model for many other museums in America and Europe.

Schwarzmann's Horticultural Hall, a magnificent glass building in the tradition of London's Crystal Palace, stood until 1954, when it was demolished after being badly damaged in a hurricane. Another survivor of the exhibition, the two-story **Ohio House** at States Drive and Belmont Avenue, is unusual for the names of Ohio stone dealers, cutters, and quarries carved in its stone blocks.

Much of the Park's sculpture dates from the exposition and the 1874 formation of the Fairmount Park Art Association to "promote and foster the beautiful in the City of Philadelphia." *The Pilgrim* by Augustus Saint-Gaudens, Frederic Remington's *Cowboy,* and Carl Milles's *Playing Angels* along Kelly Drive are just a few of the works by noted sculptors. On Aquarium Lane, the **Italian Fountain,** also known as the **Fountain of the Sea Horses,** is a 1926 reproduction of a late-eighteenth-century fountain in the Borghese Gardens in Rome, while the **Civil War Memorial** at North Concourse and Lansdowne Drive, designed by James H. and John T. Windrim, is a veritable gallery of important American sculpture. There are majestic statues of Union generals: John Reynolds by John Grafly, George Meade (Philadelphia's most prominent war hero) by Daniel Chester French, George B. McClellan by Edward C. Potter, and Winfield S. Hancock by John Quincy Adams Ward, all on pedestals; niches in the complex arrangement are filled with busts of other military figures.

As a place of recreation for the city, Fairmount Park flourished after the Centennial Exposition. In 1918, the Benjamin Franklin Parkway, in the planning stage for almost a quarter-century, finally opened from Broad Street to Fairmount Hill, and eventually attracted many cultural institutions. The Philadelphia Museum of Art, partially opened in 1928, became a Neo-classical terminus for the parkway. On the north side of the parkway above 21st Street, the **Rodin Museum** (215–763–8100), with Rodin's imposing *Gates of Hell* at the entrance, houses the largest collection of the work of the late-nineteenth-century French sculptor outside of Paris. The collection, gift of Philadelphia businessman Jules E. Mastbaum, opened in its own building in 1929.

During the Depression, Fairmount Park's roads, paths, and public areas were improved by the Works Progress Administration. In recent years public use, stimulated by concerts, outdoor theater, and additional recreational facilities, has been on the increase, bringing with it problems of overuse and fears for its future.

## PHILADELPHIA MUSEUM OF ART

By an act of the Pennsylvania legislature in 1873, the Pennsylvania Museum—its original name—was created as both an art gallery for the Centennial Exposition of 1876 and, once that had closed, as a permanent museum of art and industry "for the improvement and enjoyment of the people of the Commonwealth." The museum's first building was H. J. Schwarzmann's Memorial Hall in Fairmount Park. The legislature also created a museum art school, now the independent Universities of the Arts, with the idea of training craftsmen for the state's industries.

The museum's original collection was meager, but it expanded rapidly, bolstered by such major gifts as the Bloomfield Moore

*Thomas Eakins'* Between Rounds *(1899), from the collection of the Philadelphia Museum of Art (detail).*

collection of decorative arts; by 1910 the museum had outgrown its quarters. Work on the present building, a huge Neo-classical pile designed by Horace Trumbauer, began in 1919, and it was opened on March 26, 1928. The building, located on Fairmount, was harmonious with the design of the famous waterworks below it but was widely criticized for not being modern, and for being built of yellow, not white, marble. The museum's collection was swallowed up by the huge building—its director, an imperious but effective New Englander named Fiske Kimball, had to borrow works to fill some of the rooms.

The museum thrived under Kimball's guidance. On the upper exhibition floor, he established a series of galleries and period rooms that, in his words, "enable the visitor to retrace the great historic pageant of the evolution of art." In 1938, the name of the museum was changed to the Philadelphia Museum of Art to avoid confusion with the Pennsylvania Academy of the Fine Arts, and by the time Kimball retired in 1954 the Museum had become one of the world's greatest.

LOCATION: Benjamin Franklin Parkway at 26th Street. HOURS: 10–5 Tuesday–Sunday; until 8:45 Wednesday. FEE: Yes, except 10–1 Sunday. TELEPHONE: 215–763–8100.

# NORTH PHILADELPHIA

By the early twentieth century, North Philadelphia's Broad Street rivaled Rittenhouse Square as the address for the wealthy and socially ambitious. In 1907 the New York impresario Oscar Hammerstein commissioned a leading theatrical architect, William H. McElfatrick, to build an Opera House at Broad and Poplar streets that would rival the entrenched Academy of Music. The **Philadelphia Opera House** was a social and artistic success—for about five years. Then Hammerstein sold out, and the new owner imported New York City's Metropolitan Opera Company to fill the house for the next three years, hence its enduring nickname, "the Met." The building subsequently declined, and it no longer offers programs to the public. In the late 1990s its owner, the Holy Ghost Headquarters Church, was working to stabilize it.

OPPOSITE: *The Great Stair Hall of the Philadelphia Museum of Art is graced by a monumental mobile by Alexander Calder.*

Another North Broad Street monument is the **Widener House,** built by streetcar developer and philanthropist Peter Widener in 1887. The **Thomas Eakins House,** a four-story brick building at 1729 Mt. Vernon Street, was home to the famous artist from age thirteen to his death in 1916. Henry Ossawa Tanner, one of the best black artists to emerge in the nineteenth century, lived in the 1871 brick house at **2908 West Diamond Street** as a child, from 1872 until 1888.

## EDGAR ALLAN POE HOUSE

The three-story brick cottage is typical of the modest one-family homes built in North Philadelphia in the mid-nineteenth century. Of the six years that Poe spent in Philadelphia working as a freelance writer and editor, he only lived here for one, from 1843–1844, but it was here he wrote such celebrated short stories as "The Gold Bug" and "The Black Cat." The house, built about 1841, was declared a National Historic Landmark in 1962 and is now administered by the National Park Service.

LOCATION: 532 North Seventh Street. HOURS: 9–5 Daily. FEE: None. TELEPHONE: 215–597–8780.

## GIRARD COLLEGE

The French-born Stephen Girard was a philanthropist and financier who on several occasions restored public confidence in the American banking system. During the yellow fever epidemic of 1793, he volunteered to supervise a hospital where he nursed the sick day and night. Girard wanted a simple main building for Girard College, the school for orphan boys that he endowed in his will. But the financier Nicholas Biddle, having become chairman of the school's board, ordained that Thomas U. Walter, then still a young architect, alter his previous plans for the simple structure and instead build the best Greek Revival building Girard's money could buy. The result was Founder's Hall, a marble building that ranks as one of the best examples of the style in the country.

Founder's Hall has a Corinthian colonnade and, inside, four vaulted rooms on each of its three floors. The building houses Girard's sarcophagus and the Girard Collection of late-eighteenth- and early-nineteenth-century furniture. Girard lived in the 1750 house he called **Gentilhommière,** located on the grounds, from 1798 until his death in 1831, when he was one of the richest men in America.

LOCATION: Girard and Corinthian avenues. HOURS: 2–4 Thursday, and by appointment. FEE: None. TELEPHONE: 215–787–2600.

# SOUTH PHILADELPHIA

Although South Philadelphia cannot compete with the city's more central districts in number of historical sites, it is, in fact, the area where the Dutch first settled in 1633, along the river they named Schuylkill, meaning "hidden creek." The Dutch were followed by the Swedes, whose main legacy, the Gloria Dei (Old Swedes') Church, is the district's leading historical and architectural attraction.

The ties of the early settlement to the water are evident in the cluster of old houses on the Delaware River along South Front Street. Among the earliest are the **Finlow-Nichell House** (770 South Front Street, private), a plain, three-and-a-half story merchant's house with a brick cornice, built in 1745, and the equally tall **Nathaniel Irish House** (704 South Front Street, private), with its dormer windows and gable-end chimneys. It was built ca. 1769 by Nathaniel Irish himself, a carpenter.

## GLORIA DEI (OLD SWEDES') CHURCH

Noted for its steep roof and vaulted ceiling, Gloria Dei is the oldest church in Pennsylvania and one of the oldest still operating in the eastern United States. Built by Swedish Lutherans between 1698 and 1700 on the site of an earlier Swedish log church, it has a simple design reflecting the Quaker influence that ruled the day. Gloria Dei remained a Swedish church until 1845, when it was taken over by the Protestant Episcopal Church. In 1942, President Franklin Roosevelt signed a bill making it a National Historic Site. Located nine blocks south of Independence Hall, the brick church is now part of the Independence National Historical Park, although the building itself is maintained by its congregation. Inside, models of the ships that brought the first Swedes to this country hang from the ceiling.

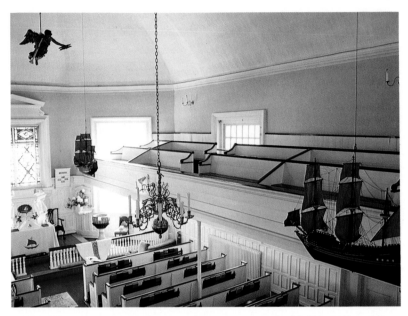

*Models of the ships that brought Swedish settlers to this country hang from the ceiling of Gloria Dei (Old Swedes') Church.*

The church is set in the middle of a graveyard where Alexander Wilson (1766–1813), the "father of American ornithology," and the artist James Peale (1749–1831), the brother of the better-known portrait painter Charles Willson Peale, are buried.

LOCATION: Delaware Avenue and Christian Street. HOURS: 9–5 Saturday, Sunday; and by appointment. TELEPHONE: 215–389–1513.

## CHURCH OF ST. PHILIP DE' NERI

This fine Greek Revival church, completed in 1841, is of particular architectural interest because it was designed by Napoleon Le Brun when he was nineteen years old and an apprentice in the office of Thomas U. Walter. The sandstone church is fronted by four giant Doric pilasters, and a cross rises from the pediment. A target of rioting anti-Irish mobs in 1844, the church escaped damage. A major restoration, including a new roof, was completed in 1996.

LOCATION: 218 Queen Street. HOURS: By appointment. TELEPHONE: 215–468–1922.

Further inland, wealthy Philadelphians built elaborate country homes such as **Bellaire Manor** (20th Street and Pattison Avenue, an eccentrically designed brick house probably constructed in 1714 by the city's former mayor Samuel Preston.

A celebrated example of the Greek Revival style is the **Ridgway Branch of the Library Company of Philadelphia** (900 South Broad Street), designed by Addison Hutton and completed in 1878. Across its broad, 220-foot front the building has a central portico entrance with eight Doric columns and two flanking porticoes, each with four columns.

# WEST PHILADELPHIA

The farms and estates that were the pride of this area in the eighteenth century are all but gone now, the victims of suburbs, industry, and commerce. A remnant of this era can be seen at The Woodlands, a late-eighteenth-century residence, and at Bartram's Garden in the house built by naturalist John Bartram in 1730. West Philadelphia is also home of the University of Pennsylvania, and some of the country's best collegiate architecture.

## BARTRAM'S GARDEN

Despite the deterioration of much of West Philadelphia, Bartram's Garden, the country's first botanic garden, has managed to survive the centuries. It was originally laid out by America's first native botanist, John Bartram, in 1728. Here he conducted hybridizing experiments, probably the first in the country, and imported plants from around the world. The **John Bartram House,** facing the Schuylkill River, was built by Swedish owners in 1689 from blocks of local stone and enlarged by Bartram in 1731 and 1770. The two-and-a-half-story house's tall Ionic columns form a recessed porch. Bartram, a freethinker expelled from his Quaker meeting for denying the divinity of Christ, had these words carved in a second-floor stone panel:

IT IS GOD ALONE ALMYTY LORD
THE HOLY ONE BY ME ADORD
JOHN BARTRAM 1770

The house and gardens were acquired by the Fairmount Park Commission in 1891; there are also a barn, stable, and cider mill on the property.

LOCATION: 54th Street and Lindbergh Boulevard. HOURS: May through December: 12–4 Wednesday–Sunday; January through April: 12–4 Wednesday–Friday. *Gardens:* Dawn–dusk Daily. FEE: Yes, for house. TELEPHONE: 215-729-5281.

Another great house on the Schuylkill is **Woodlands** (40th Street and Woodland Avenue, 215–386–2181), built about 1787 by William Hamilton, who had inherited the estate from his grandfather, Andrew Hamilton, the defender of the freedom of the press in the Peter Zenger trial of 1735 and the designer of Independence Hall. With its great Tuscan portico facing the river, Woodlands ranks among the best houses of the Federal period in the country. Hamilton also established one of the country's best gardens. Part of the estate became **Woodlands Cemetery** in 1843, and a superintendent now occupies most of the house; the interior is no longer open to the public. Philadelphia artist Thomas Eakins and Anthony Joseph Drexel, banker, newspaper owner, and founder of Drexel University, are among the notables buried on the grounds. In 1871, the University of Pennsylvania purchased part of Hamilton's former holdings for its new campus.

# UNIVERSITY OF PENNSYLVANIA

Today one of the leading universities in the country with a wealth of distinguished collegiate architecture, the university was founded in 1740 by Benjamin Franklin and a group of respected Philadelphians, including ten future signers of the Declaration of Independence and twenty-one members-to-be of the Continental Congress. In 1779, however, the trustees were accused of Toryism and the school's charter was revoked for ten years. After changing its name several times, it became the University of Pennsylvania in 1791. The law and medical schools are the oldest in the country.

In 1871, the university sold its property at Ninth and Market streets to the federal government and moved to 36th Street and Woodland Avenue in West Philadelphia. **College Hall,** its first building, was designed in the Collegiate Gothic style that year by Thomas W. Richards, then an instructor of drawing at the school, and constructed with green serpentine stone. It was large enough

OPPOSITE: *Memorial tower at the entrance to the Quad, University of Pennsylvania.*

*Benjamin Franklin, in front of College Hall, observing the University of Pennsylvania Campus.*

to house the departments of science and liberal arts in its wings and the library, chapel, and assembly rooms in its central pavilion; the building's five-and-a-half-story Gothic towers at each end have since been removed.

The university library, now called the **Furness Building** in honor of its architect, Frank Furness, is an extravagant masterpiece of the late nineteenth-century architect. One of the first libraries in the country to separate the stacks from the reading rooms, it has a five-story square castellated tower that has been a university landmark since the building's completion in 1891. It now houses the Department of Fine Arts.

The architectural firm of Cope and Stewardson, noted for other collegiate buildings, at Princeton University and Bryn Mawr College, designed the **University Dormitories,** which were built between 1895 and 1902, in the same Collegiate Gothic style. The complex of five courts has been described as "a series of architectural adventures." Cope and Stewardson collaborated with architects Frank Miles Day and Wilson Eyre, Jr., on the eclectic **University Museum,** a U-shaped building ranging in height from one to three stories (for campus tours: 215–898–1000).

Nearby **Drexel University,** founded as a technical school by the banker and philanthropist Anthony J. Drexel in 1890, has an outstanding brick academic **Main Building** (1890–1891), at the corner of Thirty-second and Chestnut streets. It was designed with rich terra-cotta detailing by the architects Wilson Brothers & Co.

At the southernmost tip of West Philadelphia, **Fort Mifflin** (215–685–4192), formerly called Mud Fort, was originally built on Mud Island in the Delaware below the mouth of the Schuylkill. Constructed, as its name implies, from mud in 1771, the fort has been called the "Alamo of the Revolution" for withstanding a British siege that began after the American defeat at the Battle of Germantown and lasted forty days, until November 16, 1777. American resistance, which prevented General Howe from bringing his supplies upriver, enraged the British commander, who called Fort Mifflin a "cursed little mud fort." It was rebuilt after the war and named for the Pennsylvania governor, Thomas Mifflin. Today it is a National Historic Site, with re-enactments of drills and skirmishes.

# G E R M A N T O W N

Now a part of the city of Philadelphia, Germantown was founded in 1683 and grew into a separate, German-speaking town with its own character and culture. In the mid-eighteenth century Philadelphians discovered its bucolic charms and began building summer residences there. More came to escape the yellow fever epidemics of the 1790s, and the influx continued, aided by the construction of better roads and railroads. The English-speaking newcomers eventually took over the town.

With the arrival of outsiders to Germantown came disputes as to which language, German or English, would predominate in school and church. The large, two-story stone **Germantown Academy** (110 School House Lane), built in 1761, had facilities for both German- and English-speaking students and faculty. By 1775, however, there were enough English-speaking residents to build the **Concord School House** (6309 Germantown Avenue, 215–843–0943), just for their children. The building, with its highly visible belfry and spire, is open by advance appointment. The fine Italianate **Trinity Lutheran Church** was built in 1857 by an English-language faction of the German Lutheran church that had dominated the town in colonial times.

Germantown was also the site of an important Revolutionary War battle on October 4, 1777, between Washington's army and forces commanded by General Howe. Hoping to take Howe by surprise, Washington's troops approached the town by four separate roads, an extremely complex strategy for an army that was poorly trained and equipped. An early morning fog at first seemed to work to the Americans' advantage; Major General John Sullivan's column drove British soldiers from an advanced post into Cliveden, Judge Benjamin Chew's mansion, and he left a detachment behind to besiege them before pressing on. However, this action and the poor visibility threw off the timing of the attack and, after two wings of the Americans fired on each other in the thick fog, a determined British counterattack threw the revolutionaries into a panicky retreat.

Although the Americans lost over one thousand men, twice the British losses, they had come so close to victory that they retreated with their morale intact, if not improved. Washington's daring as a commander impressed the French and helped bring them into the war on the American side.

## GERMANTOWN AVENUE

The first settlers, a mix of German-speaking Quakers and Mennonites, laid out the town in 1700 along a single street, Germantown Avenue, the now-historic thoroughfare lined with an exceptional collection of eighteenth- and nineteenth-century mansions.

Before the battle of Germantown, Lord Howe made his headquarters in Stenton, built in 1730 by James Logan, William Penn's secretary. Tours of the area are conducted by **Historic Germantown,** which is headquartered in Cliveden (6401 Germantown Avenue, 215–848–1777), and include the houses described here.

### Cliveden

This gracious house was built from 1763 to 1767 of local stone by a local mason and carpenter, but, far from being typical of the locality, its sophisticated design was that of English houses of the time. Complementing its elegant interior, with the immense entrance hall and panelled dining room, are such architectural details as the Doric frontispiece and pediment and the five urns placed across the front of the roof, the height of contemporary fashion.

The house is furnished with fine Philadelphia pieces of the eighteenth and early nineteenth centuries, and there are family

*Cliveden, built in 1767, was damaged by an American bombardment during the Battle of Germantown.*

portraits by such noted painters as John Smibert, John Wollaston, and Robert Edge Pine.

LOCATION: 6401 Germantown Avenue. HOURS: April through December: 12–4 Thursday–Sunday; other times by appointment. FEE: Yes. TELEPHONE: 215–848–1777.

Number 6340 is **Upsala** (215–842–1798), the rear part of which was probably built about 1755 by a Dutch settler, Dirck Jansen. From 1795 to 1798 John Johnson III transformed the simple country structure into an elegant villa, with fine interior woodwork. The house, with its original cornices as well as furnishings from the Johnson family, is named after the Swedish university town of Uppsala.

One of the oldest houses still standing in Philadelphia, **Wyck House** (6026 Germantown Avenue at Walnut Lane; 215–848–1690) was owned by nine generations of the same Quaker family from 1689 to 1973, when it was first opened to the public. The western portion of the house, constructed of local stone, was probably built between 1720 and 1730. A second, larger house was built in 1771–1773, and the two structures were joined before the Battle of Germantown in 1777, when it was used as a field hospital. In 1824, William Strickland extensively altered the house. Wyck House has never been sold, but was passed on by marriage.

## Deshler-Morris House

Because of its associations with President George Washington, who rented it as a "summer White House," the house is owned by the National Park Service as part of Independence National Historical Park. The house, which has now been restored and furnished in the style of the late eighteenth century, was built in 1772 by David Deshler, an importer of English and West Indian merchandise. Sir William Howe used it as his headquarters after his victory over the Americans in the Battle of Germantown on October 4, 1777, and President Washington rented it for the summers of 1793 and 1794 to escape the yellow fever epidemic in Philadelphia. The simple but elegant house is built on a raised stone basement and has a Tuscan doorway with a pediment, and a dentil cornice on the roof. The house was owned by a prominent Philadelphia family, the Morrises, from 1836 to 1948, when it was bequeathed to the National Park Service.

> LOCATION: 5442 Germantown Avenue. HOURS: April through mid-December: 1–4 Tuesday–Saturday. FEE: Yes. TELEPHONE: 215–596–1748.

Built in 1744 of Wissahickon schist quarried on the property, **Grumblethorpe** (5267 Germantown Avenue, 215–843–4820) was one of the first summer houses in Germantown. The simplicity of its exterior, which is marked by a pent roof and a central balcony, is reflected inside by the woodwork and the plain furnishings. During the Battle of Germantown, the house was the headquarters of British Major General James Agnew, who was killed in the fighting. The house was built by the wealthy Philadelphia merchant John Wister and marks the beginning of the "Anglicizing" of Germantown.

   **Loudon** (4650 Germantown Avenue, 215–686–2067), built between 1796 and 1801 by Philadelphia merchant and philanthropist

Thomas Armat, has been changed many times since then. The Greek portico with four Corinthian columns was added in 1830, the rear addition in 1888. The prominent Logan family also lived here, and the house is decorated with paintings and furniture from five generations of descendants.

## STENTON

William Penn's secretary and agent, James Logan, designed and built this house on more than five hundred acres in 1728. Named for his father's birthplace in Scotland, it has a simple elegance in the Quaker tradition that influenced the design of Germantown country houses built after it. The leading political figure of his day,

*Philadelphia's last surviving log house, circa 1770, was moved to the grounds of Stenton in the late 1960s.*

Logan was particularly skillful in handling Indian affairs, and Indian delegations often visited the house and camped on the grounds. The house has a wide central hallway and two panelled parlors on the ground floor. Logan's second-floor library once held the finest collection of books in the colony; the books now belong to the Library Company of Philadelphia.

The house was acquired by the city in 1908 and has been maintained by the National Society of Colonial Dames since 1910. It is furnished with William and Mary and Queen Anne pieces similar to those Logan is known to have owned. The rubblestone barn on the property was built between 1787 and 1798.

> LOCATION: 18th and Cortland streets. HOURS: March 15 through
> November: 1–4 Tuesday–Saturday. FEE: Yes. TELEPHONE: 215–
> 329–7312.

The **Fromberger-Harkness House** (5501 Germantown Avenue, 215–844–0514), often described as "the brick building on Market Square," is the home of the Germantown Historical Society. References to the building date to the end of the eighteenth century. It is rumored that the Bank of the United States occupied the house during the yellow fever epidemic of 1788–1789. The bank's holdings may have been stored in cellar vaults. The society's collections, spanning more than 300 years, include textiles, decorative arts, toys, and dolls. The society oversees the **Clarkson-Watson House** (5275 Germantown Avenue), the summer refuge of both Secretary of State Thomas Jefferson and Attorney General Edmund Randolph during the 1793 yellow fever epidemic.

Beyond Germantown, in the Chestnut Hill section of Northwest Philadelphia, is the world-famous **Morris Arboretum** of the University of Pennsylvania (Hillcrest Avenue between Stenton and Germantown avenues, 215–898–5000). John T. Morris, who made a fortune in iron, bought the 166-acre estate with his sister Lydia in 1887, and she bequeathed it to the university. The gardens include many species collected by horticulturist E. H. "Chinese" Wilson on trips to the Far East in 1899–1917. One of America's finest Victorian landscape gardens, the arboretum contains architecture and sculpture that blend with several distinct garden areas, including Azalea Meadow, English Park, the Fernery; Japanese gardens; Swan Pond and Love Temple; and the Rose Garden, the last being its most formal garden.

# PHILADELPHIA    ENVIRONS

Few cities have suburbs as lovely; no American city has seen as
much history occur in its environs as Philadelphia. Some of the
most important battles of the Revolution were fought here, as
George Washington's army struggled without success to save the
city—then the new nation's capital—from the British. Earlier in the
war, Washington crossed the Delaware on Christmas night, 1776,
from an encampment just up the river from Philadelphia to rout
the British at Trenton. A year later, his army suffered through the
winter of 1777–78 in Valley Forge, today just outside the city limits.
A plaque marks the spot in Chester, now an area of docks and
shipyards, where William Penn stepped ashore in 1682.

The suggested sequence of sites described here begins at that
landing spot, swings around the city, and ends at Andalusia, a
Greek Revival mansion on the Delaware River.

## CHESTER

The **Penn Memorial Landing Stone,** Front and Penn streets,
marks the spot where Penn stepped ashore on October 24, 1682.

*William Birch's 1800 engraving,* Preparation for War to Defend Commerce, *shows the
building of the Frigate* Philadelphia.

The ca. 1683 **Caleb Pusey House** (15 Race Street, 215–874–5665) is located in Upland, a hamlet bordering Chester that has retained the town's original Swedish name, on twenty-seven acres of the original estate. It is the only English house still standing in the state that Penn is known to have visited (the rest are reproductions). With William Penn and Samuel Carpenter as partners, Pusey operated the first mill in the province. The 1724 **Chester Courthouse** (412 Avenue of the States, 215–876–8663), built of irregular blocks of sandstone, is the fourth on this site. Its predecessors served as the seat of the first court in the colony and a meeting place for William Penn and other early leaders.

## ESSINGTON/PROSPECT PARK

**Governor Printz Park** (Taylor Avenue and Second Street, Essington, 610–583–7221) was the site of Printzhof, the Tinicum Island residence of New Sweden's first royal governor, the dictatorial, four-hundred-pound Johan Printz. The original 1643 building burned after two years, and Printz built a larger, two-story log structure on the site. After Printz returned to Sweden in 1653, the colony was seized by the Dutch. Printzhof was excavated in the 1930s, and parts of the house's foundations were exposed.

About a mile north of the park, the ca. 1650 **Morton Homestead** (Route 420, Prospect Park, 215–583–7221) may be the state's oldest surviving building. The log house was built by Morton Mortonson, a New Sweden Colony settler and great-grandfather of John Morton, a signer of the Declaration of Independence. The two-room house is a Swedish *parstuga,* which became known in America as a "dog trot" house. The Swedish and Finnish settlers introduced the log cabin to America. The house is furnished with reproductions of Swedish peasant furniture.

## SWARTHMORE

The town takes its name from Swarthmore Hall in England, the home of George Fox, founder of the Society of Friends. Quakers founded **Swarthmore College** in 1864; it became nonsectarian in 1911. The **Benjamin West Birthplace** (1724) is a simple two-story stone house with a pent roof on the exterior between the floors. West was the most famous colonial American painter and the first

OPPOSITE: *Swarthmore College, founded by Quakers in 1864.*

to study and win recognition abroad. In London, he was a founder of the Royal Academy and was sponsored by George III. His *Penn's Treaty with the Indians* hung in Independence Hall.

# MERION

The **Barnes Foundation** (300 North Latches Lane, 610–667–0290) was founded in 1922 by Albert C. Barnes, a chemist, physician, and art connoisseur who made his fortune from the invention of Argyrol, a nasal medicine popular in the 1940s. His world-renowned collection of twentieth-century paintings, including several by Matisse and Cézanne, is now open to the public by appointment. The foundation's two-story stone building, where Barnes lived, was designed by Paul Philippe Cret, a Philadelphia architect popular in the 1920s, who designed the Delaware River Bridge.

The **Arboretum of the Barnes Foundation** (610–667–3067), twelve acres of "the best woody ornamentals the temperate zones of the world have to offer," has many specimens from the Far East, including the Chinese *Davidia involucrata,* called the "dove tree" because its blossoms resemble birds.

# FORT WASHINGTON

The graceful mansion known as **Hope Lodge** (553 Bethlehem Pike, 215–646–1595) was Continental Army Surgeon General John Cochran's headquarters after the Battle of Germantown in 1777. It was built about 1750 by Samuel Morris, a successful Quaker gristmill operator, ship owner, and brewery proprietor. In 1784 Henry Hope, after whose family the Hope Diamond is named, purchased the house and gave it to his ward as a wedding gift. The house, which is administered by the state, has a symmetrical brick exterior and an arched central hallway.

# GRAEME PARK

Built in 1722 by Pennsylvania's provincial governor, William Keith, Graeme Park was purchased in 1739 as a summer residence by a successful Philadelphia physician, Thomas Graeme. He created one of the most gracious houses of the period by redoing the interior and installing panelling, marble fireplaces, and other decorative elements.

*Andalusia, the home of Nicholas Biddle, a proponent of the Greek Revival style.*

The house was inherited by Dr. Graeme's daughter, Elizabeth, who was married to a Loyalist who served the British during the Revolution. Elizabeth, however, was a Patriot and allowed American General Anthony Wayne to use the house as his headquarters in 1777. Now a house museum, Graeme Park was given to the state in 1958.

LOCATION: 859 County Line Road, Horsham. HOURS: 10–4 Wednesday–Sunday. FEE: Yes. TELEPHONE: 215–343–0965.

# ANDALUSIA

On a broad lawn overlooking the Delaware River is Andalusia, estate of the scholarly president of the Bank of the United States, Nicholas Biddle, who commissioned the distinguished Thomas U. Walter to enlarge the late-eighteenth-century mansion in 1832 and add a portico with Doric columns. Biddle, an ardent promoter of the Greek Revival style, once wrote there were two great truths, "the Bible and Grecian architecture." The house has remained in the Biddle family and is open by appointment (215–848–1777).

# EASTERN PENNSYLVANIA

The first European to venture into the interior of Pennsylvania was Frenchman Étienne Brulé, who explored the Susquehanna River to its source in 1615–1616. Brulé made the journey at the behest of Samuel de Champlain to enlist the Susquehannock Indians in an attack against the Iroquois of New York. Henry Hudson, an Englishman employed by the Dutch, had entered Delaware Bay in 1609—thereby establishing Holland's claims to Pennsylvania—but the first settlers were Swedes, in 1643. They ceded their settlement on Tinicum Island near the Schuylkill River to the Dutch in 1655, and then, in a shift of power that is so typical of the early history of the mid-Atlantic states, the English took it all over in 1664.

In 1681 Charles II made the Quaker William Penn proprietor of the lands west of the Delaware River between the fortieth and forty-third parallels. In the colony that bore his family name, Penn laid "the foundation of a free colony for all mankind"—the so-called Holy Experiment that guaranteed civil liberty, religious freedom, and economic opportunity. Soon after, the colony became the most prosperous in America, attracting not only Quakers from England and Wales, the dominant group, but also immigrants from other colonies and from abroad.

Although his influence was profound, Penn stayed in America only a short time, from 1682 to 1684 and from 1699 to 1701. Before Penn landed in America in October 1682, his representatives were laying out the city of Philadelphia, and shortly after his arrival he executed a "treaty of purchase and amity" with the Indians for their rights to the land, an agreement the philosopher Voltaire called "the only treaty never sworn to and never broken." The colony was fortunate; Penn's fair treatment of the Indians staved off serious violence until the mid-eighteenth century.

On Penn's second visit, he established a unicameral legislature and guaranteed freedom of worship to those believing in "*One almighty God*," under the democratic Charter of Privileges that would remain Pennsylvania's form of government until the American Revolution. The colony's official policy of religious toleration brought many Germans, including Amish, Mennonites, Dunkards, Moravians, and Schwenkenfelders; their hard work and farming skills made Pennsylvania an exporter of food to other colonies.

Pennsylvania began to industrialize early; even William Penn was excited by the discovery of iron ore in 1684. The first forge in the province was built in 1716, and despite England's efforts to

*Detail of a 1757 engraving, titled* A View of Bethlehem, One of the Brethren's Principle Settlements, *showing rolling farmland and orchards.*

discourage iron making in America, there were at least fifty forges and furnaces in the colony by the eve of the Revolution. By then the colonies, led by Pennsylvania, were producing one-seventh of the world's supply of iron.

With the Continental Congress in Philadelphia, Pennsylvania was naturally a pivotal state in the American Revolution—a veritable keystone, in this and all things, as the nickname Keystone State proclaims. So many shrines to American liberty—Valley Forge, Washington's Crossing, and Independence Hall, among others—are located in Pennsylvania, that it is surprising to note that the state's delegation only narrowly approved the Declaration of Independence, with Benjamin Franklin and Robert Morris among the nine Pennsylvania signers. In fact, much of the will to fight for independence came from the feisty Scotch-Irish frontiersmen. Many of the Pennsylvania Germans were either Loyalists or too isolated on their farms to care much about the issues, and the Quakers were opposed to bearing arms.

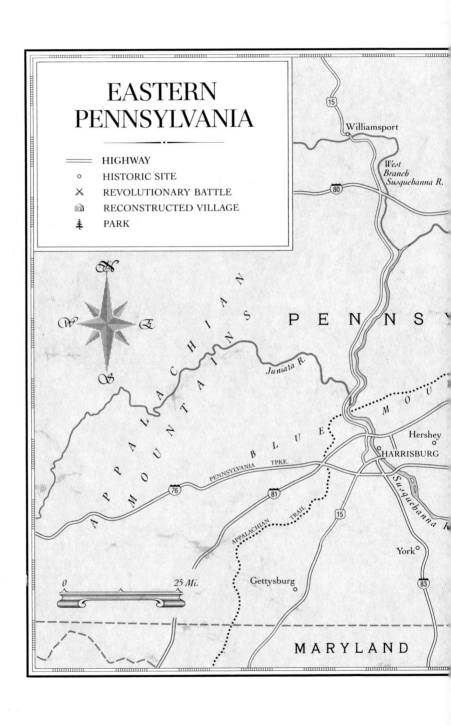

# EASTERN PENNSYLVANIA

- ═══ HIGHWAY
- ○ HISTORIC SITE
- ✕ REVOLUTIONARY BATTLE
- 🏠 RECONSTRUCTED VILLAGE
- 🌲 PARK

Williamsport

*West Branch Susquehanna R.*

15

80

P E N N S

*Juniata R.*

M O U

Hershey

HARRISBURG

B L U E

*PENNSYLVANIA* TPKE.

76

81

15

*APPALACHIAN* TRAIL

York

*Susquehanna R.*

0        25 Mi.

Gettysburg

83

M A R Y L A N D

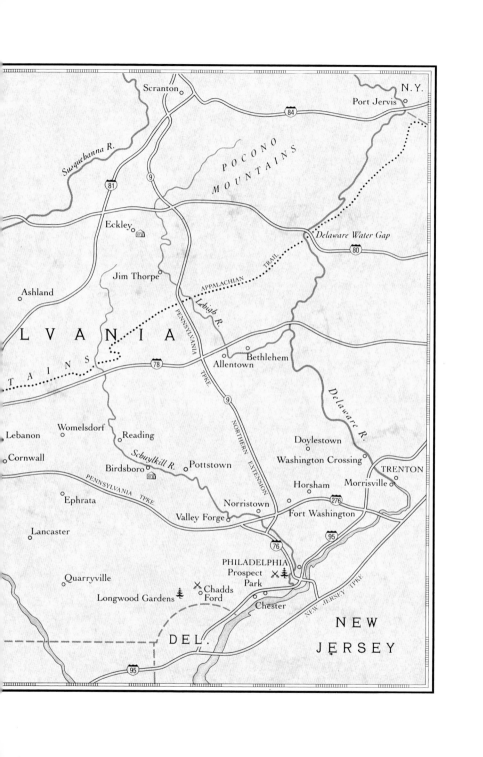

Congress left Philadelphia for Lancaster on September 18, 1777, as British General William Howe approached the city. Washington had failed to halt the advance at the important Battle of Brandywine on September 11, and on September 20 the British killed three hundred Americans in a surprise bayonet attack on the camp at Paoli. Two weeks later, on October 4, Washington's daring attack on the British at Germantown failed—mainly because of a thick morning fog—but his audacity and planning were widely admired and helped bring the French into the war on the American side. In July 1778 settlers defending the town of Forty Fort in the Wyoming Valley against a raid by Loyalists and Indians were brutally tortured and slain in the "Wyoming Massacre."

The state that emerged after the Revolution was plagued by border disputes. The matter of the Wyoming Valley on the Susquehanna River, claimed by Connecticut as its settlers had moved there in 1754, was finally settled in 1782 after considerable dispute and some bloodshed. Congress decided in favor of Pennsylvania and Pennsylvania forcefully dispossessed holders of Connecticut titles in the so-called Yankee-Pennamite War of 1784. In the same year, the quarrel with Virginia over southwestern Pennsylvania was resolved with Virginia agreeing to the Mason-Dixon Line as a common border, and in 1789 New York State accepted the forty-second parallel as its boundary. Pennsylvania assumed its present outline—and acquired a port on Lake Erie—when it purchased the Erie Triangle from the federal government in 1788 for seventy-five cents an acre.

By the 1850s coal was transforming Pennsylvania into an industrial state. The anthracite coal field of northeastern Pennsylvania, the East's largest, was discovered in 1762, but the industry didn't thrive until anthracite began to be burned commercially early in the nineteenth century.

Antislavery sentiment caused an enthusiastic response to President Lincoln's call for troops in 1861. A Pennsylvania detachment of 530 men, known as the "First Defenders," reached Washington, then threatened by the Confederates, before volunteers from any other state. During the Civil War, Pennsylvania was invaded three times: first in October 1862, when General "Jeb" Stuart's cavalry rode into the Cumberland Valley while circling General McClellan's army; again during the invasion by General Robert E. Lee that ended with the Confederate defeat at Gettysburg; and finally in the summer of 1864, when Confederate raiders burned Chambersburg in retaliation for Federal raids in Virginia.

Much of the state's history in the late nineteenth century is marked by tragedy and labor trouble. The Johnstown Flood, one of the worst disasters in American history, killed 2,200 on May 31, 1889; the state capitol at Harrisburg burned in early 1897; the same year fire caused $3 million worth of damage in Pittsburgh.

Violence had long marred labor relations in the state. The secret workers' society, the Molly Maguires, used terror and murder to gain their goals in the anthracite coal mines from about 1865 until their power was finally broken by a series of murder trials from 1875 to 1877.

Highly industrialized Pennsylvania suffered during the Depression, and an unemployment toll of almost one million helped presidential candidate Franklin D. Roosevelt sweep the state in 1932. The approach of war in Europe, however, created a demand for steel and coal and speeded the state's economic recovery.

## HARRISBURG

The state capital was originally called Harris's Ferry after John Harris, an Indian trader who settled here about 1712. His son, John Harris II, and his son-in-law, William Maclay, laid out the town in 1785 and named it Harrisburg. Harris foresaw that the

*The dome of the Pennsylvania Capitol in Harrisburg.*

town might be the state capital, and put aside "four acres and thirteen perches to be held in trust until the Legislature sees fit to use it." However, when the state tried to name the settlement Louisberg in honor of Louis XVI of France, Harris balked, declaring, "You may Louisberg all you please, but I'll not sell an inch more of land except in Harrisburg."

Harrisburg became the capital in 1812, although it was not incorporated as a city until 1860. During the Civil War, an advance party of Confederates approached the city, but turned back when Robert E. Lee met the Federal forces at Gettysburg. In February 1897, fire destroyed the capitol building.

The present-day **Capitol** at State and Third streets (717–787–6810), a 651-room Italian Renaissance edifice covering two acres, was dedicated in 1906 by President Theodore Roosevelt. The 272-foot dome that then dominated the city was modeled after St. Peter's in Rome. The marble staircase within the rotunda was drawn from that in the Paris Opera House. The well-known painter and illustrator, Edwin Austin Abbey, did many of the paintings inside the building, including *The Spirit of Vulcan*, which shows the god of metalworking presiding over a steel mill. Sculptured groups of symbolic nude figures by George Grey Barnard flank the triple arches of the entranceway. The State Law Library and "Forum" Concert Hall have exceptional Art Deco interiors.

## The State Museum of Pennsylvania

In addition to an extensive collection of pewter, ironwork, needlework, and furniture, the museum also displays one of the world's largest framed paintings, Peter F. Rothermel's *Battle of Gettysburg*. The circular modern building also houses a planetarium and exhibits on Pennsylvania's history and natural heritage.

LOCATION: Third and North streets. HOURS: 9–5 Tuesday–Saturday, 12–5 Sunday. FEE: None. TELEPHONE: 717–787–4978.

The **Harrisburg Historic District,** bounded by the Susquehanna River and Forster, Third, and Hanna streets, includes the **John Harris Mansion** (219 South Front Street, 717–233–3462), which the city's founder, John Harris II, completed in 1766. The house, overlooking the river and the original ferry site, was altered when

OPPOSITE: *Paintings by Edwin Austin Abbey, inside the rotunda of the Pennsylvania Capitol, Harrisburg, depict three spirits of industry—steel, oil, and coal—along with the spirit of religious liberty.*

Simon Cameron, U.S. senator from Pennsylvania and secretary of war in Lincoln's cabinet, purchased it in 1863. The three-and-a-half-story building, now headquarters of the Dauphin County Historical Society, is open as a house museum. Nearby, the **William Maclay Mansion** (401 North Front Street) was built about 1792. Originally a farmhouse, it was remodeled into a Georgian mansion in 1909 and now houses the state bar association.

Both Harris II and Maclay are buried in the cemetery adjacent to the **Paxton Presbyterian Church** (Paxtang Boulevard and Sharon Street). Built in 1740, it is one of the country's oldest Presbyterian churches in continuous operation. The baptismal font and the pulpit candleholder have been in use for over two hundred years.

Located along the Susquehanna River six miles north of Harrisburg, the **Fort Hunter Mansion** (5300 North Front Street, 717–599–5751) displays antiques and furnishings from the nineteenth century in a stone mansion dating from 1814. The house is on the site of a fort built in 1756 for protection against the French and Indians. The complex also includes an icehouse, tavern springhouse, two Victorian barns, and a blacksmith shop.

## HERSHEY

In 1903 Milton S. Hershey, a caramel-maker from Lancaster, purchased a cornfield here and established a chocolate manufacturing plant. Hershey is still a fine example of a planned industrial community; unique touches include streetlights shaped like candy kisses along Chocolate Avenue, the main thoroughfare. At 1 Chocolate Avenue, the **Hershey Museum of American Life** (717–534–3439) has, among its myriad collections, outstanding examples of Pennsylvania rifles, Pennsylvania German folk art, and American Indian and Eskimo artifacts. The twenty-three-acre **Hershey Gardens** (717–534–3492) on Hotel Road features 8,000 rose plants (450 varieties) in its extensive botanical displays.

## CORNWALL

In the 1730s a Cornishman named Peter Grubb began mining the famous Cornwall Ore Banks that would continue to produce prodigious amounts of magnetite ore for the next two centuries. In 1742 he built the Cornwall Iron Furnace, which was acquired by the wealthy ironmaster Robert Coleman in 1798. The furnace was enlarged to its present size in 1857 and continued operating until 1883. In 1932 Coleman's great-granddaughter gave the furnace to the state and it remains one of the world's best preserved iron-making facilities.

### Cornwall Iron Furnace

This handsome sandstone building with unusual pointed windows is built into the side of a hill so that the ore, limestone, and charcoal could be poured into the furnace from the top. The casting room, where the molten metal was run into molds, is on the ground level with the steam engine and great wheel, seventy-six feet in diameter, that produced the blast. Exhibits at the Charcoal House **visitor center** explain the processes of iron making, charcoal making, and mining. Nearby are an **open-pit mine** and **ironmaster's house.**

LOCATION: Rexmont Road at Boyd Street. HOURS: 9–5 Tuesday–Saturday, 12–5 Sunday. FEE: Yes. TELEPHONE: 717–272–9711.

# LANCASTER

The first recorded settler of Lancaster was George Gibson, who opened a tavern in 1721 near what is now Penn Square. The town was called Gibson's Pasture for twenty years until officially named Lancaster after the town in England.

By mid-century Lancaster was known as "the arsenal of the colonies" for the guns it produced. The famed Kentucky rifle was actually a Lancaster product that was sold, along with farm tools, to frontiersmen crossing the Appalachians. On September 27, 1777, the Continental Congress, fleeing the British who entered Philadelphia that same day, met in Lancaster before moving on to York. A pamphlet published in Lancaster in 1779 contained what may have been the first written reference to George Washington as "the Father of his Country."

Today Lancaster, still an important industrial and agricultural center, is the commercial hub of the Pennsylvania Dutch country. The town center remains relatively unsullied, however, and contains many buildings of historic interest. The 1852 **Fulton Opera House** (12–14 North Prince Street) has been restored to its gilded, nineteenth-century grandeur right down to the red plush seats. A wooden statue of its namesake Robert Fulton, co-inventor of the steamboat and one of Lancaster County's more famous native sons,

*The 1719 Hans Herr House, the oldest Mennonite meetinghouse in America.*

is in a niche on the second floor. The opera house is on the site of the old Lancaster Jail where the Paxton Boys from Harrisburg massacred fourteen Conestoga Indians in December 1763.

The **Heritage Center Museum of Lancaster County** (717–299–6440) is located in two historic buildings on Penn Square: the Old City Hall, which housed the state government from 1799 to 1812 before the legislature moved on to York, and the Masonic Lodge of the same period. The museum exhibits such folk and decorative arts as quilts, Fraktur, clocks, furniture, and crafts. In the center of Penn Square the 1874 **Soldiers and Sailors Monument,** a forty-three-foot-high square Corinthian column topped by a figure of Liberty, commemorates the Civil War dead.

Three miles south of Lancaster is **Rock Ford Plantation** (881 Rock Ford Road, 717–392–7223), the three-story center-hall Georgian manor built in 1792 by General Edward Hand. Born in Ireland, Hand practiced medicine in Lancaster before joining the Continental Army in 1775. He fought at Long Island, White Plains, Trenton, and Princeton, and in 1779 took part in the Sullivan campaign against the Indians of New York and Pennsylvania. The **Rock Ford–Kauffman Museum,** a collection of folk art and crafts

*A simple bedroom inside the Hans Herr House.*

gathered by noted antiquarians Zoe and Henry Kauffman, is located in an eighteenth-century barn on the grounds.

The superbly restored 1719 **Hans Herr House** (five miles south, off routes 222 and 741, 717–464–4438) is the oldest building in Lancaster County and America's oldest Mennonite meetinghouse. The building with its steeply pitched roof was built by Christian Herr for his father, the local Mennonite bishop, and has been the subject of paintings by Andrew Wyeth, a Herr descendant.

## Wheatland

James Buchanan was secretary of state under President James K. Polk when, in 1848, he purchased this Federal mansion and twenty-two acres for $6,750. The house, named for the fields of wheat that once surrounded it, has been restored to the period when Buchanan was president. Period rooms include an Empire dining room and a Victorian parlor, which contains a Chickering piano that Buchanan gave his niece, Harriet Lane, who served as his First Lady when the bachelor president was in the White House.

*The Moravian Church in Lititz, near Lancaster.*

Buchanan's study—where he planned his presidential campaign and, after his election in 1856, attended to affairs of state—contains much of his personal furniture. At the end of his term in 1861, he retired to Wheatland and wrote his only book, *Mr. Buchanan's Administration on the Eve of the Rebellion.*

LOCATION: 1120 Marietta Avenue. HOURS: April through November: 10–4:15 Daily. FEE: Yes. TELEPHONE: 717–392–8721.

## Landis Valley Museum

Brothers Henry and George Landis began collecting the artifacts of rural America about 1880. First displayed on the family farm in the 1920s, their collection of over 75,000 Pennsylvania-related objects dating between 1750 and 1900 was taken over by the Pennsylvania Historical and Museum Commission in 1953, and has since been expanded into one of the most important museum complexes in the country. The twenty-two exhibit areas include such original Landis Valley structures as the 1800s **Landis Farmstead** and the 1850 **Landis Valley Hotel.** Others like the 1890 **Schoolhouse** and the **Printing and Saddler's shops** were moved to the site, while the eighteenth-century **Tavern** and **Toll House** are period reconstructions. Now the largest museum devoted to the interpretation of Pennsylvania German rural life, it covers almost two centuries of agricultural development, from the crude buildings of the early settlers to the larger and more permanent structures put up during the prosperous years, 1815 to 1850.

LOCATION: Route 272 (Oregon Pike), four miles north of Lancaster.
HOURS: April through October: 10–5 Tuesday–Saturday, 12–5 Sunday.
FEE: Yes. TELEPHONE: 717–569–0401.

## QUARRYVILLE

Five miles south of this town, named for the local limestone quarries, is the **Robert Fulton Birthplace** (717–548–2755), a restored stone house. Fulton, who moved to Lancaster with his family when he was two years old, was a painter as well as the designer of the *Clermont,* the first commercially successful steamboat. Exhibits at the house examine both his careers.

## EPHRATA CLOISTER

From 1732 to the early nineteenth century, Ephrata was one of the country's most successful religious communities. During its heyday, about 1750, this ascetic German sect numbered some three hundred souls. Much of the original cloister still stands, including the **Saal** (chapel), a five-story frame structure that reflects the medieval character of Ephrata, with a steep gable roof and narrow slits for windows. Hand-illuminated German manuscripts produced by the sisterhood can be seen in the chapel. The sixty-two-room **Saron** (sisters' house) is at right angles to the Saal. Here the sisters slept, two to a room, on narrow wooden benches with wooden blocks for pillows. The **Almonry,** where food, money, and clothing were given to the poor, a log house belonging to founder Conrad Beissel, and several cabins and cottages are also part of the twenty-eight-acre complex. The 1837 **Academy** was erected after the order had declined.

Under the direction of Beissel, a charismatic German mystic, all property was held in common, the community was self-sufficient, and members observed the Sabbath on Saturday and dressed in white, full-flowing garments. Although Beissel permitted married couples or householders to live in the community, more emphasis was put on celibacy after he died. The community was noted for its music. It also had the third printing press in America and,

starting in 1743, produced such treasured works as the 1,514-page *Martyr's Mirror,* the story of the persecution of the Mennonites in Europe. The order's third press (1804) is still operated today. The cloister cared for American wounded during the Battle of Brandywine, although its members were pacifists.

LOCATION: 632 West Main Street, Ephrata. HOURS: 9–5 Monday–Saturday, 12–5 Sunday. FEE: Yes. TELEPHONE: 717–733–6600.

# WOMELSDORF

Founded in 1762 as Middletown, this farming, cigar-manufacturing, and textile town was named for John Womelsdorf in 1774. Henry William Stiegel, known on the frontier as Baron von Stiegel, operated the nearby Charming Forge in 1749. Stiegel was one of the colony's most successful ironmasters until he turned to manufacturing the glass that is highly collectible today.

## *Conrad Weiser Homestead*

This 1730s limestone house, expanded in 1751 by Conrad Weiser to hold his large family, is furnished with antiques from the area, most dating back to his lifetime. German-born Weiser, an important figure in maintaining peace on the frontier, began befriending Indians and studying their languages and customs two years after arriving in New York in 1710. Through his friendship with the Iroquois chief Shikellamy, he arranged the Philadelphia conferences of 1731 and 1736 that allied the Iroquois with the Penn family, and he helped form and execute the policy that kept Pennsylvania at peace with the Indians and secured Pennsylvania's borders until the French and Indian War. Weiser was also a religious leader, baptized by Conrad Beissel and for a short time a resident at the religious community at Ephrata.

The graves of Weiser, his wife, and several of their children are on a knoll near the house. There is also a statue of Shikellamy carrying a peace pipe. The twenty-six-acre park surrounding the house was designed in 1926 by the sons of Frederick Law Olmsted.

LOCATION: One mile east of Womelsdorf on Route 422. HOURS: 9–5 Wednesday–Saturday, 12–5 Sunday. FEE: Yes. TELEPHONE: 610–589–2934.

OPPOSITE: *The medieval-style building at Ephrata Cloister. Ephrata means plentiful in Hebrew.*

# BIRDSBORO

## Daniel Boone Birthplace

The rectangular stone structure was built on the site of the log cabin where Daniel Boone—frontiersman, scout, Indian fighter, and hero to generations of American schoolchildren—was born in 1734. At the age of sixteen he moved with his family to North Carolina. The restored and furnished Boone House—built in sections by three different families in the eighteenth century—and six other period buildings tell the story of the Boone family and other early settlers of Berks County. The homestead includes a visitor center, trails, and a lake on 579 acres, and is also known as the Museum of Pennsylvania Pioneers.

LOCATION: One mile north of Route 422 between Reading and Pottstown. HOURS: 9–5 Tuesday–Saturday, 12–5 Sunday. FEE: Yes. TELEPHONE: 610–582–4900.

## Hopewell Furnace National Historic Site

This outstanding example of an iron-making community, restored to its heyday of 1820 to 1840, illustrates all the steps in operating a cold-blast furnace, from producing the charcoal to firing the furnace to casting the molten iron into pig iron bars or into products such as iron stoves, a Hopewell specialty. Mark Bird, an American Patriot active in politics, built the furnace on French Creek about 1771, just in time to produce armaments for the Revolution.

At the time Hopewell was well situated to produce iron; nearby were an abundance of iron ore, forests of hardwood to turn into charcoal, and limestone for flux, to help separate the impurities from the iron ore. In time, however, Hopewell was made obsolete by anthracite coal and later coke, which produced iron much more economically. The use of these fuels was made possible by the invention in 1828 of the hot blast, which preheated the air going into a furnace.

Restoration of Hopewell, which closed in 1883, was begun in the 1930s by Civilian Conservation Corps workers. Using old furnace records, photographs taken after the Civil War, archaeological findings, and interviews with former workers, the Park Service was able to either restore or reconstruct the buildings in the complex. It includes a **charcoal hearth,** one of the hundreds used for

*The ca. 1771 furnace room at Hopewell Furnace, where cold-blast charcoal iron was made.*

producing fuel for the furnace, a **water wheel**—one of the more challenging reconstructions—which moved the blast machinery, the **connecting shed and bridgehouse** where the charcoal, ore, and limestone were dumped into the furnace, and the **cast house/furnace complex,** where castings were made.

LOCATION: Five miles south of Birdsboro on Route 345. HOURS: 9–5 Daily. FEE: Yes. TELEPHONE: 610–582–8773.

# POTTSTOWN

This town, the first in Montgomery County, was planned in 1752 by John Potts, a local ironmaster. In 1754 Potts built the lovely Georgian **Pottsgrove Manor** (West King Street, 610–326–9618), which for size, elegance, and the refinement of its Philadelphia Chippendale furnishings was the equal of any house in Philadelphia. After his defeat at Brandywine, George Washington is said to have stayed at the mansion while his troops rested nearby. The house, which became a hotel in the late nineteenth century, was acquired by the state in 1941 and restored, along with an eighteenth-century flower and herb garden.

# NORTHEASTERN PENNSYLVANIA

Although this area includes the beautiful Pocono Mountains and the lovely Delaware Water Gap, its history is dominated by the anthracite coal in the 480-square-mile section centering on Scranton. Coal fueled the area's industry, most notably the Bethlehem Steel Company, and, beginning with the Lehigh Canal in 1818, spawned an elaborate system of canals and railroads to bring the coal to other markets.

This tour through the industrial heart of northeastern Pennsylvania starts in Scranton and ends in Bethlehem, a city of cultural and industrial tradition, originally settled by the Moravians.

## SCRANTON

Located in the heart of the anthracite coal basin, Slocum Hollow was a community of five houses when brothers George W. and Selden T. Scranton arrived here from New Jersey in 1840. With their cousin, Joseph H. Scranton of Augusta, Georgia, they built the iron furnace that would later grow into the Lackawanna Iron and Coal Company. With an abundance of coal nearby, the town in the Lackawanna Valley, ringed by mountains, grew rapidly and attracted many other industries. In 1848, the Lackawanna Iron and Coal Company produced the first iron "T" rails for railroads. The city suffered from the opening up of the ore fields of the Great Lakes region early in the twentieth century, and the decline of the anthracite industry after World War II, but managed to revitalize its economy. In fact, the Scranton Plan has been a model for other cities in decline. The city has also paid particular attention to its industrial and architectural past, preserving and restoring areas of historic importance.

### Pennsylvania Anthracite Heritage Museum

This museum takes a broad look at the way of life that developed in the coal-mining regions of northeastern Pennsylvania. Changing exhibits examine transportation and industry, as well as the immigration into the area, its ethnic diversity, and the domestic and industrial uses of coal. The many artifacts in the collection are

OPPOSITE: *A red caboose in Scranton recalls the city's heritage as an important railroad center.* OVERLEAF: *Tunkkanock Viaduct traversing the countryside.*

*Restored mine at the Pennsylvania Anthracite Heritage Museum, Scranton.*

drawn from the mines, canals, railroads, mills, and factories that contributed to the region's growth.

LOCATION: Bald Mountain Road at McDade Park. HOURS: 9–5 Monday–Saturday, 12–5 Sunday. Closed major holidays. FEE: Yes. TELEPHONE: 717–963–4804.

## Scranton Iron Furnaces

The four stone blast-furnace stacks are impressive reminders of mid-nineteenth-century industrial might. The interconnected furnaces were built between 1841 and 1857 by the Scranton and Platt Company, later the massive Lackawanna Iron and Coal Company, once the second largest producer of steel in the country. The furnaces, located in the heart of the city, were closed in 1909 after coke replaced anthracite coal in iron and steel production.

LOCATION: Cedar Avenue. HOURS: 8–dusk Daily. FEE: None. TELEPHONE: 717–963–3208.

Other historic sites in Scranton include the **Scranton Public Library** (Albright Memorial Building, North Washington Avenue at Vine Street, 717–348–3000), a gift of the Albright family of Buffalo, formerly of Scranton. The elaborate, gray limestone edifice of Renaissance design is noted for its stained-glass windows illustrating the art of bookbinding, its marble mosaic floors, marble fireplaces, and other examples of fine craftsmanship. At 232 Monroe Avenue, the **Catlin House** (717–344–3841) is a Tudor Revival house museum with furnishings, memorabilia, and an archival library relating to the Scranton area; it serves as headquarters of the Lackawanna Historical Society. It is the former home of banker George Henry Catlin, cousin of George Catlin, an artist and explorer known for his portraits of American Indians, who was born in nearby Wilkes-Barre.

The **Steamtown National Historic Site** (South Washington Avenue, off I-81 exit 53, 717–340–5200) celebrates what has been called "the biggest business of nineteenth-century America"—railroading. As railroads expanded, so did the country. The Steamtown collection includes locomotives, freight and passenger cars, and maintenance equipment. Visitors may take rail excursions.

## ECKLEY MINERS' VILLAGE

Eckley was settled in 1854 and remained a company-owned "patch" town until 1971. (Coal in the area was supposedly discovered in 1818 when a deer pawing the earth uncovered a vein of anthracite.) In 1968 Paramount Pictures rebuilt the mine's breaker, or processing plant, and restored the town to film *The Molly Maguires,* about labor unrest in a company mining town after the Civil War. The town has fifty-eight buildings on one hundred acres. The **visitor center,** a **miner's double house** from 1890, and two **churches** are among the buildings open to the public.

LOCATION: Off Route 940, Eckley. HOURS: 9–5 Monday–Saturday, 12–5 Sunday. FEE: Yes. TELEPHONE: 717–636–2070.

## ASHLAND

Established in 1847, Ashland was named after the Kentucky estate of Henry Clay. Today it is the site of the **Museum of Anthracite Mining** (17th and Pine streets, 717–875–4708), which has a

*The mining town of Eckley was restored to make* The Molly Maguires, *a film about labor violence in the coal mines.*

diverse collection of tools, machinery, and photographs of the coal-mining process. Nearby the **Pioneer Tunnel Coal Mine,** a shaft running 1,800 feet horizontally into the ground, can be toured on open cars while former miners explain the process of mining. Visitors can also ride along the side of the mountain on a narrow-gauge train pulled by a steam locomotive called a "lokie."

## JIM THORPE

The town of Mauch Chunk, a railroad, canal, and mining town on the Lehigh River, took the name of the great Indian athlete Jim Thorpe when it merged with its sister community, East Mauch Chunk, in the mid-1950s. The new community erected a monumental mausoleum, the **Jim Thorpe Memorial,** a half mile outside of town on Route 903. Thorpe, a graduate of the Carlisle Indian College, had won more than a half dozen events at the 1912 Olympic Games in Stockholm, but his medals were taken away

*Restored miner's home along a street in Eckley.*

when he was accused of professionalism. His records, however, were later reinstated and his medals returned to his family.

The town's tourist information office is located in the restored brick **New Jersey Central Railroad Station** (717–325–3673) of 1888. Among the other architectural landmarks are the red brick **Lehigh Coal and Navigation Building,** 1882, on Hazard Square and **St. Mark's Church** on Race Street, an outstanding Gothic Revival building designed by a leading proponent of the style, Richard Upjohn, Sr. Its stained-glass windows are by Tiffany and Company. **Stone Row,** also on Race Street, consists of sixteen townhouses, some open to the public, that were built for the engineers on the Lehigh Valley Railroad.

The 1860 **Asa Packer Mansion** (717–325–3229) on Packer Road was the home of the founder of the Lehigh Valley Railroad and Lehigh University in Bethlehem. The flamboyant three-story brick mansion is in original condition, and next door to the **Harry Packer Mansion,** built in 1874 by Asa for his son.

# BETHLEHEM

A Moravian legacy is still strong in this small city, known for its music, historic architecture, and steel. Bethlehem was founded in 1741 by Moravians sent over to this country by their protector, Count Nikolaus Ludwig von Zinzendorf. During his Christmas visit that year the town was named Bethlehem. From the beginning the city was noted for its music. Several Bach scores were printed in Bethlehem before they appeared in Europe, and today the Bach Festival each spring is considered a continuation of the Moravian "service of song" that Zinzendorf began in 1742. The Moravians had excellent relations with the Indians, and many settlers came here for protection during the French and Indian War.

## Moravian Community

Bethlehem's oldest building, **Gemein Haus,** now the **Moravian Museum of Bethlehem** (66 West Church Street), is the focal point of the cluster of eighteenth- and early nineteenth-century structures that make up the Moravian Community. The five-story log

*St. Mark's Church in Jim Thorpe, designed in the Gothic Revival style by Richard Upjohn, Sr.*

*Moravian College, Bethlehem.*

building, built in 1741, once housed married Moravians. The museum stresses the Moravian skill in the decorative arts with displays of needlework, furniture, and silver. The Moravians' earliest place of worship is on the second floor.

When it was built in 1806, the Georgian-style **Central Moravian Church** with a tower set on a square platform was large enough to hold the entire community three times over. The **Sisters' House** (1744) and the **Brethren's House** (1748) were built for "those who chose to live in a state of single blessedness," while the **Widows' House** was for the widows of Moravian ministers. A dried apple dish called *schnitz* was made in the **Schnitz House** each October. The house, erected in 1801, is made of logs covered with stucco. The **Moravian Cemetery** has only flat stones of equal size, in accordance with the Moravian belief that all people are equal before God.

LOCATION: From Main Street to West Church Street. HOURS: 1–4 Tuesday–Saturday. FEE: Yes. TELEPHONE: 610–867–0173.

## Eighteenth-Century Industrial Area

The commercial center of the Moravian settlement, where at least thirty colonial industries were once located, has been re-created on a ten-acre site on the Monocacy River. Here interpreters in Moravian dress demonstrate eighteenth-century trades and crafts. Restored buildings like the 1762 **Waterworks,** believed to be the first municipal pumped water system in the country, illustrate the progressive nature of the Moravian settlers.

Included in the area are the reconstructed 1764 **Springhouse,** the **Tannery** with its restored vat room, where hides were processed for clothing, shoes, and other leather goods, and a **Miller's House.** The 1869 **Luckenback Mill,** the most recent restoration, houses the center's main offices along with a gallery of contemporary crafts, interpretive exhibits, the Bethlehem **visitor center,** and the **Chamber of Commerce.**

LOCATION: 459 Old York Road. HOURS: Varied; call for information. FEE: Yes, for guided tour. TELEPHONE: 610–691–5300.

The **Kemerer Museum of Decorative Arts** (427 North New Street, 610–868–6868) houses a collection of colonial and Victorian furniture, oriental rugs, Bohemian and other glass, nineteenth-century regional paintings and prints, many fine grandfather clocks, and changing gallery exhibits. Also open to the public, the **Goundie House** (501 Main Street, 610–691–6055) was built in 1810 by John Sebastian Goundie, a former Bethlehem brewer. The kitchen and dining room have been restored and decorated with period antiques. The Moravian Society's **Sun Inn,** built in 1758, hosted many notables of the colonial era; John Adams called it "the best inn I ever saw." (564 Main Street, 610–974–9451).

# SOUTHEASTERN PENNSYLVANIA

## LONGWOOD

Once known as Long Woods, the area was heavily populated by antislavery Quakers. The land was originally given to George Pierce by William Penn in 1701, and Pierce's grandsons planted the

OPPOSITE: *Grass, ferns, and flowers thrive in Longwood Gardens.*

original arboretum, which Pierre S. du Pont purchased as part of his estate in 1906. Du Pont oversaw the development of Longwood Gardens into one of the great gardens of the world and bequeathed it to the public upon his death in 1954. Pierce's brick mansion, built in 1730, is now part of the du Pont mansion.

## Longwood Gardens

Longwood Gardens consists of three hundred landscaped acres, seven hundred acres of meadow and woodland, and four acres of the country's finest glass conservatories. More than 14,000 different types of plants are grown here. After a visit to Italy in 1925, du Pont began to incorporate water fountains into the gardens' designs. The **Main Fountain Garden,** a formal geometric garden with fountains that spray water 130 feet into the air, has dramatic displays of fountains and fireworks on summer evenings. Among other highlights are the **Topiary Garden** with three species of yew, and the **Main Conservatory** of 1921.

LOCATION: Route 1. HOURS: Varied; call for information. FEE: Yes. TELEPHONE: 610–388–1000.

*A freshly-killed deer adds a jarring element of realism to Andrew Wyeth's* Tenant Farmer, *which also shows the Barns-Brinton House.*

*Lafayette's quarters on the Brandywine battlefield.*

## CHADDS FORD

Today this pleasant town in the Brandywine Valley is as well known for being the 1917 birthplace of the eminent American artist Andrew Wyeth as it is for being the scene of the bloody Battle of the Brandywine in 1777 during the Revolution. The Brandywine River Museum displays the work of the entire Wyeth family and a number of other important illustrators who settled in the valley. It is one of the country's most successful regional museums.

Chadds Ford was named for John Chads, a ferryman and farmer, whose two-story fieldstone house, the **John Chads House** (Route 100, 610–388–7376), has been beautifully restored by the Chadds Ford Historical Society. The Brandywine Creek apparently used to be a more difficult stream to cross than it is now; as early as 1736 Chad operated a flatboat ferry that moved back and forth along a line strung between the banks. The landmark **Barns-Brinton House** (1.5 miles west of town on Route 1, 610–388–7376) appears in Andrew Wyeth's painting *Tenant Farmer*. Built in 1714 as William Barns's tavern, the building is distinguished by its Flemish bond brickwork and interior woodwork.

## Brandywine Battlefield Park

This fifty-acre state park contains the two buildings Washington and Lafayette used as quarters during the Battle of Brandywine on September 11, 1777, although most of the fighting took place elsewhere in the vicinity. The clash became inevitable when British General William Howe and some 18,500 men landed at Head of Elk, Maryland, on the Chesapeake Bay on August 4 and moved toward Philadelphia, while Washington sought to cut him off by positioning his 10,500-man force on the Brandywine Creek.

On the day of the battle, Howe sent the Hessians under General Knyphausen toward Chadds Ford, while he and General Charles Cornwallis, with the main force, swung north and crossed the Brandywine above the Americans' right wing. Washington, hampered by faulty intelligence, didn't realize that he had been outmaneuvered until his right was already under attack from the rear. A column he sent north under General Nathanael Greene prevented a rout—even though the Continentals suffered heavy casualties—and allowed the Americans to retreat in an orderly fashion with their morale preserved. The story of the battle is told in exhibits in the **visitor center** near the entrance to the park.

**Washington's Headquarters** was an early eighteenth-century stone house belonging to Quaker Benjamin Ring, a prominent farmer and miller. The house later burned, but has been rebuilt on the site. The **Lafayette Quarters,** furnished with period antiques, is the original farmhouse belonging to Quakers Gideon and Sarah Gilpin. When he returned to tour the United States in 1825, Lafayette visited with Gilpin, who was then on his deathbed.

LOCATION: Route 1. HOURS: 9–5 Tuesday–Saturday, 12–5 Sunday. FEE: Yes. TELEPHONE: 610–459–3342.

## Brandywine River Museum

This converted century-old gristmill on the Brandywine River houses works by Howard Pyle, the first American illustrator of note, and teacher of more than one hundred students. Others represented in the collection are N. C. Wyeth, father of Andrew Wyeth and a famed illustrator in his own right, Maxfield Parrish, and Frank Schoonover. Also on view is a comprehensive selection of American landscape and still-life paintings by William Trost Richards, Edward Moran, William Michael Harnett, George Cope, and John Frederick Peto. In 1971, the mill was converted into a museum with glassed-in towers that connect the floors. Besides the changing exhibitions that attract national attention, the museum has one gallery devoted to the works of Andrew Wyeth, and another to works of other Wyeth family members, including Andrew's accomplished son, Jamie.

LOCATION: Route 1. HOURS: 9:30–4:30 Daily. FEE: Yes. TELEPHONE: 215–388–7601 or 610–388–2700.

# VALLEY FORGE

Although no battles were fought here, some two thousand American soldiers died of disease and exposure to cold during the winter of 1777–1778. For this reason there is no more important shrine to the sacrifices made during the Revolution for the cause of independence. When George Washington brought his men here on December 19, 1777, the British were occupying Philadelphia, and his ragged, ill-equipped army was worn out from the battles of Brandywine and Germantown.

*Washington's Headquarters at Valley Forge.*

The encampment, which has been preserved as the Valley
Forge National Historical Park, was well situated on high, wooded
ground, far enough away from Philadelphia to prevent surprise
attack but close enough to keep an eye on the enemy. On arrival
the men set about constructing two thousand huts, but with the lack
of winter uniforms and shortages of food and other supplies, these
primitive shelters were hardly adequate to protect them from the
snow, freezing temperatures, and relentless winds. Congress ig-
nored Washington's pleas for assistance until the commander began to fear that the army would "inevitably" be forced to "dissolve
or disperse in order to obtain subsistence in the best manner they
can."

Surprisingly, the army emerged from the ordeal as a better
fighting force. Much of the credit goes to Prussian drillmaster
Friedrich von Steuben, who undertook to train the poorly prepared Americans. In the meantime, new supplies and reinforcements reached the camp and, in May, news of the alliance with
France that guaranteed military aid to the Americans. To celebrate
Alliance Day, a well-trained, well-equipped army, its morale high,
passed in review on May 6, 1778. On June 19, a day after the
British left Philadelphia, the Americans set off after them, and
nine days later fought them to a standstill at Monmouth, New
Jersey, in one of the fiercest conflicts of the war.

## Valley Forge National Historical Park

Starting with the modern **visitor center,** which has audiovisual
presentations and exhibits of artifacts such as Washington's sleeping marquee, a road loops through the historical park, following in
places the perimeter of the **Grand Parade,** the drill ground where
von Steuben successfully trained the ragtag army. It also passes the
abatis, redans, redoubts, and other field fortifications that made up
the **Outer Line Defenses** to the south and the **Inner Line Defenses**
on the slopes of the encampment's highest point, **Mount Joy.**
**Redoubt 4,** which has been reconstructed, helped guard northern
approaches.

Early in the tour, guides in period uniforms demonstrate the
soldier's life at the reconstructed huts of the **Muhlenberg Brigade,**
which was assigned the outer line of defense. A short distance
farther the road passes the **National Memorial Arch,** dedicated in
1917, which bears George Washington's words: "Naked and starv-

*Cannons at Valley Forge.*

ing as they are, we cannot enough admire the incomparable patience and fidelity of the soldiery."

Near the Schuylkill River, in the far northwestern corner of the camp, was **Washington's Headquarters,** a small, sparsely furnished stone house belonging to gristmill owner Isaac Potts. Nearby are reconstructions of huts that housed the 150 men assigned to guard Washington. Another stone house, **General James Varnum's Quarters,** overlooking the Grand Parade, is open to the public, while the houses that quartered other members of the high command—Lord Stirling, Henry Knox, Lafayette, and William Maxwell—are closed but can be seen from the roads and trails. A bronze equestrian statue honors General Anthony Wayne.

> LOCATION: Junction of routes 23 and 422. HOURS: 9–5 Daily. FEE: Yes, to buildings. TELEPHONE: 610–783–1077.

The **Washington Memorial Chapel,** with its fifty-eight-bell carillon, and the **Museum of the Valley Forge Historical Society** (215–783–0535), containing firearms and other artifacts of the period, are on privately owned land within the park.

# DOYLESTOWN

Settled in 1735, this former stage stop between Philadelphia and Easton is now the seat of Bucks County. It is known today for the three somewhat bizarre concrete buildings that make up **Mercer Mile,** the unusual legacy of Dr. Henry Chapman Mercer, a collector, archaeologist, and manufacturer of tiles and pottery. The mammoth **Mercer Museum** (Pine and Ashland streets, 215–345–0210), built between 1914 and 1916, houses a vast quantity of early Americana, including some 25,000 implements, tools, and machines that trace the early industrial development of the country.

Mercer's own home on East Court Street, now the **Fonthill Museum** (215–348–9461), is an equally eccentric 1910 stone and concrete structure that contains tile collections and other memorabilia relating to Mercer's life. The **Moravian Tile and Pottery Works** (East Court Street and Swamp Road, 215–345–6722) still produces tiles as in Mercer's day and offers guided tours.

Northwest of Doylesville, in Dublin (Route 313, 215–249–0100) is the **Pearl S. Buck House,** home of the first American woman to win both the Nobel and Pulitzer prizes. The author's foundation aids displaced and disadvantaged children of many nations.

# WASHINGTON CROSSING

In the darkest of the dark days—December 1776—George Washington was forced to cross the Delaware River from New Jersey to Pennsylvania to evade the advancing British. Once encamped there between the hills and the river, he faced the likelihood that most of his army would depart for home once their enlistments were up at the end of the year, leaving him with a mere 1,200 regulars. "You may as well attempt to stop the winds from blowing or the sun in its diurnal as the regiments from going when their term is expired," he wrote.

His daring plan to recross the river on Christmas night and attack the British at Trenton is commemorated in the state historical park. The crossing began in darkness; according to the plan, Washington and General Nathanael Greene were to cross with the main force of about 2,400 men at McKonkey's Ferry, about nine miles upstream, while two smaller forces crossed directly at Trenton and farther south to cut off the road to Burlington. Worsening weather caused the river to freeze and delayed the passage; Washington's complete contingent did not reach the opposite shore until

*Detail from Emanuel Gottlieb Leutze's* Washington Crossing the Delaware, *painted in 1851.*

4 AM, some four hours behind schedule. Although he would soon lose the advantage of darkness, Washington pressed on, "as I was certain there was no making a retreat without being discovered and harassed on repassing the river." His victory at Trenton, one of the most important of the war, is commemorated in the state historical park on the New Jersey side of the Delaware River.

## Washington Crossing Historic Park

In the Washington Crossing section of the five-hundred-acre park, **McKonkey's Ferry Inn** is a ca. 1780 building on the site of an inn where Washington might have dined before crossing the Delaware on December 25, 1776. A short distance to the north are replicas of **Durham boats** of the sort that Washington used to ferry his men across. These shallow-draft boats, which ranged from forty to sixty feet in length, were designed to transport ore and pig iron down the river to Philadelphia. During the crossing, they were manned by the same fishermen from Marblehead, Massachusetts, who evacuated Washington's troops after the Battle of Long Island.

The actual **embarkation point** is marked by a fieldstone monument; from here the crossing is reenacted every Christmas Day. In the nearby **Memorial Building,** built from fieldstone in 1959, is an exact copy of Emanuel Leutze's famous, if somewhat inaccurate, painting *Washington Crossing the Delaware* that hangs in the Metropolitan Museum of Art in New York City. The event is also depicted in a film and exhibits.

The **Bowman's Hill** section is named for the highest of the hills along the Delaware that Washington's army used as an observation post. There is now a one-hundred-foot-tower on the hill with spectacular views of the surrounding countryside. Parts of the **Thompson-Neely House,** a large fieldstone home with four brick chimneys, date from 1702. During the encampment it was used as headquarters by some of Washington's officers, including General William Alexander, Lord Stirling; Captain William Washington, a relative of the general; and a future president, Lieutenant James Monroe. Many of the house's antique furnishings were donated by the Thompson and Neely families.

The **Memorial Flagstaff,** also in the Bowman's Hill section, marks the graves of unknown American soldiers, buried before the army embarked on Christmas Day, who died of exposure and disease. One hundred acres of the park have been set aside as the **Bowman's Hill State Wild Flower Preserve** and contain flora and fauna native to Pennsylvania.

LOCATION: *Washington's Crossing:* Seven miles south of New Hope on Route 32; *Bowman's Hill:* two miles south of New Hope on Route 32. HOURS: 9–5 Monday–Saturday, 12–5 Sunday. FEE: Yes. TELEPHONE: 215–493–4076.

# MORRISVILLE

Named for Robert Morris, the financier of the Revolution who had an estate here, Morrisville was once seriously considered for the nation's capital; a resolution before Congress in 1783 proposed a site "on the banks of the Delaware at the falls near Trenton, on the New Jersey side, or in Pennsylvania on the opposite." William Penn's "beloved manor" is reconstructed on its original site.

## Pennsbury Manor

The two-and-a-half-story manor house with truncated hip roof was the only home Penn ever built for himself, although his stay here,

*Pennsbury Manor, a reconstruction of William Penn's home on the Delaware River.*

starting in 1699, lasted just two years. The house was rebuilt in 1938–40 on the foundations of the original building through clues to the original dimensions and details of the construction found in William Penn's letters. Hardware uncovered in the ruins was duplicated and original tiles were used for the reconstructed fireplaces. Today, the forty-three-acre estate includes a smokehouse, bake-and-brew house, blacksmith shop, stables, farm animals, and formal gardens.

The land on which the house stood was given to Pennsylvania in October 1932 on the 250th anniversary of Penn's arrival in America in 1682. That year Penn acquired the land from the Indians for a price that included currency, clothing, utensils, rum, cider, and beer. Penn's fairness in dealing with Indians won their loyalty and spared the colony the problems of Indian warfare in its early days.

LOCATION: 400 Pennsbury Memorial Road. HOURS: 9–5 Tuesday–Saturday, 12–5 Sunday. FEE: Yes. TELEPHONE: 215–946–0400.

# WESTERN PENNSYLVANIA

OPPOSITE: *A view of Pittsburgh, once the nation's "Gateway to the West."*

The Susquehanna River, south of the junction of its two branches at Northumberland, effectively splits Pennsylvania into unequal parts, with two-thirds of its territory lying west of the river. The early settlers of western Pennsylvania were the independent-minded Scotch-Irish Presbyterians, some of whom settled as far as present-day Pittsburgh in the early 1760s, and who would eventually take control of the state from the Quakers.

The relative tranquility of the colony's early days ended as the rivalry between the French and the English over control of the frontier trade and the territory west of the Ohio River intensified. In late 1753, George Washington, then a twenty-one-year-old major in the Virginia militia, was sent to Fort Le Boeuf near Lake Erie to warn the French to cease fortifying the area around the headwaters of the Ohio, and to assert Virginia's own claims to the area.

The next year Washington was back on the frontier commanding troops at Great Meadows. After attacking a small company of French nearby, he withdrew to build a fortification that he called Fort Necessity. On July 3 came his first taste of real combat: an attack by a larger force of French and Indians caused him to surrender, albeit on honorable terms. This was the opening battle of a war for empire known in America as the French and Indian War, and in Europe as the Seven Years' War. "A volley fired by a younger Virginian in the backwoods of America," Voltaire observed, "set the world on fire."

After peace was attained the frontier almost immediately erupted again in warfare when the Ottawa chief Pontiac led an uprising known as Pontiac's Rebellion to drive the English out of the country. From May to October 1763, the fighting spread over a thousand miles of frontier. The end of the rebellion reopened the frontier to settlers, who pushed over the Appalachians to the Ohio Valley, taking with them two famous products made by the Pennsylvania Germans in Lancaster—the Conestoga wagon and the misnamed Kentucky rifle.

The independent spirit of the state's frontiersmen surfaced again after the Revolution when grain farmers and small distillers in four southwest counties opposed the excise law of 1791 taxing rye whiskey. In 1794, with the farmers threatening to· march on Pittsburgh, President Washington sent 13,000 federalized troops to the area, and after twenty insurgents were jailed, the so-called Whiskey Rebellion quietly ended.

Lemon Inn on the Portage Railroad, *by George Storm, ca. 1850.*

The problem of transporting goods and travelers across the mountains that divided the state became particularly vexing when Pennsylvanians realized that New York's Erie Canal, begun in 1817, would put them at a competitive disadvantage for western trade. In 1826 the legislature authorized the building of the Pennsylvania Canal system to link Philadelphia and Pittsburgh, and by 1840 the system consisted of 606 miles of canals and 118 miles of railroads and included the ingenious Allegheny Portage Railroad between Hollidaysburg and Johnstown.

The vast bituminous fields of western Pennsylvania began to yield significant amounts of coal about 1840. Other industries also flourished in Pennsylvania, among them lumber, paper, textiles, shipbuilding, and, after the coming of the railroad, the manufacturing of rail equipment. Glassmaking began on a small scale in the late seventeenth century, but the first quality product, today treasured by museums and collectors, was made by "Baron" von Stiegel in a glassworks erected in 1765.

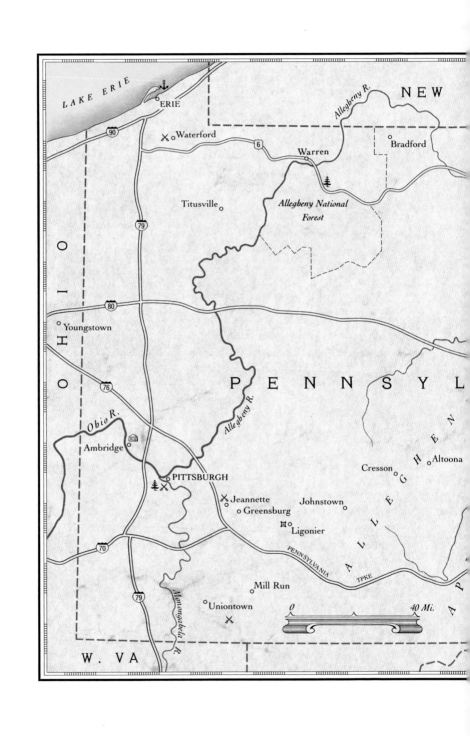

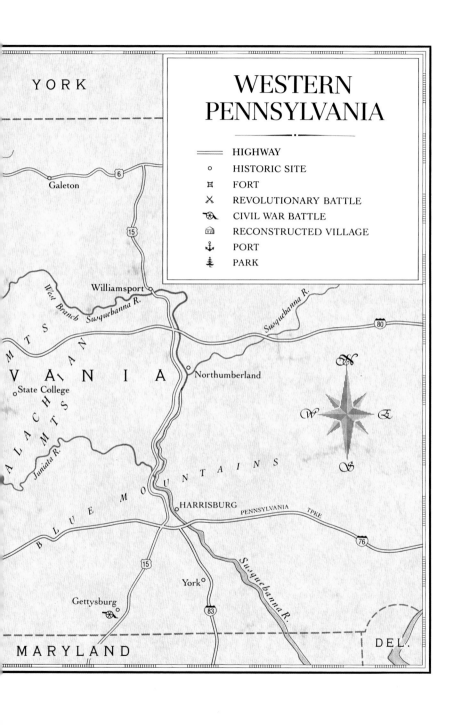

YORK

## WESTERN PENNSYLVANIA

| | |
|---|---|
| ═══ | HIGHWAY |
| ○ | HISTORIC SITE |
| ☷ | FORT |
| ⚔ | REVOLUTIONARY BATTLE |
| ⚔ | CIVIL WAR BATTLE |
| ⌂ | RECONSTRUCTED VILLAGE |
| ⚓ | PORT |
| ⚕ | PARK |

Galeton

West Branch Susquehanna R.

Williamsport

Susquehanna R.

State College

Northumberland

Juniata R.

BLUE MOUNTAINS

HARRISBURG

PENNSYLVANIA TPKE.

Susquehanna R.

York

Gettysburg

MARYLAND

DEL.

In 1859 E. L. Drake, a middle-aged railroad conductor, drilled the first gusher near Titusville. Drake's discovery set off a flurry of exploration and production that created many a fortune, most notably that of John D. Rockefeller. For years Pennsylvania's oil men were so confident that theirs was the country's only oil field that they boasted they would drink every drop of oil found west of the Alleghenies. Production in the state, however, peaked in 1891 with 31.4 million barrels. After the Civil War, coal and steel brought Pennsylvania full force into the Industrial Age. In Pittsburgh, the Scottish-born telegraph operator Andrew Carnegie organized steel production on a worldwide basis and made that city the leading producer of steel in the world.

# CENTRAL PENNSYLVANIA

Few areas in the eastern United States are as wild or as sparsely inhabited as Central Pennsylvania, particularly in the heavily forested regions of the north. Here the lumber industry built such river towns as Lockport and Williamsport. The Susquehanna River is the area's eastern border, extending from where the river forks at Northumberland north to the New York border. On the west the border follows county lines through the Allegheny National Forest on the north, passes just west of Johnstown, and ends at the Maryland border. In its history, topography, culture, and economy, the area around Gettysburg and York belongs to the Piedmont Plateau lying east of the Susquehanna, and has little in common with the wooded, mountainous areas of the state's central region.

## GETTYSBURG

It was Gettysburg's position at the hub of four major highways that brought together the armies in the most decisive and bloodiest battle of the Civil War. General Robert E. Lee, having entered Pennsylvania from Virginia in early June, was heading toward the state capital on the afternoon of June 29, 1863, when he said to his officers: "Tomorrow, gentlemen, we will not move to Harrisburg as we expected, but will go over to Gettysburg and see what General Meade is after." Actually, the goals of General George Gordon Meade, the Army of the Potomac's new commander, were clear to everyone involved: the North wanted to destroy General Lee's

OPPOSITE: *Figures on the base of the Soldiers' National Monument, Gettysburg.*

Confederate Army of Northern Virginia and bring about the end of the war. For its part, the Confederacy wanted a decisive victory on northern soil.

Adjoining the Military Park is the **Gettysburg National Cemetery,** where 3,706 Civil War dead, more than a third of them unknown, are buried with nearly as many from later wars. The sixty-foot, marble **Soldiers' National Monument** stands near the spot where President Abraham Lincoln, on November 19, 1863, delivered his most famous speech, the brief but eloquent Gettysburg Address. The speech was not written on the back of an envelope on the way to the battlefield, as the story is often told; rather, it was originally drafted on White House stationery in Washington. Each summer one of the first two drafts, on loan from the Library of Congress, is displayed at the National Military Park.

*A statue of Gouverneur K. Warren, chief engineer for the Union Army, stands on Little Round*

## Gettysburg National Military Park

Created by Congress in 1895, the 3,500-acre park, which nearly surrounds the town of Gettysburg, today consists of thirty-five miles of roads and 1,300 monuments, many erected by the states. The **Virginia Monument,** with its statue of General Robert E. Lee, stands where he observed Pickett's Charge on July 3, 1863. The **North Carolina Memorial,** also on Seminary Ridge, was carved by Gutzon Borglum, sculptor of Mount Rushmore. The **Pennsylvania Memorial,** a four-arched granite monument erected in 1910, honors the 34,530 Pennsylvanians who fought in the battle.

The battle was joined on July 1, with a skirmish west of town between the brigade of Confederate General Ambrose P. Hill and General John Buford's Federal calvary, which quickly escalated

*Top, which he saved for the Union line at the Battle of Gettysburg.*

into full-scale battle. Hill pushed forward to **Seminary Ridge,** while
General Richard Stoddert Ewell's troops drove the Union forces
out of Gettysburg to the high ground of **Culp's Hill,** the northernmost point of the hook-shaped **Cemetery Ridge.** Although the first
day was a Confederate victory, General James Longstreet's late-
afternoon attack on the Federal southern flank the next day failed
to dislodge the enemy from the high point called **Little Round
Top,** nor did Confederate commanders Hill and Ewell succeed in
driving the Union forces from Cemetery Ridge.

On July 3, after an hour's artillery duel, General Lee attacked
General Meade's center with full force. The gallant but hopeless
advance against the Federals on Cemetery Ridge was led by General George Edward Pickett and has gone down in history as Pickett's
Charge. Despite devastating frontal and cross fire, the Confederates briefly penetrated the Union lines at a stone wall on the
ridge—a point known as the **High Water Mark**—before they were
beaten back. When Pickett reported, "General Lee, I have no
division now," his commander replied, "Come, General Pickett,
this has been my fight and upon my shoulders rests the blame."

The final victory, a defensive one, was the North's, but at a
terrible cost. Of the 88,000 Federal troops in the battle, 3,155 were
killed, 14,529 wounded; of the 75,000 Confederates, 3,903 were
killed and 18,735 wounded. Meade's army was too exhausted to
press its advantage, so on the night of July 5, Lee began his retreat
to the south. Throughout the park, interpretive markers explain
such landmarks of the battle.

At the main entrance to the park on Route 134, the **visitor
center** holds the Rosensteel collection of Civil War artifacts, exhibits explaining the three-day battle, and an electric map orientation
program. The nearby **Cyclorama Center** features the cyclorama
painting of Pickett's charge by Paul Philippoteaux.

> LOCATION: On Route 134. HOURS: Roads open 6 AM–10 PM Daily.
> FEE: For visitor and Cyclorama centers only. TELEPHONE: 717–334–
> 1124.

A number of the older buildings in and about town are interesting
both in themselves and for the connection with the Civil War. The
Italianate **Adams County Courthouse** (Baltimore and West Middle
streets), with restored, fresco-walled ceremonial courtroom and a
clock tower; the **Old Dorm** of the Lutheran Theological Seminary,
an 1832 brick building on Seminary Ridge; and **Pennsylvania
Hall,** an 1837 brick building at Gettysburg College, all served as

*Interior of Golden Plough Tavern, York.*

hospitals for men wounded in the fighting. The 1858 **Western Maryland Railroad Passenger Depot** (Carlisle and Railroad streets), where President Lincoln arrived to deliver his speech at the cemetery, now houses the Gettysburg Travel Council.

The farm designated as the **Eisenhower National Historic Site** (717–334–1124) was General Dwight D. Eisenhower's weekend retreat from the White House, a refuge in time of illness, and a gathering place for the family. Tours begin at the visitor center at the Gettysburg National Military Park, which offers a brief orientation program and shuttle bus service to the site.

## YORK

Settled in 1741 at the point where Monocacy Road, an important trading route, crossed Codorus Creek, York was the first settlement west of the Susquehanna River. In colonial days, its fields were so fertile and well-farmed that York was known as the "breadbasket of America." While the British occupied Philadelphia during the Revolution, York served as the nation's capital. From September 1777 to June 1778, the Continental Congress conducted the affairs of state in York's **Colonial Courthouse** (717–846–1977), now reconstructed at the corner of West Market Street and Pershing Avenue, one block west of York's Continental Square. It was here Congress adopted the Articles of Confederation, the nation's first constitution. Congress also ratified the country's first international treaties and issued the first national Thanksgiving Proclamation in York. Exhibits, multimedia shows, and historic memorabilia interpret this era.

During the Revolution, York was also one of the settings for the so-called Conway Cabal, an attempt on the part of a faction in Congress to replace George Washington with General Horatio Gates and to regain control of the army and the war. While in York, Gates stayed at the **General Gates House** (157 West Market Street, 717–848–1587), a 1751 stone building that adjoins the **Golden Plough Tavern,** an unusual log and half-timbered building. Tradition holds that it was in the Gates House that Lafayette thwarted the cabal by pledging his loyalty to Washington in a toast. Behind the adjoining buildings, the **Barnett Bobb Log House,** an outstanding example of the homes built by German settlers in the early nineteenth century, has period painted furniture.

The extensive collections of the **Historical Society of York County** (250 East Market Street, 717–848–1587) present an excellent picture of early York. The museum includes a re-creation of the original village square, with an apothecary shop, firehouse, settler's cabin, tavern, and silversmith shop, among other places of business. Also displayed are period costumes and the 1804 Tannenberg organ. The **Horace Bonham House** (152 East Market Street, 717–848–1587) was built in 1840 and extensively remodeled around 1880. Bonham was a gentleman artist known for his paintings of York residents. There are original furnishings that belonged to the family in the late nineteenth century.

## JOSEPH PRIESTLEY HOUSE

The eminent English scientist and freethinker Joseph Priestley built this two-and-a-half-story Georgian house in 1794 and lived here until his death. Restored by the state, the house contains period furnishings as well as laboratory equipment, letters, and documents. Priestley had discovered oxygen and eight other gases before falling into disfavor in England through his support of the French Revolution and his liberal theological views. Greeted with acclaim in both New York City and Philadelphia, he preferred the country life and built his home in Northumberland, a town on forks of the Susquehanna River. Exhibits include antique scientific equipment.

LOCATION: 472 Priestley Avenue, Northumberland. HOURS: 12–4 Friday–Sunday. FEE: Yes. TELEPHONE: 717–473–9474.

# PENNSYLVANIA LUMBER MUSEUM

The heyday of lumbering, once one of Pennsylvania's principal industries, is re-created in this museum. Exhibits include a reconstructed logging camp complete with bunkhouse/mess hall, laundry, blacksmith shop, and steam-powered circular sawmill from the 1890s, and displays of tools and equipment used to fell trees.

At first the state's abundant pine forests were considered obstacles to westward expansion. But in the 1830s the lumber industry was born and the trees harvested with such energy that the forests were all but depleted by the end of the century. The Susquehanna River, its branches reaching deep into the wilderness, was a natural corridor for floating logs, causing towns like Lock Haven and Williamsport to boom. In the early days logs were lashed together in rafts, sometimes up to three hundred feet long. These were replaced in the mid-1860s by "booms," or river traps for free-floating logs.

The Lumber Museum's collection includes a Shay locomotive—a geared locomotive designed in the 1880s by Michigan lumberman Ephraim Shay, to be operated on the steep grades and sharp curves of the crudely built logging railroads.

LOCATION: Route 6, ten miles west of Galeton. HOURS: April through November: 9–4:30 Monday–Saturday, 10–4:30 Sunday. FEE: Yes. TELEPHONE: 814–435–2652.

# BRADFORD

Oil was discovered here in 1875, bringing the predictable influx of prospectors and sending land prices soaring. For a period, oil wells were everywhere, even in backyards and front lawns, and by the late 1930s Bradford fields were producing three million barrels of prime crude a year. Today, the days of the oil boom are re-created in the **Penn-Brad Oil Museum** (south on Route 219, 814–368–5574), which includes a tool museum and an 1890s-style wooden drilling rig reconstructed with antique tools.

# P I T T S B U R G H

Many vestiges remain of Pittsburgh's rich and important past, when the city was a strategic frontier outpost, a crucible of industrial growth, and the nation's "Gateway to the West." The city is located on the triangle of land formed by the Allegheny and Monongahela rivers where they join to form the westward-flowing Ohio. In 1753 George Washington, on his expedition to warn the French away from Fort Le Boeuf, noted in his journal: "I spent some time viewing the rivers, and the land in the fork, which I think extremely well situated for a fort, as it has the absolute command of both rivers."

The French obviously thought so too—no sooner did the English occupy the fork early in 1754 than the French took the point of land away and built their own fortification, Fort Duquesne. From then on, the fork became a prize in the contest for control of North America known as the French and Indian War.

From Fort Duquesne, the French controlled the upper Ohio Valley for three years, sending troops to defeat Washington in 1754 at Great Meadows and Braddock in 1755 near where Turtle Creek runs into the Monongahela River south of Pittsburgh. Finally, in 1758 the French burned and abandoned the fort at the approach of General John Forbes and a force of 6,500 men, including a company under the command of Colonel George Washington. Forbes Road, the wagon-wide track that Forbes's expedition hewed through the wilderness from Fort Bedford through Ligonier to Pittsburgh, became the principal highway between the East and Ohio and helped secure Pittsburgh's future as a commercial and transportation center.

Named for the British statesman William Pitt the Elder, the formidable five-sided fortress called Fort Pitt was begun in 1759 and completed two years later. The only remaining part, called the Blockhouse, was added in 1764 and is now preserved as the Fort Pitt Museum. The small village that grew up around the fort was destroyed during Pontiac's Rebellion in 1763. The four downtown blocks on the point of land today known as the Triangle were laid out the next year. No sooner did the Treaty of Paris end the French and Indian War in 1763, making Pittsburgh indisputably English, than the city was claimed by both Pennsylvania and Vir-

OPPOSITE: *Downtown Pittsburgh with Henry Hobson Richardson's Allegheny County Courthouse and Jail in the foreground.*

ginia. After the Revolution, Congress settled the conflicting claims to the city in favor of Pennsylvania.

In 1804 a banker from Philadelphia described Pittsburgh as "a fine Country Town" with "tolerable goods & cheap markets, dear stores & bad society." Boatbuilding, distilling—producing a whiskey that George Washington pronounced "excellent" during a prewar visit—glassmaking, and cotton weaving were among the fledgling industries that bolstered the area's expanding economy. Pittsburgh thrived in selling goods to settlers passing through, and as an entrepôt for goods moving east and west.

The iron industry was also developing rapidly, pointing to the next century when Pittsburgh would become the world's leading producer of steel. About 1830 anthracite coal, being mined in abundance in western Pennsylvania, came to replace charcoal in smelting iron. The adaptation of the puddling furnace and rolling mill were other critical technological changes that speeded the development of this key industry. By the end of the Civil War, which had accelerated demand, Pittsburgh was producing half the iron and one-third of the glass in the country.

In the post-Civil War era, the Scottish-born Andrew Carnegie, a former telegrapher on the Pennsylvania Central Railroad, foresaw that steel would replace iron in the building of railroads and bridges. Carnegie modernized steel production, bringing all the steps—smelting, forging and rolling, cutting, and founding—under one roof. By 1870 Carnegie had become both the number one steelmaker and the richest man in the world.

Carnegie once observed that his epitaph should read: "Here lies the man who was able to surround himself with men far cleverer than himself." Carnegie's associates included brilliant young Henry Clay Frick, Henry Phipps, and Charles M. Schwab. Phipps was Carnegie's longtime associate and adviser. Frick made a million dollars in the coal business by the time he was thirty, merged his interests with Carnegie's, and became president of Carnegie Brothers in 1889. Schwab started as an engineer's helper and became president of Carnegie Steel in 1897. He then helped J. P. Morgan form the United States Steel Corporation, which bought out Carnegie in 1901. Schwab later founded the Bethlehem Steel Company.

Like Carnegie, all three men eventually moved to New York, but Pittsburgh has been enriched by their legacy. Restoration of **Clayton** (7227 Reynolds Street), the mid-Victorian home that Frick purchased in 1882 in the now-less-than-fashionable East End section of Pittsburgh, was completed in 1990. The house, which was redesigned in the French chateau style by Frederick J. Osterling, then a young Pittsburgh architect, stayed in the family. Frick's daughter, Helen, provided funds when she died in 1984 so that "future generations may better understand the kind of life that was lived within its walls." The **Frick Art Museum** (412–371–0600) on the grounds contains her important collection of Italian, Flemish, and French paintings and decorative arts.

The amalgamation Carnegie brought to the steel industry was also occurring elsewhere in the city. In 1881, for example, eight national trade unions under Samuel Gompers met in Pittsburgh to form the Federation of Organized Trades and Labor Unions of the United States and Canada, later renamed the American Federation of Labor. In 1907 Pittsburgh itself took over the neighboring city of Allegheny (population 150,000); in the census of 1910, its population had risen to 534,000.

Although the city suffered during the Depression, increased demand for steel from the automobile industry and from abroad as World War II approached aided in its recovery. Pittsburgh's much-heralded renaissance began in May 1950, with the demolition of a 103-year-old building, followed by the razing of almost everything west of Stanwix and Ferry streets. The widespread demolition of older buildings led one citizen to observe: "The town has no worship of landmarks. Instead it takes pleasure in the swing of the headache ball and the crash of falling brick." After a somewhat slow start, however, the forces of preservation rallied to save many architecturally important buildings.

A tour of Pittsburgh logically starts downtown at Point State Park, where a 150-foot fountain symbolizes the confluence of the Allegheny, Monongahela, and Ohio rivers, and proceeds to the areas and neighborhoods north, across the Allegheny River; south, across the Monongahela; and east, where Schenley Park and the city's many cultural institutions are located.

## POINT STATE PARK

Markers throughout the park explain the development of the site's fortifications, but the only remaining structure is the **Fort Pitt Blockhouse,** built as one of five redoubts on the western side of Fort Pitt. In the late nineteenth century, the Blockhouse was saved from demolition by the Daughters of the American Revolution, who restored it and maintain it today.

## Fort Pitt Museum

Located in a re-created eighteenth-century bastion of the English fort, the museum tells the story of Fort Pitt and the events that led up to the French and Indian War, with dioramas, scale models, and gallery displays. There is also a full-size reproduction of a barracks room. During the summer the Royal American Regiment puts on drills and concerts of eighteenth-century band music.

LOCATION: Point State Park. HOURS: 9–5 Tuesday–Saturday, 12–5 Sunday. FEE: Yes. TELEPHONE: 412–281–9285.

The three-story Greek Revival **Burke's Building** (209 Fourth Avenue) was built in 1836 by John Chislett, an English-trained architect. The small but dignified office building was the only building to survive the 1845 fire that devastated the Triangle area. At the turn of the century, Fourth Avenue was Pittsburgh's Wall Street, and many of the early skyscrapers put up by financial institutions survive, such as the 1905 **Machesney Building** (number 221), the 1928 **Arrott Building** (at Wood Street), and the 1906 **Union Bank Building** (also at Wood Street).

**Pennsylvania Station** (Grant Street and Liberty Avenue), completed in 1903, is the fourth station built by the Pennsylvania Railroad as a terminal for the lines running to such important cities as Philadelphia, St. Louis, Cincinnati, and Chicago. The well-known Chicago architect Daniel Burnham designed both the building and the much-admired Beaux-Arts rotunda at the entranceway.

**Grant Street,** the easternmost street of the Triangle, is a mix of modern and historic buildings and a "showplace thoroughfare," according to the city's effective preservation organization, the Pittsburgh History and Landmarks Foundation. Many of the Grant Street buildings were built by Henry Clay Frick, including the **Frick Building** at the corner of Fifth Avenue, an austere but classic example of early skyscraper design by Daniel Burnham in 1901; the original part of the 1916 **William Penn Hotel** at Sixth Avenue; and the massive but delicately designed 1917 **Union Arcade** at Grant Street and Fifth Avenue. The last, ornamented in stone-colored and white terra-cotta, was designed in the Flemish Gothic style by Pittsburgh architect Frederick J. Osterling, and had space for 240 shops facing open arcades and seven hundred offices. It is

OPPOSITE: *The dome of Pennsylvania Station, Pittsburgh.*

*Smithfield Street Bridge, Pittsburgh, spanning the Monongahela River.*

now called Two Mellon Bank Center, and the arcades have been floored over, but the ten-story-high central court covered by a stained-glass dome remains.

Also at this junction is the city's most famous set of buildings, the **Allegheny County Courthouse and Jail,** completed in 1888, also known as the "County Buildings." Although the architect, internationally known Henry Hobson Richardson of Massachusetts, did not live to see the buildings completed, the Romanesque Revival complex, with its prominent courthouse tower, many arches, and generous ornamentation, is considered among his best works. The jail and the courthouse are connected by the arched "Bridge of Sighs," spanning Ross Street.

As a river city, Pittsburgh has many bridges, but none more notable than the **Smithfield Street Bridge.** This is one of the country's oldest truss-type bridges and one of the best works of the Austrian-born Gustav Lindenthal, who built the Queensboro Bridge over New York City's East River. The bridge, which crosses the Monongahela River and leads to Mount Washington and the Southside, was widened in the same design style in 1889 and 1911.

# SOUTHSIDE

Starting in the 1760s, much of the coal that fueled the city's early industry was mined from the four-hundred-foot Mount Washington, across the Monongahela River from the Triangle. In the late nineteenth century, twelve cable cars, called inclines, carried coal and passengers up and down the slopes; of these, two remain in operation. The **Monongahela Incline,** between West Carson Street and Grandview Avenue at Wyoming Street, was the city's first, built in 1870. It rises 367 feet at a thirty-five-degree angle along two parallel tracks and provides a spectacular view of the city. A mile away, the 1877 **Duquesne Incline** (1197 West Carson Street to 1220 Grandview Avenue) still has its original cars with cherry and maple interiors. The waiting room of the Grandview Station displays photographs of old Pittsburgh and other trolley lines and inclines.

Beneath Mount Washington is the former **Pittsburgh & Lake Erie Railroad Terminal,** now an adaptive-use complex known as **Station Square.** The railroad, which specialized in hauling coal,

*View from the base of the Duquesne Incline, built in 1877.*

built the terminal in stages between 1897 and 1918 along the shore opposite the Triangle. When the operation declined in the 1960s, the complex survived demolition until 1975, when the Pittsburgh History and Landmarks Foundation's proposal for the forty-three-acre site began to put the historic buildings to new use and created open areas for the public along the waterfront. Thus far the 1897 freight house has been converted into a commercial and retail arcade; the 1901 passenger station has become the **Landmarks Building,** with offices and a five-hundred-seat restaurant under the stained-glass ceiling of the Grand Concourse. Several other buildings have been put to office and commercial use. Displayed outdoors are railroad rolling stock, a Bessemer converter, an ingot mold, and an original car from the Monongahela Incline.

# OAKLAND

To the east of the Triangle, on a two-hundred-foot-high plateau that overlooks the Monongahela River, wealthy Pittsburghers began to build mansions. Oakland is the location of Pittsburgh's Civic Center, Schenley Park, and The Carnegie. All this began in 1889 when the expatriate heiress Mary Croghan Schenley donated three hundred acres for a park, and Andrew Carnegie gave the city a cultural institution for the park's main entrance.

## The Carnegie

The original building of The Carnegie (formerly the Carnegie Institute), constructed from 1892 to 1895, is a simple, dignified, Italian Renaissance–style structure with a music hall flanked by two Venetian campaniles. The Forbes Avenue section, built between 1903 and 1907 in a more ostentatious Beaux-Arts tradition, includes a sumptuous foyer for the music hall adorned with different kinds of marble, elaborate bronze work, and plaster ornamentation. Carnegie supposedly insisted the foyer cost more than any throne room, as a tribute to the sovereignty of the American people. Both parts were designed by the firm of Longfellow, Alden & Harlow.

The Carnegie includes the **Carnegie Library of Pittsburgh** (412–622–3114), one of the nation's most important libraries, with more than four million items, and the **Carnegie Museum of Natural History,** whose collection includes outstanding exhibits of dinosaurs, mammals, North American Indian artifacts, and a display of Inuit culture. The **Carnegie Museum of Art** has European and American decorative arts in the Ailsa Mellon Bruce Galleries and

*The gilt and marble foyer of the Carnegie Music Hall.* OVERLEAF: *A portion of The Carnegie's collection.*

changing exhibits in the Heinz Galleries. The addition in 1974 of the Sarah Scaife Gallery significantly expanded the museum.

LOCATION: 4400 Forbes Avenue. HOURS: 10–5 Tuesday–Saturday, 1–5 Sunday. FEE: Yes. TELEPHONE: 412–622–3131.

## Schenley Park

In 1889 Mary Croghan Schenley, an expatriate who had been living in London for forty years, gave three hundred acres for a park. According to local legend, this occurred after representatives of the city and a development company raced across the Atlantic to be the first to request the land. The city won, and the park, later expanded to 456 acres, was designed by the English architect William Falconer. The late-eighteenth-century **Neil Log House** on East Circuit Road, now restored and furnished with frontier items, is one of the few remaining pioneer structures in the Pittsburgh area. The restored and modernized greenhouses of the **Phipps Conservatory** (Curto Drive, 412–622–6914) were built by the de-

signers Lord & Burnham of Irvington, New York, starting in 1892. Phipps was a partner of Andrew Carnegie. The conservatory specializes in seasonal floral displays and is open year-round.

Near the Carnegie entrance to the park, the **Christopher Lyman Magee Memorial** is a granite stele designed in 1908 by Henry Bacon, who later did the Lincoln Memorial in Washington, DC. The bronze cornucopia bas-relief is by Augustus Saint-Gaudens. Another great American sculptor, Daniel Chester French, did the bas-relief bust on the **George Westinghouse Memorial** at West Circuit and Schenley drives.

LOCATION: Forbes Avenue.

## Civic Center

The developer of the Civic Center, Franklin Felix Nicola, was undoubtedly influenced by the City Beautiful movement of the late nineteenth century, an attempt at sane city planning inspired by the wide boulevards and open spaces of the great European cities. Nicola purchased an Oakland cornfield in 1897 and the next year built the **Hotel Schenley,** for years the city's finest hotel. In 1956 the University of Pittsburgh acquired the building as a student union, and in 1983 the William Pitt Union was restored to its former Schenley splendor.

The centerpiece of the Civic Center is also the city's best-known historic building, the impressive **Cathedral of Learning** (Bigelow Boulevard and Fifth Avenue). The textured limestone building containing classrooms for the University of Pittsburgh soars in a pinnacle of irregular setbacks to 535 feet. The building is not without its detractors; Frank Lloyd Wright supposedly called it "the world's largest 'Keep off the Grass' sign."

Built between 1926 and 1937, the cathedral was designed by the Philadelphia architect Charles Zeller Klauder, who also did the nearby **Heinz Chapel** built from 1934 to 1938 in an unusual Gothic design with an apse at each end, and the **Stephen Collins Foster Memorial** (412–624–4100), housing a museum, archive, and research library of Foster's works, and a small theater. The Gothic monument to the Pittsburgh-born Foster seems inappropriate for the folksy American songwriter. Foster is buried in **Allegheny Cemetery** (4734 Butler Street, Lawrenceville), along with actress Lillian Russell, financier and philanthropist Andrew Mellon, and Harry K. Thaw, the jealous husband who shot and killed architect Stanford White in 1906.

At 4338 Bigelow Boulevard, **The Historical Society of Western Pennsylvania** (412–681–5533) is housed in a 1912 Italian Renaissance villa of white brick and matching terra-cotta, and has displays of local glass, documents, furniture, and paintings.

Oakland is also the location of some of the best work of colorful New York architect Henry Hornbostel, who first worked in Pittsburgh in 1904 when his firm won the competition to design the Carnegie Technical School, now **Carnegie Mellon University** at Tech and Frew streets. His plans for the school were never fully realized, but the most notable buildings on campus, such as **Hammerschlag Hall,** with the great arches front and back, and the 1906 **Margaret Morrison Carnegie College,** with a circular Doric colonnade, are by his hand. Hornbostel, who later became the school's first professor of architecture, also designed the Civic Center's monumental 1911 **Allegheny County Soldiers' and Sailors' Memorial** (Fifth Avenue and Bigelow Boulevard). The Beaux-Arts edifice, modeled after the mausoleum at Halicarnassus, features a 2,500-seat auditorium.

## NORTHSIDE

Now the Northside section, the city of Allegheny once rivaled Pittsburgh across the river to the south. Before the Civil War, the city was the terminus for the Pennsylvania Canal and the Ohio and Pennsylvania Railroad, and in 1889 H. J. Heinz moved his plant there. After annexation by Pittsburgh in 1907, however, Allegheny declined. Although much of the old city has been destroyed by redevelopment, certain important landmarks survive and many sections are being restored and revitalized.

The 1897 **Allegheny Post Office** in Landmarks Square is a domed Italian Renaissance building of pale gray granite that once dominated a major intersection of the city. In the late 1960s the building was marked for demolition before the Pittsburgh History and Landmarks Foundation stepped in to save and restore it. Artifacts from demolished Pittsburgh buildings, as well as Charles Keck's 1915 portal sculptures from the Manchester Bridge, are exhibited in the garden court. The buildings now house the **Pittsburgh Children's Museum** (412–322–5059).

On Allegheny Square, the former Allegheny Library, now the **Carnegie Library of Pittsburgh, Allegheny Regional Branch** (412–321–0389), was the first of the 2,811 libraries Carnegie eventually built. Topped by a tower and an urn, the 1889 granite building is across from a Daniel Chester French statue of Colonel James Anderson. This iron magnate had opened his library to Andrew Carnegie and other young employees, and eventually gave his collection to the city. Henry Hobson Richardson designed the **Emmanuel Episcopal Church** (West North and Allegheny avenues) in brick after the congregation rejected a plan for a more costly stone building. Built in 1886, it has an expansive slate roof, broken only by six gables and rounded at one end.

# WESTERN PENNSYLVANIA

## JOHNSTOWN

Since 1800, when Swiss immigrant Joseph Schantz (later anglicized to Johns) laid out the town in the narrow valleys formed by the Conemaugh and Stony Creek rivers, Johnstown has been flooded many times; 85 people died in 1977. However, it was the flood that devastated the steel town after the South Fork Dam broke on May 31, 1889, that has gone down as one of the worst natural disasters in American history. The dam, built in 1852 to supply water to the Pennsylvania Canal system, had been raised to a height of eighty feet in 1881 to increase the size of a lake used by a sportsmen's club. When the earthen barrier gave way, a wall of water seventy-five feet high and a half mile wide descended on the city. The 2,209 lives that were lost included 777 unknowns who are buried beneath small, white marble headstones, laid in precise rows, in **Grandview Cemetery,** one mile west of town.

The **Johnstown Flood National Memorial** (Route 869, 814–495–4643) is a National Park Service site on the location of the South Fork Dam. The visitor center houses a museum with exhibits on the flood and the local geography. In Johnstown itself, the **Johnstown Flood Museum** (304 Washington Street, 814–539–1889) is housed in the library Andrew Carnegie donated to the town after the flood. It contains photographs, maps, and other material on the major floods of 1936 and 1977 as well as the disaster of 1889. Built in 1891, the **Johnstown Inclined Plane** (Johns Street and Edgehill Drive, 814–536–1816) has since provided residents with a quick way to higher ground, saving many lives. The 896-foot-long, cable-pulled railway has a grade of 71 percent, one of the steepest in the country.

OPPOSITE: *In the aftermath of the Johnstown flood in 1889, a resident poses on the wreckage.*

# ALLEGHENY PORTAGE RAILROAD NATIONAL HISTORIC SITE

This system of tracks rises 1,400 feet on inclined planes over the summit of Allegheny Mountain, linking the eastern and western canals of the Pennsylvania system. The portage railroad was built between Johnstown and Hollidaysburg to facilitate commerce with the West and meet the competition posed by the completion of the Erie Canal in New York state in 1825. Completed in 1834, it consisted of ten inclined planes, five on each side of the mountain; at each incline, cars were attached to thick hemp ropes, which were moved up and down the tracks by stationary steam engines. On the levels between the planes, steam locomotives pulled the cars.

In 1842 Charles Dickens wrote of his trip on the railroad: "It was pretty traveling thus at a rapid pace along the heights of the mountain and with a keen wind, to look down into a valley full of light and softness and catching glimpses through the treetops . . .

*The railroad, historically important to Pennsylvania's economy, employed innovative*

and we riding onward high above them like a whirlwind." The portage railroad was abandoned in 1854 after the Pennsylvania Railroad completed its line, which included Horseshoe Curve, over Allegheny Mountain.

Near the mountain summit, **Lemon House,** now a visitor center, was a tavern and rest stop for travelers on the railroad. Its owner, Samuel Lemon, became a wealthy man selling coal and supplies to the railroad. Other sites within the park include **Planes 6, 8, 9, and 10,** stone culverts, and excavated engine-house foundations. Also still standing are the **Skew Arch Bridge,** once called "the most famous piece of masonry in America," which was built—without mortar—to carry traffic over Plane 6, and **Staple Bend Tunnel,** a 901-foot passage, much of it through solid rock.

LOCATION: Three miles east of Cresson on Route 22. HOURS: June through Labor Day: 9–6 Daily; September through May: 9–5 Daily. FEE: None. TELEPHONE: 814–886–6150.

*technology to facilitate trade by linking the state to both the east and the expanding west.*

# ERIE

Pennsylvania's northernmost city and its only port on Lake Erie was named after the Eriez Indians, who were wiped out by the Seneca in the mid-seventeenth century. As a port, the city is well protected by the seven-mile-long Presque Isle, a peninsula that curves around the harbor. In 1753 the French built a fort on Presque Isle, which was then abandoned to the English and finally burned by Indians in 1763 at the start of Pontiac's Rebellion.

The town was first laid out in 1795, the year after General "Mad" Anthony Wayne defeated the Indians in the Battle of Fallen Timbers, opening the Erie Triangle to settlement. In March 1813, Lieutenant Oliver Hazard Perry was sent to Erie to oversee the building of the small American fleet, including the *Niagara*.

## Flagship Niagara

Commanded by Lieutenant Oliver Hazard Perry, the 110-foot, square-rigged, two-masted brig *Niagara* turned the tide in favor of the Americans in the Battle of Lake Erie on September 10, 1813. The battle, which took place off Put-in-Bay, Ohio, ended the British threat to the northwest and was an important American victory

*His first flagship heavily damaged by British fire, Oliver Hazard Perry is rowed to the* Niagara *during the Battle of Lake Erie.*

in the War of 1812. The present ship was reconstructed for the centennial of the battle using the timbers of the keel of the original vessel. The eighteen carronades—thirty-two-pound guns for fighting at close quarters—were cast in Erie at the time of the centennial.

LOCATION: 164 East Front Street. HOURS: June through Labor Day: 9–5 Tuesday–Saturday, 12–5 Sunday. Phone to verify ship is in port. FEE: Yes. TELEPHONE: 814–452–2744.

Two of Erie's most notable buildings stand side by side on State Street. The **Old Custom House** (number 411), a Greek Revival structure whose finely proportioned portico has six Doric columns, was built in 1839 as the Erie branch of the United States Bank of Pennsylvania. The bank failed before the building was finished and in 1849 it became a customhouse. It is now the **Erie Art Museum** (814–459–5477). The **Cashiers House** (number 417), built in 1838 for the bank's first cashier, houses the collections of the Erie County Historical Society (814–454–1813).

On the grounds of the Pennsylvania Soldiers' and Sailors' Home (560 East Third Street, corner of Ash Street), is the **Anthony Wayne Memorial Blockhouse Museum** (814–871–4531), a replica of the blockhouse where General Anthony Wayne died on December 15, 1796; his body was later removed to Radmore, Pennsylvania. The grave of Captain Charles Vernon Gridley is marked by four Spanish cannon in **Lakeside Cemetery** (1718 East Lake Road). Gridley, who died in Japan, began the Battle of Manila Bay in 1898 after Admiral George Dewey spoke the famous line: "You may fire when you are ready, Gridley."

# WATERFORD

The tensions that led to the French and Indian War surfaced dramatically here in the winter of 1753, when Governor Robert Dinwiddie of Virginia sent George Washington, then a twenty-one-year-old major, to warn the French away from Fort Le Boeuf, the fortification at Waterford. As Washington later reported, the French replied that "it was their absolute design to take possession of the Ohio." The following year, the first battle of the war was fought at Great Meadows. A scale model of the fort is displayed at the modern **Fort Le Boeuf Museum** (123 High Street, 814–796–4113), along with other exhibits that tell the story of Washington's initial confrontation with the French.

# DRAKE WELL MUSEUM

This replica of an oil well, derrick, and well house marks the site on fabled Oil Creek where Edwin L. Drake built the first commercial oil well in August 1859. Drake's discovery precipitated an oil boom of unprecedented proportions, spawning an industry that literally changed the face of America.

Long before Drake's discovery, Indians and early settlers had known about the light coating of oil found on Oil Creek. Occasionally it was skimmed off and sold as "Seneca Oil," a patent medicine claiming to cure such ills as blindness, rheumatism, and baldness. As early as 1840, Pittsburgh druggist Samuel M. Kier produced a lamp fuel, a forerunner of kerosene, by distilling petroleum. In 1854 an entrepreneur named George H. Bissell formed an oil prospecting company and in 1858 hired Drake, a former railroad conductor, to drill on a plot of land he leased on Oil Creek near Titusville. Drake struck oil at 69½ feet on August 27, 1859. At the rate of about twenty-five barrels à day, the well produced close to two thousand barrels of oil before the year was out.

The museum, housed in a modern building, includes a unique collection of books, documents, photographs, and artifacts, including a four-wheeled wagon with its volatile cargo clearly identified on the side: "Nitro-Glycerine."

LOCATION: Off Route 8, Titusville. HOURS: 9–5 Monday–Saturday, 12–5 Sunday. FEE: Yes. TELEPHONE: 814–827–2797.

# AMBRIDGE

Founded as a company town by the American Bridge Company, Ambridge was built on the site of Economy, a communal brotherhood of labor established in 1825 by members of the Harmony Society. The Harmonists were followers of George Rapp, a German Pietist who had come to America in 1803. To prepare for the millennium, Rapp and about six hundred followers established a community at Harmony, Pennsylvania, about twenty-five miles north of Pittsburgh, where they lived simply and practiced celibacy.

In 1814 the society moved to a site on the Wabash River in Indiana—later named New Harmony by the English reformer Robert Owen—but returned to Pennsylvania in 1825 to be closer to major markets. Here they established a three-thousand-acre agricultural and manufacturing center, producing shoes and cotton and wool textiles. The community they called Economy was so successful that it came to dominate commerce in western Pennsylvania and eventually it invested large sums in oil drilling, railroads, and other businesses. The society continued to prosper after Rapp died in 1847, but celibacy, a lack of new members, and increased commercial competition brought about its demise in 1905.

## Old Economy Village

Now located on just under seven acres, Old Economy Village, restored and administered by the state, is one of the best-preserved utopian communities in the country. The eighteen buildings remaining were once the administrative, cultural, and economic center of the Harmonist community and include the **Great House,** a twenty-two-room structure, where Rapp and his adopted son and business manager, Frederick Reichert, lived. The society's cultural center was the **Feast Hall,** which now houses the **Harmonist Museum.** The **church,** designed by Reichert and completed in 1831, has a distinctive octagonal clock tower and cupola topped by bell-shaped domes. Several of the community's shops are restored and open to the public, as are the large formal garden with boxwood-lined paths, and the Great House kitchen garden.

LOCATION: Great House Square, Fourteenth and Church streets. HOURS: 9–5 Tuesday–Saturday, 12–5 Sunday. FEE: Yes. TELEPHONE: 412–266–4500.

# HANNA'S TOWN

Three miles north of the small industrial city of Greensburg is Hanna's Town, a once-important settlement in western Pennsylvania that had all but disappeared. In recent years, the site has been extensively excavated by the Westmoreland County Historical Society in Greensburg, including the fort built in 1774 by General Arthur St. Clair, a British colonial officer who fought on the American side during the Revolution and later served in the Continental Congress. A Conestoga wagon is displayed. St. Clair and his wife are buried in Greensburg.

LOCATION: Off Route 119, three miles north of Greensburg. HOURS: May through Labor Day: 10–4 Tuesday–Saturday, 1–4 Sundays. FEE: Yes. TELEPHONE: 412–836–1800.

# JEANNETTE

Once known as the "Glass City," Jeannette was named for the wife of H. Sellers McKee, who established a glass factory here in 1889.

## Bushy Run Battlefield

The Battle of Bushy Run turned the tide of Pontiac's Rebellion in favor of the British, relieved the Indian siege of Fort Pitt, and opened up western Pennsylvania to future settlement. Colonel Henry Bouquet of the British Colonial army was en route with five hundred men to relieve and resupply Fort Pitt, when he was attacked by Indians on the afternoon of August 5, 1763, and suffered many casualties. The next morning Bouquet, employing Indian tactics, drew the Indians into an ambush and routed them. Four days later, he arrived at Fort Pitt.

Exhibits at the visitor center tell the story of the battle; there are also tours through the 183-acre grounds.

LOCATION: Bushy Run Road (Route 993). HOURS: 9–5 Wednesday–Sunday. Grounds open until 8 PM during Daylight Saving Time. FEE: Yes. TELEPHONE: 412–527–5584.

# UNIONTOWN

In 1784 General Ephraim Douglas wrote: "This Uniontown is the most obscure spot on the face of the earth." Today the town, which became a bituminous coal center, is better known as the nearest major community to the Fort Necessity National Battlefield. The battle here on July 3, 1754, opened the French and Indian War in which the French and the English fought for control of North America. Fort Necessity was built by George Washington, then a twenty-two-year-old lieutenant colonel, and the battle in its defense—as well as a skirmish that preceded it—was his first experience under enemy fire.

After his arrival at Great Meadows on May 24, Washington learned of a small French force camped on Chestnut Ridge—later called Jumonville Glen after the French commander—only a few miles away, and on May 28 Washington overran the encampment in a surprise attack. He then returned to Great Meadows and strengthened the fortification, which he first called Fort Necessity in his journal on June 25.

On July 3, the French, commanded by Louis Coulon de Villiers, brother of Jumonville, attacked with superior manpower and, by nightfall, forced Washington to surrender. Although allowed to withdraw the next day with "honors of war," Washington had shown himself to be an inexperienced commander. But perhaps more importantly, points out his modern-day biographer, James Thomas Flexner, he demonstrated at Fort Necessity that he was a natural leader.

## Fort Necessity National Battlefield

The site of Fort Necessity became a National Park in 1933; the stockade, storehouse, and entrenchments were reconstructed later. The story of the battle is told in an audiovisual room at the **visitor center.** Major General Edward Braddock, captain general of all British soldiers in America, is buried in a separate part of the battlefield. Mortally wounded in the Battle of Monongahela on July 9, 1755, Braddock died on the retreat and was buried in an unmarked grave about one mile west of Fort Necessity. (In the same fight, George Washington had two horses shot out from under him.) In 1804 workmen came across what are believed to be his remains. A monument now marks **Braddock's Grave,** where they were reinterred.

The park complex includes **Mount Washington Tavern** on Route 40 overlooking the site of Fort Necessity. The restored tavern, built about 1817, includes a barroom, parlor, kitchen, and bedrooms. The dining room has exhibits about the National Road (now Route 40).

LOCATION: Eleven miles southeast of Uniontown on Route 40. HOURS: 8:30–5 Daily. FEE: Yes. TELEPHONE: 412–329–5512.

# FALLINGWATER

In 1936 Frank Lloyd Wright designed this house, built in cantilevered sections over the waterfall of Bear Run, for the civic-minded Pittsburgh department store owner Edgar J. Kaufmann. The house, which enhances the natural landscape of waterfalls and rock formations as it blends into them, is one of the most honored examples of twentieth-century architecture. Called "the best-known private house for someone not of royal blood in the history of the world," Fallingwater has been the subject of countless articles, treatises, and books. An exhibit at the Museum of Modern Art

OVERLEAF: *Fallingwater, a milestone of modern architecture, designed by Frank Lloyd Wright to mesh with its environment.*

in New York City was devoted to it, and it has been endlessly photographed. In 1963 Edgar Kaufmann, Jr., donated the house and 1,543 surrounding acres to the Western Pennsylvania Conservancy with the words: "Such a place cannot be possessed. It is a work by man for man, not by a man for a man."

LOCATION: Off Route 381 South, Mill Run. HOURS: April through mid-November: 10–4 Tuesday–Sunday; mid-November through March: 11–4 Saturday–Sunday. FEE: Yes. TELEPHONE: 412–329–8501.

# LIGONIER

This resort town in the hills of western Pennsylvania was named for Sir John Ligonier, the first commander of the important British outpost, **Fort Ligonier,** which has been reconstructed on its original 1758 site. The fort was built by Colonel Henry Bouquet of the Forbes Expedition, sent to seize French-held Fort Duquesne, which later became Pittsburgh. To delay the expedition, which included George Washington among its commanders, the French and Indians attacked Fort Ligonier on October 12, 1758, but were driven off. Forbes proceeded to Duquesne, arriving there on November 25, just after the French had abandoned it.

The fort's modern museum contains an excellent collection of military artifacts, an officer's mess, armory, and storehouse.

LOCATION: South Market Street. HOURS: April through October: 10–4:30 Monday–Saturday, 12–4:30 Sunday. FEE: Yes. TELEPHONE: 412–238–9701.

Three miles east of Ligonier in Laughlintown, the **Compass Inn** (Route 30, 412–238–4983) was built in 1799 and became a popular hostelry for stagecoach travelers and drivers on the Philadelphia–Pittsburgh turnpike during the first half of the nineteenth century. The two-story log-and-stone building has been restored and is open as a museum filled with furniture and utensils of the period. On the grounds are a reconstructed cookhouse, a barn, and a blacksmith shop.

Nearby is **Mount Braddock,** still in private hands and needing restoration. Built around 1802 by the inventor and iron merchant Isaac Meason, it is the grandest Georgian house west of the Appalachians.

OPPOSITE: *Fort Ligonier, a reconstruction in western Pennsylvania. George Washington was a member of the expedition that built the original fortification.*

## Notes on Architecture

### EARLY COLONIAL

In the eastern colonies, Europeans first built houses using a medieval, vertical asymmetry, which in the eighteenth century evolved toward classical

symmetry. Roofs were gabled and hipped, often with prominent exterior chimneys. Small casement windows became larger and more evenly spaced and balanced on each facade.

### GERMAN COLONIAL

In Pennsylvania, Southern Germans built one- and two-and-a-half-story houses of stone, with thick walls, slightly arched doorways and windows, and no stair halls.

### DUTCH COLONIAL

The distinctive Dutch houses of the Hudson Valley, built of wood or stone, feature overhanging gambrel roofs that shelter porches. Viewed from the side, the flaring roofs have the appearance of a broad-brimmed hat. The architectural origin of the porches was more likely Caribbean than Dutch.

### GEORGIAN

Beginning in Boston as early as 1686, and only much later elsewhere, the design of houses became balanced about a central axis, with only careful, stripped detail. A few

large houses incorporated double-story pilasters. Sash windows with rectilinear panes replaced casements. Hipped roofs accentuated the balanced and strict proportions inherited from Italy and Holland via England and Scotland.

### FEDERAL

The post-Revolutionary style sometimes called "Federal" was more flexible and delicate than the more formal Geor-

gian. It was rooted in archaeological discoveries at Pompeii and Herculaneum in Italy in the 1750s, as well as in contemporary French interior planning principles. As it evolved toward the Regency, rooms became shaped as polygons, ovals, and circles and acquired ornamentation in the forms of urns, garlands, and swags. Lacking the strong color of English and Scottish prototypes, this style was sweetly elegant; a fan-shaped window over the door is its most characteristic detail.

### GREEK REVIVAL

The Greek Revival manifested itself in severe, stripped, rectilinear proportions, occasionally a set of columns or pilasters, and even in a few instances Greek-temple form. It was used in official buildings and

in many private houses. It combined Greek and Roman forms—low pitched pediments, simple moldings, rounded arches, and shallow domes.

### GOTHIC REVIVAL

After about 1830, darker colors, asymmetry, broken skylines, verticality, and the pointed arch began to appear. New machinery produced carved and pierced trim along the

eaves. Roofs became steep and gabled; "porches" or "piazzas" became more spacious. Oriel and bay windows became common and there was greater use of stained glass.

## ITALIANATE

The Italianate style began to appear in the 1840s, both in a formal, balanced "palazzo" style, and in a picturesque "villa" style. Both had round-headed windows and arcaded porches. Commercial structures were often made of cast iron, with a ground floor of large arcaded windows, and smaller windows on each successive rising story.

## SECOND EMPIRE

After 1860, Parisian fashion inspired American builders to use mansard roofs, dark colors, and varied textures, including shingles, tiles, and increasing use of ironwork, especially on balconies and sky-

lines. With their ornamental quoins, balustrades, pavilions, pediments, columns, and pilasters, Second Empire buildings recalled many historical styles.

## QUEEN ANNE STYLE

The Queen Anne style emphasized contrasts of form, texture, and color. Large encircling verandas, tall chimneys, turrets, towers, and a multitude of textures are typical of the style. The ground floor might be of stone or brick, the upper floors stucco, shingle, or clapboard. Specially shaped bricks and plaques were used for decoration. Panels of stained glass outlined or filled the windows. The steep roofs were gabled or hipped, and other elements like pediments, Venetian windows, and front and corner bay windows were typical.

## SHINGLE STYLE

The Shingle Style bore the stamp of a new generation of professional architects led by Henry Hobson Richardson (1838-1886). Sheathed in wooden shingles, its forms were smoothed and unified. Verandas, turrets, and complex roofs were sometimes used, but thoroughly integrated into a whole that emphasized uniformity of surface rather than a jumble of forms. The style was a domestic and informal expression of what became known in town mansions and official buildings as Richardson Romanesque.

## RICHARDSON ROMANESQUE

Richardson Romanesque made use of the massive forms and ornamental details of the

Romanesque: rounded arches, towers, stone and brick facing. The solidity and gravity of masses were accentuated by deep recesses for windows and entrances, by rough stone masonry, stubby columns, strong horizontals, rounded towers with conical caps, and botanical, repetitive ornament.

## RENAISSANCE REVIVAL OR BEAUX ARTS

Later in the 1880s and 1890s, American architects who had studied at the Ecole des Beaux Arts in Paris brought a new Renaissance Revival to the United States. Sometimes

used in urban mansions, but generally reserved for city halls and academic buildings, it borrowed from three centuries of Renaissance detail, much of it French, and put together picturesque combinations from widely differing periods.

# I N D E X

494

Composed in Basilia Haas and ITC New
Baskerville by Graphic Arts Composition, Inc.,
Philadelphia, Pennsylvania. Printed and bound
by Toppan Printing Company, Ltd., Tokyo,
Japan.